MENCKEN

MENCKEN

A STUDY OF HIS THOUGHT

❖❖

By CHARLES A. FECHER

With a Foreword by Alfred A. Knopf

ALFRED A. KNOPF

NEW YORK · 1978

THIS IS A BORZOI BOOK
PUBLISHED BY ALFRED A. KNOPF, INC.

Library of Congress Cataloging in Publication Data
Fecher, Charles A. (Date)
Mencken: A study of his thought.
Bibliography: p.
Includes index.
1. Mencken, Henry Louis, 1880–1956.
2. Authors, American—20th century—Biography.
PS3525.E43Z553   818'.5'209   [B]   77-21154
ISBN 0-394-41354-7
Manufactured in the United States of America
First Edition

GRATEFUL ACKNOWLEDGMENT is made to the following firms for
their kind permission to quote from previously published material:

A. S. Abell Co., publishers of the Baltimore *Sunpapers:* various "Monday Articles" and other
columns by H. L. Mencken.

Delacorte Press: *The Constant Circle* by Sara Mayfield, copyright © 1968 by Sara Mayfield.

Dial Press: *The Smart Set, A History and Anthology,* copyright © 1966 by Carl R. Dolmetsch and
copyright © 1966 by S. N. Behrman.

E. P. Dutton & Co., Inc.: *The Confident Years* by Van Wyck Brooks, copyright © 1952 by Van
Wyck Brooks.

Harcourt Brace Jovanovich, Inc.: *On Native Grounds* by Alfred Kazin.

Harold Matson Co., Inc.: *Disturber of the Peace* by William Manchester, copyright © 1950,
1951 by William Manchester.

For
HAROLD S. HATTON
cousin, friend,
and fellow Menckenian

CONTENTS

Eight pages of photographs will be found following page 104

FOREWORD

IT IS A PLEASURE and a privilege to have the following brief notes on H. L. Mencken as I knew him appear
with Charles Fecher's study, which is so far and away the best work of
any kind I have ever read on Henry as to leave the competition
nowhere. I read Mr. Fecher's manuscript chapter by chapter, as he
completed them over a period of several years, with ever-increasing
admiration. And in the end I had seen in the round a picture of the
friend I knew.

I have always assumed that we probably met, as Henry has stated,
in 1913, when I was working in a very humble capacity for my first
employer, Doubleday Page & Co. Frank Doubleday had just arranged
to become Joseph Conrad's exclusive American publisher. I had begun
reading Conrad when still an undergraduate, and later, with John
Galsworthy's urging, had read all his books. We were to publish
Chance, his new novel, and Mencken had been for a long time, as
Conrad put it in a letter to me, "beating a drum" for him in *The Smart
Set*, of which he was co-editor and to which he contributed a monthly
article on the current books. Once Conrad wrote a friend about "dear
Mencken's amazing article about me, so many-sided, so brilliant, and
so warm-hearted. For that man of a really ruthless mind, pitiless to all

shams, has a great generosity. My debt of gratitude to him has been growing for years."*

So we may be certain that it was our common admiration for Conrad that led me to the newsroom of the Baltimore *Sun*, where I found Henry in his shirtsleeves, pounding out copy on his typewriter.

We had plenty to talk about at this birth of a friendship that soon became, with that of my wife, Blanche, the closest and most influential in my long life. We did not meet with any frequency for a long time, but then I had married Blanche in 1916 and the year before that had planned and founded my own firm, which I hoped would become Mencken's publisher. But let him tell it in his own words:

"In 1915 he acquired somehow a dubious-looking Master's certificate and set sail, but I remained supinely ashore, sitting on previous contracts that, at least in theory, could not be broken. By the end of 1916, however, I managed to get purged of them, and Alfred and I have been publisher and author ever since, and not only publisher and author, but also a great many other things, including publisher and editor, penitent and confessor, confessor and penitent, fellow slaves alike of the grape and of the three B's, and political enemies.

"A childless man, with no more talent for pediatrics than for poverty, chastity and obedience, I advise him about the education of his son (who disregards, and with good sense, both of us), and he on his part, though he is as innocent of politics as a newly-hatched Dalai Lama, unloads his counsel in that great science upon me, who began to sniff at politicians so long ago as 1902."

So in 1917 we published his *A Book of Prefaces*.

Even then he had the reputation, chiefly with those who did not know him well—and I didn't know him well—of being a burly, loud, raucous fellow, rough in his speech and lacking refined manners. How mistaken this opinion was I learned a little later, when on a visit to Washington I introduced Blanche Knopf to him. He met her with the most charming manners conceivable, manners I was to discover he always displayed in talking with women. And shortly he handed her a box of cigarettes—Milos, I think they were called—and we both remembered that their paper was purple and their tips gold. I knew Mencken for more than forty years, intimately for well over thirty. His public side was visible to everyone: tough, cynical, amusing, and exas-

---

*For permission to quote from this letter I am indebted to the trustees of the Joseph Conrad estate.

perating by turns. The private man was something else again: sentimental, generous, and unwavering—sometimes almost blind—in his
devotion to people of whom he felt fond.

Devoted to his mother, Henry lived with her in the Hollins Street
house—red brick with white front marble steps. He left the house only
after his mother's death and his marriage to Sara Haardt. When she
died barely five years later he returned to it, occupying it with his
younger brother, August, and dying in it. Here one invariably ate and
drank well. Mencken was marvelous in his handling of domestic help,
and the black cook always served him devotedly. He liked to putter
around the yard and particularly to break up wood—discarded packing
cases, wine boxes, and what not—to burn in the living room fireplace,
and he took special pride in his skill as a bricklayer, to which the wall on
one long side of what he always called "the yard" still bears witness.

When we moved to the country, he always stayed overnight and
often for a weekend. Invariably he read himself to sleep, never with
anything he was tackling in a serious way but with some odd volume he
had picked up somewhere, frequently in a secondhand bookstore. His
pajamas were of the brightest solid colors, as one could see since he
never closed the door of his room. He endeared himself to our domestic help, and after his illness brought an end to his visits, the couple
who had been with us for many years expressed great sorrow that they
were not to see him again. No other house guest of mine ever moved
them that way.

He was as close to Blanche as he was to me and got along as well
with my father, eighteen years his senior, as he did with me, twelve
years his junior. He shared with us for more than thirty years books and
music, good food and drink when we were well, and gave freely the
most thoughtful and expert kind of help on those occasions, happily
rare, when we were ill. In Baltimore, he cultivated all his life the wise
medical men at Johns Hopkins, and he spent a fantastic amount of his
time getting friends to and from doctors' waiting rooms and hospitals,
comforting them and keeping them company there.

Mencken's first visit to the Bach Festival at Bethlehem, Pennsylvania, was with Joseph Hergesheimer in 1923. He wrote: "The Bach
jaunt turned out to be very pleasant. We found excellent beer on
draught at ten cents a glass. The choruses were superb, but the solo
voices singed by kidneys. Joe turned up in a golden orange kimona with
a purple lining—the perfect Borzoi."

Later, I went regularly to the festival with Mencken, staying wherever we could find accommodations: the local hotel, a semiresidential hotel in nearby Allentown, and one time at the Elks Club in Bethlehem. During the Prohibition years he boasted that he could find beer within ten minutes of his arrival in any town. But once in Bethlehem he was stumped, and only at the end of twenty-four hours did a taxicab driver overhear his complaint and drop us off at the right place. We rang a bell, and the door opened. Henry pointed to the scores of the B Minor Mass that we were carrying and asked politely, "Can you do anything for two poor, thirsty musicians?" The fellow looked us over with two glass eyes, decided we were all right, and told us to come in and turn left. At the end of the hall we found a bar about thirty feet long serving good beer and sandwiches at ridiculously modest prices. Henry was enchanted.

His advice was always ours for the asking; he frequently suggested authors for us to approach and books to publish, and was the first to call my attention to and recommend Thomas Mann's *Buddenbrooks*. But the idea that this was anything but a normal relationship between a writer and a friend who happened to be his publisher would have shocked him beyond words. He was not a unique example of this. Carl Van Vechten, Thomas Beer, and Joseph Hergesheimer acted toward us the same way.

In 1921, Mencken sent in the revised version of *In Defense of Women*. I suggested publishing it the following spring, but said that I would try for the immediate fall if he so desired. His reply was characteristic: "You are the publisher; not I. I leave all such matters to your judgment." And as we had the second edition of *The American Language* in the works at that time, he added, "All I ask is that you make 'The American Language' good and thick. It is my secret ambition to be the author of a book weighing at least five pounds."

A Baltimore clergyman had sent us a manuscript with the suggestion that Mencken might write an introduction for it if we published it. I sent the manuscript to him, and he wrote me: "The ——— book is psychical crap, but it might sell. ——— is a High Church Episcopal Rector in a fashionable suburb. Most of his congregation are rich ex-Methodists, Presbyterians, Dunkards, Jews, Lutherans, etc. I shall certainly write no introduction for it. More, ——— is well aware that I shall not. Never believe a clergyman."

Once Mencken was in Berlin, where Blanche and I had been a

year earlier. He ended a letter to me: "Tell Blanche that the Sohlers always refer to her as 'die schöne Frau Knopf.' On the question of your own beauty, they are polite but not enthusiastic. I told them that you and Harding were regarded as the handsomest living Americans."

Once we must have drawn up an organization chart and shown it to him, for he ended another letter: "It cost you thirty or forty dollars to draw up that Stammbaum you showed me. Read Henry Ford on the subject of office diagrams and abscissae. His overhead is only one eighth of one percent. In sso. corde Jesu."

In 1928, I went with him to the Republican National Convention at Kansas City. He collected political conventions the way other men collect books or paintings. We met at lunch on the opening day. He asked where I was sitting and I told him up in the gallery, nearest the roof. He acted with his usual briskness, and since I was carrying a small Bell and Howell movie camera, he quickly procured me a photographer's badge, and from then on I sat with the Baltimore *Sun* crowd in the midst of all the hubbub on the floor. It was all great fun, but my fondest recollection is of Henry at his typewriter in the suite that Paul Patterson, publisher of the *Sunpapers*, had engaged—a sailor hat on his head, a corncob pipe between his teeth, clad only in his B.V.D.'s.

I used to attend the meetings of the famous Saturday Night Club with some frequency. Until ten o'clock there was music, chiefly arrangements of classical symphonies. The players, I am sure, enjoyed it far more than the listeners, who were few, but the listeners surely did enjoy the players. Two at the piano: Henry secundo and Max Broedel primo. Raymond Pearl with his French horn. A cello, a flute, a viola, a few violins, and Willie Woollcott (Alec's brother), author of a song that suited the crowd to a T called "I Am a One Hundred Percent American," as a sort of Greek chorus. At ten o'clock sharp, *los mit Musik*, and serious beer drinking began. It was Prohibition, and each member of the club was host in turn and supplied bottled home brew enough to half-fill a bathtub. After Repeal the members repaired to Schellhase's, Henry's favorite cafe or, as he preferred to call it, saloon. Schellhase's has now moved to very different quarters, but still displays the mugs of the club members on one of its walls.

How well I remember one Saturday when Frank Hazlehurst was host. He was to remove my tonsils next morning. As the evening advanced and the drinking continued, one member after another came up and spoke words of reassurance to me: "Don't worry about Frank,

the more he drinks of this the steadier his hand will be in the morning."
Next morning, Henry accompanied me to St. Agnes' Hospital. And
when a sister turned up soon after I had been put to bed to ask why a
tonsillectomy had to be done on the Sabbath, Henry told her in his
sweetest and most disarming manner something that satisfied her that
this one Sunday was the only day on which any operation could ever be
performed on me. And then he advised me that if priests came to talk
with me after the operation, as they undoubtedly would, I had only to
point to my throat, nod my head from side to side, and say nothing.

To indicate the nature of our very special personal and professional relationship, I fall back again on Henry's own words. In very
early days, he sometimes thought of the young firm of Knopf as a ship,
and ten years after its founding he wrote:

"It had two masts, and new sails, and a new and challenging ensign
under the main-truck: on a field of white a spectral dog, leaping into
space. This dog, I learned, was a borzoi; I know no more about it to this
day. The ship now began to appear off my coast more frequently. It
sprouted a third mast, and then a fourth. Sailors began to show on the
deck, apparently well filled with proteins and carbohydrates. A
smokestack arose, and belched smoke. Deck grew upon deck. I began
to hear a band, and the shuffle of dancing in the evening. There were
stewards, officers in blue and brass, a purser, a boots. A bar opened. In
an imperial suite lolled the sybarite, Joe Hergesheimer. In 1917 I
engaged passage myself, taking a modest room on D deck. It seemed
only polite to pay my respects to the skipper. I found him immersed in
books up to his neck—big books and little books, books sober and staid
and books of an almost voluptuous gaudiness, books of all ages and in all
languages, books in the full flush of beauty, ready for the customer and
books stripped down to their very anatomical elements. And all the talk
I heard, to the end of that first voyage, was of books, books, books.

"One day, quite by accident, I discovered that he was also interested in music. We launched into Brahms instantly—but in ten
minutes we were back to books. I tried Beethoven: he lasted longer.
Bach: longer still. But even old Johann Sebastian, in the end, yielded to
books.

"That was in the days of hard struggle. Of late, with the waters
calm, the decks crowded with passengers, and the holds full of—
books!—I have noticed a growing expansiveness. There is more time to
listen to the band, even to grab a clarinet and essay a few toots. One

night, lately, we put in a solid hour belaboring Richard Strauss; not a
type clicked, not a rose fluttered upon William Heinemann's grave.
There have been conferences, too, on the subject of Moselle, its snares
and mysteries, and on the hotels of London, Paris and Berlin, and on
dogs, and even on the Coolidge statecraft. If I were younger and less
bilious in my prejudices, there would be discourse, I suspect, on golf: I
have seen the grotesque clubs of the game in a corner. There is a son to
think of. There is a large and complicated organization, evergrowing."

Throughout all my long and complicated dealings with Henry, I
was perhaps in the end most impressed by the sheer competence with
which he tackled every problem we had to face together. He might
indeed have been writing about himself when he wrote of competence,
"I can imagine no higher praise. Competence is almost as infrequently
encountered on this earth as virtue." But *his* competence rose to
heights to which I could never attain. I doubt that we shall see his like
again.

ALFRED A. KNOPF

PREFACE

I AM OLD ENOUGH to remember those last few years,
just prior to the outbreak of the second World War, when
Mencken's "Monday Articles" still lit up the editorial page of the Baltimore *Evening Sun*, but I was young enough then to be dazzled by the
brilliant style, the incomparable humor, and the virtuosity of language
that caused one, while the tears of laughter streamed down one's face,
to grope for the dictionary. The first book of his that I ever bought (it is
still in my library) was the fourth edition of *The American Language*
when it came out in 1936, and this in turn led me to the volumes of
Prejudices and to *Treatise on the Gods* and *Treatise on Right and
Wrong*. As they appeared a bit later, I eagerly devoured the *Days*
books and the two Supplements. I became a Mencken buff, and my
allegiance has not wavered from that day to this.

The reader of the following pages will perhaps note that I have felt
under no obligation to apologize for the fact. It is customary nowadays
to speak in patronizing tones of Mencken (when one speaks of him at
all) as a professional "debunker" of half a century ago who employed his
rather questionable wit in exposing some of the sillier aspects of life in
the twenties, but whose humor is now as hollow as his ideas are dated.
If this book makes any point at all, I hope it is the point that such a view
is wrong. The enormous influence which he exercised in the twenties

(and for a while before and after) helped to shape the world in which we live today, and it is not necessary to agree with all of his ideas to admit the role which they played in that shaping. His style is unique enough in American literature to make him worthy of study on that ground alone, if no other.

Moreover, there is the undeniable fact that interest in him has always continued to be high; he has never needed a "revival" such as Henry James had, and, still later, Scott Fitzgerald. Since his death in 1956 there has been a steady stream of books about him and of anthologies of his uncollected writings; going through my own "Bibliographical Note" in the present work, I count up a total of twenty-three such volumes, or an average of slightly more than one a year—not bad at all for an author presumed to be "dated," and the stream shows no sign of drying up.

The idea of writing a book about him myself goes back so far that I can scarcely recall a time when I did not have it; but in the course of the years my conception of its nature inevitably underwent some changes. One thing, at least, I never intended it to be—I was always willing to leave the writing of his biography to other hands. From the outset it was visualized as "a study of his thought," but originally it was to have been a relatively brief work, done in the informal manner of his own two *Treatises* and, like them, with no visible scholarly apparatus. It got out of hand, of course, and has turned into what the reader sees before him.

The writing of it thus took a forbiddingly long time—so long, in fact, that three people to whom I would have wished to present copies upon its publication died while it was in progress. First among these was Miss Betty Adler, custodian of the H. L. Mencken Room in Baltimore's Enoch Pratt Free Library, a greater "authority" than any of us who have written about him, and the person to whom every Mencken scholar living today is most deeply in debt. It was Betty Adler who opened the Room to me and pointed the way through its vast resources, and who encouraged me to go ahead with my own work. Another was her successor, Maclean Patterson, with whom I had a number of pleasant and profitable meetings. The third was A. D. Emmart of the *Evening Sun*, whose long career on the paper went back to Mencken's own time, who was helpful to me in innumerable ways, and of whom I can only say today that he was the kindest man I have ever known.

Both before and after Betty Adler's death other members of the Pratt Library staff were interested and helpful. Mr. Richard Hart, now retired as director of its Humanities Department, was always most considerate, and Mr. William Forshaw, the assistant director, acted well beyond any reasonable call of duty to help me run down this, that, or the other little detail. My indebtedness to him is greater than I can well record.

I am grateful, too, to Mr. G. Albert Puliafico and Mr. Henry L. Meledin of Mercantile-Safe Deposit & Trust Company, Trustee for the Estate of H. L. Mencken, for their kindness in seeing to it that I was able to make use of unpublished materials in the Room.

Various members of the firm of Alfred A. Knopf, Inc., have been of invaluable help, most notably my editor, Ms. Jane Garrett, and her assistant, Ms. Alice Quinn. But to no member of the Knopf firm am I more indebted than to its founder, the dean of American publishers, Mr. Alfred Knopf himself. His interest in the book has been unfailing since the day that a portion of the manuscript was first shown to him; he has encouraged me and inspired me, and on more than one occasion he has gently needled me to get it done. Among other things, he supplied me with information and reminiscences that could have come from no other source than Mencken's publisher and personal friend of many years' standing. I can only hope that in its final form the book does not let him down.

It is, of course, the tritest of clichés to express gratitude in a preface like this to the members of one's own family, but every married person who has ever written a book knows how literally true such an expression is. My wife, Muriel, and my daughters, Betsy and Charlotte Ann, believed in it even when I did not; they put up with me when the putting up must have been difficult indeed; and they provided the proper atmosphere and made sure that I got the time needed to write. Sometimes they must have felt that they were living with H. L. Mencken rather than with me, but their patience and understanding never gave out and their encouragement is the chief reason that the book was ever finished at all.

CHARLES A. FECHER

BALTIMORE, MD.
July 4, 1977

M E N C K E N

INTRODUCTION

. . . it would be difficult to imagine anyone agreeing with everything Mencken said; but it is all but inconceivable that anyone could be indifferent to him.

—William H. Nolte,
H. L. Mencken: Literary Critic

◇◇

1 A STUDY OF MENCKEN'S THOUGHT —a study, for that matter, of the thought of any man—inevitably presupposes two things. The first is that he had a "thought"—that is to say, a unified and coherent body of ideas treating of ultimate questions and perennial issues, either set forth explicitly in his writings or abstractable from them by others. It is the sort of thing that, among philosophers, we usually call a "system." And the second presupposition is that that thought or system is worth studying.

In the case of Mencken, it may be necessary to defend both halves of this thesis. The unity and coherence are there, all right: from the 1905 book on Shaw to the collection of notes published posthumously in 1956 as *Minority Report*, his ideas exhibit an internal consistency and lack of contradiction that must be without parallel in literature. They exhibit, too, an absolute clarity; there will never be any need for an English professor or a candidate for the Ph.D. to busy himself with a tortured analysis of what Mencken meant. What he meant is exactly what he said, and it leaves no room for doubt.

He himself noted the essential unchangeableness of his opinions in a letter of January 22, 1940, to Jim Tully:

On all known subjects, ranging from aviation to xylophone-playing, I
have fixed and invariable ideas. They have not changed since I was four
or five years [old].[1]

He called attention to the fact again, perhaps a half-dozen years
later, in *Minority Report:*

I can't recall ever changing my mind about any capital matter. My
general body of fundamental ideas is the same today as it was in the days
when I first began to ponder.[2]

Hamilton Owens, for long associated with him on the Baltimore
Sunpapers, pointed out the same thing almost wonderingly:

Most of us arrive at maturity with no notion of life's significance or lack
of it, no understanding of its myriad complexities, no philosophic system to guide us save copybook and Biblical maxims. As we grow older,
we adopt first this rule of thought and then that one, only to discard each
in turn as experience proves it false or inadequate. . . . Mencken, more
than any man I have ever heard of, avoided this painful intellectual
progress through life. Read some of his earlier writings and you will see
what this means. When he wrote about Nietzsche in 1908, he displayed
in his comments not only understanding of that tortured philosopher but
also an ability to see his shortcomings. He was meticulously careful to
underwrite only those attitudes that conformed to his own. The point of
view thus expressed is precisely the same as that set forth in his posthumous *Minority Report.* . . . the evidence all suggests that the young
Mencken's concept of the world and of the men and women in it, whatever its source, was complete when he first contemplated the great out-
doors from the windows of the red brick house on Hollins Street. He
gathered facts to support his congenital prejudices and filled out the details as he went along. He learned how to express himself in ever more
resounding phrases, but the point of view never altered.[3]

Of course, the mere fact that a man's point of view never alters is
no reason to regard it as either intelligent or worthy of respect. The
opposite could very well be true. There are thousands of men and
women who have never changed their minds about anything, either
because they were too ignorant, or too narrow, or because they
absorbed a certain body of ideas early in life and simply never came
in contact with any others. But it must be obvious that Mencken does
not belong in this category. Throughout his entire career he was ex-

posed to ideas differing very greatly from his own; the omnivorous reading which he had to do as a reviewer and critic certainly made him aware of them; he knew personally many of the people who held them. He even liked some of these people: there is no doubt whatever, for example, that he had a humorous affection for such an out-and-out adversary as the Methodist Prohibition advocate Bishop Cannon, and he wrote with fairness and understanding of that "emperor of wowsers," Anthony Comstock. He numbered among his friends clergymen of every denomination, but he could not for an instant believe what they believed and was never tempted to succumb to their blandishments.

In this intransigence there was without doubt a certain amount of attitudinizing, of playing for effect. It is surely not without significance that he chose *Prejudices* as the generic title for the series of volumes in which he set forth his own opinions. But the effect was never dishonest and the prejudices were not irrational ones, held blindly and obtusely in the face of all contrary evidence. They were simply his, worked out in his own mind and tested by his own experience, and in the whole range of that experience he had never seen any plausible reason for changing them. They suited him better than any others he had encountered. Converting to any of those others, he would no longer have been the man he was.

2 MENCKEN IS NOT USUALLY considered, nor did he consider himself, a "thinker." He has been called a newspaperman, a journalist, an editor, a critic, a philologist, a scholar, a satirist, and a humorist. In his lifetime he was also called a lot of other things, some of them less balanced but more vivid. It is safe to say, though, that neither those who regarded him as one of the great figures of American literature nor those who looked upon him as Antichrist ever thought of his work as having any kind of philosophical implications.*

---

*To be sure, Ernest Boyd in his book *H. L. Mencken* (New York: Robert M. McBride & Co., 1925) had treated of Mencken's thought, and one of his chapters is even entitled "The Philosopher." But it deals only with some of Mencken's political ideas, and his writings about religion are scarcely touched upon even in passing. Moreover, the book, despite its undeniable merits, runs to only 89 pages and it appeared at a time when Mencken still had a quarter of a century of his career ahead of him.

His own view of philosophy was a dim one, and that branch of it which is known as metaphysics he thought "very hollow. Half of it is a tremendous laboring of the obvious, and the other half is speculation that has very little relation to the known facts."[4] Observing that when the weather on his "estates in the Maryland jungles" became too hot for serious mental activity he always gave over a couple of weeks to a rereading of the philosophical classics, he went on:

> Out of the business, despite its high austerity, I always carry away the feeling that I have had a hell of a time. That is, I carry away the feeling that the art and mystery of philosophy, as it is practiced in the world by professional philosophers, is largely moonshine and wind-music—or, to borrow Henry Ford's searching term, bunk.[5]*

What made it, for him, moonshine and wind-music and bunk was the fact that the professional philosophers, from Socrates down, were engaged in the pursuit of something that Mencken simply could not believe in—Truth. Their whole lives had been spent trying to establish the existence of an "Absolute"—a truth, in other words, that was independent of the beliefs and opinions of any individual person, or even of mankind as a whole, and was true *a priori* and before all human experience. Such a truth would be true for all men, at all times, and would be true even if no one had ever discovered it. Opinions could change, and as a matter of fact they did; one fashion of thought might go out and another come in; but Truth, not being dependent on opinions or fashions, was forever unchangeable.

It was just this point of view that Mencken, his whole life long, found it utterly impossible to accept. "The absolute," he maintained,

> . . . is a mere banshee, a concept without substance or reality. No such thing exists. When, by logical devices, it is triumphantly established, the feat is exactly on all fours with that of the mathematician who proved that twice two was double once two. . . . There is, in fact, no idea in any man that may be found certainly in all men.[6]

This, from an article published in 1927, was simply an echo of

---

*He also wrote: "Philosophy consists very largely of one philosopher arguing that all others are jackasses. He usually proves it, and I should add that he also usually proves that he is one himself." (*Minority Report*, p. 48.)

what he had already written twenty-two years earlier in his first prose book, the one on George Bernard Shaw:

> No two men see the same thing in exactly the same way, and there are no fixed standards whereby we may decide whether one or the other or neither is right.[7]

Errors, of course, might be exposed, but as he quite rightly pointed out, this did not necessarily mean that a truth was established thereby:

> Nine times out of ten, in the arts as in life, there is actually no truth to be discovered; there is only error to be exposed. In whole departments of human inquiry it seems to me quite unlikely that the truth ever *will* be discovered. Nevertheless, the rubber-stamp thinking of the world always makes the assumption that the exposure of an error is identical with the discovery of the truth—that error and truth are simple opposites. They are nothing of the sort. What the world turns to, when it has been cured of one error, is usually simply another error, and maybe one worse than the first one. This is the whole history of the intellect in brief.[8]

The exposure of error and the establishment of fact ("fact" as distinguished from Truth in the philosophical sense) was the business of science. We shall have occasion a bit later to study Mencken's attitude toward science and to account for it in terms of that nineteenth-century *Weltanschauung* which was still very much in the air as he grew up; here it suffices only to note his firm conviction that each new scientific discovery reduced the area in which philosophy could function and pushed it further and further back up against the wall. It was a conviction that he had held from the beginning and that never left him: "To me," he wrote late in life, "the scientific point of view is completely satisfying, and it has been so as long as I can remember. Not once in this life have I ever been inclined to seek a rock and a refuge elsewhere."[9]

There is in all this an element of paradox which he seems not to have noticed, but which was pointed out long ago in a famous fragment attributed to Aristotle (whom Mencken, incidentally, admired very much): "You say that you must philosophize; very well, then, you must philosophize. You say that you should not philosophize; then (in order to prove your point) you must philosophize. In either case, you must philosophize."[10] In other words, it is impossible to deny—or even to belittle—philosophy without making use of philosophical arguments. And the statement was echoed, many centuries later, in a somewhat different vocabulary, by St. Thomas Aquinas when he observed that "whoever denies the existence of truth grants that truth does not exist: and, if truth does not exist, then the proposition 'Truth does not exist' is true: and if there is anything true, there must be truth."[11]

Mencken, of course, would contemptuously dismiss this as mere logic-chopping, and perhaps in a sense it is; nevertheless, it contains an argument that even the most thoroughgoing skeptic—and he considered himself the most complete one since Pontius Pilate[12]—must find some difficulty in getting around.

For the paradox is that he devoted his entire life, and most of his fantastic energies, to exposing ideas he believed to be wrong and men who he was convinced were frauds; and that in order to do this he had to believe in himself and believe, too, that the ideas he held were right. These ideas might not constitute a philosophy in the technical sense of the word; still less would they make up a "system," since the chief characteristics of a philosophical system are that it is very carefully worked out in the mind of the man who creates it and that he is convinced of its truth not only as a whole but in each of its parts. But they certainly constitute an impressive body of thought, and it is that thought which is the subject matter of this book.

Moreover, if Mencken was not a system-builder as Kant was, or Hegel, he can with some justice be called a "universal man" as the phrase is applied to Leonardo or to Goethe. The range of his interests and activities was all but illimitable. Throughout most of his life he was a practicing newspaperman, not only in the fields of writing and editing but also, to a degree at least, in management. Parallel to this, and at the same time, he was a magazine editor, which again meant not only writing and editing but involving himself to some extent in the details of layout, production, advertising, circulation, and business direction. Either one of these might have made a career; yet they were really just unavoidable by-products of his main energies.

Those main energies manifest themselves in his books and in the incalculable quantity of his journalistic writings. Let us turn to the books first. Set aside *The American Language*, whose four editions and two supplements, totaling some 3,800 pages, would in itself have constituted a lifework for almost any other man. Set aside the 1,347-page *Dictionary of Quotations*, on which he labored intermittently for a quarter of a century. Set aside, finally, the *Days* books as the record of his own personal experiences, and the six volumes of *Prejudices* on the ground that they roam over such a wide variety of subjects as literally to defy cataloguing. What remains is still an impressive testimony to the breadth of his intellectual curiosity and his knowledge.

There is a philosophical study *(The Philosophy of Friedrich Nietzsche)*. There is a volume of literary criticism *(A Book of Prefaces)*. There are studies of political theory *(Notes on Democracy)* and of the position of women in modern society *(In Defense of Women)*. Finally, there are the two works which he himself regarded as among his most important achievements but which have fallen into ill-deserved neglect: one on religion *(Treatise on the Gods)* and one on ethical theory *(Treatise on Right and Wrong)*. Each of these represents a truly immense amount of reading, study, assimilation, and reflection; one may disagree with their positions in part or in whole, but one cannot deny the mastery of subject matter that they exhibit.

But even the books do not bear a complete witness to Mencken's versatility. For that, one must turn to the newspaper and magazine work. The writing on literature and literary criticism is, of course, a virtual library in itself. His pieces about music were so numerous that his friend Louis Cheslock was able to assemble a whole volume of them and still not collect everything by any means. And beyond that the field is wide open. I turn, for example, to the listing of "Monday Articles" in Betty Adler's *H.L.M.: The Mencken Bibliography*, and select at random just one year—1923; again setting aside those that treat of national or local politics, there are columns on disarmament, birth control, teaching, higher education, censorship, criminology, legal theory, tourism, Anglo-Saxondom, the Bethlehem, Pennsylvania, Bach festival, and the proposal to build a new art gallery in Baltimore—to pick out only a few.

Naturally, not everything—books, articles, reviews—is of equal quality. The mere chore of grinding out the weekly column for the *Sun*, or the monthly pieces first for *The Smart Set* and then *The American Mercury*, must at times have lain heavily on him, so that, as he said of Wagner, "one detects . . . days when [he] felt, as the saying goes, like a fighting cock, but one also detects days when he arose in the morning full of acidosis and despair."[13] This is inevitable. But the variation in quality is astonishingly narrow, and in the whole incredible output there is scarcely anything that is less than good. In the very least of it there is always a thought, an expression, a turn of phrase, that is characteristically and quintessentially Mencken.

And from first to last it holds together. Whether he is writing about free will or the chances of Al Smith's election to the Presidency, about Puritanism in the national letters or the advantages to be gained from traveling in a Pullman car, the same approach and the same relatively small set of principles illumine his work. They give it, as I have indicated, a consistency almost unique in literary and cultural history. Those principles were to him what Euclid's axioms are to his system of geometry, and while they may not set forth philosophical profundities in philosophy's technical vocabulary, they come as close as anything in our time to offering a complete and reasoned view— Mencken's view, of course, with which others may violently disagree— of the cosmos and of man's role in it.

3 TO ALL THIS, however, an objection may be raised, and as a matter of fact Mencken himself raised it very honestly. It is that the vast bulk of his work was journalism, and hence by that token both superficial and ephemeral. He called it "journalism pure and simple—dead almost before the ink which printed it was dry."[14]

With the possible exception of *The American Language* (and there are critics, like Charles Angoff, who refuse to grant any merit or real importance even to this), his writings, it is argued, lack scholarship and profundity and make no significant contribution to the sum total of human knowledge. Even in a field like the history and criticism of literature, where he functioned as a professional, there were whole areas in which he was unforgivably ignorant or, what is worse, violently prejudiced. And he tried to cover up both ignorance and prejudice by writing in a highly sensational style that relied for its effects on wild exaggeration, humor in rather doubtful taste, vituperation, and *ad hominem* attacks that should have been beneath the dignity of a serious writer.

Finally, the argument runs, whereas it is the mark of a truly original thinker that his ideas are of lasting interest and value, most of Mencken's work deals with issues that are not only dead but in most cases all but forgotten.

None of this can be lightly dismissed. It is true that there were gaps in his knowledge—though they were no greater, and probably nowhere near as great, as the gaps to be expected in the stock of knowledge of any well-educated person. It is likewise true that many of the ideas he held have been modified in the light of subsequent research and discoveries, and that this process of modification was already well under way in his own lifetime. Too, he was undeniably a man of very strong likes and dislikes: what he liked he praised and campaigned for to the limit of his energies, as in his crusading for Dreiser,* and what he disliked he ridiculed sometimes quite unjustly, as in his attitude toward the whole nineteenth-century New England school of which Emerson was the chief figure. He admitted that he was not fair and was not interested in hearing both sides of an argument.[15] But there will be occasion often in the pages that follow to point out these limitations, and so it serves little purpose to stop and deal with them here.

On the other hand, the charge that he wrote about matters that were of only passing import and that as a result his thought badly dates is somewhat more serious and had better be considered before we go any further. On the surface it may seem to be true, and certainly it accounts for the sharp decline in his popularity during the thirties and early forties. Of the writers prominent during the first decades of this century whom Mencken hailed and enthusiastically supported, who today reads Dreiser or Sinclair Lewis or Sherwood Anderson or James Branch Cabell? They are almost as forgotten as the Henry Sydnor Harrisons, Robert W. Chamberses, and James Lane Allens of a still earlier generation on whom he poured out his ridicule. What of the American Presidents whom he castigated as a matter of standing policy—Harding, Coolidge, Hoover? They survive, if at all, only as minor names in history texts, and even Woodrow Wilson and Franklin Roosevelt have been eclipsed to a degree as Democratic leaders by later figures like John F. Kennedy. What significance today has the New Thought? Does anyone have any really strong feelings about Socialism in a world where one-third of the earth's surface and one-half of its people are ruled by Communism? Even in the remoter reaches of the Bible Belt, are there very many Fundamentalists left? Prohibition,

---

*Yet he never permitted either admiration or personal friendship to blind his critical judgment. No man wrote more unmercifully of Dreiser's shortcomings as a literary artist; Mencken's comments on the Dreiserian style, in fact, led to a break between the two men that lasted for years.

about which Mencken wrote scores of articles and columns running to thousands of words, is hardly a burning issue in a country where the annual per capita consumption of alcoholic beverages is 31 gallons and where the tax revenue alone on such beverages is well in excess of a billion dollars.

All this is undeniable. Yet far from disposing of Mencken, much of it actually constitutes a powerful argument in favor of his force and influence.

The social and political scene on which he came as a young news-paper reporter in 1899 was as undistinguished as was, *mutatis mutandis,* the literary scene which he entered as book editor of *The Smart Set* in 1908. Both were marked by complacent mediocrity. The United States, in the century or so since its achievement of independence, had survived a bloody civil war, had spread across 3,000 miles from the Atlantic to the Pacific coast, and emerged as a major, wealthy, and ever-growing power. Save for an occasional minor altercation like the war with Spain in 1898, it had known peace and the comfort, assurance, and self-satisfaction that come with peace. Its inhabitants were unanimously convinced that the democratic principles enunciated in the Declaration of Independence, the Constitution, and the writings of the Founding Fathers gave the nation a virtue and strength that no other land on earth could boast, and that these principles were infinitely superior to any other system of government that had ever existed or could possibly be imagined. Glorying in the fact that the will of the majority ruled and that the least person had a perfect right to express himself, it looked upon any contrary opinion as being not only heresy but treason. As Mencken was to put it:

> What, then, is the spirit of Americanism? I precipitate it conveniently into the doctrine that the way to ascertain the truth about anything, whether in the realms of exact knowledge, in the purple zone of the fine arts or in the empyrean reaches of metaphysics, is to take a vote upon it, and that the way to propagate that truth, once it has been ascertained and proclaimed by lawful authority, is with a club.[16]

The underlying metaphysic of this national spirit was Puritanism. It is not easy to define Puritanism, in spite of Mencken's classic definition of it as "the haunting fear that someone, somewhere, may be happy."[17] We commonly think of it as a dour and half-frightened conviction that the sexual impulse in man is ineradicably evil and that every slightest manifestation of it must be put down, and certainly its attitude toward sex was a large and important part of it. But there was much more to it than that. Starting out originally in England as a reform movement within the Established Church, it spread over here beyond any kind of denominational barriers and evolved into an attitude of narrowness and intolerance, a conviction that whatever was opposed to its own gloomy doctrines was by that token wicked, and "a delusion of moral duty"[18] that led the Puritan to believe he was called upon to play policeman to the world and compel all others to be good by his standards. Santayana was but echoing Mencken when he described it as being "at enmity with joy."

Mencken's lifelong aversion to Christianity—and neither Voltaire nor Nietzsche ever said harsher things about it—was based in part at least on the fact that he tended to identify it with this Puritanism that he so much despised. In this he was mistaken, but it was not really his fault. Puritanism is as much a perversion of genuine Christianity as, at the opposite extreme, would be unbridled libertinism, but it cannot be denied that the Christian Churches of the United States, Catholic as well as Protestant, had long been corrupted by its grim theology. Protestantism was either drably Fundamentalist or else, as Mencken saw it, flirted with "the Roman harlot" and played with incense, candles, and Gregorian chant; the Catholic Church of the period was pitiably mediocre, and except for Cardinal Gibbons—Mencken's fellow townsman, by the way—had not a single distinguished figure to boast. Both branches, while remaining implacably hostile to one another, were united in a common assault upon anything that could be considered a natural human impulse or pleasure.

This "luxuriant demonology," in which "God himself was transformed into a superior sort of devil,"[19] thrust itself ferociously into every corner of American life. In the specific area of religion it emphasized man's incurable sinfulness; in that of morals, as has been said, it maintained a ceaseless vigilance over the weakness of his flesh. So uncompromising was its attitude toward sex that the very language people spoke had to be purged of everything that might conceivably arouse an impure thought in the mind: newspapers and magazines could not print a word like "leg" even if they were referring to furniture but had to use "limb" in its place; "bosom" was substituted for "breast"; and terms like "prostitute," "pregnant," "syphilis," and "gonorrhea" were got around with absurd euphemisms.[20] In political and social life

Puritanism manifested itself in such things as Sunday "blue laws" and ordinances against blasphemy, and its crowning triumph was, of course, Prohibition.

But setting aside Prohibition, it was perhaps on literature that its hand lay heaviest. Suspicious of beauty of any kind, it took a particularly dim view of the beautiful in art. Both implicitly and explicitly it held that the purpose of fiction was to edify and improve and that that of criticism was to uphold the principles of the moral law, and the notion that the artist might live only to create beauty was anathema to it. The result was that it sternly put down anything that did not conform to its own aesthetic and encouraged the production of work in which artistry was very definitely secondary to purity of content. Whitman it castigated and then ignored; Mark Twain it dismissed as a hollow clown; even men like Henry James, perhaps the one unquestioned giant that American fiction has as yet produced, and William Dean Howells, at least a serious and respectable craftsman, did not dare revolt against its canons. It was the Chamberses and Harrisons, or—what is worse—the Harold Bell Wrights and John Fox, Jr.'s, who achieved fame and success because they depicted life as the Puritan imagination believed life ought to be.

Mencken described the situation at length in the great essay "The National Letters," which introduces *Prejudices: Second Series:*

> We have achieved no prodigies of the first class, and very few of the second class, and not many of the third and fourth classes. Our literature, despite several false starts that promised much, is chiefly remarkable, now as always, for its respectable mediocrity. . . . Viewed largely, its salient character appears as a sort of timorous flaccidity, an amiable hollowness. In bulk it grows more and more formidable, in ease and decorum it makes undoubted progress, and on the side of mere technic, of the bald capacity to write, it shows an ever-widening competence. But when one proceeds from such agencies and externals to the intrinsic substance, to the creative passion within, that substance quickly reveals itself as thin and watery, and that passion fades to something almost puerile. In all that mass of suave and often highly diverting writing there is no visible movement toward a distinguished and singular excellence, a signal national quality, a ripe and stimulating flavor, or, indeed, toward any other describable goal. What one sees is simply a general irresolution, a pervasive superficiality. . . . One is conscious of no brave and noble earnestness in it, of no generalized passion for intellectual and spiritual adventure, of no organized determination to think things out.[21]

Around the turn of the century certain authors like Frank Norris and Theodore Dreiser began to grow impatient under the restraints of Puritanism and to try to turn out work that reflected American life honestly, truthfully, and naturally. But their efforts were met by a reaction of pious horror and, in the case of Dreiser at least, by persecution and a deliberate attempt to prevent publication of his books on the ground that they were mere pornography.

To say that Mencken came into the midst of this oppressive atmosphere like a breath of fresh air is really a meteorological understatement. He came into it like a cyclone, or, at all events, like the gust of wind that heralds a summer thunderstorm. Almost before anyone knew of his presence he was leveling hammer blows at the Puritans, and before very long he had them reeling and breathless. Everything they had held sacred for a couple of generations came under his relentless attack. He denounced the political figures of the time as hollow posturers, and ridiculed without mercy the fourth-rate novelists and dramatists whose work had been gravely accepted as modern American literature.

In the beginning, of course, both his audience and his influence were local—at first in the pages of the old Baltimore *Morning Herald* and then a bit later in the *Sunpapers.* But as early as August 1906—the year in which he went to work for the *Sun*—Colonel Henry Watterson of the Louisville *Courier-Journal* was facetiously complimenting the staid old paper on having gotten itself a real "Whangdoodle," and the reputation that was launched then would build up through the "Free Lance" column, which he wrote almost daily from May 1911 to October 1915, and attain solid permanence with the famous "Monday Articles" from 1920 until 1938. As he himself wrote many years later, with some understatement, the "Free Lance" column "was highly controversial and every statement I made in it was instantly attacked."[22]

Very early, too, he began to branch out. With his acceptance of the post of book editor of *The Smart Set* in 1908, he achieved a national audience. *The Smart Set* was never a really respectable magazine and doubtless it would be stretching the truth a bit to say that it was an influential one, but Mencken's reviews, together with the drama criticism of George Jean Nathan, speedily gave it a prestige that older periodicals, with much larger circulation and infinitely greater dignity, could and did envy. In 1914 he and Nathan became its co-editors, and for the next nine years they waged their war against all the forces of

Puritanism, patriotism, and 100% Americanism. It was a war that they themselves never took quite seriously, and the very lightness with which they carried it on was infuriating to those opposing forces, who took it seriously indeed.

Thus by the time they founded *The American Mercury* in 1924, Mencken was well established as a critic of national reputation and importance. Behind him lay not only a vast mass of newspaper and magazine work but the Nietzsche volume, the *Book of Prefaces*, the slighter *In Defense of Women*, three volumes of the *Prejudices* series, and above all the first three editions of *The American Language*. The academic critics might look down their noses at him, deploring his vulgarity and his lack of proper intellectual credentials, but however much they tried they could not possibly ignore him. He was too influential and important, he was simply too big, to be dismissed.

He had not, to be sure, deliberately sought fame for its own sake. "If I really believed," he once wrote, "that I had Left a Mark upon my Time I think I'd leap into the nearest ocean."[23] Yet by 1926 Walter Lippmann could call him "the most powerful personal influence on this whole generation of educated people,"[24] and *The New York Times*, of which he seldom spoke well, frankly admitted that he was the most powerful private citizen in America. Somewhat later, in a literary history of the period, Alfred Kazin summed it up admirably: "But if Mencken had never lived, it would have taken a whole army of assorted philosophers, monologists, editors, and patrons of the new writing to make up for him";[25] and his biographer Carl Bode is quite right in saying that by the early twenties Mencken was on the way to becoming a national institution.[26]

What had he done, in those roughly two decades, to bring himself to a position of such eminence?

For one thing at least, he had raised criticism to the level of a fine art—and America, unlike the Germany of Goethe or the France of Sainte-Beuve or the England of Coleridge, had not thus far known a body of critical writing that enjoyed an existence distinct from that of the literature it studied. We had had earlier critics, of course: Poe comes to mind at once, and there was also James Gibbons Huneker, who was to exert a considerable influence on the shaping of Mencken's own body of ideas. But neither of these, despite the fact that they wrote original and sometimes even profound criticism, achieved anything like a lasting reputation in the field; Poe is certainly much better known in this country as a clever versifier and a writer of detective and horror stories, and whatever fame Huneker may still have rests chiefly upon a novel that in his day was considered to be pornographic. And save for these lonely exceptions to the rule, American criticism was a dry, juiceless pursuit which threw a very dim light on the literature (principally the English literature) of the past: it considered that it was making a significant contribution to human knowledge if it counted the number of irregular verbs in *Beowulf* or located some Latin source for an obscure passage in *The Faerie Queene*. It could not be bothered, it felt that it would be beneath its dignity to bother, with the literature that was taking shape around it.

Mencken's criticism differed from this not just in degree but in kind. There had simply never been anything like it before. Though he was extraordinarily well read, he gave little time to mining the classics of earlier generations; his work is notably free of both quotation and learned allusion. He preferred to deal with the contemporary—and in his role as a book reviewer this meant dealing as much or more with the bad, the third- and fourth-rate, as with the good. Indeed, it was the attention that he gave to the bad, and the ridicule he poured upon it month after month after month in *The Smart Set*, that exposed it for what it was and so cleared the path for better and more honest work.*

When he wrote about the good—Conrad's novels, for example, or Dreiser's—he illumined it superbly for the benefit of those who had read or would read it, but at the same time he was at an infinite remove from that tribe that Hemingway would later call "explainers." That is to say, however much insight he might bring to bear upon an author's craftsmanship and thought, he never looked for symbolism or two or three layers of hidden meaning. His analyses, in fact, could be read with pleasure and profit by people who had no particular interest in Conrad or Dreiser. Often—there are those who complain that it was too often—his consideration of the work of other men was only a point of departure for setting forth his own ideas; such great essays as "The National Letters," "Puritanism as a Literary Force," and "The Sahara of the Bozart" not only trace the history of American literature but are a part of it.

---

*Benjamin De Casseres once wrote: "My God!, the years Mencken has spent—wasted—in mentally rolling in tons and tons of dried dung: American fiction! Can he ever be cleansed? Such is the price an honest workman must pay for thoroughness." *Mencken and Shaw* (New York: Silas Newton, 1930), pp. 76–77.

In addition, however, there is an aspect to Mencken's critical writing that places it in a category even above and beyond that of the three great European authors whom I mentioned earlier. Goethe, Sainte-Beuve, and Coleridge wrote important and original criticism; without them German, French, and English literature would be much the poorer. The point is, however, that they would not be essentially different,* whereas Mencken's criticism literally changed the whole course of literature in the United States. When he began writing, it was one thing, and by the time he finished, it was something else again; and the difference is attributable to him more than to any other one man or any other single force.

So it does not really mean anything if Dreiser, Lewis, and the other writers whom he championed are in eclipse—an eclipse which may very well be only temporary, as that of Henry James turned out to be temporary. If Mencken cleared the path for them, they were able to clear it in turn for the men who would come after: Dreiser and Lewis made possible Thomas Wolfe and Ernest Hemingway and William Faulkner, and these in their turn made possible every significant American novelist and short-story writer of the past generation—John Steinbeck, Robert Penn Warren, John O'Hara, James Gould Cozzens, Norman Mailer, John Updike, to name but a handful of very different and unrelated men. There is not one among them without a debt to Mencken for his literary freedom and the quality of his audience. To some of the more recent figures he may be scarcely more than a vague name, but the debt is there nonetheless. And while Mencken himself might have little interest in their work, as he had little in that of Wolfe or Faulkner, he is, to use one of his own favorite terms, the *Stammvater* of them all.

To open the way for them he had first to destroy the Puritanism which would have been as much their foe as it had been their predecessors . And destroy it he did, without ever giving quarter for an instant. The war began, as we have seen, in the Baltimore *Morning Herald* at the turn of the century and it went on for a long time—there and in the *Sunpapers*, in *The Smart Set* and *The American Mercury*, in half a dozen books, in the defense of Dreiser's *The "Genius"* and Cabell's

---

*I am perfectly well aware, of course, that Goethe to a supreme degree, and Coleridge to a somewhat lesser one, enriched the creative literatures of their native lands. The above statement is made strictly with regard to their critical writings—which, in each case, is of much less importance than their imaginative work.

Jurgen. The final mortal blow was not struck until 1925, when "the infidel Scopes" was tried at Dayton, Tennessee, for violating the state's law against the teaching of evolution; the fact that Scopes was found guilty and fined one hundred dollars had nothing to do with who won. Even then, a year later, Puritanism could lash out in its death throes at its ancient enemy in the famous "Hatrack" case, but that was the end; thereafter it could no longer be taken seriously, nor could it impede the growth of a new, honest, and characteristically American literature.

Concomitant with this, and really another campaign in the same war, was Mencken's unceasing attack upon sham and hypocrisy in American politics. William H. Nolte writes that while he has met English teachers who knew next to nothing about Mencken, he has never yet met a political scientist who was unaware of him.[27] In itself this may not mean anything, because the political scientist and the politician belong to two entirely different species and the mere fact that the former are familiar with Mencken's work is no necessary proof that the latter have ever read him or, reading him, been moved to mend their ways. But it would at least seem to indicate that his political writings are known in academic circles, and that such respect as they have stems not only from his theorizing (which here and there is rather shaky) but from their practical repercussions.

In this battle, of course, the effect is much harder to gauge; in the very nature of things it was one that neither he nor anybody else could ever decisively win. Just as it would be senseless to argue that Mencken was responsible for the repeal of the Eighteenth Amendment, though he had as much to do with it as any man, so it would be equally senseless to argue that before him the nation's political life was corrupt and that after him it was pure and undefiled. But if today's public and governmental figures are a cut above the Bryans and Hardings and Coolidges of a past generation, if the American people do not take "beaters of breasts" quite as seriously as their fathers did, he must deserve a large share of the credit for these facts—so that here, too, his influence has been considerable.

This was also, as I have indicated, part of the struggle against Puritanism, for the same forces that repressed the arts and dictated what a man might and might not drink were responsible likewise for the laws and the lawmakers that gave their dismal philosophy practical application. By attacking such laws and the men who made them, Mencken was striking blows for freedom on yet another front—just as, in his writings on religion and ethics, he helped vanquish the absurd Fundamentalism that made it difficult for any intelligent person to take religious faith seriously, and, in *The American Language*, freed the living tongue of more than a hundred million people from bondage to archaic rules and pointed it in the direction of a power, growth, and vigor that it had not known since Elizabethan times.

To say that the issues about which Mencken wrote are dead is true enough. But they are dead precisely because he killed them—because the battles that he fought he so thoroughly won that the very memory of the war tends to fade into a distant past. Anyone who has ever had to undergo even minor surgery takes it for granted that he will be given something, generally or locally, that will enable him to endure the experience without pain; yet he seldom stops to think of how much he is indebted for that fact to Dr. W. T. G. Morton, the inventor of anesthesia. In the same way, the man who buys a case of beer at a neighborhood store to take with him and enjoy at home, or who sips a martini appreciatively in a cocktail lounge, or who buys a book without having to ask himself whether someone else has first passed upon it, may never have heard of Mencken but he owes to him much of the freedom that he enjoys. The world he lives in is, in very large part, one that Mencken made.

4 ONE FINAL ARGUMENT REMAINS. It is possible to admit Mencken's great influence but to hold that it was bad—to take the position, in other words, that the world he made is full of evils and that he is responsible, directly or indirectly, for them. This argument would maintain that the literary freedom he advocated broke down all standards of decency and good taste and eventually opened the way to unrestrained pornography. It would maintain that his campaign against Prohibition and the Volstead Act led to the alcoholism and possibly even to the drug abuse that loom so large among present-day social problems. It might even maintain that his ridicule of religion did irreparable damage to the nation's moral codes, and is thus a contributing factor to the crime, violence, and sexual looseness that we see everywhere about us today.

Even assuming this argument to be true, it would simply not be valid. Influence cannot be measured in terms of good and bad. Probably no man has had a greater influence on Western politics and diplomacy than Niccolò Machiavelli, who achieved the ultimate honor of having his name turned into a common adjective, but it would have to be admitted that the influence he had did not exactly conduce to honesty and upright conduct. Most Americans and Western Europeans would probably regard Communism as an evil, but they could not on that account deny that Karl Marx has had a greater influence on the course of history than anybody else since Christ. There are scores and hundreds of people of whom it could be said that the world would have been better off it they had not lived, but they are there in the record nonetheless.

So even if it were possible to demonstrate with mathematical precision and beyond any doubt that Mencken was directly responsible for all the ills of modern times, such a thing would not diminish in the least the importance of studying him. It could, on the contrary, increase it.

It is, needless to say, the thesis of this book that Mencken's influence was all to the good—that the things he attacked deserved to be attacked, and that America is a cleaner, saner, more healthy place today because he attacked and disposed of them. It is part of the same thesis that, by virtue of their effects, the ideas that inspired him to his work and guided him in carrying it out are eminently worthy of serious consideration. Such a position need not hold that he was always right, or even that he was always reasonable; he was obviously neither. But it does hold that even when he was wrong and even when he was being quite unreasonable, he was having an immense impact on his time. That impact puts him among the giants in our cultural history, and his place there is secure.

I

BACKGROUND

I come of a family that has thought very well of itself for 300 years, and
with some reason.

—Autobiographical Notes, 1925

◇◇◇

THERE ARE AT LEAST FIVE full-length biographies of Mencken, and it is not the intent of this book to add another one to the list. None comes anywhere near being definitive, but all have their merits. Just as it is impossible to write a critical study of a man without giving some biographical background to indicate whence his ideas arose, so it is likewise impossible to write a straight biography without including at least some treatment of his beliefs and how he arrived at them; and all those who have told the story of Mencken's life have dealt with his thought as well. Some, needless to say, have done it better than others.

In general, the biographies tend to get better as they go along; that is to say, the later ones are superior to the earlier. The first was Isaac Goldberg's *The Man Mencken*, published in 1925. This, it will be recalled, was the same year that saw the appearance of Ernest Boyd's book *H. L. Mencken*, but Goldberg had several advantages over Boyd. Whereas the latter's work runs to only 89 pages, Goldberg could spread out over a leisurely 388 and thus include immensely more material. Unhappily, like Boyd, he wrote at a time when his subject still had twenty-three years of development and tremendous productivity ahead of him. In some respects, no better book on Mencken has been written to this day; in others, it naturally dates very badly.

Mencken—who was then forty-five—must have been quite impressed by the thought of a book coming out about him, for he collaborated with Goldberg to a degree quite unusual among living biographical subjects. In answer to the latter's questions he prepared a 200-page typescript setting forth in detail his ancestry, his family background, an account of his boyhood and early newspaper experiences, and his ideas and feelings on an infinite variety of matters. In addition he made available to him youthful poems that had not been included in *Ventures into Verse*, manuscripts of early short stories, and some of the columns of "Knocks and Jollies" and "Untold Tales" from the Baltimore *Morning Herald;* little of this has ever been published in book form elsewhere. In effect, as Carl Bode says, he wrote a good part of Goldberg's book for him.

In a letter of July 28, 1925, Mencken told Goldberg that "I can only congratulate you sincerely on a very remarkable piece of research"[1] (though under the circumstances it is difficult to see just what research Goldberg had to do). He also tells him that "your facts, so far as I know them, are exactly accurate." Nevertheless, and in spite of Goldberg's unique firsthand source, he does occasionally nod: he gives "Otterheim" instead of "Otterbein" as the name of the church in Mencken's first published news story,* and February 4, 1904, as the date of the Great Baltimore Fire, whereas it actually broke out on February 7. Admittedly, these things are trivial, but one would expect that Mencken himself, with his newspaperman's respect for accuracy, would have caught them.

In spite of his gratitude and compliments, it is to be wondered whether Mencken really did have any very high opinion of the book and whether he was completely honest with Goldberg about it. Writing to Raymond Pearl on December 3 of the same year, he calls it "mainly applesass."[2] To Jim Tully he confided on May 4, 1927, that "Goldberg is a learned man, but has no humor."[3] This latter criticism comes quite close to the truth: Goldberg took Mencken much more seriously than Mencken ever took himself and so tended to invest him with the role of messiah—a role that Mencken could never stand in others and would have indignantly disclaimed for his own person.

---

*As a matter of fact, this would seem to have been Mencken's *second* news story. Preceding it by at least a few minutes was the account of the theft from the stable of Howard Quinlan, near Kingsville. (Cf. *Newspaper Days*, pp. 7–8.) On this detail, at least, Mencken's own memory faltered; he has nothing about it in the manuscript that he prepared for Goldberg.

Years later, in a letter which he wrote on July 27, 1947, to another biographer, William Manchester, he declared: "Goldberg is anything but reliable. He was a charming fellow but a Socialist and hence couldn't understand my politics at all."[4]

Exactly a quarter of a century was to go by before there would be another life of Mencken, and then two came out almost simultaneously—Edgar Kemler's *The Irreverent Mr. Mencken* and Manchester's *Disturber of the Peace.* To both of these men, while their work was in progress, he showed almost—if not quite—the same courtesy and helpfulness that he had shown to Goldberg; he met with them on numerous occasions, answered their questions patiently and at length, and placed at their disposal information which no research would have enabled them to uncover. (There were, as we shall see, certain things that he apparently did not tell them and which one can only suppose they did not ask.) Unhappily, he was in no position to pass judgment or express an opinion on their finished products—both books were completed and published after his incapacitating stroke in November 1948.

Kemler's is the least satisfactory of all the biographies; certainly it is the briefest, so that many very important things are mentioned only in passing or not treated at all. Sara Mayfield states that Mencken was skeptical of the project from its beginning,[5] but he made no effort to dissuade the young man and, as has just been said, provided him with all the data he wanted. His misgivings may have been due in part, at least, to the fact that he sensed that Kemler was not going to be the hero-worshipper Goldberg had been, or that Manchester was showing himself to be during this same time. His judgments were far more critical, and this means that the failure of his work is especially unfortunate because instead of being the worst biography it could so easily have been the best.

One gets the impression that Kemler simply did not understand Mencken either as man or as writer. He considers him a skeptic of the first order and compares him to Rabelais, Swift, and Shaw, but feels that he abused his gifts and produced little—excepting the *Days* books and *The American Language*—that would be likely to endure. This opinion, after all, is hardly original: others, both before and since Kemler, have said the same thing. But to his mind this abuse of gifts made Mencken, after having swept away the delusions of one generation, a spokesman for those of the next. He accuses him of "flirting" with Nazism and Fascism, of agreeing with the racial theories of the Nazis, and of sympathizing with Hitler's program for European conquest—statements for which there is no slightest basis either in Mencken's published writings or in his private letters.*

William Manchester's *Disturber of the Peace* is without doubt the best of the five book-length studies we are considering here—but this is not exactly the same thing as saying that it is definitive. Like Mencken, the author was a practicing newspaperman, which meant that he was used to writing in a clear, direct style that was admirably suited to his task. He had already laid a considerable groundwork for it in "A Critical Study of the Work of H. L. Mencken as Literary Critic of *The Smart Set Magazine*, 1908–1914," which he did as a thesis for his master's degree at the University of Missouri. When the idea came to him of expanding the thesis into a book he wrote to Mencken, who was eventually instrumental in securing a job for him with the *Sunpapers;* thereafter, settled down in Baltimore, he was able to work in close contact with his subject, ply him with questions, and from time to time submit sections of the work to him for factual verification and comment.

Unhappily, it was Manchester's infatuation for Mencken and his ideas that, in the end, really disqualified him for the work he had set himself. This is in no sense to say that he is hopelessly uncritical—he really is not. But the influence of Mencken led him into a trap that, over the years, has proven fatal to many men—that of trying to write in the Menckenian style. It is a futile undertaking, though none of those who have succumbed to the temptation seem ever to have realized it. When Manchester refers to "the damp cells where [Paul Elmer] More, [Irving] Babbitt, and other such creeps dismally fretted," he sounds only like a pale imitation of the master; when he speaks of Catholics as "Christers," he is showing nothing but bad manners and poor taste. If Mencken were to do the latter (and I can find no place in his writings where he does), it would not be offensive because it would simply be quite typical of the man.

---

*One might reasonably expect that a biographer would get the date of his subject's birth right even if nothing else, but Kemler manages to err on this elementary point. He gives Mencken's birthday as September 9, whereas it is actually September 12. Even in the paperback reprint published thirteen years later (1963), the error remains uncorrected.

Yet it has to be admitted that no other book gives us more of Mencken's own spirit, or re-creates him more vividly, than *Disturber of the Peace.*

Sara Mayfield's *The Constant Circle* is in a class by itself, since of all the biographies it is the only one written by somebody who had known Mencken well and been in regular contact with him during his most important and active years. Actually Miss Mayfield began as a friend of his wife, Sara Powell Haardt, rather than of Mencken himself, but by virtue of that fact she saw him often and for extended periods during the twenties and thirties; he depended on her for assistance during Sara's prolonged illness, and continued to correspond with her afterward. Hers is the most authentically firsthand portrait of all; even though the book is sometimes rambling and anecdotal—perhaps because of that fact—it makes genuinely delightful reading. It reveals much about him that we would not otherwise know.

By long odds the biggest, most comprehensive, and most heavily documented life is the *Mencken* of Carl Bode. This is a labor of both scholarship and love, and despite certain shortcomings (one cannot help but feel that Mencken himself would have referred to the author as "the Herr Professor-Doktor") it is likely to stand as the most nearly definitive work for a long time to come. Bode had access to an enormous amount of material in the Mencken Room of Baltimore's Enoch Pratt Free Library that had not yet been catalogued when Manchester and Kemler wrote their books; and in addition he interviewed practically everybody who had ever known Mencken or been in close contact with him. This included his brother August; his secretary, Mrs. Rosalind Lohrfinck; the Knopfs, Alfred and Blanche; Hamilton Owens, Paul Patterson, and other luminaries of the *Sunpapers;* surviving members of the Saturday Night Club; the doctors who had attended or examined him during the years of his incapacity; and numerous other friends, acquaintances, and associates. Since most of these people have since died, he was the last biographer who could have such direct and firsthand information made available to him.

The result is that he adds to the others' accounts things about which they scarcely so much as hint. Mencken was apparently willing to answer Kemler's and Manchester's questions with perfect honesty and to check their manuscripts for factual correctness, but he did not volunteer information for which they did not specifically ask. Bode, writing after he had died, did not have to show quite the same concern for his sensibilities that they did, and, as we have just said, he could make use of material that Mencken simply did not open up to them.

He is particularly valuable and interesting, for example, on the subject of Mencken's relationships with women. The other two, and Miss Mayfield even more so, naturally treat in great detail of Sara, but they say nothing about any other women in his life and one can only conclude that Mencken, much more reticent here than anywhere else, offered them no information. Marion Bloom is not even listed in Manchester's index; Aileen Pringle, the actress, is simply someone whom he met on a trip to Hollywood and to whom some gossip columnists thereupon linked him romantically; Marcella Du Pont and her husband are family friends whose home he would occasionally visit on weekends in his later years. Yet from Bode we learn that Mencken was very close to Miss Bloom, that they dated over a long period of time, and that if he did not actually propose marriage to her he was at least once on the brink of doing so. (According to the account, he abandoned the idea when she was converted to Christian Science.) His feelings toward Miss Pringle were of such a nature that, when he became engaged to Sara Haardt, he sent back the letters that she had written to him and asked for his in return. And though Marcella Du Pont was much younger than he, and married (not too happily) to a scion of the immensely rich Wilmington, Delaware, chemical firm, their friendship was a warm and intimate one and her letters to him often began with "Henry dearest." To these women, and to a few others about whom Bode tells us, Mencken was something more than the "Sage of Baltimore," the greatest newspaperman of his day, and the *enfant terrible* of American literature; he was a kind and considerate friend, a very masculine man, and a figure—despite his bourgeois appearance and what he himself called his "matronly" build—of glamour and romance.

But Bode is valuable for other reasons too. Besides these friendships with women, he has a great deal of information not readily available elsewhere on Mencken's relationships with such people as Philip Goodman, the Philadelphia advertising man and publisher; Alfred and Blanche Knopf; and Dr. Howard Kelly, the Johns Hopkins physician and member of the "Big Four" who was a friendly enemy for a quarter of a century or more. There is much on his association with and involvement in the work of the *Sunpapers.* And Bode was able to include fascinating data on those last years following the stroke when, his work cut off and his life empty, Mencken waited helplessly for death; from him, for example, we get the statement, undocumented and unsubstantiated, that when Mencken himself realized the extent to which his faculties had been impaired he threatened to commit suicide.

All of these books attempt, and for the most part quite successfully, to delineate the cultural and intellectual climate in which Mencken was born and grew to maturity, and the effect which he then had on that climate. In synthesizing and weighing the body of his ideas, however, they fall somewhat short. Almost inevitably their authors, like everyone who ever came in contact with him, were spellbound by the tremendous personality, the vast bulk of his production, the surface virtues of superb writing and uproarious humor. For them the man was more important than his work.

One cannot fault them, of course, for failing to do something that they did not set out to do anyway. But the task of burrowing beneath that surface to the bedrock of thought that it adorned and judging whether it also had the virtue of truth, and judging, too, whether that truth was for a day or all time—this task remains to be done.

2 WHEN WE TURN from the books that other people wrote about Mencken to his own works, we are, of course, on somewhat different ground. In a sense everything that he wrote was about himself, which is to say that he may well have been the most autobiographical author who ever lived. It was impossible for him to keep himself out of his books, articles, and columns, and he seldom made the attempt. His own likes and dislikes, his violent prejudices, his dogmatic certainties and gay skepticism, permeate whatever subject he happened to be discoursing upon, whether the preposterous antics of a national convention or the teleological argument for God's existence. His book reviews are often simply points of departure for setting forth his own opinions on the topic treated in the book, and it was not at all unusual for him, two or three paragraphs under way, to lose sight of the book completely. This tendency even carries over into the immense scholarship of *The American Language* —here and there in the text, and certainly in many a mischievous footnote.

It was a tendency that manifested itself at the very outset of his career: the 1905 critical study of Shaw, his first book except for the uncharacteristic *Ventures into Verse,* is as much Mencken as it is Shaw. The work on Nietzsche, coming three years later, may have been the pioneer treatise, at least in English, on its subject, but on many pages Nietzsche's philosophy is little more than a convenient base from which to expound the philosophy of Mencken, which by that time was pretty well formed. And so with everything that was to come after. What chiefly infuriated the staid bourgeois readers of the Baltimore *Sunpapers,* as they crumpled the "Free Lance" columns and later the "Monday Articles" in their fists, was his insistence on projecting himself into every one of them, and his seeming smug assurance that any person who had any intelligence at all would of course agree with him!

The result, as I have already indicated, is that we have no difficulty knowing what Mencken thought on almost any conceivable subject. A concordance of his writings (and one is not only badly needed but would be a delightful work in its own right) would undoubtedly run to thousands of rubric headings, with in some cases hundreds of perfectly consistent entries under each one. This makes him an almost ideal subject for the researcher,* who does not have to cast about among mutually contradictory statements to try to determine which one represents his earlier and which one his later beliefs.

This wealth of material in his critical writings is all the more helpful because the specifically autobiographical volumes tell us, as a matter of fact, very little. *Happy Days, Newspaper Days,* and *Heathen Days* remain the most continuously popular of his works, and they also rank among the very best, but they are about as far from the uninhibited *Confessions* of, say, St. Augustine or Jean-Jacques Rousseau as it would be possible to get. He himself, on the very first page of the first one, called them "casual and somewhat chaotic memoirs" and pointed out that they were not offered as "coldly objective history."[6] They are a series of anecdotes and genre pieces, brilliantly written and re-creating an era of Americana as it has perhaps never been re-created elsewhere, but they are almost as remarkable for what they leave out as for what they put in.

A case in point may be found in Chapters 18 and 19 of *Heathen*

---

*This, and the fact that almost (if not quite) everything that one needs is assembled and carefully catalogued in one place—the H. L. Mencken Room of Baltimore's Enoch Pratt Free Library.

Days. Both of these are dated 1934, and they describe two episodes on a Mediterranean cruise—the first, a visit to the site of ancient Carthage, and the second, some days spent in the Holy Land. So far as one could gather from the text, Mencken was traveling entirely alone. But the facts surrounding the trip are that in the early winter of that year, following the difficult negotiations by which he had divested himself of *The American Mercury*, he felt so completely worn out and Sara's health was in such a precarious state that he thought an ocean trip would benefit both of them. She was thus with him throughout the whole journey. Yet in the two chapters there is not only no mention of the fact that he was accompanied by his wife—there is not the slightest indication that he was or ever had been married!

So in many other instances throughout. He speaks of his friends, but never of friendship. He tells of his reading, but—save perhaps in the case of *Huckleberry Finn* and the impact of Huxley—gives no hint of how these books influenced him and helped mold his own thought. He describes his rapid advance in the newspaper business, but if he experienced either elation or misgivings over his increasing responsibilities he tells us nothing about it. He recounts stories that are sidesplittingly funny, but he is always on the outside of them, narrating the events with a detached and cynical air and his gravelly chuckle.

One is forced to conclude that Mencken set out with the deliberate intention of being as selective and impersonal as possible in his memoirs, and that what he did include he treated, as was typical of him, with an extremely light touch. What could not be treated that way was simply left out. When, following the great success of *Happy Days*, Knopf suggested that he do a companion volume on the second decade of his life, he demurred; with the coming of adolescence it seemed to him that "existence began inevitably to take on a new and more sinister aspect."[7] The sensational pouring out of callow romances and youthful sexual exploits, and the discovery of freedom that comes to every youth, were not for him; certainly he went through all of this, as every young man does, but he simply felt that it was nobody else's business.

Did he maintain this same reserve in his other autobiographical writings? It will be some time yet before we know. But the memoirs, remember, do not stop with the three published *Days* books. In a fireproof vault at the Pratt Library there is a five-volume *Diary* and four volumes entitled *Letters and Documents Relating to the Baltimore Sunpapers*, which may not be opened until 1981, along with four volumes of *My Life as Author and Editor* and three volumes entitled *Thirty-five Years of Newspaper Work,* which are similarly restricted until 1991. One can only speculate on what they contain, and the speculation is rather useless until the appointed times roll around. Perhaps he may have been a bit more frank about certain persons who, like himself, would be sure to be dead by that time, but it is not likely that even under these circumstances he would engage in any scandalous revelations or gossip-mongering. Mencken was always Mencken, and this sort of thing was utterly alien to him; these works may tell us more about him and about other people than we now know, but it seems improbable that they will tell us anything essentially different.

3 TO SOME DEGREE, at least, every man is what he is because his ancestors were what they were. The Menckens, for almost as far back as the family can be traced, were intellectuals, scholars, teachers, jurists, and even theologians! "There are more Ph.D.'s on my family tree," Mencken once wrote, "than even a Boston bluestocking can boast; there was a whole century when even the most ignorant of my house was at least *Juris utriusque Doctor.*"[8]

To be sure, the first ones of whom we know anything were merchants—a class of men of whom the Sage of Baltimore was to have an opinion hardly very much higher than his opinion of politicians. Helmrich Mencke,* who, if not the patriarch of the clan, was at least the earliest one of whom any record seems to have survived, was apparently a quite successful one. He died at Oldenburg, in Hannover, in 1570, leaving two sons, Gerd (d. 1614) and Otto (d. 1617). Eilhard, the only son of Gerd to live to maturity, became archpresbyter of the cathedral of Marienwerder, and when he died there of the plague in 1657 he created by the terms of his will a *Familienstipendium* which almost to this day has provided for the higher education of all European Menckens. Otto's son Johannes (1607–1688) followed the now established tradition by becoming a successful and prosperous merchant who traveled widely and achieved the eminence of *Rathsherr* (town councillor) in the family's native Oldenburg.

Johannes' son, who again bore the name Otto, presumably after his grandfather, lived from 1644 to 1707 and carried the Menckens in

*The final "n" was not added to the name until a generation or so later.

one generation from *Geschäft* to the realms of scholarship. He received his degree from the University of Leipzig at the age of twenty, and five years later, after a brilliant lecturing career throughout Germany and Holland, returned to his alma mater as professor of morals and politics. Five times during his life of service to the institution he served as its *rector magnificus*. In 1682 he founded the *Acta eruditorum*, one of the earliest of learned journals and, as Isaac Goldberg says, a remote ancestor of *The American Mercury*. Almost every important intellectual figure of Western Europe for the next century or more appeared in this periodical; among its contributors were men like Boyle, Pascal, Descartes, Locke, and Sir Isaac Newton, and in 1684 the great philosopher and mathematician Leibniz published in its pages his first paper on the differential calculus. It remained in the possession of the family until 1754, with Otto's son Johann Burkhard (1674–1732) and grandson Friedrich (1708–1754) as successive editors, and even after it passed into other hands it continued to appear until 1782.

Johann Burkhard Mencken surpassed even his father in scholarship and literary renown. He took his Ph.D. at Leipzig when he was twenty-one, and three years later, after traveling throughout Europe and England, was elected a member of the British Royal Society. A year later, he was back in Leipzig with a full professorship in history at the university, and was embarked upon a career of immense productivity. In addition to taking over the editorship of the *Acta* from his father, he published numerous works of history, biography, and poetry: his library, says Goldberg, "was so superior to that of the university that he threw it open to the students"; and it was at this university, at the conferral of degrees on February 9, 1713, and again on February 14, 1715, that he delivered two lectures which have retained a certain measure of fame to this day under the title of *De charlataneria eruditorum*, or *The Charlatanry of the Learned*.

This unique and delightful little work, which astonishingly prefigures the whole career of H. L. Mencken two centuries later, was a merry but nonetheless deadly assault upon quacks and frauds in every field. Johann Burkhard aimed his shafts at teachers, philosophers, theologians, scientists, doctors, lawyers, writers, and critics, ranging in time from Greece and Rome to men who may have been in the audience listening to him—at those very groups, in short, that his descendant would later make the objects of his own special ridicule. He exposed their hollow pretensions to learning, their real ignorance, their scholastic hairsplittings, their craving for adulation, and their bitter envy of each other. He showed by frequent example that most of the books they had written were worthless.

De charlataneria created a sensation at the time—so great a one, in fact, that it offended some Leipzig dignitaries and for a while its sale in the town was forbidden. But that did not prevent its distribution elsewhere in Germany. As befitted a learned disquisition given to a university audience, it had been delivered in Latin, but it was quickly translated into German and went through numerous editions, acquiring an ever-increasing mass of notes with each one. Over the years it appeared, too, in French, Dutch, Spanish, and Italian.*

Otto and Johann Burkhard, however, were not direct but collateral ancestors of H. L. Mencken. They were descended from Johannes, who had been the elder son of Otto Mencken, who had in turn been the son of old *Stammvater* Helmrich. Otto, however, had also a younger son, again named Helmrich (1609–1669), and it is from this branch of the family that the Baltimore Menckens have come down. Helmrich had five sons, one of whom died in infancy, and five daughters. Of the four sons who survived, the eldest, Otto (1654–1703), entered the diplomatic service, married well, and was elevated to the nobility, putting a *von* in front of his surname; two lapsed into business; but the fourth son, Lüder (1658–1726), followed in the tradition of his by-this-time distant cousins. In his day, in fact, his fame as a scholar was on a solid level with theirs.

Like them, he entered the University of Leipzig (being tutored, in fact, by Uncle Otto of the *Acta eruditorum*) and received his A.M. in 1680 and his Ph.D. in 1682. Thereafter, for forty-four years he was a dominant figure in the university's life; a professorship in Saxon law was created for him, he was a chief judge, and he served two terms as *rector magnificus*. In his capacity as head of the municipal committee of the Thomaskirche, he hired Johann Sebastian Bach to be the church's

---

*At some time prior to 1923 H. L. Mencken apparently had an English translation of it made by a "decayed priest," but was quite dissatisfied with it. Cf. his letter of February 20, 1923, to Carl Van Doren (Forgue, *Letters*, p. 243). In 1927 he asked Dr. Francis E. Litz, of the faculty of Catholic University in Washington, to make another English version. Dr. Litz did so, but it was not until ten years later that Mencken got around to preparing it for publication. He wrote a 43-page introduction and supplied copious notes. It was published as *The Charlatanry of the Learned* (New York: Alfred A. Knopf, Inc., 1937).

organist. "So great was his renown," says Goldberg, "as an author and expounder of legal subjects that he was known as *Viva Lex* (The Living Law-Book) and *Das Orakel des Rechtes* (The Oracle of the Law)." It is Lüder Mencken whom H. L. claims as his direct ancestor—a rather odd thing for a man who once wrote that "few men are less learned in the law than I am, or have less respect for it."[9]

It would doubtless serve little purpose to follow the genealogical trail down through succeeding generations, except to remark that H. L. Mencken, who usually exaggerated a great deal, was not exaggerating in the least when he spoke of the number of Ph.D.'s in his family history. For the next century virtually all of them held this degree, and all were distinguished usually as teachers and practitioners of law. Eventually we get down to Johann Christian Mencken, born at Wittenberg on December 3, 1797, whose exact occupation is unknown but who, again to quote Goldberg, "signals the recession of the Menckens to commercial activity." He had a son, christened Burkhardt Ludwig, who was born at Laas, in Saxony, on June 7, 1828; and on November 5, 1842, he apprenticed this youth to one Heinrich Berger, a merchant of Oschatz, who in return for the sum of 100 Thalers was to take Burkhardt Ludwig into his home and give him a thorough grounding in business practices. This Berger dealt in tobacco, so that the young man learned not only about business in general but apparently acquired a good knowledge of the tobacco industry in particular.

He seems to have stayed with Berger for just about six years. On November 1, 1848, bearing in his pocket a certificate of proficiency in business and 500 Thalers (the equivalent, at that time, of $350 in American money), he set sail for the New World and landed, a couple of weeks later, in the port of Baltimore.

What brought Burkhardt Ludwig Mencken to America? In later years his grandson used to maintain that he came over to derive a sardonic pleasure from observing the spectacle of democracy at first hand, but it seems somehow improbable that this could have been his only motive. Even the fact that it was 1848—a year, it will be remembered, of profound and often violent political and social upheaval in Europe—does not necessarily mean anything. He was not a revolutionary and he did not flee Germany, like so many of his compatriots, because he was in danger of being caught up as one. More likely he came for the simple reason that, to his common sense and solid if modest ambitions, America seemed to offer better opportunities than his tired and war-torn homeland.

Why Baltimore, and what made him stay there? The first part of this question is easier to answer than the second. Baltimore was the second-largest seaport in the country at the time, being surpassed in tonnage only by New York, and a special set of circumstances made it the almost natural point of debarkation for ships coming from Germany. These circumstances were that the Baltimore & Ohio Railroad, as it thrust its tracks ever farther westward by land, sought also to extend its empire eastward across the ocean; and a fleet of its own ships, carrying both cargo and passengers, plied regularly between the port of Bremen and the B. & O. terminal at Locust Point, just southeast of the city. Germans, as a matter of fact, had been coming to Maryland since long before the Revolutionary War, but the number was to keep increasing steadily all through the nineteenth century.

Not all of them, of course, stayed in Baltimore. Many promptly continued on westward, so that for several generations Maryland towns like Frederick, Hagerstown, and Cumberland had large German settlements. Others went on to Pennsylvania, West Virginia, Ohio, Indiana, and the Middle West. But large numbers did remain in Baltimore, perhaps for no other reason than that the long and arduous ocean voyage had left them exhausted and they were only too eager to settle down in the first place they reached.

Thus by 1848 the city already had a sizable German colony, and in the 1880's, when H. L. Mencken was a boy, it is estimated that out of its total population of 425,000 approximately 100,000 were Germans or of German descent. When Burkhardt Ludwig arrived there were German churches, both Protestant and Catholic, schools where instruction was entirely in the German language, and daily and weekly German newspapers. But above all there was an immense number of social clubs, or *Vereine*, where the members could meet regularly and keep alive the tongue and traditions they had brought with them from their native land. Some of these, like the Germania and the Concordia, were deliberately of very limited and exclusive membership; only wealthy merchants and professional men could even afford to belong to them; but below this level there were innumerable groups which met regularly for dances, songfests, picnics, and other general merrymaking. Many—indeed most—of these remained in existence down to the First World War, and a few managed to survive that holocaust and keep going until the Second.

In all this, however, though the opportunity must certainly have been open to him, Burkhardt Ludwig Mencken played no part, just as he had played no part in the revolutionary activities of the land he had left. "He belonged to no organization save a lodge of Freemasons," his grandson wrote later, "and held himself diligently aloof from the German societies that swarmed in Baltimore in the eighties. Their singing he regarded as a public disturbance, and their *Turnerei* as insane."[10] He seems to have been a rather withdrawn and lonely person, and his family, as it grew first into children and then with the years into grandchildren, was the principal and perhaps the only object of his interest and solicitude: "No man on this earth ever believed more innocently and passionately in the importance of the family as the basic unit of human society, or had a higher sense of duty to his own."[11]

In Baltimore the knowledge of the tobacco business that he had gained from Heinrich Berger served him in good stead, and he was soon seated at a bench rolling cigars. Within a short time he opened up his own grocery and general store, and then, with the money accumulated from that venture, he returned to tobacco as a wholesaler. In 1851 he married a sixteen-year-old girl named Harriet McClellan, whose family, of English-Scottish ancestry, had come from Kingston, Jamaica; since his bride spoke no German, English became the language of the household. She bore him five children, of whom the last died shortly after birth in 1862; and in that same year Harriet herself succumbed to tuberculosis. Their eldest son, August, born June 16, 1854, was the father of H. L. Mencken.

There is no reason to suppose that Burkhardt Ludwig was intellectual or scholarly: those traits had been recessive in the family for at least a couple of generations before him, and would not reappear until two more after him. But he was certainly a man of above-average intelligence with a keen business sense; though an agnostic in religion, he had his own demanding personal code of ethics; and he was apparently well enough grounded in the science of moral theology to debate it for hours on end (in German) with the Xaverian Brothers who ran St. Mary's Industrial School near his home in West Baltimore. These characteristics were to be repeated in his oldest son. August Mencken was very much like his father, except that he was far more gregarious and by all accounts had a broad, almost slapstick sense of humor.

The photographs of him that have survived show a handsome, even dashing-looking man of youthful appearance, clean-shaven save for the kind of mustache that was typical of the period, with large, bright eyes and a genial smile that seems to be an integral part of his features. There is a picture of H. L. Mencken at the age of eighteen which, minus the mustache and with a rather more serious expression, bears a resemblance that is striking even between father and son. August looks precisely like what he was: a successful businessman, solid and respectable, sure of himself and of the world about him, and one would guess, even if one did not know, that he had a home and wife and family, and that he was very much the center of this universe.

It was but natural that he should follow his father into the tobacco business, but for reasons about which we can only guess he did not remain with him for long. In 1875, when he was twenty-one, he and his brother Henry, three years his junior, struck out for themselves as "August Mencken & Bro." Their initial capital investment was thirty-five dollars; by the middle eighties the company was worth well over a hundred thousand. Henry was in charge of sales; August supervised production and prepared elaborate cost analyses "long before they began to be whooped up at Harvard. They showed precisely what it stood the firm to produce 1000 of any one of the twenty or more brands of cigars on its list."[12] Once the business was solidly established, August had to devote little more than half his time to it; for the rest he was free to pursue other interests, the chief of which was baseball.

Sometime in the late 1870's at a West Baltimore picnic— doubtless it was an affair of one of those *Vereine* which old Burkhardt Ludwig held in such complete contempt—he met a slim, blond, serious-looking but attractive young girl named Anna Margaret Abhau. Anna's background was even more thoroughly German than August's; her father, too, had emigrated in 1848, and her mother's family, the Gegners, had operated coach lines in Bavaria until the coming of the first railroads there had destroyed their business. It was a love match: they were married in November 1879 and moved into an apartment on West Lexington Street near Fremont. Today it is a slum of Baltimore's inner city; then it was an attractive and respectable middle-class neighborhood, naturally almost entirely German.

Here, ten months later, Anna Mencken gave birth to her firstborn son. He was "fetched into sentience" at precisely 9 P.M. on Sunday, September 12, 1880 (the date was already celebrated in Baltimore as Defender's Day, commemorating the repulse of an invading British force during the War of 1812), and the delivery was made by Dr. C. L. Buddenbohm, who subsequently rendered a bill of ten dollars "to one confinement."[13] The child was named Henry Louis—Henry after his uncle of course, the other half of the firm of August Mencken & Bro., and Louis after that unfortunate infant who had been Harriet McClellan Mencken's last child and who had died shortly after birth in 1862. August's views on religion and its observances were hardly more sympathetic than his son's were to be, but under wifely pressure he yielded and the baby was duly baptized in the Lutheran Church.

Three years later, with little Henry having been succeeded by a brother Charles and with the tobacco business prospering, August Mencken decided that the time had come for the family to have a home of its own. Accordingly, they moved from the small apartment to a new, spacious, three-story row house, with the red brick trim and white marble front steps that then and ever since have been regarded as typical of Baltimore, at 1524 Hollins Street. It was to be the home of Menckens for almost a century: here August and Anna would live out their lives; here too, except for the five years of his marriage, H. L. Mencken would live out his, dying there in his sleep at the age of seventy-five; and even after that it would remain the home of his surviving youngest brother, August, until the latter's death in 1967.

4 THE BALTIMORE OF THE 1880's in which August and Anna Mencken raised their family was a tranquil city, where existence was simple and the pace of things unhurried. Its population of 425,000 made it big, and yet not quite so big and cosmopolitan as New York or Chicago, Boston or Philadelphia. Lying north of the Potomac River, it was not part of the South; but lying south of the Mason-Dixon Line, it was not northern either. This in-between position had created for it a cultural and political ambivalence that goes at least as far back as the Civil War, and persists in some measure to this day: large numbers of Americans undoubtedly look upon it as being in the South, and yet it seems safe to say that no native Baltimorean ever thinks of himself as a Southerner.

Like any major seaport, the city had expanded over the years from its harbor, and its "downtown" commercial section lay only a few blocks from the sluggish basin formed by the northwest branch of the Patapsco River as it moves out into Chesapeake Bay. Of this area as it was in the eighties, with its narrow streets, stores, banks, hotels, and other business establishments, little if anything survives today; virtually all of it was destroyed in the Great Fire of 1904, which leveled 140 acres and more than 1,300 buildings, and even what arose on the ashes of that went through an inevitable cycle to dilapidation and decay, and within the past couple of decades has yielded to "urban renewal."

From here Baltimore moves out naturally enough in the four directions of the compass, and each of these four sections is referred to by its appropriate geographical designation. South Baltimore is the section directly adjacent to the port, and it depends upon the port for its life and livelihood; it is given over chiefly to shipping and heavy industry. East Baltimore is a middle-class residential neighborhood, characterized by block after block after block of identical row houses, each with its white steps; even today, three or four generations after their ancestors arrived, this part of the city contains deep ethnic pockets of Italian, Polish, Bohemian, and Czech families which retain much of their native culture. West Baltimore is physically very similar, except that the homes tend to be a bit larger and originally represented a somewhat higher degree of affluence; in recent years, however, this section has been more affected by racial change than its counterpart to the east. For some reason the term "North Baltimore" is seldom heard, perhaps because there is no one community that can be identified in this way; but in general, as one moves northward one gets into an area of larger, wealthier, more exclusive dwellings and eventually into the rolling farmland of Baltimore County.*

In the 1880's, of course, the city was much smaller than it is now. Since the Second World War the whole section that encompasses the 1500 block of Hollins Street has gone through a process of blight and decay, and efforts are being made at present to restore it; but when August Mencken bought his new home there in 1883 the area was still almost rural, and open country began just a few blocks away. The streets, major as well as minor, were laid with cobblestones, with

---

*It should perhaps be explained that Baltimore County is politically distinct from the city. The city of Baltimore is not within any county.

perhaps a dirt road down the middle of the wider ones for the convenience of vehicles; and the pavements in front of the houses were usually of red brick laid out in herringbone fashion. Very often, at the curb which separated pavement from street, trees were planted and grew as high as or higher than the houses themselves.

Children played unsupervised in the streets with perfect safety, for the first automobiles had yet to put in their appearance and the horse-drawn wagons with their iron wheels made such a terrific clatter on the cobblestones that they could be heard even before they could be seen. Streetcars were horse-drawn too, and like today's buses they carried their crowds downtown to work in the morning and home again at night; but a man in August Mencken's economic bracket would have his own buggy for this purpose, and when not in use it would be kept at one of the numerous livery stables that dotted every neighborhood. One would think that the trip would have been interminable, but a reading of H. L. Mencken's *Happy Days* and other memoirs of the period gives the impression that it was accomplished just as quickly, and perhaps even more so, than the same expedition in today's traffic.

Save for the varying ingenuity and resources of their mistresses, the row homes tended to be as identical within as without. Central heating was still almost entirely unknown, but a versatile Baltimore figure named John H. B. Latrobe had perfected a small coal-burning stove which was perhaps the first rudimentary principle of the idea; fitted into one of the living-room walls, it heated that room and, in theory if not in actual practice, also sent additional warmth via a flue to the room directly above. This device, known from its inventor as the Latrobe stove, graced thousands of Baltimore homes. In the late eighties August Mencken installed the first steam-heating plant seen on Hollins Street. Some of the newer homes were connected with public or private sewers, but then and for several decades thereafter the sanitary facilities in most of them consisted of an outdoor privy in which a wooden seat was constructed over a pit; the accumulation in these pits was hauled off about once a year by what was known as the O.E.A.—"odorless excavating apparatus." "Every now and then," says Mencken, "some child in West Baltimore fell into such a sink, and had to be hauled out, besmeared and howling, by the cops."[14]

The front room of the house—the one, that is, looking out on the street—was the living room, except that in those days it was usually called the "parlor"; actually little living was done in it, and in many homes it was so strictly off limits that its sole occasional purpose might be to "lay out" a member of the family who had died. The room behind it was the "dining room," which was rarely if ever used for dining. Behind this lay the kitchen, where meals were not only prepared but usually also served; it was presided over, of course, by the mistress of the household, but here, too, most of the ordinary life of the family ran its course. Outside the kitchen was the "back yard" (the ones in the 1500 block of Hollins Street had the unusual length of a hundred feet), and on the other side of the back-yard fence was an "alley." Across the alley were the backs of another row of houses. Down this narrow and not quite public thoroughfare came garbage collectors, junk dealers, and the itinerant vendors of fruits and vegetables whom Baltimoreans always called "Arabers" (pronounced *ay-rabbers*).

Winter could be a time of paralyzing cold; summer brought with it heat of almost tropical intensity. Baltimoreans usually advise any out-of-town visitor who complains about the weather to wait around for another twenty-four hours, since it is sure to change; and it is a fact that meteorological conditions in the city have always been extremely unstable. The housewives put up ivory-colored or "ecru" window shades in winter to take advantage of what dim sunlight there was, and along about April they took these down and replaced them with dark blue ones that would keep out the sun's ferocious glare in the coming months; this, along with a change of rugs, was part of the semiannual "housecleaning" routine that each fall exactly reversed what had been done in the spring.

Every neighborhood had its little corner grocery store, where meats, produce, dairy products, baked goods, and penny candy for children were to be had. In the summer months there dangled from the ceilings of these stores long strips of "fly paper," so that the city's incredible population of *Musca domestica* could be lured away from the meat counter and trapped. Since the day when such foods could be either bought frozen or conveniently stored in freezers still lay in the womb of an undreamed future, housewives had to do much of their purchasing on a day-to-day basis. In all probability, of course, these stores did not greatly differ from their counterparts in any American city, large or small, of the period; but an institution that seems to have been peculiar to Baltimore was the "market" to be found in each section. These were conglomerations of "stalls" gathered under a single roof (and in those days open on all sides) where each dealer specialized in some particular delicacy; they were always thronged on Saturday afternoon and evening in preparation for the major meal of the week on Sunday. Most of these markets are still in existence and most of them still do a fairly thriving business, though the nature of their products has changed very considerably. Hollins Market was just a few blocks from the Mencken house, and here Anna did much of her shopping.

Baltimore, as Mencken was to write much later, "ate divinely." Just to the south was Anne Arundel County (always known to the inhabitants of the city as *Ann'ran'l*), and from its fields there came in season luscious strawberries and peaches, tomatoes and corn. The farmland to the north, including the fertile Pennsylvania Dutch counties that lay just over the state line, lavished upon it an even more varied bounty. Canvasback duck came from the Eastern Shore, and "fried chicken à la Maryland" was already legendary. But it was, of course, the "immense protein factory of Chesapeake Bay" that gave the city and the state a reputation for gastronomic eminence that they still enjoy; the very name "Maryland" automatically couples in the mind with the word "seafood." Crabs, both hard and soft, were the prime delicacy, and they could be prepared and served in a very large number of ways; oysters ran a close second. The former disappeared from menus as soon as summer was over, and Baltimoreans piously believed that oysters could not be eaten in those months that did not have an "r" in them.

Such things naturally go down the human throat much more easily and gratefully if they are assisted by some form of alcohol, and the result was that the natives of the town drank almost as well as they ate. Baltimore had many breweries, most of them founded by early German immigrants and in the 1880's still owned by their families, and the fame of some of them had spread far. August Mencken, however, regarded all local beers as poisonous, and kept them on hand only to serve to visitors of the less distinguished sort; his own favorite was Anheuser-Busch. The city had also a name for its whiskeys: in those days "Maryland" was associated with "rye" almost as readily as with "seafood," though here again since the Second World War virtually all of the great Maryland ryes have disappeared or been replaced by spirit blends. Among the old receipted bills which H. L. Mencken found in his father's files was one showing that on December 27, 1883, August had paid four dollars for a gallon of Monticello; it is no longer made, but a comparable whiskey would retail today for about six or seven dollars a fifth.

The male portion of the citizenry did its drinking and took its simple masculine pleasures in the saloons that dotted every neighborhood, where a sixteen-ounce glass of beer was to be had for five cents and "free lunches" always stood upon the bar. But family life was also very close, and a favorite form of relaxation for father, mother, and children, at least in summer months, was an outdoor picnic at one of the city's many parks, all of them conveniently accessible by horsecar and affording urban residents a brief contact with Nature. Most families, too, enjoyed a "cruise" on the bay steamer *Louise* to the resort town of Tolchester on the Eastern Shore; the return trip by moonlight was believed to do much for romance.

In politics Baltimore was (and is) overwhelmingly Democratic, though not in quite the same way that the "Solid South" is said to be Democratic. Nevertheless, it remains true that, save for an occasional figure who achieves eminence primarily by the force of his own personality, the Republicans have seldom been able to put up anything more than token opposition in any campaign or election. So far as religion was concerned, Catholics were by far the largest single group, which was perfectly understandable since the huge blocs of Irish, Polish, Bohemian, and Italian immigrants who had come over in the previous couple of generations were Catholic almost to a man; but there were substantial segments of all of the larger and more established Protestant denominations, and together they probably equaled the Catholics in number. Some 10 to 15 percent of the town's inhabitants were Jewish. Beginning in the middle eighties and continuing for almost forty years, the figure of Cardinal Gibbons, who was admired and respected as much by non-Catholics as by his fellow believers, gave the city a tolerance and ease in religious matters that were remarkable for the time and virtually a foretaste of today's "ecumenical movement."

Of the population figure mentioned earlier, approximately one-quarter was black. They lived then, as most of them do now, in conditions of abject poverty; although the word "ghetto," insofar as it was used at all, was little more than a historical reference to European Jewry and there were no solidly black neighborhoods as there are today, the Negroes of the city were nevertheless confined to obscure side streets and alleys. The women provided domestic help for families that could afford such a thing, and the men worked in the meaner sort of jobs. But there was apparently no consciousness on either side of racism or racial prejudice; both accepted the arrangement as part of the God-given order of things, which it would be folly to try to change.

Blacks lived in the alley behind the 1500 block of Hollins Street, and the Mencken boys, Harry and Charlie, along with their white chums, had no hesitation about playing with the black children and saw nothing out of the way in doing so. "It was not at all unusual for a colored boy from the alley behind Hollins Street to be invited to join a game of one-two-three, or a raid on Mr. Thiernau's potatoes and turnips." Writing this as late as 1939, Mencken went on: "There have been no race riots in Baltimore to this day," but then, with a prescience that is all the more chilling because he did not live to see the changes that would come, he immediately added: "though I am by no means easy about the future."[15]

Other things on the Baltimore scene might come and go (though change of any kind was likely to be slow and imperceptible), but there was one institution as solid and enduring as the earth on which the city rested. This was the *Sunpapers*. There were other local papers, of course—in fact, at that time there were five *—but none of them had ever achieved anything like the enormous prestige and authority of the *Sun*. Founded in 1837 by Arunah S. Abell and still controlled by members of the family, it was in those days a morning paper: the evening and Sunday editions would not be added until H. L. Mencken's time. Fiercely independent, it jealously guarded not only its own right of free speech but the rights and liberties of the people; during these very years it was engaged in a bitter struggle with the Democratic party bosses to keep the city's judiciary free of political control, and it won so thoroughly that the matter has scarcely been an issue since. Baltimoreans might disagree with the *Sun*, they might hate it (and many of them did), but no literate resident would have dreamed of sitting down to his breakfast without it.

---

*It is commonly said that today there are three, but this is true only if the *Sun* (morning) and the *Evening Sun* are regarded as two separate papers. As a matter of fact they are, but few Baltimoreans ever bother to make this subtle distinction.

Altogether it was a smug and complacent city, proud of itself, its history, its people, of the fact that it was such a pleasant place to live. Baltimore knew and enjoyed the good things of life, and saw no reason to suppose that anything was ever going to change.

One of the things that gave it such solidity was the fact that its residents, by and large, were homeowners. The houses they lived in were theirs, and in many cases had been paid for by hard toil and over a long period of years. A newly married couple, like August and Anna Mencken, might start out their family life in an apartment, but this was almost always viewed as a temporary expedient, and the day when such a couple made the settlement on their own home was perhaps the greatest event in their lives. This gave neighborhoods not only a stability which they would not otherwise have had, but an attractiveness too: the man of the house took pride in his property and assumed a responsibility for keeping it neat and in good repair, and the housewives scrubbed the white front steps until they fairly glistened in the sunlight.

This was the aspect of Baltimore that would most impress H. L. Mencken. Over a period of almost fifty years he was to say some rather caustic things about it, but no man ever loved it more or regarded it more as home. In a *Sunpapers* article of 1925 which was subsequently reprinted and expanded in *Prejudices: Fifth Series,* he wrote:

A home is not a mere transient shelter: its essence lies in its permanence, in its capacity for accretion and solidification, in its quality of representing, in all its details, the personalities of the people who live in it. In the course of years it becomes a sort of museum of these people; they give it its indefinable air, separating it from all other homes, as one human face is separated from all others. It is at once a refuge from the world, a treasure-house, a castle, and the shrine of a whole hierarchy of peculiarly private and potent gods. . . . I believe that this feeling for the hearth, for the immemorial lares and penates, is infinitely stronger in Baltimore than in New York—that it has better survived there, indeed, than in any other large city of America—and that its persistence accounts for the superior charm of the town. . . . A Baltimorean is not merely John Doe, an isolated individual of *Homo sapiens,* exactly like every other John Doe. He is John Doe *of* a certain place—of Baltimore, of a definite *house* in Baltimore. It is not by accident that all the peoples of Europe, very early in their history, distinguished their best men by adding of this or that place to their names.[16]

5 IT WAS IN THAT SAME ARTICLE that Mencken also remarked:

> I have lived in one house in Baltimore for nearly forty-five years. It has changed in that time, as I have—but somehow it still remains the same. No conceivable decorator's masterpiece could give me the same ease. It is as much a part of me as my two hands. If I had to leave it I'd be as certainly crippled as if I lost a leg.

He left it for a period of five years, from 1930 to 1935, when he was married to Sara Haardt and they lived in an apartment at 704 Cathedral Street. Within a short time after Sara's death he moved back. Carl Bode is authority for the story that when, somewhat earlier, he was seriously considering marriage to Marion Bloom, he suggested to her that they could live on the third floor of the house at Hollins Street.[17] It was indeed an integral and vital part of him.

It had become so very early in life, as he grew up in a family "encapsulated in affection."[18] The house itself, large, gracious, with wide, bright, high-ceilinged rooms handsomely furnished by August's expenditures and kept spotless by Anna's housewifely craft, afforded all the creature comforts that the late nineteenth century knew or could have conceived of. The neighborhood itself was pleasant above the average. There are whole sections of Baltimore's row houses where a tree or a spot of grass may not be encountered for miles on end, but on Hollins Street this was definitely not the case. In the backyard were a grape arbor and several kinds of fruit trees. Directly across the street from their front door was the wide green of Union Square, with trees, a pond, and a pseudo-Greek temple. Less than a block away was the House of the Good Shepherd, a home for troubled girls run by an order of Catholic sisters; its walls were high and forbidding, but the upstairs windows of the Mencken home afforded a view of its leafy courtyards, where the nuns could be seen moving back and forth on their nameless errands.

"In Hollins Street, save in Winter," Mencken wrote years later, "I am surrounded by green. . . . I suspect that this enclosure in green may have had a good deal to do with formulating my view of life. . . . I can grow angry and fretful on occasion, but it is seldom for long."[19]

At the center of this household, a more than benevolent despot whose authority was never for one instant seriously called into question, stood August Mencken. Beside him, formulating "a large programme of desirable improvements in him,"[20] but a tender, loving, and devoted wife and mother nonetheless, was Anna. In the background (perhaps not quite as far in the background as one might have wished) was the patriarchal figure of old Burkhardt Ludwig. It was these three who overshadowed everyone else in the boy's world, and who were to form in his mind by their lives and example the ideas that would ever afterward be a part of him.

Burkhardt Ludwig, "as undisputed head of the American branch of the Menckenii,"[21] took his duties with exceptional seriousness. No family problem was so trivial, even though it might involve nothing more than selecting a pattern of wallpaper, that he did not weigh it carefully and hand down a decision. If a grandchild fell ill, he had to be notified; if a new one arrived, the task of picking out a name for it fell to him, and from his choice there was no appeal. In the backyard at No. 1524 there was a summer house, and here, on Sunday mornings, Burkhardt Ludwig, August, and Uncle Henry would meet to discuss family affairs; "in these councils," says Mencken, "my grandfather's vote counted for 100, and my father's and uncle's for one each."[22]

Yet this authority was never exercised in any harsh and dictatorial manner; the old man simply regarded all such things as part of the inevitable burden of his office, and it would not have occurred to him that anyone else would dare hold a differing opinion. Occasionally his daughters and daughters-in-law might murmur, but this never reached the stage of open rebellion. Toward young Henry he showed an especial interest and affection, for as the *Stammhalter*, or oldest son of his oldest son, the boy would in the normal course of events succeed him someday on the throne. He lavished presents upon him at Christmas and on birthdays, took him on wild, careening buggy rides over the cobblestones of Baltimore, and in the quiet return moments of such rides would regale him with accounts of the past glories of the Mencken family in faraway Oldenburg and Leipzig.

Anna Mencken sometimes found herself in silent conflict with him. She had wanted, for example, to name their youngest son Albert, but Burkhardt Ludwig sternly overruled her and announced that he was to be called August, and once, when he took it upon himself to give Harry and Charlie haircuts in the backyard, she "professed politely to admire the result, but there was very little enthusiasm in her tone."[23] Yet she had a sympathetic understanding and a deep affection for him, and would defend the strict legality of his decisions even when they ran counter to her own wishes. He had long since remarried, but the memory of his child-bride, Harriet McClellan, was still poignant within him, and he would often drop in of an afternoon at the house on Hollins Street to reminisce to Anna about her. Anna's own feminine tenderness was moved by this, and it accounted in large part for the fond recollections of him that she afterward communicated to her oldest son.

Anna was, indeed, the heart and mainstay of the household. August, according to his son's account, could not put a new washer in a spigot or mount a ladder without falling off, but Anna cared for the three floors and basement of a large house, raised four children, supervised the hired girls who came and went in endless succession, and, dressed in a long gingham apron and a slat bonnet, pulled up a million weeds from the back yard and the pavement out front. She was, Mencken tells us, a great worrier: if guests were expected she would be fearful until their arrival that something terrible might happen to them on the way, and she could conjure up all kinds of objections and hazards to anything that another member of the family might propose.[24]

She was but forty-one when August died very suddenly in 1899, leaving her with three sons and a daughter, of whom the eldest, Henry, was himself only eighteen at the time. Thereafter she lived for a quarter of a century in widowhood until her own death in 1925. During those years Henry would become a famous author and editor with more than a dozen books to his credit, none of which she ever read; Charles and August would become highly successful engineers; but Anna was the matriarch of the house and ruled it with a firm if loving hand. "One Christmas," says William Manchester, "while his mother was entertaining guests in the living-room, Mencken quietly wandered in and began to fuss with a vase of flowers. Anna stopped in the middle of a sentence and turned around. 'Harry!' she snapped. 'Stop that!' And Harry, after a perceptible start, backed away from the vase and meekly sat down."[25]

It was perhaps only natural that, as a small boy, Mencken should be closer to his mother than to his father, and the fact that he lived under the same roof with her, unmarried, for twenty-five years after August's death only enhanced this closeness. In a letter to Dreiser shortly after she had herself died, he wrote:

I begin to realize how inextricably my life was interwoven with my mother's. A hundred times a day I find myself planning to tell her something, or ask her for this or that. It is a curious thing: the human incapacity to imagine finality. The house seems strange, as if the people in it were deaf and dumb.[26]

But August, while he lived, was very much the center of the boy's life and the one of whom, as a man, he retained the most vivid memories. It is significant that in the lengthy manuscript which he wrote for Goldberg there is a whole chapter entitled "My Father" but no corresponding one on his mother.

In the pages of *Happy Days* August is sometimes made to seem like a clown and buffoon. In part, this is due to Mencken's own tendency to humorous exaggeration, but in larger part it is due, too, to the fact that the man really did like to clown and play buffoonish roles. He once went so far as to prepare a completely bogus but very authentic-looking Dun & Bradstreet report on a business acquaintance, alleging that the man drank heavily, gambled, and that his company was on the verge of bankruptcy. When he purchased a summer home for the family at Mount Washington in the suburbs of Baltimore, he announced to his horrified new neighbors that he intended to use the place to breed pigs and actually gave the name "Pig Hill" to the location. Perhaps the most elaborate of all his jokes was the invention, in collusion with his brother Henry, of a third and entirely mythical brother named Fred, who was reputed to be a clergyman. This was supposed to be a source of great sorrow and disgrace to old Burkhardt Ludwig, who was a thoroughgoing agnostic, and August and Henry would go to great lengths to beg their friends not to mention Fred in the old man's presence, lest the mere reminder of this wayward son distress him. Over the years "Fred" was promoted to the post of chaplain in the United States Senate and eventually became a bishop! "To this day," Mencken wrote in 1939, "a rheumy old Baltimorean sometimes stops me on the street to ask what has become of him."[27]

It is easy to see from this whence Mencken derived his own sense of humor and his love of elaborate practical jokes, but just as his own nature was at bottom a serious one, so was August's, and it was this aspect of the older man that he himself chiefly remembered. "My father," he wrote for Goldberg, "was a very good business man—a shrewd buyer and a competent manager of men."[28] "I never saw him," he remarked elsewhere, "in a place of disadvantage or embarrassment: in the small world that he inhabited he always sat at the head of the table."[29] "There was never an instant in my childhood when I doubted my father's capacity to resolve any difficulty that menaced me, or to beat off any danger. He was always the center of his small world, and in my eyes a man of illimitable puissance and resourcefulness."[30]

August's success as a manager of men did not, however, embrace any recognition of the rights of organized labor. He paid union wages, but would not for an instant tolerate the intrusion of a union into his company. He scanned the newspapers daily for accounts of the conviction and hanging of labor leaders. His political views went little further than a conviction that free trade would ruin the cigar business, and he was a high-tariff Republican of the extreme wing. As such he took a very dim view of any radical movements for social reform; to his mind, all such things were only a conspiracy of charlatans to mulct the taxpayers. "I picked up this idea from him," his son wrote, "and entertain it to the present day."[31] August believed that "political corruption was inevitable under democracy, and even argued, out of his own experience, that it had its uses."[32] "He regarded all borrowing as somehow shameful, and looked confidently for the bankruptcy and probable jailing of any business man who practised it regularly."[33]

Like his father, and with even better reason (for he was himself only half German, and had grown up in an English-speaking household), August cared nothing for the German social and cultural groups that swarmed in the Baltimore of the eighties. In fact, he disliked clubs and associations of any sort, and would not even join trade organizations that might have been advantageous to him in the conduct of his business. The sole exception to this rule was his membership in the Freemasons; he was an enthusiastic Shriner, attended their conventions, and marched proudly in their parades. Looking back, his son saw him as "in some ways, a curious mixture of snob and Philistine."[34]

He was but twenty-six when Henry was born, and so as the boy grew into adolescence it was not difficult for the two of them to come together on a more or less man-to-man basis. During the last couple of years of his father's life young Harry worked, however unwillingly and incompetently, in the firm of August Mencken & Bro. Even at that time he was already much attracted to the newspaper business, and this was the chief point of contention between them; August was willing enough for his son to study law, but his chief desire was for the youth to succeed him someday in the management of the business, and one gets the impression that there were some strained and painful scenes between them. Once August confessed to Henry that he was himself not in the profession that he would freely have chosen; as a young man his ambition had been to be an engineer, but he had had to forgo this and follow his father into the tobacco trade, and he saw no good reason why his son could not do likewise.

Following the move to Hollins Street in 1883, two more children had come along—Gertrude, born in 1886, and August, born in 1889. In middle and old age the relationship between Henry and August was proverbial among their friends and associates: from the time that Henry came back to the house after Sara died in 1935 until his own death in 1956, they lived together, alone save for domestic help, and when Henry became incapacitated following his 1948 stroke August literally devoted his whole life to caring for him. Yet August receives only brief and passing mention in *Happy Days*—by the time he reached the age of boyish play Henry would already have been in adolescence and the two would thus have had little in common. It is Charlie, separated from him by only twenty months, who was his constant companion of that period, supplemented by his cousins who lived just next door and a whole host of children in the neighborhood.

Together the two boys played in the long backyard and cozy cellar of the house. At an appropriate age they were initiated into the Hollins Street gang, and they "went for" the fire company at No. 14 engine house a few blocks away (which meant that it was their sworn duty to drop everything and follow the fire trucks whenever they responded to a call). As small children they spun tops on the cement pavements of Union Square and as older boys they played ball in the street. They were supplied with roller skates and, later, with bicycles. There was always a dog, and usually a cat, and for a period of years the two of them shared a pony. They walked the tops of backyard fences, jumped out of stable haylofts, and enjoyed the illicit thrill of stealing potatoes from Mr. Thiernau's grocery store; in later years, Henry suspected that the grocer deliberately left a quantity of his less edible ones outside as a kind of accommodation for them.

In 1889, and again the following year, August took his family and Uncle Henry took his and the two groups spent their summer vacations in a double home at Ellicott City, to the west of Baltimore. Today it is a thriving, modern community lying athwart U.S. Route 40, with the new and fashionable homes of lawyers, doctors, and other professional people, swimming pools, shopping centers, and all the other accouterments of suburbia; but in those days it was a remote and sleepy little village, and to get from it daily to their place of business in the city August and Henry had to use a B. &O. train of Civil War vintage that took the better part of an hour to make the trip. It was a new and wondrous experience for a boy born and raised in the city, and Mencken has described his reaction to it in a passage that, setting aside *Ventures into Verse*, is the closest thing to sheer poetry to be found in the whole body of his writings:

> The impact of such lovely country upon a city boy barely eight years old was really stupendous. Nothing in this life has ever given me a more thrilling series of surprises and felicities. Everything was new to me, and not only new but romantic, for the most I had learned of green things was what was to be discovered in our backyard at Hollins Street, and here was everything from wide and smiling fields to deep, dense woods of ancient trees, and from the turbulent and exciting life of the barnyard to the hidden peace of woodland brooks. The whole panorama of nature seemed to take on a new and larger scale. The sky stretched further in every direction, and was full of stately, piled up clouds that I had never seen before, and on every side there were trees and flowers that were as strange to me as the flora of the Coal Age. When a thunder-storm rolled over the hills it was incomparably grander and more violent than any city storm. The clouds were blacker and towered higher, the thunder was louder, and the lightning was ten times as blinding. I made acquaintance with cows, pigs and all the fowl of the barnyard. I followed, like a spectator at a play, the immemorial drama of plowing, harrowing, planting and reaping. Guided by the Reus boys, who had been born on the place, I learned the names of dozens of strange trees and stranger birds. With them I roved the woods day after day, enchanted by the huge aisles between the oaks, the spookish, Grimms' Fairy Tale thickets, and the cool and singing little streams. There was something new every minute, and that something was always amazing and beautiful.[35]

Only those two summers were spent there, but Mencken never forgot them and in later years he and August (who would have been an infant at the time) would make occasional pilgrimages back to Ellicott City simply to revisit its scenes. The place remained for him, sophisticated city man that he was, the epitome of pastoral loveliness and peace.

One event took place during that time which would, in a very real sense, determine the whole course of his future life. Occasionally his mother would send him down into the village proper to pick up some things at the general store, and on one of these trips he discovered the printing office of the weekly Ellicott City *Times*. Gaping and silent, the nine-year-old boy watched the press foreman and his assistant turn out an edition of the paper (an edition was about 400 copies, and it had to be printed one side at a time) on a hoary old Washington hand press, and there and then the smell of printer's ink swirled up into his sinuses. The paper went to press every Thursday, and if his mother did not have an errand for him on that day he would try to think up one.

The Ellicott City house was rented, but in 1892 August bought a second home in Mount Washington and from then until his death the family lived there each year from May to October. While school was in session the boys made the trip into the city each day by train. Here again, an area that was originally remote and wholly rural has become a rather commonplace suburb within the city proper, but for a good many years young Harry and Charlie roamed its woods in complete abandon, fished in the Jones Falls, and set traps for rabbits without ever catching any.

It was, in brief, as utterly typical and normal a life as an American boy of that period could live. Not without reason, when *Happy Days* came out and he described it with a humor and irony unexpectedly gentle for him, did both reviewers and readers compare it to his own favorite American novel, *Huckleberry Finn*. "My early life," he wrote at that time, "was placid, secure, uneventful and happy";[36] he remembered some griefs and alarms, but they were all trivial and vanished quickly. Family life was marred neither by domestic discord nor by financial worries; August and Anna, like any couple, may have had problems, but if so they did not communicate them to him.

But though his childhood may have been normal, it was in no sense intellectual. The scholarship of the Menckenii of Leipzig was only dimly remembered and not emulated at all; no branch of the family in America at least, during this period, was engaged in any pursuit that could be said to require learning. Mencken himself noted this in an unpublished autobiographical fragment: "For a man," he said, "whose life has been mainly given over to letters I grew up in an amazingly unliterary environment. There had been no author in my family for a century, and my immediate relatives, though very far from illiterate, showed little interest in books."[37] August had accumulated a small and rather miscellaneous library, ranging from Shakespeare's plays and the novels of Dickens to *One Thousand Proofs That the Earth Is Not a Globe* and a history of Freemasonry in Maryland; he was fond of Mark Twain and bought each of his works as they appeared; but his "taste for literature in its purer states was of a generally low order of visibility,"[38] and his actual reading was confined pretty much to the daily papers. Anna had subscribed to *The Ladies' Home Journal* from its charter issue and read it from cover to cover, but she, too, seldom looked into a book.

Mencken was to start exploring, along about his ninth year, the somewhat limited riches of the old-fashioned secretary in the sitting room—but of that, more in the next section.

It is easy to see whence he derived in his boyhood the ideas that were to be a part of him for the rest of his life. There was, first of all, the era itself—a time, as has already been said, of peace, progress, and complacent prosperity. It was dominated by a set of bourgeois social values that were universally accepted and would not be called into question for a long time. Values in other fields might be—in particular, as the domain of scientific knowledge increased, religious belief came to play less and less of a part in men's lives—but the code of social mores remained constant. Oddly enough, these same mores were based on the Judaeo-Christian religious and cultural tradition, even though they might be little more than a distortion of it, but the tradition at least provided a foundation by which men lived and worked, thought and dealt with each other.

There was, secondly, the city. Too big for the simplicity of a small town and not quite big enough for the sophistication that characterizes a metropolis, it envied neither one its kind of life. Its geographical location put it at the exact spot where the industrial bustle of the North and the aristocratic leisure of the South met and blended. It was self-assured and comfortable, and conveyed that assurance to all who lived in it. Baltimore has had wealthy men, of course; a few philanthropists have endowed it with hospitals and universities, libraries and art galleries; but basically it was a city of middle-class people, of upper bourgeoisie who lived by that set of values we have just mentioned and passed them on to each new generation as a proud heritage.

Thirdly, there was his family. Here the influences ranged from the Germanic solidity and seriousness of his grandfather, Burkhardt Ludwig, to the varied and almost contradictory influences of his father. August's essential conservatism in matters political and social became a part of Mencken quite early, but so, too, did his sense of humor, his broad wit, and his love of practical joking. On the sidelines was his mother, serious too, worrying herself about things that were never likely to happen, but providing both before and after August's death a quiet, well-ordered life in which Mencken could pursue his work and interests without distraction and with a maximum of regularity and comfort.

Last of all, there was the house itself. It is almost impossible to live in one of Baltimore's row homes without absorbing into one's marrow something of its solidity, its air of permanence, its quality of being both itself and a part of its neighborhood and section. If not today, then at least in the 1880's and down through the first half of the twentieth century such homes imparted dignity to the people who lived in them, and they felt a responsibility to give dignity to them in turn. "I was a larva," Mencken wrote,

> of the comfortable and complacent bourgeoisie, though I was quite unaware of the fact until I was along in my teens, and had begun to read indignant books. To belong to that great order of mankind is vaguely discreditable today, but I still maintain my dues-paying membership in it, and continue to believe that it was and is authentically human, and therefore worthy of the attention of philosophers, at least to the extent that the Mayans, Hittites, Kallikuks and so on are worthy of it.[39]

6 IN EARLY SEPTEMBER 1886, just a few days before reaching his sixth birthday, young Harry was enrolled as a pupil at F. Knapp's Institute, a private school located in downtown Baltimore just opposite the City Hall. Uncle Henry's daughter Pauline, who was thus not only his cousin but his next-door neighbor as well, entered at the same time, and on the opening day Uncle Henry conducted the two of them along the entire route (it was a mile-and-a-half ride by horsecar) and pointed out the landmarks by which they should be guided. On the second day they went alone and managed to make it as far as the correct point of debarkation, but thereafter they took a right turn instead of a left and even-

tually wound up down around the harbor. A kindly policeman came
to the rescue and delivered them, frightened and tearful but only a
few minutes late, to Professor Knapp.

The school was of a type that has long since vanished from the
American pedagogical scene but which flourished widely in the latter
half of the nineteenth century, particularly in a city like Baltimore with
its heavy German population. Friedrich Knapp was a contemporary
and compatriot of Burkhardt Ludwig Mencken, and of much the same
austere temperament. He had emigrated in 1850 and opened his "institute" shortly thereafter, and it had prospered for many years as a
refined and efficient school whither the upper-class bourgeoisie of the
town could send their children. In the beginning instruction had been
carried on in German (though by the eighties English had won out), but
despite this fact and the professor's name and origins it was in no sense
limited to those of German ancestry; among the student body were
Irish-Americans, Italian-Americans, Jewish-Americans, and even, as
Mencken was to remark later on, some American-Americans.

By the time the boy entered, the place was already beginning to
be a bit frayed about the edges. Its competition came, naturally
enough, from the public schools. The professor firmly believed and
frequently argued that sooner or later, and more likely sooner, the
public-school system would collapse under the sheer weight of its own
inherent and incurable infamy; whenever there was a hanging at the
city jail he liked to point out that the condemned had been a product of
the public schools and not of a place like Knapp's Institute. Nevertheless, he was really fighting a hopeless battle, and as enrollment and
income declined he had eventually to leave the downtown location and
take up quarters in a building on Hollins Street a half-dozen blocks or
so from the Mencken home.

He was a strict disciplinarian who ran the place with an iron hand
and a rattan switch that was in pretty constant use. Every morning,
before class began, the pupils had to line up for his personal inspection,
and woe betide the unfortunate one who failed to pass it. Did telltale
dirt marks on the knees of stockings or the seat of pants betray the plain
fact of having sneaked a ride on a horse truck? Was there evidence of
having been involved in a street fight along the way? Were shoes not
properly shined? The professor would order the culprit to come forward and would carefully select a switch from the large armamen-
tarium that he carried with him at all times. *"Eins!"* he would order,

and the poor victim would raise both arms above his head; "*Zwei!*" and he would lower them until they were stretched straight out in front of him; "*Drei!*" and he would bend over until his fingertips touched his ankles. Then came the vigorous application of the switch to his bottom. Girls were punished less frequently, and much less severely, and of course on a less intimate part of the anatomy.

It was in this spartan atmosphere that the young Harry Mencken received his introduction to "the educational process." Yet neither the school nor old Knapp was as bad as the foregoing might suggest. The professor may have been strict, but he was not cruel; he may have been a disciplinarian, but he was not a tyrant. He much preferred to give praise instead of blame, "grinned like a Santa Claus" whenever a boy or girl did well in recitation, and was generous in handing out "merits" for exceptional performance. He took an individual interest in each of his pupils; his own personal notations on some of Henry's report cards show the way in which he followed his progress: "*Henrys Fleiss und gutes Betragen machen den Lehrern Freude*" ("Henry's diligence and good conduct make it a pleasure to teach him"), he wrote, and "*Macht tüchtige Fortschritte*" ("Makes excellent progress"). When, years later, Mencken came to write of him, it was with real affection and respect.

Young Henry was, in fact, one of the star pupils of the place. Besides his good marks in conduct and deportment, he excelled in penmanship, English, and drawing. Surprisingly enough, the only subject in which he was really weak was German, and for a time this troubled the old man; but toward the end he was able to reassure the boy's parents that at last he was making progress here too. Mencken's writings are so thoroughly interspersed with German words and idioms, and with such typical honorifics as *Professor-Doktor*, that the legend grew and long persisted that he was as much at home in that language as in his native English; but in point of fact he always disliked it, never attained to any great proficiency in it, and regarded it as being of "a generally preposterous and malignant character."[40]

Despite the professor's dreadful predictions about the public-school system, it was to such a school that Henry proceeded upon leaving Knapp's. This was the Baltimore Polytechnic Institute (or Poly, as it has been known to generations of the city's residents), a school which was and still is devoted to teaching boys the manual arts. It was the only part of his education that later he regarded as a complete and utter waste of time. "All I learned at the Polytechnic," he wrote in the manuscript that he supplied to Isaac Goldberg, "was forgotten within a year after my graduation. I can't imagine a more useless education than that I received there."[41] He had only the very mildest interest in subjects like woodworking or steam engineering, and his aptitude for them was not very much greater than his father's.

One subject in Poly's curriculum, to be sure, did fascinate him, and to such an extent that for the entire four years he was there he vacillated between it and journalism as a possible choice for a career. This was chemistry, and apparently the only reason it did not win out in the end was that the man who taught it had little knowledge of it and even less ability to communicate that knowledge to others. Had the youth been in different hands, chemistry might have carried the day and he would eventually have had "a swell job on the staff of the Du Ponts and maybe a couple of new synthetic rubbers or super-cellophanes to my credit."[42] We may perhaps be grateful that this nameless and forgotten pedagogue was as incompetent as he was; had he managed to impart any enthusiasm for the subject to Mencken, the staff of the Du Ponts might indeed have been enriched, but American literature would certainly have been much the poorer.

In later years the teachers at Poly stood out more clearly in his mind than the courses they taught. One was an eccentric old bachelor named Uhrbrock, whose specialty was algebra and who firmly believed that this branch of mathematics was the most important and essential of all intellectual disciplines. It chanced that algebra was the very subject in which Mencken lacked enough knowledge, upon entering, to put him into an advanced class. Uhrbrock, who really did not know the boy and even had difficulty remembering his name, thereupon offered to tutor him after school hours until he had mastered it sufficiently to take a special test in it, and his own blazing enthusiasm for his subject enabled Mencken not only to master it in six weeks but to get a mark of 100 in the examination. He never forgot Uhrbrock's kindness; when, more than a decade later, he was a city editor and the teacher was in trouble with his superiors, he was able to repay him with some small kindnesses. He refers to him without naming him in an essay on education first printed in the New York *Evening Mail* in 1918 and subsequently gathered in *Prejudices: Third Series,* and when he came to write *Heathen Days* in 1942 he declared that "I owe [Uhrbrock] a massive debt, and it is a pleasant privilege to acknowledge it gratefully after fifty years."[43]

He remembered, too, a couple of other teachers whom he does not name and who, he says, were by the academic standards of the time probably pretty bad. One chewed tobacco incessantly and the other had an unhappy weakness for the bottle, but both, despite their lamentable shortcomings, were genuinely interested in reading and good writing. One set him to reading *The Spectator* and the other introduced him to Thackeray. It was doubtless their interest in and enthusiasm for literature, as much as the incompetence of the "brother" who taught chemistry, that caused the pendulum to swing in favor of journalism.

The four years at Poly not only continued the formal education that had begun at Knapp's Institute, they also finished it. After his graduation from there in 1896 he never attended any kind of school again.

But meanwhile another form of education was under way at home, and indeed it had begun many years before. In 1888 he had read his first long story, an adventure tale called "The Moose Hunters," in the pages of an English annual named *Chatterbox*, which had been given to him as a Christmas present by his grandmother Mencken. It opened to him, as he says, "a new realm of being and a new and powerful enchantment,"[44] and thereafter books began to exert a powerful pull. He tried *Grimm's Fairy Tales* and some of the juvenile fiction popular at the time, but was repelled by their improbable fantasy. Slowly he gravitated toward the secretary in the sitting room, where the volumes of his father's library were assembled, but Shakespeare, Dickens, George Eliot, *Ben Hur*, and the five-volume *History of Freemasonry in Maryland* were rather heavy going for a boy of nine. One book, however, seemed a bit more promising, and he took it into his bedroom and began it. It introduced him to a world whose delights would remain undimmed for sixty years: the book was *Huckleberry Finn.*

"If I undertook to tell you the effect it had upon me," he wrote much later, "my talk would sound frantic, and even delirious. Its impact was genuinely terrific. I had not gone further than the first incomparable chapter before I realized, child though I was, that I had entered a domain of new and gorgeous wonders, and thereafter I pressed on steadily to the last word. My gait, of course, was still slow, but it became steadily faster as I proceeded. As the blurbs on the slip-covers of murder mysteries say, I simply couldn't put the book down."[45]

He did not put it down for the rest of his life. He continued to reread it not less than annually until he was well over forty, and returned to it on frequent occasions even after that. Repeatedly, in his days as a literary critic, he referred to it and used it for purposes of comparison, no matter what the particular book before him at the moment. In *The Smart Set* for February 1913, he wrote: "I believe that *Huckleberry Finn* is one of the great masterpieces of the world, that it is the full equal of *Don Quixote* and *Robinson Crusoe*, that it is vastly better than *Gil Blas*, *Tristram Shandy*, *Nicholas Nickleby* or *Tom Jones*. I believe that it will be read by human beings of all ages, not as a solemn duty but for the honest love of it, and over and over again, long after every book written in America between the years 1800 and 1860, with perhaps three exceptions, has disappeared entirely save as a classroom fossil."[46] In a column in the Chicago *Tribune* dated February 8, 1925, he declared that "we have produced absolutely nothing to put alongside *Huckleberry Finn*, or to offer it even the feeblest challenge. In the whole range of the English novel, indeed, there are not five books to put alongside it."[47]

Huck naturally sent him back to look into the other volumes by Mark Twain that stood side by side in the old secretary, though some of them, like *The Gilded Age* and *A Tramp Abroad*, turned out to have rather less instantaneous appeal for a juvenile reader. But he had discovered a world surpassing even that of "The Moose Hunters," and as the months and years went by, its exploration became one of the principal activities of his life. He gave careful attention to such things as *Boys' Useful Pastimes* by Professor Robert Griffith, A.M., and conscientiously carried out many of the experiments described therein; he plowed through the volumes of *Chambers' Encyclopaedia*, and even glanced at such things as *Life Among the Mormons* and *One Thousand Proofs That the Earth Is Not a Globe*; but meanwhile he was also discovering for himself the glories of English literature. Slowly and with considerable effort he got through much of Dickens; he tried George Eliot, but developed for her an aversion that lasted for the rest of his life. It was not until he was in Poly that, under the guidance of one of the teachers mentioned earlier, he read Thackeray and the riches of the English novel were really opened up to him.

He was probably no more than twelve when this happened, but thereafter he proceeded in a manner so orderly and systematic that it would be cause for admiration even in a much older person. In that one winter after discovering Thackeray he moved backward through Addison, Steele, Pope, Johnson, and Pepys. Continuing onward in reverse chronological order, he was soon in the Restoration and then the great Elizabethan dramatists, and—eventually—among the poets of the Middle Ages. Almost everything he read was a source of fresh delight: the word "almost" is used advisedly because two things at least— Milton's *Paradise Lost* and Spenser's *The Faerie Queene*—failed to make the slightest impression upon him. He read not only the classics themselves but a huge number of historical and critical works of the second, third, and fourth orders of importance which provided background and enlightenment on them.

"Altogether," he told Goldberg, "I doubt that any human being in the world has ever read more than I did between my twelfth and eighteenth years."[48]

Somewhere in the course of all this reading he discovered the four men who were to have the most powerful influence not only on his own ideas but on the evolution of his prose style as well. They were James Gibbons Huneker, George Bernard Shaw, Nietzsche, and Thomas Henry Huxley.

William Nolte is probably right when he says: "Of all American critics, the one who exerted the greatest influence on Mencken's thought was undoubtedly James Huneker."[49] He encountered him first in the pages of *M'lle New York*, an urbane and arty magazine of the period, founded by Vance Thompson and lasting for only the three years from 1895 to 1898. The critic's vigorous style, irreverent sophistication, and seemingly limitless erudition, together with his championship of new figures in literature, music, and painting, made a deep impression. We shall have occasion later, in considering Mencken's own criticism, to study in somewhat greater depth the older man's influence on him; here it suffices to note that although at the time of that first discovery "he was as far out of [Mencken's] world as Betelgeuse,"[50] later on, toward the end of Huneker's own active career, the two men were to become good friends. Three of Mencken's finest pieces are about him: the third chapter of *A Book of Prefaces*, an essay collected in *Prejudices: Third Series*, and the introduction which he wrote to an anthology of Huneker's critical writings.

It was but natural that his studies in the English drama should lead him quickly to Shaw. In later years he would lose all interest in the theater and his opinion of Shaw was to be revised very radically, but at the moment he seemed a kindred spirit and a source of inspiration. Shaw, like Huneker, was an iconoclast, engaged in smashing many an old and hitherto revered idol and exposing the absurdity of many generally accepted ideas. His plays were effecting a revolution on the English stage, and the prefaces that he wrote to them were shocking readers as much as the plays themselves shocked audiences. He was witty and clever, and—above all—he wrote clearly; this last in itself was enough to attract Mencken to him, although it seems safe to say that he would not have been thus attracted if it had not seemed to him that beneath the style there was a solid body of ideas.

Mencken's first prose work was to be a critical study of Shaw's plays. In 1891 the Irish dramatist had published a book entitled *The Quintessence of Ibsenism,* and Mencken found it fascinating because, apart from the fact that it was by Shaw, he was also keenly interested in the work of the great Norwegian. In 1904, by which time he was city editor of the Baltimore *Evening Herald,* he wrote to Brentano, Shaw's American publisher, to suggest that he do a similar volume on Shaw himself. Brentano was not interested, and so Mencken turned to the Boston publishing firm of John W. Luce & Co. Harrison Hale Schaff, the company's editor, replied expressing a willingness to consider the project, and Mencken labored at it during the next few months, submitting the manuscript section by section and showing a surprising reasonableness about editorial suggestions and revisions. The day that he received the galley proofs had an "unparalleled glow" that he remembered for years.

It is a slim volume, running to but 107 pages, and it must be borne in mind, of course, that Shaw himself would go on for almost another half century, so that it could make no pretense to completeness and would speedily become dated. Nevertheless, it is an impressive enough achievement. The style is a bit immature (for Mencken) but by no means hesitant; he is in firm command of his subject matter and of the way that he wants to treat it. A passage like

> For six thousand years it had been necessary, in defending a doctrine, to show only that it was respectable or sacred. Since 1859, it has been needful to prove its truth . . .[51]

might have come out of one of the volumes of *Prejudices*, and his description of *Man and Superman* has been quoted so often and in so many places as a harbinger of his later work that I abjure the pleasure of quoting it once again. He admires Shaw's wit, his treatment of novel and unorthodox themes, his dramatic sense and technical mastery; but even then he was unwilling to consider him a profound thinker—his object, he says, is "to exhibit the Shaw plays as dramas rather than as transcendental treatises."[52]

He sent a copy of the book to Shaw, apologizing in the inscription for its shortcomings and his own inexperience, but never received any acknowledgment.

Setting Nietzsche aside to the end, it is to Thomas Henry Huxley that we must turn as really the greatest single influence on the development of Mencken's own attitude toward man, life, and the universe, and as exerting a powerful impress on his literary style as well. Huneker he would far outdistance in critical acumen, Shaw he would come to regard as an "Ulster Polonius" whose lifework was "to announce the obvious in terms of the scandalous," and he was at no time unaware of weaknesses and inconsistencies in Nietzsche's thought. But his admiration for Huxley never flagged—it remained as strong at the end of his career as when he first encountered him during that youthful reading.

There were, in fact, notable resemblances between them. Certainly Mencken was not a family man in the same sense that Huxley, with a wife and eight children, was, but he had the same deep respect for the virtues of home and family, and held to the same solid middle-class values. Like Huxley, he viewed with a skeptical eye most of the commonly accepted beliefs of the day. Like him, too, he was to be engaged his whole life long in controversy and would succeed in making bitter enemies, and would be regarded by those enemies as Antichrist or an emissary of Satan.

The Englishman, it will be recalled, was known as "Darwin's bulldog." Charles Darwin had published the most epochal book of the nineteenth century; but he was himself a very shy and retiring person, who had little stomach for the fierce controversy that his work inevitably aroused, and even less ability to take part in it. Huxley thereupon stepped into the breach. In books, debates, lectures, and teaching he defended the theory of evolution against the savage opposition put up to it by the entrenched forces of the religious establishment, and endeavored to clarify Darwin's difficult and thorny text for men of average intelligence. In the process he succeeded in making some of his opponents—for example, Bishop Wilberforce, the Anglican prelate of Oxford—look like fools, and this was a technique that would naturally commend itself to Mencken. Finally, he handled his highly abstruse subject matter with a superb lucidity and a style that is one of the landmarks of modern English literature.*

Just when Mencken encountered him, and which books he read, are not entirely clear from the record. But it must have been fairly early, and the influence must have made itself felt almost at once. At that youthful age his opinions were still vague and unformed, but he later told Goldberg that "Huxley gave order and coherence to my own doubts and converted me into a violent agnostic."[53] In *A Book of Prefaces* he writes of "Huxley with his devastating agnosticism, his insatiable questionings of the old axioms, above all, his brilliant style."[54] On the occasion of the hundredth anniversary of the great scientist's birth in 1925, he devoted one of the "Monday Articles" to him, and at that time he wrote:

> Huxley, I believe, was the greatest Englishman of the Nineteenth Century—perhaps the greatest Englishman of all time. When one thinks of him, one thinks of him inevitably in terms of such men as Goethe and Aristotle. . . . Huxley was not only an intellectual colossus; he was also a great artist; he knew how to be charming. No man has ever written more nearly perfect English prose. There is a magnificent clarity in it; its meaning is never obscure for an instant.[55]†

In later years Mencken could not recall who first introduced him to Nietzsche, and when in 1937 a young student at the University of Texas named Edward Stone besought his help on a master's thesis

---

*There is an excellent account of Huxley's efforts on behalf of Darwinism in *The Huxleys*, by Ronald W. Clark (New York: McGraw-Hill, 1968), pp. 45–77. This admirable work covers four generations of this amazing family, with special emphasis, of course, on Thomas Henry and his two most famous grandsons, Sir Julian, the biologist, and Aldous, the novelist.

†Compare his remark about his own style, written toward the very end of his active career: "The imbeciles who have printed acres of comment on my books have seldom noticed the chief character of my style. It is that I write with almost scientific precision—that my meaning is never obscure." (*Minority Report*, p. 293.)

entitled *H. L. Mencken's Debt to F. W. Nietzsche*, he provided the desired assistance but remarked: "In my own mind my debt to Nietzsche seems very slight."[56] At the time his interest in him began, much of the philosopher's work had not yet been translated into English, and Mencken's German hardly qualified him to tackle the original. But after the success of the book on Shaw, Schaff of John W. Luce & Co. suggested to him that he do a similar work on Nietzsche, and according to Schaff's own account Mencken wrote back saying that there must be something to mental telepathy, for he had been thinking of writing an article about Nietzsche just when the letter arrived. Encouraged by Schaff's proposal, he spent most of the following winter studying Nietzsche's prodigious output in the German editions available at the Pratt Library (his proficiency in the language was by now, apparently, much improved) and reading the biography of him by his sister—a thoroughly unreliable and deceptive piece of work, though not even Nietzsche scholars were aware of this fact at the time. The result was his largest and most impressive accomplishment to date, a book that far outstrips the Shaw volume in size and in importance. It may have been replaced by more authoritative treatises, but to this day no more readable study of Nietzsche has appeared.

Despite Mencken's disclaimer, the influences are obvious and are very great. Nietzsche's *Sklaven-Moral* ("slave morality") certainly corresponds to Mencken's description of the great majority of men as "goose-stepping ignoramuses and poltroons." The "intelligent minority" of which Mencken repeatedly wrote may not be what the German philosopher had in mind when he spoke of the "Superman," but it undoubtedly points toward his coming. Above all, Nietzsche's savage attacks on Christianity and its whole moral and ethical system find an echo on page after page of Mencken's works; this is not to say, of course, that he took the idea over bodily from Nietzsche and simply carried it on, but certainly the latter clarified Mencken's own thinking on these matters and perhaps gave him some of the courage needed to set down such unconventional and unpopular thoughts.

But there will be occasion often in the pages that follow to note the ways in which Mencken, even if unconsciously, drew upon Nietzsche. Here it may be of interest to focus on a few things that show resemblances rather than influences, but which illustrate how the lives of the two men ran curiously parallel.

"Nietzsche at 40 and Nietzsche at 25," Mencken noted in the biographical section of his study, "were essentially the same. The germ of practically all his writings lies in his first book."[57] This statement is obviously just as true of him; we have already seen that his ideas were formed early and that he never substantially changed them. It is also true that the major themes of his writing, whether theological, political, or literary, were sounded in that first book on Shaw.

On another page he writes that "Nietzsche did not belong to the majority."[58] No more did Mencken—and he belabored the fact in countless books, articles, columns, and reviews. "Nietzsche saw that the philosophers and sages of the day, in many of their most gorgeous flights of logic, started from false premises, and he observed that certain of the dominant moral, political and social maxims of the time were mere foolishness."[59] It was Mencken's contention that half the world's problems were the result of defective thinking that started from false premises, and he never ceased to question most of the commonly accepted beliefs in the American culture of his time.

"Nietzsche," he says on another page, "wrote verses before he was ten: pious, plaintive verses that scanned well and showed rhymes and metaphors made respectable by ages of honorable employment."[60] Mencken began writing poetry at a very early age, too, holding himself for a while to a schedule of one complete poem a day, and like Nietzsche's they were highly derivative and based upon traditional forms. His own first book, *Ventures into Verse,* was a collection of them—exhibiting for the most part the influence of Kipling, whom he adored at the time, but drawing, too, upon various old English and French meters. He abandoned verse completely and forever even before the book itself was published, but there is no reason to suppose that had he pursued it he would have made any more of a name for himself as a poet than Nietzsche did.

"There arose in [Nietzsche]," he says, "a fiery loathing for all authority, and a firm belief that his own opinion regarding any matter to which he had given thought was as sound, at the least, as any other man's. Thenceforth the assertive '*ich*' began to besprinkle his discourse and his pages. '*I* condemn Christianity. *I* have given to mankind . . . *I* was never yet modest . . . *I* think . . . *I* say . . . *I* do . . .'"[61] If possible, this is even truer of Mencken; no man ever used the first personal pronoun more than he did, and it has already been pointed out that

his writings tell us as much about him, and about his likes and dislikes, as they do about whatever may be his ostensible subject of
the moment.

But there is a final resemblance which is the most striking and
sobering of all. In 1888, it will be recalled, Nietzsche went hopelessly
insane.* The remaining twelve years of his life he spent in a kind of
twilight world, physically sound enough and occasionally having brief
lucid moments but forever cut off from any kind of intellectual work or
contact. During most of that time he was devotedly cared for by his
sister, following her around and meekly obeying her instructions.

Mencken, of course, did not go insane, but in 1948, at the age of
sixty-eight, he was stricken by a cerebral hemorrhage that put an end to
his active career in just as cruel a way. Physically he too recovered, but
the stroke permanently damaged certain brain areas and left him without the ability to read and write. The written word had been his inspiration and the source of all his activity since he had first encountered it at
the age of eight in "The Moose Hunters," and its absence left his life a
sick and lonely void. He could only sit amid his own books and the
books of others, and amid his vast collection of letters, papers, and
other memorabilia, unable to make any more intelligible sense out of
them than if they had been written, say, in Sanskrit. His brother
August watched over him and took care of his needs and wants for the
next eight years.

There is thus something gruesomely prophetic in Mencken's account of Nietzsche after the onslaught of his insanity, in a passage
written, remember, in 1908:

> There he would sit day after day, receiving old friends but saying little.
> His mind never became clear enough for him to resume work, or even to
> read. He had to grope for words, slowly and painfully, and he retained
> only a cloudy memory of his own books. His chief delight was in music
> and he was always glad when someone came who could play the piano for
> him.[62]

---

*The cause of his insanity is generally believed to have been paresis, resulting from an infection
contracted years before on a youthful visit to a brothel, but this has never been established beyond
all doubt. There is a discussion of the matter in *Nietzsche: Philosopher, Psychologist, Antichrist*,
by Walter Kaufmann (New York: Random House, 3d ed. 1968), pp. 67–71.

Mencken's own old friends came to see him regularly and doubtless he appreciated their visits, but he, too, had to grope for words and for the names of people he had known well for years, and because his helplessness was so embarrassing to him it was embarrassing to the visitors also. Like Nietzsche—and perhaps even more so—he had always loved music, and listening to it now filled many a long and empty hour. Here he had something of an advantage over the philosopher, for in the intervening decades the radio and the phonograph record had made music much more readily accessible. On the Saturday that he died he spent part of the afternoon listening to the broadcast of Wagner's *Die Meistersinger* from the stage of the Metropolitan, and for dinner he and August had invited one of their good friends, Louis Cheslock, a professional musician and member of the Saturday Night Club. Later Mencken excused himself, remarking that he did not feel well, and went up to bed. He was found dead there the next morning; the parallels between him and Nietzsche had carried through virtually to the end.

7 ON NEW YEAR'S EVE, 1898, August Mencken, then just forty-four years old and apparently in the full prime of life and vigor, was seated with his wife in the living room at Hollins Street when he suddenly collapsed and fell unconscious on the floor. Young Henry was himself upstairs in bed with influenza at the time, but the frightened Anna roused him and he went out into the night for Dr. Wiley, the family physician. On examination, the attack was diagnosed as a kidney infection. Today's drugs and techniques would doubtless have cleared it up in short order, but the medical science of that era was still just a bit too primitive and August wasted away very rapidly. He died on Friday, January 13, 1899, and was buried on the ensuing Sunday.

In *Newspaper Days*, published in 1941, Mencken states that on the next evening—Monday—he dressed carefully in his best suit of clothes and presented himself at the offices of the Baltimore *Morning Herald* to apply for a position as reporter. In the autobiographical notes which he prepared in 1925 for Isaac Goldberg he says that it was two weeks later. Whichever it was, the parental opposition to a career in

journalism had disappeared with bewildering suddenness and on a
note of tragedy; he was free to divest himself of the cigar business
(which in any case now passed wholly into the hands of his Uncle
Henry) and to pursue his chosen interest.

Max Ways, city editor of the *Herald*, received the youthful appli-
cant civilly enough, but admitted that he had no openings and that
the chances of there ever being one were incalculably remote. He
suggested, however, that Mencken keep dropping around at regular
intervals just to remind the editor of his existence. So he accordingly
went back the next evening, and the one after that, and again and again
for what seemed an interminable period. Finally, on a night when the
whole city and all of the surrounding countryside lay wrapped in a
blizzard of monumental proportions, Ways called the young man over
to him, explained that the paper had heard nothing for days from its
Govanstown correspondent, and suggested that he might go out there
to see if there was anything in the way of news.

Govanstown was a remote little village lying far to the north of the
city, and to get there by horsecar in such appalling conditions was not
easy. Arriving, Mencken banged on the door of the volunteer firehouse
and then routed out the local undertaker and the druggist to see if
either had anything that might make a story. The druggist proved an
obliging source. Then came the long trip back into Baltimore with his
scoop, and on the next morning, February 24, 1899, the following story
appeared in the *Herald* under the headline "Team Stolen":

> A horse, a buggy and several sets of harness, valued in all at about $250,
> were stolen last night from the stable of Howard Quinlan, near Kings-
> ville, in the Eleventh district. The county police are at work on the case,
> but so far no trace of either thieves or booty has been found.

Just below it, with the heading "Exhibited War Scenes," was
another item, which the discerning Ways had given to him to rewrite
after he had turned in his first story:

> At Otterbein Memorial U. B. Church, Roland and Fifth avenues,
> Hampden, Charles H. Stanley and J. Albert Loose entertained a large
> audience last night with an exhibition of war scenes by the cineograph.

That was the beginning. There was nothing, to be sure, remark-ably auspicious about it, and it has to be admitted that it did not lead to instant recognition and promotion. For the next several months Mencken continued to work for the *Herald*, if indeed "work" is the proper term to use, on an unpaid volunteer basis, putting in a long day at August Mencken & Bro. and then dashing home for dinner and a change of clothes before going back downtown to the newspaper offices. Finally, in late spring, a vacancy did occur and he was made a full-fledged reporter covering the Southern police district, at a salary of seven dollars a week with a book of passes for the trolley cars and the use of an expense account. In July he was moved to the Central district, a much more important assignment since it included Police Headquar-ters, the courts, and the city jail. Within a year he was assigned to cover "the more subtle skullduggeries of the City Hall."

It would serve no purpose in this study to trace Mencken's long newspaper career step by step; William Manchester and Carl Bode have both covered it in all necessary detail, and the interested reader is referred to their books. It may suffice here to note that by 1901, two years after going to work for the *Herald*, he was editor of its Sunday edition; in 1903 he became city editor of the regular morning paper. In 1904, the year of the Great Baltimore Fire, he covered his first pair of national political conventions, the Republican one in Chicago during June and the Democratic one in St. Louis a month later. A few weeks after that the *Herald* decided to inaugurate an evening paper and he was named its city editor, having for a time equal responsibility for both the morning and evening editions. He was managing editor of the paper and secretary of the company when the *Herald* ceased publica-tion in 1906. He worked for a few weeks for the Baltimore *Evening News* and in July transferred to the *Sunpapers*, thus beginning an association that would last, with two rather longish and awkward inter-ruptions during the World Wars, for the remainder of his days.

The point is that during those early years he was absorbing the experiences and acquiring the practical outlook that would guide both his life and his work forever after. The reading of Huneker and Shaw, Huxley and Nietzsche, however strong its influence, was nevertheless intellectual and abstract; what he gathered in as a reporter was the raw stuff of life itself. He never saw any reason to regret that he had not acquired a college education:

At a time when the respectable bourgeois youngsters of my generation were college freshmen, oppressed by simian sophomores and affronted with balderdash daily and hourly by chalky pedagogues, I was at large in a wicked seaport of half a million people, with a front seat at every public show, as free of the night as of the day, and getting earfuls and eyefuls of instruction in a hundred giddy arcana, none of them taught in schools. . . . It would be an exaggeration to say that I was ignorant, for if I neglected the humanities I was meanwhile laying in all the worldly wisdom of a police lieutenant, a bartender, a shyster lawyer, or a midwife.[63]

Whether Baltimore was an especially "wicked" seaport, in the sense that Marseilles and Port Said and Singapore are popularly believed to be wicked, is perhaps open to question. But it is an occupational hazard of the newspaper reporter's job that he encounters far more wickedness than goodness, and Mencken speedily took in his share. In after years he could no longer recall his first murder, but his first suicide stood out quite clearly: "the victim was a lovely young gal who had trusted a preacher's son too far, and then swallowed poison: she looked almost angelic lying on her parlor floor, with a couple of cops badgering her distracted mother."[64] He rode in patrol wagons with captured burglars. At the City Hospital he saw "people with their legs cut off, their arms torn off, their throats cut, their eyes gouged out. It was shocking for a little while, but then no more."[65] On July 28, 1899, when he was less than nineteen years old, he covered his first hanging: it was, moreover, one of "the very first chop," since on this particular occasion no less than four men followed one another to the gallows. Once, half in jest, Max Ways sent him out to cover a Polish Jewish wedding, and he interviewed the bride and her mother while the girl stood in the middle of the floor "with nothing on save a diaphanous vest and a flouncy pair of drawers."[66]

In the police courts he learned early the distinction between justice and law and the fact that there is no necessary connection between them. When he moved on to City Hall he had ample opportunity to observe the nature of politicians and the workings of the democratic process; here, while still a youth, he began to formulate the attitude that he would always have toward both. He came in contact with party bosses, city councilmen, mayors, governors, and eventually congressmen and senators. The time arrived when he sat among the most distinguished and exalted stratum of newspapermen in the press gallery of the United States Senate: "to this day," he wrote as late as 1939, "though reason may protest bitterly, I still revere the gentlemen of the Washington corps."[67]

It was, as he would remark in *Newspaper Days*, a "crusading time," and he not only had to cover but occasionally got involved in some examples of what he would later characterize, with supreme contempt, as "the uplift." "I recall," he says,

> crusades against sweat-shops, against the shanghaiing of men for the Chesapeake oyster fleet, and against dance-halls that paid their female interns commissions on the drinks sold. I had a hand in all of them, and if they filled me with doubts they also gave me some exhilarating experiences. With the cops I toured the bastiles of the waterfront crimps, and examined the jails that they maintained for storing their poor bums, and with health department inspectors I saw all the worst sweat-shops of the town, including one in which a huge flock of hens was kept hard at work laying eggs in a filthy cellar.[68]

But he had been born "with no more public spirit than a cat,"[69] and he decided early on that all attempts to improve those who had no wish for improvement, or to free those for whom liberty would have been only a burden, or to ram virtue down the throats of the "congenitally sinful," was a complete and utter waste of time. His "true and natural allegiance," he concluded, "was to the Devil's party, and it has been my firm belief ever since that all persons who devote themselves to forcing virtue on their fellow men deserve nothing better than kicks in the pants."[70] Much later he ventured to formulate this idea scientifically, in what he proposed as Mencken's Law:

> Whenever A annoys or injures B on the pretense of saving or improving X, A is a scoundrel.

He developed a similarly dim view of "the gospel of service." This happened in May 1901, when he got his first really big out-of-town assignment: the great fire that had destroyed 450 acres of the city of Jacksonville, Florida. "Busy-bodies" all over the country immediately began to collect money and goods for the relief of the victims, and in this work the city of Baltimore was of course not wanting. Mencken's job, in addition to covering the disaster, was to assure the people of Jacksonville that succor was on the way. Included in the relief train were 100 secondhand horse blankets from the Pimlico racetrack, and when he arrived he found the residents refreshing themselves in the waters of the St. Johns River in 80-degree temperatures. Another kindly gift on the train was 100 cases of Maryland rye, which made chills run up and down the spine of Jacksonville's mayor, since he would have to post guards to watch it and was reluctant even to trust them. It was such imbecilities as these that led Mencken to conclude "that Service is mainly only blah."[71]*

Fortunately, however, not all his assignments, and thus not all his experiences, lay in the area of politics and public events. In September 1901 he was made drama critic of the *Herald;* this was not really a promotion, since he had asked for the job and the work that it involved was something over and above his duties as Sunday editor. Robert I. Carter, who had come to the paper as managing editor the year before, reserved to himself the more serious plays that reached town, and this meant that Mencken was left with second-string productions, comedies, musicals, melodrama, vaudeville, and burlesque. But he covered them diligently, enjoying them the more the worse they were, and in the process he got to know and associate with many of the recognized theatrical celebrities of the time—managers like Daniel Frohman, Clyde Fitch, and Augustus Thomas, press agents like Channing Pollock, Herbert Bayard Swope, and Bayard Veiller, and fellow critics like the enormously influential dean of the craft, William Winter. Actors themselves he avoided on the ground that they were all idiots.

Carter, a graduate of Harvard with a game leg and a red Vandyke beard, looked more like a college professor than a newspaperman, and when he first appeared in the *Herald*'s editorial rooms the staff did not quite know how to take him. But Mencken learned very quickly to have a deep respect for him, for he possessed both an expert knowledge of the theater and a fine critical sense. "The first job of a reviewer," he told the young man, "is to write a good story—to produce something that people will enjoy reading. If he has nothing to say, he simply can't do it. If he has, then it doesn't make much difference whether what he

---

*Three years later, when Baltimore had its own Great Fire, the citizens of Jacksonville had an opportunity to reciprocate. "They proposed to send up enough oranges (some of them almost fresh) to supply 500,000 people for 100 days, but the Baltimore authorities declined them." (*Newspaper Days*, p. 105.)

says is fundamentally sound or not." This, in essence, was to be the cardinal principle that would guide Mencken's own literary criticism for the next two generations.

Though his opportunities for serious playgoing were as yet limited, he continued to do an immense amount of reading in the subject. It was at this time, of course, that his interest in Shaw began to develop, and along with it an equally strong interest in Ibsen. He not only began a collection of Ibseniana (which he gave many years later to the University of Leipzig) but also projected a translation of the Norwegian dramatist's work which would be much superior to the standard English version by William Archer then on the market. Since Mencken naturally knew no Norwegian, he worked with the Danish consul in Baltimore, a man named Holger A. Koppel, and together they brought out editions of *A Doll's House* and *Little Eyolf*, with introductions and notes. The series, however, proved commercially unsuccessful, and was abandoned after these two volumes.

His work as a drama critic continued when he went to work for the *Sun*, and in the winter of 1905–6 he wrote, according to his own account, twenty-three unfavorable reviews in a row. The manager of Ford's, Baltimore's leading theater, complained bitterly that Mencken was ruining his business and that the quality of the plays was not really his fault, since he had to take whatever was sent out on the road by the New York agents. Mencken found himself in sympathy with this position; he withdrew as the *Sun*'s reviewer, and never wrote a line of drama criticism again.

Very early, too, in his cub-reporter days, Wilberfoss G. Owst, the *Herald*'s music critic, discovered that Mencken could play the piano and "knew how many sharps were in the key of C Major." Owst, an Englishman and "an abyss of thorough-bass," not only was an indolent man but also had a very sensitive ear, and it was painful to him to have to listen to the inferior performances put on by church choirs, soloists on something less than a professional level, and visiting Italian bands. What better idea, therefore, than that he should borrow Mencken to cover such things for him? As in the case of the theater, this arrangement left him with only "third-, fourth- and fifth-string concerts" to attend, and, also as in the case of the theater, it was something to be done in his spare time and after his regular reportorial duties were out of the way. In his first summer at this assignment, he says, he heard the whole repertoire of bad opera from *Cavalleria Rusticana* to *The Chimes of Normandy*, not once but three or four times, and in the intervals dropped in on half a dozen Italian bands.

But he enjoyed it thoroughly, for he was already an ardent music-lover. A piano had come into the sitting room at Hollins Street when he was only seven years old, and he had started taking lessons very shortly thereafter. When he was yet in his mid-teens he composed a number of waltzes, the manuscripts of which still survive in the Pratt Library's Mencken Room. But during the unhappy years in his father's cigar business and the first press of his newspaper work, music had been rather forgotten; now his interest revived, and it revived all the more strongly when he discovered that a number of his colleagues on the paper were amateurs in the genuine sense of the word and played for the sheer love of it.

Joe Callahan, his assistant, was a violinist, though "perhaps the worst who ever lived," and through Joe he got to know Fred Gottlieb, a wealthy brewer who was also an amateur flautist, and Albert Hildebrandt, a maker and dealer in violins who played the cello. Then there was Isidor Goodman, the *Herald*'s night editor, who played the flute too, and the assistant sporting editor, Emanuel Daniel, "who passed in the office under the nickname of Schmool, and was a violinist." They began to join forces on occasional evenings to play, and as time went on they were joined by others, some of them professional musicians: for example, Theodore Hemberger, who had at one time been conductor of the Scranton Symphony Orchestra and was now a violin instructor at Baltimore's Peabody Conservatory of Music. Gradually more men, both professional and amateur, came in, and they began to meet on a regular basis. Mencken played the piano, but he was also the heart and leader of the group and most of the programs were of his devising. Two hours were devoted to music-making, and then another two to the "twin and inseparable art of beer-drinking." This was the origin of the famous Saturday Night Club, which, with scarcely any interruption though with a considerable succession in membership, would meet continuously for the next forty-six years.

Somehow, too, in the midst of these backbreaking newspaper duties, he yet found time to do a considerable quantity of writing on his own. It has already been mentioned that he began to compose verse while scarcely more than a boy, holding himself for a while to a schedule of one poem a day. Kipling was his inspiration and model, and as a matter of fact the very first thing that he ever published in a magazine was a poem, "To R. K.," which appeared in the *Bookman* for December 1899. He had sent it in anonymously and without even a return address, but when the *Bookman* actually used it he modestly wrote in and admitted his authorship and received a check for ten dollars in return.

Much, though by no means all, of this early poetry was eventually collected into *Ventures into Verse*, his first book and the only one that has since become a rare and costly collector's item.* It is a fascinating volume to dip into, not just for the foretaste it gives us of the later Mencken but also and equally for the directions it points in but which were never afterward traversed. The poem entitled "A Madrigal," for example, expresses emotions which are certainly typical of adolescent youth, but they hardly seem typical of the youth who would become the hard-boiled and cynical critic of *The Smart Set, The American Mercury,* and the *Sunpapers*. Some West Baltimore belle undoubtedly inspired it:

> How can I choose but love you,
> Maid of the witching smile?
> Your eyes are as blue as the skies above you;
> How can I choose but love you, love you,
> You and your witching smile?
> For the red of your lips is the red of the rose,
> And the white of your brows is the white of the snows,
> And the gold of your hair is the splendor that glows
> When the sun gilds the east at morn.
> And the blue of your eyes
> Is the blue of the skies
> Of an orient day new-born;
> And your smile has a charm that is balm to the soul,
> And your pa has a bar'l and a many-plunk roll,

---

*Only 100 copies were printed, and of these 50 were given to the author and 50 offered for sale by the publishers (who appear on the title page as Marshall, Beek & Gordon, with the improbable addresses of New York, London, Toronto, Sydney, and Baltimore). The only known actual sale was of two copies to a book dealer in Portland, Maine. In later years the legend spread that Mencken bought up all the copies he could get hold of for the specific purpose of destroying them, but he himself denied this (cf. *Newspaper Days*, p. 65). Forty-two copies are known to survive, which is not at all bad for a book of which only 100 copies were printed in the first place; their location and provenance are given in *Census of Ventures into Verse* by Betty Adler (Baltimore: Enoch Pratt Free Library, 1965; 2d ed. 1972). The most recent copy to come upon the market (1972) sold for $1,050.

So how can I choose but love you, love you,
Love you, love you, love you?

Even here, of course, humor and cynicism come through in the last few lines. They are even more evident in the "Rondeau of Statesmanship," which states a theme that Mencken would develop in a thousand variations through a lifetime of writing:

In politics it's funny how
A man may tell you one thing now
        And say tomorrow that he meant
        To voice a different sentiment
And vow a very different vow.

The writ and spoken laws allow
Each individual to endow
        His words with underground intent
                In politics.

Thus he who leads in verbal prow-
Ess sports the laurel on his brow—
        So if you wish to represent
        The acme of the eminent
Learn lying ere you make your bow
                In politics.

He stopped writing poetry as early as 1902, and although he gives the press of his newspaper work as an excuse there is no doubt that he had really lost all interest in it. "If I had kept on writing verses," he observed to Isaac Goldberg, "the chances are that I might have produced very fair stuff." [72] This is one of the rare instances where his own self-judgment may quite possibly have gone astray; there is not the slightest reason to suppose, on the basis of this *Jugendwerk*, that he would ever have established any reputation as a poet. Certainly he would not have found it possible to adapt to the new forms which, within the next decade or so, would manifest themselves in the work of Frost, Pound, and Eliot.

From poetry he turned to the short story. This was a field in which, just on the superficial basis of the number of them that he managed to sell, he was eminently successful. His first one, "The Woman and the Girl," was accepted by *Short Stories* in February 1900, but for some reason was not actually published until a year later; in the meantime the magazine accepted another entitled "The Cook's Victory" and included it in its issue for August 1900, so that, going purely by publication date, it was his first prose piece other than newspaper work to see the light. *Short Stories* thereafter became one of his steadiest outlets, and he also sold work to *Red Book, Criterion,* and *Frank Leslie's Popular Monthly,* the last-named edited by Ellery Sedgwick, who would later spend a generation or more as editor of *The Atlantic Monthly.* Sedgwick was so impressed by his work that he offered him a job on the periodical's staff at a salary considerably greater than he was making on the *Herald,* but Mencken turned it down because it would have involved living in New York and he did not feel that he could conscientiously leave his mother and the rest of his family in Baltimore.

The stories, almost without exception, are interesting and well told, and the characters deftly enough drawn. His handling of dialogue shows a keen ear for vernacular speech, thus presaging the immense and scholarly treatment that the subject would receive in the pages of *The American Language.* The Menckenian clarity is already in evidence, and there is plenty of the humor that would enliven his later work. Yet in spite of these virtues they seldom rise above the conventional, formalized fiction of the time; they are all cut pretty much out of the same cloth, and that cloth is in the pattern required by the popular magazines that constituted his market. There is no promise that the man who wrote them, however competent he showed himself to be, would go on to do anything better; he admitted much later that they were "hollow things, imitative and feeble."[73]*

Along with the short stories he also began a novel, of which about fifty pages of manuscript survive, laid in Elizabethan England. It was a perfect example of the historical romances so in vogue at that period, filled with "what-ho's!" and "'sdeath's," and Shakespeare was one of the principal characters. He would even talk in the language of the plays, which the real Shakespeare in all probability never did. The project

---

*An interesting and amusing sidelight on the short stories is the fact that in 1901 Mencken sold two of them to *Youth's Companion,* then and for long thereafter an immensely popular periodical for boys. Somehow or other they got lost in the office and did not come to light until almost thirty years later. The editor thereupon returned the manuscripts to Mencken and asked if he would care to make any changes in them in the light of a generation of additional experience in writing and editing. Mencken passed them without changing a word.

blew up when he "discovered that [he] knew no more about Elizabethan England than about the M. M. III age of Crete."[74]

He abandoned fiction, he says, for the same reason that he gave up
the writing of poetry—because it finally dawned on him that he simply
had no talent for it. In this he was undoubtedly right, but another and
more positive reason may have been that he was beginning to discover
now what he did have the talent for. He had been contributing more or
less regular columns to the *Herald* for some time, commenting upon
the local political and social scene and to some degree on the national
one too. He loved setting down his opinions on politicians and the
workings of government; these opinions were unusual and unorthodox,
and in turn they were eliciting reaction from the paper's readers. He
was already by way of becoming "controversial."

His music and drama criticism was opening new worlds too. His
coverage of the theater led to the discovery of Shaw, and this discovery,
as we have seen, led in turn to his first real book, the 1905 *George
Bernard Shaw: His Plays.* Three years later came the book on
Nietzsche. After what he calls a "lack of direction" and "various false
starts," he had at last found himself: he was a critic of ideas, and would
remain one ever after.

It is to a study of his ideas, after this brief treatment of background and formation, that we now turn.

II

THE PHILOSOPHER

Religion is fundamentally opposed to everything I hold in veneration—courage, clear thinking, honesty, fairness, and, above all, love of the truth. In brief, it is a fraud.

—*Autobiographical Notes, 1925*

◇◇◇

BURKHARDT LUDWIG MENCKEN was an agnostic with no membership in any church and no kind of religious belief whatever; but he had nothing against the clergy as such, and as a matter of fact rather enjoyed engaging with them in theological disputation. His son August, on the other hand, was not only antireligious but vigorously anticlerical as well. In this respect, H. L. Mencken was something of a mean between his grandfather and his father: he numbered among his acquaintances Baltimore clergymen of every denomination, and for some of them he undoubtedly had a very high regard, but this regard was not accompanied by any kind of respect for their convictions. Just as it was impossible for him to take seriously any postulate of religion, so it was also impossible for him to believe that anybody else could take it seriously either, and this included even men for whom the religious life was a chosen vocation. If they were "liberal" and wore their beliefs lightly, then there was some chance that he could meet with them on equal terms; if they were persons of deep faith who honestly believed what they preached to others, an unbridgeable gap existed and he was likely to have for them nothing but contempt.

He analyzed his feelings toward religion many times and in many places, but nowhere more clearly and succinctly than in a 1924 "Clinical Notes" column in *The American Mercury:*

My essential trouble, I sometimes suspect, is that I am quite devoid of what are called spiritual gifts. That is to say, I am incapable of religious experience, in any true sense. Religious ceremonials often interest me esthetically, and not infrequently they amuse me otherwise, but I get absolutely no stimulation out of them, no sense of exaltation, no mystical *katharsis*. In that department I am as anesthetic as a church organist, an archbishop or an altar boy. When I am low in spirits and full of misery, I never feel any impulse to seek help, or even mere consolation, from supernatural powers. Thus the generality of religious persons remain mysterious to me, and vaguely offensive, as I am unquestionably offensive to them. I can no more understand a man praying than I can understand him carrying a rabbit's foot to bring him luck. This lack of understanding is a cause of enmities, and I believe that they are sound ones. I dislike any man who is pious, and all such men that I know dislike me.[1]*

It is interesting to speculate on whether Mencken would have been different if the home in which he grew up had been imbued with any kind of religious atmosphere at all. Unhappily it is also quite useless, for the plain fact remains that it was not. August's own attitude has just been mentioned; Anna Mencken, as later her daughter Gertrude, attended church on occasion, but for them it was chiefly a social event where one encountered friends and neighbors, and the spiritual imperatives of religion meant nothing to them. Like their older brother, Charles Mencken and August, Jr., never went to church at all.

The point hardly needs to be labored that there was nothing unusual about such a thing, any more then than now. Membership in the various churches might have been high, but the enrollment figures were no real index to the number of persons who actually believed in Christianity, and even less to the number who practiced it as a way of life. It may even be that religious faith reached its nadir in the United States during the latter part of the nineteenth century, for that peaceful, smug, and prosperous society had no particular need of God. Few problems plagued it, and it was confident that the ones that did would eventually be disposed of by scientific progress. A belief in science had taken the place of belief in God.

---

*He expressed himself even more briefly and forcibly in a letter of December 2, 1927, to Charles Green Shaw: "I am completely devoid of religious feeling. All religions seem ridiculous to me, and in bad taste. I do not believe in the immortality of the soul, nor in the soul. Ecclesiastics seem to me to be simply men who get their livings by false pretenses. Like all rogues, they are occasionally very amusing." (Forgue, *Letters*, p. 306.)

This change had set in with the Renaissance, which Mencken calls "a reversion to the spacious paganism of Greece and Rome,"[2] but it did not really get well under way until science as we now know it began its triumphant advance in the seventeenth century. Thereafter it proceeded rapidly, the conquests of science and the decline of religion moving in a kind of inverse proportion. Mencken singles out Bacon, Galileo, Newton, Leibniz, Harvey, and Leeuwenhoek as worthy of special mention, and declares that as a result of their work "the universe ceased to be Yahweh's plaything and became a mechanism like any other, responding to the same immutable laws. . . . Man became an animal—the noblest of them all, but still an animal. Heaven and Hell sank to the level of old wives' tales, and there was a vast collapse of Trinities, Virgin Births, Atonements and other such pious phantasms. The Seventeenth Century, and especially the latter half thereof, saw greater progress than had been made in the twenty centuries preceding—almost as much, indeed, as was destined to be made in the Nineteenth and Twentieth."[3]

By the middle of the nineteenth this progress had come so far that men began to conceive of it as a law of nature or history—the idea, in other words, that there was something inevitable about it and that it would ultimately lead to human perfection. The French philosopher Auguste Comte (1798–1857) gave it a name—"positivism."* Comte believed that there had been three stages in human development: a first, which he called the "theological," in which man's ignorance of the causes behind natural phenomena had led him to ascribe every happening to the will of the gods; a second, the "metaphysical," when supernatural explanations gave place to natural laws and the new race of philosophers sought to account for things along purely rational lines; and finally the "positive," which occurred when men became convinced that all such causes were ultimately unknowable and decided to rest content with mere facts—facts which could be obtained by observation and experiment and then made the basis for scientific hypotheses and laws. It was this third and final stage, Comte thought, that mankind was just entering upon in his own time.

---

*The *Random House Unabridged Dictionary* defines "positivism" as "a philosophical system founded by Auguste Comte, concerned with positive facts and phenomena, and excluding speculation upon ultimate causes or origins." It was precisely such speculation that Mencken dismissed as "metaphysics."

This was the view that H. L. Mencken accepted wholeheartedly and unquestioningly. Knowledge, for him, meant the verifiable facts of science; whatever was not capable of being thus verified lay in the realm of metaphysics and theology, and thus did not deserve being dignified by the name of knowledge at all. Moreover, every time that science added a new fact, however seemingly trivial, to its store, metaphysics and theology were thrust further back into a corner. Such a view might seem narrow and constricted, and undoubtedly it is, but it was one that he never saw any good reason to change:

> To me the scientific point of view is completely satisfying, and it has been so as long as I can remember. Not once in this life have I ever been inclined to seek a rock and a refuge elsewhere. It leaves a good many dark spots in the universe, to be sure, but not a hundredth time as many as theology. We may trust it, soon or late, to throw light upon many of them, and those that remain dark will be beyond illumination by any other agency. It also fails on occasion to console, but so does theology; indeed, I am convinced that man, in the last analysis, is intrinsically inconsolable.[4]

Yet it must be remembered that many scientists themselves, as they worked on their hypotheses and formulated their laws, felt a sense of dissatisfaction, a desire to penetrate further and look for ultimate explanations. In Mencken's own time this was true of such figures as Robert Millikan, Sir Arthur Eddington, and Sir James Jeans. He himself, however, contemptuously dismissed such speculation as "metaphysics"; the danger in it, he felt, was that in the process of looking for such causes, scientists might also be tempted to make moral judgments—to interpret their facts, in other words, in terms of good and bad, right and wrong. And this sort of thing lay entirely outside its province, since in itself science "has no more interest in the moral significance of [its] facts than it has in the moral significance of a streptococcus. It must be amoral by its very nature: the minute it begins separating facts into the two categories of good ones and bad ones it ceases to be science and becomes a mere nuisance, like theology."[5]

Thus it seemed to him that men of this sort were not scientists in the true sense at all. They might, of course, make important and even original contributions to its work, but the moment they let their Christianity take precedence over their scientific judgment they were lost. They looked for some intelligible design or meaning in the universe, and he was convinced that there was none; they invariably found it in a God made to their own image. "Dr. Robert A. Millikan's is an elderly Unitarian born in Morrison, Ill., who took his Ph.D. at Columbia in 1895, got the Nobel Prize in 1923, and is a member of the Valley Hunt Club of Pasadena, Calif. Dr. A. S. Eddington's is a Quaker imperfectly denaturized at Cambridge and now a don there. By the same token, Sir James Jeans's is a mathematician."[6]

Huntington Cairns is probably right in saying that Mencken's respect for science was limited to the practical kind that predicts eclipses, builds bridges, conquers disease, and enhances the safety and comfort of man.[7] For science in its pure state—the higher reaches of mathematics and physics, that is—he had only a mild interest. Much of its work involved, after all, that very speculation in which he put no faith; and when, in his own late years, it did produce a gruesomely practical result in the atomic bomb, he reacted with the same horror that thousands of his fellow men did. In a 1946 interview in *Life* magazine he expressed his views in language unusually sarcastic even for him:

> As for the atomic bomb itself, I believe it is the greatest of all American inventions, and one of the imperishable glories of Christianity. It surpasses the burning of heretics on all counts, but especially on the count that it has given the world an entirely new disease, to wit, galloping carcinoma. I have been reading with great edification in the medical journals of the clinical pictures presented at Hiroshima. Large numbers of the victims, I was proud to note, were women and children. They were slowly fried or roasted to death like people burned by radium or X-rays. In many cases their agonies were prolonged, and they suffered worse than any bishop will ever suffer in hell.[8]*

He had, of course, a great interest in biology and medicine—the latter because he was, according to the accounts of all who knew him, one of the world's greatest hypochondriacs—and through the early influence of his literary idol, Huxley, he accepted without reservation the Darwinian hypothesis of natural evolution. But although from the beginning to the end of his days he studied human nature, and never

---

*Roger Butterfield, the interviewer, writes as though he were sitting chatting with Mencken while the latter ate breakfast in Manhattan's Stork Club. In actual fact, one of the volumes of miscellaneous typescripts and clippings in the Mencken Room shows that he submitted his questions in advance and that Mencken replied to them in writing.

ceased to be amused by its weaknesses and foibles, he had surprisingly little belief in the particular branch of science that specializes in it—namely, psychology. He viewed it with a skepticism that frankly bordered on contempt, and regarded most psychologists themselves as charlatans. It was, he maintained,

> the youngest of the sciences, and hence chiefly guesswork, empiricism, hocus-pocus, poppycock. On the one hand, there are still enormous gaps in its data, so that the determination of its simplest principles remains difficult, not to say impossible; and, on the other hand, the very hollowness and nebulosity of it, particularly around its edges, encourages a horde of quacks to invade it, sophisticate it and make nonsense of it. Worse, this state of affairs tends to such confusion of effort and direction that the quack and the honest inquirer are often found in the same man. It is, indeed, a commonplace to encounter a professor who spends his days in the laborious accumulation of psychological statistics, sticking pins into babies and platting upon a chart the ebb and flow of their yells, and his nights chasing poltergeists and other such celestial fauna over the hurdles of a spiritualist's atelier, or gazing into a crystal in the privacy of his own chamber.[9]

This is from a review written for *The Smart Set* in 1915. It may be true that clinical psychology was still in a rudimentary state at the time, but although it would advance rapidly over the next several decades there is no evidence that he ever modified his opinion. A dozen years later, in 1927, he thought that it "was in chaos, with no sign that order is soon to be restored."[10]* In the recorded interview which Donald Kirkley, of the *Sunpapers*, did with him on June 10, 1948, for the Library of Congress, he spoke of "psychologists and other such frauds." And this attitude extended even to the man who was unquestionably one of the most seminal and influential figures of modern times and who did more for the science of psychology than anybody since Aristotle—Sigmund Freud.

---

*However, in the same review he admitted that it might someday achieve greater respectability. Psychologists, he said, "paddle around in what ought to be a science, but they are not quite scientists. Some day, perhaps, they will make the grade, and so become brothers to the pathologists. But at this moment they are nearer the osteopaths."

Mencken's approach to Freud was a curiously ambivalent one. In spite of his frequently scoffing attitude toward many figures who are usually revered as great, he was willing enough in serious moments to admit the importance of most of those men who have contributed to human progress in some significant way. He admired Aristotle, Leonardo, Galileo, Newton, Harvey. He could admit the genius, without in the least subscribing to any of his ideas, of somebody like St. Thomas Aquinas; and there is scarcely any need to tell again of his enthusiasm and support for Darwin and Huxley. But when it came to Freud, who certainly did as much to unravel the mysteries of the human mind as Darwin did to explain the evolution of the body, he drew back. There was something about psychoanalysis that he simply could not take. His most-used phrase for it, occurring again and again throughout his writings, was "the Freudian rumble-bumble."

In the beginning, to be sure, he was inclined to grant it value, if only because, like his own writings, it flew in the face of almost universally accepted beliefs. Some of Freud's earlier pronouncements, he wrote in 1918, had seemed extravagant, and some of them undoubtedly were,

> but the more his fundamental ideas have been put to the test the more plain it has become that they are essentially sound. . . . On the one hand they blow away the accumulated psychological rubbish of centuries, both "scientific" and popular, and on the other hand they set up a new psychology that meets the known facts exactly, and interprets them logically, and diligently avoids all the transcendental pish-posh of the past. The process of thought, under this new dispensation, becomes thoroughly intelligible for the first time. It responds to causation; it is finally stripped of supernaturalism; it is seen to be determined by the same natural laws that govern all other phenomena in space and time. And so seen, it gives us a new understanding of the forces which move us in the world, and shows us the true genesis and character of our ideas, and enormously strengthens our grip upon reality.[11]

Yet as time went on he became more and more doubtful. In *Treatise on the Gods* he referred to it in passing as containing "a great deal of racy nonsense."[12] Amid the philological scholarship of *The American Language* he paused long enough to observe in a footnote that in the United States the popular craze for psychoanalysis had followed upon

Couéism, the Emmanuel Movement, and paper-bag cookery.[13] In *Heathen Days*, which came out as late as 1943, he spoke of "the Freudian sewage."[14] And there can be little doubt that the chief reason for his reservations about it, and the fact that it never seemed to him quite respectable, was the heavy emphasis placed by Freud and his followers on sex.

As a normal American male, Mencken was perfectly well aware of the power and drive of the sexual impulse. There is not the slightest reason in the world to suppose that, prior to his marriage to Sara Haardt at the age of fifty, he had lived a life of dedicated celibacy. One of the chief causes for his implacable war against the Puritans, quite aside from the fact that he felt they were trying to force *him* to live according to *their* idiotic ideas, was their pretense that sex did not exist, or their insistence that if it did the fact ought not to be generally admitted.

Yet, as we shall see, in his general attitude toward women and sex he was curiously old-fashioned and straitlaced. Charles Angoff, who is for the most part very undependable, is probably right at least in the passage where he says that "Mencken denounced conventional morality at every opportunity, but he himself entertained some notions that even conventional morality would have looked upon as overly puritanical."[15] In New York, when he went up to join Nathan in putting out an issue of *The Smart Set* or the *Mercury*, he was inclined to let down the barriers and take sex as he found it, with all the insouciance of an unobligated bachelor out on the town. In Baltimore, where he was a person of some note with an important position on an influential daily paper, he was much more reserved. But above all, he would never permit sex, any more than he would permit alcohol, to interfere with his work. That always came first, and both women and drinking were but pleasant forms of diversion to be engaged in after it was out of the way.

Thus it was simply impossible for him to accept or see any truth in Freud's dictum that sex was the overmastering impulse that not only gave direction to all of man's activities but was the master key explaining all his mental and emotional processes. In Mencken's view this was going much too far. In addition, it was in bad taste. Finally, the evidence failed to support the theory. So, for him, psychoanalysis was not really a form of scientific knowledge, and its founder had always about him a touch of the quack.

2 IT FOLLOWED THAT IF SCIENCE deals with the known, or at all events with what is knowable, religion deals with the unknown, or—in Mencken's terms—the "not worth knowing." Unlike many who dismiss it loftily with little knowledge of either its history or its content, he was really quite learned in it; he laid claim to being "a theologian of considerable gifts" and a lifelong "student of the sacred sciences," and if *Treatise on the Gods* shows nothing else, it at least evidences an immense amount of reading and study and a thorough mastery of the materials. In one place he tells of having put to rest the doubts of a Catholic who had great difficulty accepting the doctrine of papal infallibility; Mencken showed him that if he were willing to accept the other tenets of Catholic belief, this one followed logically enough.[16]

But his knowledge of the subject never for one instant brought him to the brink of faith,* which he once defined as "an illogical belief in the occurrence of the improbable." "There is thus," he went on, "a flavor of the pathological in it; it goes beyond the normal intellectual process and passes into the murky domain of transcendental metaphysics. A man full of faith is simply one who has lost (or never had) the capacity for clear and realistic thought. He is not a mere ass; he is actually ill."[17] Rather, his studies had exactly the opposite effect: he was convinced that religion represented an early and immature stage in man's development, and that its steady decline since the Renaissance was a mark of genuine progress.

Yet even though he may have been born devoid of spiritual gifts, religion fascinated him from the beginning to the end of his career. Sometimes—perhaps most often—that fascination showed itself in the form of pure buffoonery, as in his habit of enclosing holy pictures and pious tracts in letters to his friends, or ending such letters "Yours in Xt," or assuring those same correspondents that, all other remedies for hay fever having failed, he was falling back on prayer. In a bit more

---

*However, Carl Bode says that Marcella Du Pont told him that Mencken told her that when his mother and his wife died he had deeply wanted to believe but had not been able to. Bode goes on: "He also told Marcella once that when he had shared a room, at convention times, with Frank Kent, Kent had always knelt to say his prayers before going to bed. Then Mencken had watched sardonically but later wished that as a child he had been taught to pray that way." (*Mencken*, p. 333.)

serious vein, it showed itself in the impressive number of religious and theological works that he reviewed over the years in *The Smart Set* and the *Mercury*, where, despite his usually bantering tone, he yet managed to write with comprehension, reasonable fairness, and —above all—honesty. Lastly, the fascination shows itself in the sizable proportion of his own output devoted to the subject, coming to a climax in *Treatise on the Gods*.

This was his own especial favorite among all his books. It was, he thought, "smooth, good-tempered, and adroitly written, and during all the years since it was published no one has ever successfully challenged a statement of fact in it. It is a model of condensation."[18] To his brother August he confided that it was "the first work of art on the anti-religious side after Huxley." He brought to it a degree of preparation and research surpassing that for any other of his works except *The American Language*, and the ten pages of bibliography in the back doubtless only suggest the total amount of reading that he must have done. Since one of his principal objects was to show how religious beliefs and practices had entered into human culture almost at its very beginning, he is particularly good on primitive man and savage tribes. He is rather less than satisfactory on such things as Hinduism and Buddhism, but it has to be remembered that an American interest in Far Eastern religions would really have to wait for another generation. He is better on Islam and Judaism, and at his characteristic best on Christianity. On page after page he shows himself to be quite *au courant* with the most advanced Scripture scholarship of the time.

Thus he could never quite understand or forgive the rather cool critical reception that it got. For the outcries and assaults of believers he was naturally prepared (a Baltimore priest, Father John E. Graham, wrote another whole book, *The Way of the Skeptic*, to refute it), but what nettled Mencken was that respectable critics, with no more religious belief than he had, tended to dismiss it out of hand. They called it unscholarly, or a mere potpourri of the more authoritative analyses to be found in works of scholarship, or they claimed it said nothing that had not already been said. This last may be true enough, but it should be added that here it is said as only H. L. Mencken could say it.

Happily, though, neither professional indifference nor ecclesiastical hostility prevented the book from becoming a commercial and popular success. It appeared at a rather unpropitious time, early in 1930 as the Depression was settling down on the land, but by the end of that year it had already sold 13,000 copies. Thereafter it went through nine reprintings, including a cheap dollar edition. When it finally went out of print in 1945, Alfred Knopf suggested to Mencken that a revision might be in order, and a second edition, with minor changes throughout the first four chapters and the final one substantially rewritten, appeared the following year. This second edition continues in print down to the present day, along with a paperback reprint of the same text.

His general approach is very much in the tradition of that nineteenth-century positivism described a few pages back.* Religion is treated, in other words, as a natural phenomenon and on a purely natural level. It represents an effort, one among several, on the part of man at the very dawn of his history to penetrate the unknowable, and its long development since then is to be studied and explained in precisely the same way that one studies the development of political and social ideas, or philosophy and art. Such an approach is, of course, not necessarily illegitimate, and some excellent histories of the subject have been based upon it, but one may argue that it is incomplete in the sense that it fails to take into account the specific claim made by many major religions—namely, that their beliefs constitute a revelation made by God to man, or at least that they are the teachings of a divine or semi-divine being.

If Mencken gives little time to disposing of this position, it is because he simply cannot take it seriously in the first place. He mentions it briefly in the preface to the second edition of the *Treatise* and passes on: "Religion," he maintains, "was invented by man just as agriculture and the wheel were invented by man, and there is absolutely nothing in it to justify the belief that its inventors had the aid of higher powers, whether on this earth or elsewhere."[19] After all, the answer of the positivist to any such claim of supernatural origin must be that there is no scientific evidence for it, and that therefore it cannot be considered knowledge. The response of the believer to this—that it is something that has to be accepted on faith—is essentially meaningless to the positivistic mind.

His own position, he asserts, is one of "amiable skepticism," for

---

*I am not suggesting that Mencken formally belonged to the school of philosophy known as positivism (or, for that matter, to any other school), or that he could be considered a disciple of Auguste Comte. In all his writings the only place where I can find any mention of Comte is in the early Nietzsche book, and the references there are merely in passing. Nevertheless, it remains true that his beliefs and his theory of knowledge are in strict accord with positivistic principles.

though he has no belief in any of the current theologies, neither does he have any active antipathy toward them. Nevertheless, his feelings about religion are set forth in the frankest possible manner throughout, and there are moments when they are very far from amiable.

He offers a definition of religion in his opening section:

> Whether it happens to show itself in the artless mumbo-jumbo of a Winnebago Indian or in the elaborately refined and metaphysical rites of a Christian archbishop, its single function is to give man access to the powers which seem to control his destiny, and its single purpose is to induce those powers to be friendly to him. That function and that purpose are common to all religions, ancient or modern, savage or civilized, and they are the only common characters that all of them show. Nothing else is essential.[20]

In this pure and simple form religion is seldom encountered today, for what we have now are the accretions of countless ages built upon this original function and purpose, and many of these accretions have only a very indirect connection with religion as such. Both function and purpose, in the beginning, were two-pronged. There were certain powers—flood, for example, wind, fire, lightning, large and dangerous animals—which were obviously inimical to man and which seemed to him, in his then untutored state, to have a life and volition of their own. Some means had to be devised to placate them, or at least to ward off the dangers that they threatened. Other powers—sunlight, warmth, the gentle breeze—were friendly and beneficent; their continued favor had to be assured. Both tasks fell upon the priest.

Mencken paints a picture—rather charmingly and poetically, in fact—of how both religion and the priesthood probably came into being. The universality of the Flood legend in ancient mythologies provides him with the inspiration for it.

He imagines a stretch of grassland bisected by a small river, with, on one bank, a bit of higher ground broken by rock masses and covered by trees. There are caves amid the rocks, and in them, at the very earliest beginnings of a human form of life, a small tribe has found shelter and home. One spring, following the melting of heavy winter snows, there come torrential rains and the river overflows its banks. As the waters rise higher and higher, they sweep away some hapless members of the little band—perhaps a woman and a child. Still they keep rising, threatening now to pour into the very caves that hitherto had been a safe retreat from the elements.

While the people huddle miserably on the highest point of land and watch the flood advance upon them like a living, menacing thing, one man, braver or more desperate than the rest, decides to do something about it. He goes forward to meet the flood, and hurls defiance at it. He throws stones into it, and venturing in some distance, belabors it with his club. Then he scrambles back up the slope, proud if still a bit frightened, as the others flock about him with awe and acclaim. . . . "And next morning the flood begins to recede."

Such, in essence, according to Mencken, was the beginning of religion. He does not pretend, of course, that this account is to be taken literally, any more than one would take literally that "state of nature" about which the eighteenth-century philosophers of the Enlightenment liked to write, but it does offer an explanation of how early man may first have reacted and related to the unknown. The man who seemingly bested the flood was the first priest. The words and gestures that he used constituted the first liturgy. The people who watched him with the sneaking envy called admiration were the first congregation, and it was natural for them to assume that he was wielding some supernal power over the waters just as their successors of today assume that a priest wields some supernal power when he engages in the ritual of a religious service.

His success on this occasion gave him an exaggerated sense of his own importance and potency, but his path was not destined to be wholly an easy one. There were, says Mencken, skeptics in that remote day even as in this, and they tended to set him down as a fraud and impostor. By his own claim he was supposed to have some special knowledge of and influence upon these inscrutable forces, but as time went on it became obvious enough that there were many occasions when it did not work. Why, for example, did someone die in spite of the priest's incantations to drive the demons of illness from him? Why (after the invention of agriculture) did crops fail despite his petitions for a successful harvest? His initial explanations for these failures were bound to be lame and not altogether convincing, but after a while, being an adroit fellow, he came up with a reason to which they had no ready answer. The fault lay not with him but with them. They had offended the gods by doing something that they should not have done, or omitting to do something that they should have, and that was why the divine favor was withheld.

Thus the science of moral theology was born, and the priest became its adept and interpreter. He, and he alone, was privy to what pleased the gods and what displeased them, and the rules that he laid down would assure that their will was obeyed. But these rules carried with them, as yet, no real punitive measures. A man who had incurred the gods' displeasure might be struck down by disease or killed by some wild beast, but that was as far as it went. For the men of that day had, as yet, no conception of the entity which we have since come to call the "soul." The notion that there was a part of him separate and distinct from the body, which went on living after the body had died, came in later, and the notion that this part was immortal and never died at all was a very late development, reached at a quite advanced stage of religious and metaphysical speculation. When it did finally arrive the priest had in his hands a weapon of unimaginable power, for now there was simply no escaping the gods: anyone who broke their laws could be pursued even beyond the portals of death and into the next world for all eternity.

Such was the origin of hell, which Mencken believed considerably antedated the idea of heaven and has certainly had a vastly greater influence upon human conduct. "It is Hell, of course," he says,

> that makes priests powerful, not Heaven, for after thousands of years of so-called civilization fear remains the one common denominator of mankind. At the bottom of every approach to the gods, even in the most enlightened societies of today, lies the ancient motive of propitiation. . . . [W]hat remains, however brave, lofty, and metaphysical its terms, is no more than lagniappe, and of no serious import. When men cease to fear the gods they cease to be religious in any rational sense. . . . The essence of all priestly morality is retribution, and without a Hell of one sort or another retribution becomes mere rhetoric, signifying nothing.[21]

As one might expect, he is at his best and most entertaining in his descriptions of the hells of the various religions. For the Buddhist, he remarks, "going to Hell was not the simple matter that it is to a Christian," for the Buddhist religion had not one hell but eight, and each of these had sixteen subsidiary hells, making a total of 136 in all. In the deepest of these, Avichi, the standard sentence for the crime of killing a priest was 149,504,000,000 years! This may seem a trifle severe, but on the other hand it has to be borne in mind that it does eventually come to an end and the inmate, having expiated his offense, passes into the merciful annihilation of Nirvana. The Tibetan Buddhists, living on the windy and frozen roof of the world, conceived hell not in terms of fire but in the form of geysers of icy water, where the damned were so thoroughly refrigerated that their jaws froze tight, their tongues were so paralyzed that only the exclamations "Kyi-u" and "Ha-ha" were possible, and their bodies were dissolved in horrible chilblains. The Christian hell, Mencken thought, was the deepest and hottest of them all, for in the course of its development it gathered in the best features of all the other hells of antiquity and bent them to its constabulary purposes. Its tortures, he says, "are the bulwarks of all sacerdotal authority, whether Catholic or Protestant."[22]

In the very earliest stages of what, using the term a bit loosely, may be called religion, such forces as wind, rain, lightning, and so on were envisaged as having their own sentience and volition. The notion of "gods," invisible and superior beings who dwelt in the skies, was again a subsequent development, and the first gods were thought of as female in form. The oldest and most universal was the "Earth Mother," who appears in virtually all religions. This was because women brought forth children, and by analogy the earth brought forth trees, plants, and crops. Among these early tribes, as among some savage tribes even today, no connection was made between sexual intercourse and female pregnancy and childbirth, but eventually "some primeval and forgotten Harvey" stumbled upon the male role in reproduction, and it was the most epochal discovery in all history. The role of the man in society, hitherto secondary and quite unimportant, was completely altered, and as a logical result the gods began to be conceived of, too, as masculine in form—Rê the sun god in Egypt, Zeus in Greece, and Odin or Wotan in the northern regions.

For many ages, too, they existed in large pantheons and hierarchies, arranged in orders of greater and lesser dignity and with each having differently assigned responsibilities. The notion that there was only one God, a Supreme Being who ruled the entire universe and everything in it by His own power and might, had to wait for the Jews, and even among them its development took place over a very long period of time. Mencken believes, probably rightly, that they got many of their ideas from the Egyptian Pharaoh Amenhotep IV, also known as Akhenaten, a religious reformer who had tried (unsuccessfully) to introduce monotheism into Egypt.

But whether a given religion had one god or many, whether they were limited or omnipotent, whether they were thought of as human in form or as some vague kind of spirit, the function and purpose common to all of them meant that they would also have certain beliefs and practices in common too. The pages in which Mencken discusses the resemblances to be found among them show how deeply he had probed into his subject. "What the Bakua medicine-man seeks to accomplish by rattling stones in a cocoanut-shell," he says,

> or the Tibetan *lama* by whirling his prayer-wheel, or the Yakut *shaman* by going into a sweat-bath, or the Crow Indian devotee by chopping off a finger is precisely what the Pope seeks to accomplish by saying Mass in St. Peter's. All desire, first, to attract the notice of the gods, and, second, to induce them to be amiable.[23]

The Catholic rosary obviously has its analogue in the Tibetan Buddhist prayer wheel. The abstention from meat practiced by Catholics on Fridays (at least during Mencken's lifetime) is matched by Jewish dietary laws and by very similar taboos among Polynesian and other tribes. He quotes the American anthropologist Lewis Spence to the effect that the Aztec priests had heard confessions and given absolution for sins. The Eucharist, central mystery of the Christian faith, has many parallels elsewhere, he says, and in its earliest form constituted what students of comparative religion speak of as theophagy, or god-eating. Its *raison d'être* lay in the belief that by eating the god, or at all events a totem animal which represented him, the devotee would be filled with the divine attributes and strength. All such practices have a tendency to freeze into formulae, and these formulae may continue after the original purpose and intent have long been forgotten.

Religion began, as we have seen, in an effort to penetrate and explain the unknown, and, for Mencken, the unknown has at all times remained its special province. Consequently, he thought, it is by its very nature the implacable enemy of knowledge and of all attempts to increase it among men, for it must be obvious that as knowledge grows the area of the unknown tends to diminish, and thus the area controlled by religion diminishes too. The Church has vigorously resisted every attempt to expand the frontiers of human knowledge. In the sixteenth century it condemned Galileo; in the nineteenth it fought tooth and nail against the theory of natural selection propounded by Darwin; in the twentieth, so far as it understood it at all, it protested that Einstein's theory of relativity raised the specter of atheism. For its argument that there is a limit beyond which science cannot go and that this constitutes its special preserve, Mencken has only contempt; he knows perfectly well, of course, that there are questions which science has not yet answered, but this is by no means to say that they are unanswerable—it is simply to say that in the present state of our knowledge we do not yet know the answers to them.

There is, he maintains (though here he is really quoting from Andrew White's *History of the Warfare of Science with Theology in Christendom*), a consistent pattern in the way that the Church deals with new ideas that seem to threaten it. First, it denounces them ferociously and brands those who promulgate them as heretics. Second, as soon as it sees that the idea is not going to be easily disposed of but will be around for some while and enter into the general stream of human thinking, it stands back and adopts an attitude of watchful waiting. Third, it makes the discovery that holding the idea is not sinful or heretical after all, and finally it manages to prove that it was never really against it in the first place!

When Mencken claims that he has no antipathy toward religion or toward any particular Church, he is probably speaking the truth. He admitted—a bit grudgingly—its utility in human life, and respected some of the great figures in its history. For the pomp and ceremony surrounding a Roman cardinal he had no use whatever, but on the other hand he had a very great admiration for the nameless nun giving her life to the care of the sick and helpless. Nevertheless, he was convinced that it must be combated, and to that task he gave an immense amount of his time and energies. The combat was joined as far back as the "Free Lance" column in the *Sunpapers;** when he began it he was told that he could attack anything except the churches, but when some Baltimore ministers attacked him for his irreverent ideas and ribald style he was released from this restriction. He could never see any reason for treating it diffidently or with kid gloves just because it was religion. "Why," he demanded to know, "should religion not be attacked when it is idiotic? What gives a theological imbecility superi-

---

*As a matter of fact, it probably began much earlier. In the manuscript that he supplied to Isaac Goldberg, he wrote (p. 122): "So early as March, 1900, I had an article in Brann's Iconoclast, which then had an enormous sale. It is perhaps worth recording that the subject of it was the clowning of the Methodist preachers of Baltimore. I have no copy of it but I recall clearly that it was a very violent slating."

ority over any other imbecility? Why should a moron dressed up as a Methodist preacher get any more respect than a moron behind a plow?"[24]

He knew, of course, that it was so deeply entrenched in man's mind and in human culture that it would be centuries before there was any chance of effectively exorcising it. But that it would be thus exorcised someday he did not doubt. Late in life he wrote:

> The time must inevitably come when mankind shall surmount the imbecility of religion, as it has surmounted the imbecility of religion's ally, magic. It is impossible to imagine this world being really civilized so long as so much nonsense survives. In even its highest forms religion embraces concepts that run counter to all common sense. It can be defended only by making assumptions and adopting rules of logic that are never heard of in any other form of human thinking.[25]

3 NEVERTHELESS AND IN SPITE of all this—in spite even of the fact that the discovery may come as a bit of a shock to those who thought they knew him—Mencken was not an atheist. An atheist, after all, is someone who knows that God does not exist, and such knowledge is quite incompatible with the skeptical position. In terms of the Menckenian epistemology, it is no more capable of scientific verification than the contradictory one that God does exist. Earlier I quoted from one of the "Clinical Notes" columns in *The American Mercury* where he sets forth his basic attitude toward religion; it is rather curious that when he selected this passage for inclusion in the *Chrestomathy* he omitted and gave no hint of the paragraph that immediately follows:

> Nevertheless, it seems to me to be plain that atheism, properly socalled, is nonsense, and I can recall no concrete atheist who did not appear to me to be a donkey. To deny any given god is, of course, quite reasonable, but to deny all gods is simply folly. For if there is anything plain about the universe it is that it is governed by law, and if there is anything plain about law it is that it can never be anything but a manifestation of will. Do the stars spin in a certain way and no other? Then it is simply because some will ordains that they shall spin that way.[26]*

---

*The passage is not wholly consistent with other places where he denies that there is any evidence whatever of design or purpose in the universe.

What he found impossible to stomach about religion was its unqualified assurance that it knew God existed, and its blatant and unsubstantiated claim that for the benefit of believers it could mediate between Him and them. What he found impossible to stomach in each individual religion was its even more unqualified assurance that the God it believed in was the only one there was, and that to believe in any other was wicked and immoral.

In his approach to these various faiths he managed to be completely unprejudiced: he was against all of them. On occasion he might say something kind about one of the non-Christian religions in comparison to Christianity, as when he remarks that Moslemism is superior "if only because its ethical system forms a connected and consistent whole,"[27] but this does not mean that he was drawn to Islam or felt any special admiration for it, since in other places he could be quite caustic about it. So, too, with the Far Eastern religions: "The so-called philosophy of India is even more blowsy and senseless than the metaphysics of the West. It is at war with everything we know of the workings of the human mind, and with every sound idea formulated by mankind. . . . It has absolutely nothing to offer a civilized white man."[28] Buddhism seemed to him "complete hooey."[29] The Judaic Law was full of "harsh prohibitions, . . . savage pains and penalties, [and] general irrationality."[30]*

But it was only natural that most of his writings about religion should be concerned with Christianity, since he "was [himself] educated in its doctrines in youth, though not urged to believe them,"[31] and he could reasonably assume that most of his readers were in the same case. Here again his approach is positivistic in tone and leans heavily on that "Higher Criticism" of the Bible which few Scripture scholars, whether Protestant or Catholic, take very seriously anymore.

---

*There is in the Mencken Room a manila folder on which another and later hand has written: "The nature of most of this material may make it unsuitable for publication." The judgment is a prudent one. It is a collection of miscellaneous brief notes, of the kind that later made up *Minority Report*, setting forth Mencken's opinions of the Jews, and some of them are harsh indeed. If they ever saw the light they would undoubtedly give rise to the accusation, which he had to face a number of times while he was living, that he was anti-Semitic. Actually, and in spite of these notes, I think it is safe to say that he was not, but anyone seeking to defend him from the charge would admittedly have his hands full if the prosecution were permitted to introduce the folder in evidence.

It should be added that these thoughts on the Jews of his own time have no necessary connection with his attitude toward ancient Judaism as a religion.

Christian theology, it seemed to him, was no more—and possibly much less—persuasive than the theologies underlying other civilized religions, and it leaned upon irrational supernaturalism to a much greater degree than any of its rivals. What Christians were called upon to believe would, if put in the form of an affidavit, "be such shocking nonsense that even bishops and archbishops would laugh at it."[32]

What, then, made it so superior to all other existing religions, and had enabled it to hold sway over the heart, if not necessarily the mind, of Western man for almost two thousand years? The answer was not far to seek. There would never be any need to put it in the form of an affidavit, for the simple reason that it was already put in the form of the most lush and lovely poetry ever written. Mencken believed that "the Bible is unquestionably the most beautiful book in the world." No other literature, he thought, could offer a match for either the Old or the New Testament. The 23d Psalm was the greatest of hymns, the story of the woman taken in adultery in John 8:3–11 (the authenticity of which, by the way, is doubted by most scholars) was "the most poignant drama ever written in the world," and "the story of Jesus, as it is told in the Synoptic Gospels, and especially in Luke, is touching beyond compare." Other religions have, of course, produced great art too: for example, there are Buddhist temples that are certainly as magnificent as any of the cathedrals of the Age of Faith, but "Christianity, alone among the modern world religions, has inherited an opulent aesthetic content, and is thus itself a work of art."[33]*

Yet the beauty of Christianity was no guarantee whatever of its

---

*It should be borne in mind that when Mencken calls the Bible "the most beautiful book in the world," he is talking specifically about the Authorized or King James Version in English, for which he had an unashamed admiration. It is, of course, one of the great glories of English literature, but he was perfectly well aware that it was "archaic, sonorous and often unintelligible" at the time it was published in 1611. He bitterly resented any attempt to put Scripture into more modern, and hence less poetic, terms; see, for example, his article "Holy Writ" in the Chicago *Tribune,* July 18, 1926 (included in McHugh, *The Bathtub Hoax,* pp. 165–69), in which he inveighs against the translations of Goodspeed, Ballantine, Moffatt, and Weymouth.

In recent years there have been many new translations of the Bible—the Revised Standard Version and the New English Bible among Protestants and the Jerusalem Bible and New American Bible among Catholics, to say nothing of the projected fifty-volume nondenominational Anchor Bible and a number of others. Most of these are wholly new versions made from the original texts and conveying far more accurately than any of their classical predecessors the meaning of the original authors. All are good and some are very good indeed, but admittedly even the best lack the majestic poetry of the King James. One wonders how Mencken would have reacted to them.

truth. Quite the contrary, in fact. For, as he immediately goes on in the passage just quoted, "it is of the essence of poetry that it is not true: its aim is not to record facts but to conjure up entrancing impossibilities." No heart could resist the tender loveliness of the Christian story; no rational mind could possibly accept its nonsensical theology.

As it exists today, Mencken believed, that theology contains little if anything that can be traced with certitude to its Founder. In his lifetime he had never heard or conceived of such doctrines as the Trinity, Original Sin, or the Virgin Birth. Though he may possibly be credited with putting forth the idea of the Apostolic Succession, his flailing attacks on the institutionalized Jewish priesthood of the day give us some idea of how he would have regarded the grandiose hierarchy of the Church that claims to speak in his name. He would have had no patience whatever with Puritan moralists, since he was known to associate with sinners and wine was to him a more natural drink than water.

It is not easy to tell just how Mencken felt about Jesus. Sorting out and putting side by side the various places in his work where he speaks of him, one finds them to be inconsistent and even contradictory. Now and again he writes in terms that must certainly set the teeth of any genuine believer on edge: Jesus' "stupendous ignorance," he says, "must be obvious even to Christians, for His false assumptions were gross and innumerable. He was probably dirty in person and He was certainly superstitious, for he believed in devils."[34] Yet in another place he describes him as "not only of aristocratic blood but a man of learning to boot," and a little later on adds that he was "a man of great personal dignity and virtue."[35] There is one passage where he says that "the doctrine he preached differed very little from that now whooped up from soap-boxes by Communists and other such simpletons";[36] there is another where he declares that "the thing He taught mainly, first and last, was simple good-will between man and man—simple friendliness, simple decency."[37]

One can only take one's pick among these various quotations. All in all, it may be said that what he writes about Jesus in any given place depends upon the point he wants to make in that place, and whether, in order to make it, he has to present him in a favorable or unfavorable light. Basically, though, there can be little doubt that he was in agreement with Nietzsche, who wrote in *The Antichrist* that "in truth there was only one Christian, and he died on the cross."

For Christ and his teaching were one thing; the organized religion that developed from his teaching was something else again. That development Mencken credits first of all to "Paul and his attendant rabble-rousers."[38] The gentle tolerance that Jesus had advocated was already gone in Paul, who was anything but a tolerant man and who cracked the heads of heretics wherever he found them. As the Church grew in numbers and strength, and as the temporal sovereignty of the Popes gradually brought them more power than any Roman Caesar had ever had, it insisted on complete conformity with its ideas and doctrines and would not permit the slightest deviation from them. Thus for centuries it stood squarely in the way of any genuine progress.

Of the two main branches of Christianity in the Western world, Mencken exhibited toward the Catholic Church a curious reserve and almost an untypical respect. True, he enjoyed referring to it jocosely as "Holy Church" and "the Harlot of the Seven Hills," but for the most part he all but goes out of his way to avoid offending it. He objected to Nathan about publishing a short story in *The Smart Set* on the ground that "it would offend the Catholics, and set every priest in the land to whooping against us. I dislike to outrage the Catholics needlessly, not only because they are the only lodge of Christians who never try to get us barred off the newsstands, but also because they are fundamentally very decent and detest the uplift almost as much as I do myself."[39] When, much later and at his behest, Charles Angoff did a series of articles in the *Mercury* on the various churches and wanted to include one on the Catholics, Mencken demurred on the ground that they were mainly a decent lot "and why hurt them?"[40]

"The Latin Church," he wrote, "which I constantly find myself admiring, despite its frequent astounding imbecilities, has always kept clearly before it the fact that religion is not a syllogism, but a poem." He was impressed by its liturgy and thought that a Solemn High Mass was a thousand times more imposing as sheer spectacle than any Protestant service;* it did nothing for him spiritually, of course, but he confessed that it gave him the same kind of sensuous delight as came over him

---

*Here again it is interesting to speculate on how he would have reacted to the liturgical changes that followed in the wake of the Second Vatican Council. In an article in *The Smart Set* (LXXII, 2, Oct. 1923, p. 142), again entitled "Holy Writ," he showed a remarkable prescience when he wrote: "If they [i.e., the Catholics] keep on spoiling poetry and spouting ideas, the day will come when some extra-bombastic deacon will astound humanity and insult God by proposing to translate the liturgy into American, that all the faithful may be convinced by it."

upon hearing *Tristan und Isolde* or Brahms's Fourth Symphony. Canon law, he thought, was far more rational than civil law, and exhibited a much deeper understanding of human nature; civil law would do well to model itself upon it. The Catholic clergy "pursue an intelligible ideal and dignify it with a real sacrifice."[41] Now and again he errs on some point of the Church's doctrine, as in his statement that Pius XI's encyclical *Casti connubii* is infallible, or that the Pope can dispense from the prohibition against even such serious sins as murder or adultery; but, all in all, it may be said that he had as good a knowledge of both Catholic theology and Catholic law as any priest.

Yet he was not blind to its defects, and considered that the rule of the Church over its people was an unendurable form of intellectual tyranny:

> It would be hard to find, in civilized history, a match for the power that . . . lies in the hands of the Catholic clergy. . . . Obviously, such a system is a formidable impediment to the free functioning of the intelligence. The Catholic is not only forbidden to do any effective thinking for himself on matters of faith and morals; he is also discouraged from speculation in the fields adjacent, which include those of history, anthropology, sociology, psychology, philosophy, and many of the physical sciences. . . . the truth is that the Catholic system is in its very essence inimical to intelligence, and commonly either throttles it or drives it out of the fold.[42]

"I get an aesthetic pleasure out of some of the Catholic ceremonials," he told Isaac Goldberg. "When I say so I am accused of leaning toward Mother Church. But Catholicism in general seems to me to be a preposterous and degrading fraud."[43]

This judgment may sound harsh, and no doubt it is, but it is as nothing compared to the things that he wrote about Protestantism. This, for him, was the very nadir of human intelligence, the subcellar of theology. Catholicism might not be true, but it was at least beautiful; one could imagine an otherwise rational person yielding to its aesthetic attractions. Protestantism, on the other hand, had not even the slightest touch of beauty to redeem it. It was, Mencken thought, "either a banal imitation of Catholicism or a cruel burlesque upon it. It is almost too incoherent to be discussed seriously."[44] It had forgotten the kind and forgiving Jesus of the New Testament and turned back to the harsh, vengeful Jahweh of the Old—or, where it had not abandoned Jesus altogether, it had converted him "into a Y.M.C.A. secretary, brisk, gladsome and obscene."[45]

To be sure, he could understand and even sympathize with the motives that brought on the Reformation and the break with Rome. The Catholic Church had simply become too big and too powerful; it straddled Europe like a colossus, and there was no level of society, from a peasant in his hut to an emperor on his throne, where its laws and its clergy did not penetrate. To the extent that the Reformers defied this power and the corruption that had become part of it, they were men of courage; but unhappily, says Mencken, "not many of them were intelligent [and] the new theology that they brought in was quite as silly as the old." Luther was "the theologian *par excellence* — cocksure, dictatorial, grasping, self-indulgent, vulgar and ignorant"; his greatest successor, John Calvin, "was the true father of Puritanism, which is to say, of the worst obscenity of Western civilization."[46] Moreover, no sooner had the reformed Church come into being than it split up into endless sects and subsects, each quarreling with the others and grounding itself infallibly upon the "interpolations, mistranslations and typographical errors" in Scripture. The result in a very short time was sheer chaos.

Thus it seemed to him that Protestantism, whatever its strength numerically, was a very feeble force in the world and had had small influence upon the mainstream of human thought. Its chief contribution, in fact, was "its massive proof that God is a bore."[47] Here in the United States, in his own time, it was "down with a wasting disease." One half of it furtively imitated Rome and indulged in such things as candles, incense, liturgical vestments, and holy water; this high-toned and generally respectable segment carried with it the greater part of Protestant money. The other half was sliding inexorably down the road to sheer voodooism; this carried with it the bulk of Protestant energies and enthusiasms. "What remains in the middle may be likened to a torso without either brains to think with or legs to dance—in other words, something that begins to be professionally attractive to the mortician, though it still makes shift to breathe."[48]

It was the second, Fundamentalist half of Protestantism that Mencken particularly scorned and—so far as he ever felt the emotion at all—feared. It was also the body or area of activity for which he brought into play the ultimate resources in his incomparable vocabulary of invective. "No more shocking nonsense," he declared, "has ever

The Sage of Baltimore, age eight.

In the Baltimore Sun *office, 1913.*

*Mencken and George Jean Nathan at Alfred Knopf's summer home,
Port Chester, N.Y. (Photo by Alfred A. Knopf)*

*Mencken relaxes on the grounds of Alfred Knopf's home at
Purchase, N.Y., 1940. (Photo by Alfred A. Knopf)*

*Portrait photograph
taken in August 1940.
(A. Aubrey Bodine; used
by courtesy of Mrs. A.
Aubrey Bodine)*

*In his study, with the
index cards and typescript
for the* Dictionary of
Quotations, *1942.*

At work in his Hollins Street study. (Otto Hagel, Life, 1941)

Mencken in a moment of relaxation. (Helen K. Taylor,
New York Herald Tribune, *March 1942)*

Checking a reference. (Otto Hagel, Life, *1941)*

*Mencken in the living room at 1524 Hollins Street. The bookcase
behind him contains rare volumes of works by earlier generations
of Menckenii. (Otto Hagel, Life, 1941)*

On a raw winter day, Mencken mounts the steps at 1524 Hollins Street. (Otto Hagel, Life, 1941)

been put into words by theoretically civilized men."[49] Its practitioners were "backwoods Wesleys," "sorry bounders of God," "sordid," "swinish," "ignoramuses." They received their knowledge, he charged, from "a faculty of half-idiot pedagogues" in one-building "seminaries" out on some bare pasture lot in that region which he delighted to call the "Bible Belt"—the South and the Midwest—and then went forth to preach not God or love but fear and hatred of every idea that they themselves were incapable of understanding. Fundamentalism was responsible for Comstockery, for such an outrage as Prohibition, for the degrading farce of the Scopes "monkey trial" at Dayton, Tennessee, in 1925. It was "the implacable enemy of all rational pedagogy and free speech."[50] "The evangelical sects plunge into an abyss of malignant imbecility, and declare a holy war upon every decency that civilized men cherish."[51]

Upon no denomination did these strictures fall more often or more fiercely than upon the Methodists. The Episcopalians he tended to dismiss out of hand as mere slavish imitators of the Catholics. He could be rather hard on the Baptists and Presbyterians. Yet despite his aversion to Protestantism in general, and however insulting his remarks about it, the fact remains that for the most part he could write about it with the same high humor that characterizes the great body of his work. (It may not, of course, have sounded humorous to them, but all the same there was no real malice in it.) But when it came to the Methodists, his humor deserted him. If he had any prejudice at all, it was here. He writes about them more frequently than any other Christian Church, and everywhere there is a touch of real savagery in his tone.

One gets the impression that this feeling must have gone back a long way, to the days of his boyhood. In commenting to Goldberg on the fact that his mother used to go to church occasionally out of a sense of social duty, he remarked that she "detested Methodists and other such psalm-singers." When he was quite young his father packed him and his brother Charlie off to a Methodist Sunday school, not for any moral improvement or training in divinity but simply to get them out of the house so that he might enjoy an afternoon nap; and his subsequent attitude may well have stemmed from that unhappy experience. When, in his days as a reporter on the *Herald*, it turned out that a new managing editor, Lynn Meekins, was a Methodist, he claims that the entire staff was ready to rise up in protest, for it was a known fact that any member of that Church "was necessarily and *ipso facto* a devious, inimical and mean fellow, bent only on afflicting and injuring the human race";[52] but this statement may simply be one of the many that sets the *Days* books apart from "coldly objective history."

He considered the name of St. Methodius, the ninth-century apostle to the Slavs, a "significant" one. An intelligent woman "can no more be an actual Methodist than a gentleman can be a Methodist."[53] "So far as I am aware," he maintained, "no man of any genuine distinction in the world today is a Methodist; if I am in error, I apologize most humbly."[54] He blamed them particularly for Prohibition: "It was among country Methodists," he declared, "practitioners of a theology degraded almost to the level of voodooism, that Prohibition was invented, and it was by country Methodists, nine-tenths of them actual followers of the plow, that it was fastened upon the rest of us, to the damage of our bank accounts, our dignity and our ease."[55]

"Who gives a damn," he wanted to know, "for the Coolidge idealism if its chief agent and executor, even above the Cabinet, is the Board of Temperance, Prohibition and Public Morals of the Methodist Episcopal Church, i.e. a gang of snooty ecclesiastics, committed unanimously to the doctrine that Christ should have been jailed for the business at Cana, that God sent she-bears to 'tare' forty-two little children because they had made fun of Elisha's bald head, and that Jonah swallowed the whale?"[56]

In the November 1924 issue of *The American Mercury* he printed an editorial, gathered two years later into *Prejudices: Sixth Series* under the title "Invitation to the Dance," in which he lumped the Baptists and Methodists together as the chief begetters and supporters of both the Anti-Saloon League and the Ku Klux Klan, and described the conditions which he claimed were the results of their work. After a long and careful study of the Menckenian canon, I have concluded that this piece represents the absolute peak of his vituperation, a height to which he had never climbed before and which even he would never achieve again:

> This connection, when it was first denounced, was violently denied by the Baptist and Methodist ecclesiastics, but now every one knows that it was and is real. These ecclesiastics are responsible for the Anti-Saloon League and its swineries, and they are responsible no less for the Klan. In other words, they are responsible, directly and certainly, for all the turmoils and black hatreds that now rage in the bleak regions between

the State roads—they are to blame for every witches' pot that now brews in the backwoods of the Union. They have sowed enmities that will last for years. They have divided neighbors, debauched local governments, and enormously multiplied lawlessness. They are responsible for more crime than even the wildest foes of the saloon ever laid to its discredit, and it is crime, in the main, that is infinitely more anti-social and dangerous. They have opposed every honest effort to compose the natural differences between man and man, and they have opposed every attempt to meet ignorance and prejudice with enlightenment. Alike in the name of God, they have advocated murder and they have murdered sense. Where they flourish no intelligent and well-disposed man is safe, and no sound and useful idea is safe. They have preached not only the bitter, savage morality of the Old Testament; they have also preached its childish contempt of obvious facts. Hordes of poor creatures have followed these appalling rogues and vagabonds of the cloth down their Gadarene hill: the result, in immense areas, is the conversion of Christianity into a machine for making civilized living impossible. It is wholly corrupt, rotten and abominable. It deserves no more respect than a pile of garbage.[57]

How much of all this was just, or even true? Allowing for his characteristic exaggeration, it is probably safe to say that a great deal of it was. We have come so far in such a relatively short time that it is not easy to recall the low state to which religion had sunk among the American people during the last decades of the nineteenth century and the first ones of the twentieth. This applies to both major branches of Western Christianity, Catholic no less than Protestant. The former, a distinct minority, lived an isolated ghetto existence in their parishes and parochial schools, and were much too much on the defensive against what they conceived to be Protestant hostility to make any kind of real contribution to either religious or national life; in their way, they were just as Fundamentalist and Puritanical as their neighbors. The latter, just because they were a majority that had given American culture its peculiar cast and temperament, were too smug and self-assured even to be aware of the spiritual barrenness in their midst. No thinkers of any power—or at least of any genuine influence—existed in either group, and the day was still a generation or more off when men of the stature of Jacques Maritain among Catholics or Paul Tillich among Protestants would come from Europe to stimulate religious thought and inspire followers by their presence on the scene.

In part, too, this low state was the result of a condition that Mencken alludes to in several of the passages just quoted, and which we shall have occasion to glance at in more detail a little later on. It is a phenomenon which scarcely exists anymore, but which was real enough at the time—the gap between city and rural life. The affluent and relatively well-educated membership of city churches paid Christianity only lip service, if, indeed, they paid it any service at all. It was among country people, cut off by the distances and paucity of communications of that day from any effective contact with enlightened thought, that religion did flourish, and here the Bible was unquestionably taken very seriously and literally, here Fundamentalism reached its height as a way of life, here moral concepts were buried beneath the heavy shroud of Puritanism. As Mencken never tired of pointing out, it was a native of Nebraska—a man who, moreover, had once held the office of Secretary of State and been three times a candidate for the presidency—who, under oath at Dayton, Tennessee, had made the astounding declaration that man is not a mammal!

This was the debased Christianity that Mencken fought in books, articles, reviews, and columns from the beginning to the end of his career. Today he might admit that it is a better thing than it was. He may even be entitled to claim some of the credit for its improvement if, in the inscrutable designs of Providence, he was given to it as a gadfly. But this is not to say that he would find it any more worthy of belief now than then. "Of all religions ever devised by man," he wrote,

[Christianity] is the one that offers the most for the least money to the average man of our time. . . . It is a transcendental solace in the presence of the intolerable. It is a stupendous begging of questions that nevertheless disposes of them. Of all such answers Christianity is at once the simplest and the most reassuring. It is protean and elastic; it has infinite varieties; it has comfort both for the man revolting despairingly against reason or congenitally incapable of reason, and for the man whose capacity for reason stops just short of intelligence. It is, at its best, a profound inner experience, a kind of poetry that is lived—call it Catholicism. It is, at its worst, a game of supernatural politics—call it Methodism. But in either case it organizes and gives a meaning to life. In either case it soothes the man who is too weak to stand up single-handed against the eternal and intolerable mysteries.[58]

4 IF, AS MENCKEN HELD, the sole function and purpose of religion are to give man access to the powers that control his destiny and induce those powers to be friendly to him, then it must logically follow that there is no necessary connection between religious beliefs and practices on the one hand and human conduct on the other. That is to say, religion and morality are specifically distinct. This was his own firm position: "I have paid relatively little attention to the ethical aspect of religion," he wrote in the preface to the first edition of *Treatise on the Gods*, "for I am convinced that that aspect is largely fortuitous. Men simply credit to the gods whatever laws they evolve out of their own wisdom or lack of it. Religion itself is something quite different; it is primarily a theory of causes and only incidentally a scheme of conduct."[59]

Yet in actual fact almost every religion, including even very primitive ones, has had built into it some moral code which seeks to regulate more or less explicitly the actions of its believers. The more advanced and civilized the religion, as a general rule, the more complex and embracing its code is likely to be. This tendency is perhaps most marked of all in Christianity, and only slightly less so in Christianity's ancestor, Judaism. Such a code usually holds that certain acts are good and virtuous, and hence pleasing to God, and that certain other acts are evil or vicious, and hence displeasing to Him. Virtuous acts are rewarded with an eternity of bliss in heaven, while wicked ones are punished by everlasting banishment from God's presence amid the inconceivable torments of hell.

But while it is rare to find a religion which does not include a system of ethics, it is not at all unusual to find systems of ethics which do not rely in any way on the teachings of a revealed religion. The ancient Greek philosophers, and most especially Aristotle, worked out very noble systems which did not involve the slightest belief in the Olympian deities, and so, after them, did the Stoics and Epicureans. With the appearance of Christianity on the scene, religion and morality became inextricably intermingled for almost two thousand years; good and evil, and the rewards and punishments for them, were thought of in exclusively Christian terms. At the time of the Enlightenment a separation occurred again, and philosophers have been putting forward purely rational ethical systems ever since. One of the highest and most demanding, as everyone knows, was elaborated by Kant in his *Fundamental Principles of the Metaphysic of Morals* and *Critique of Practical Reason.*

Though it may be argued that there is no essential connection between the two subjects, there is at least very considerable overlapping, and so Mencken's "inquiries into the embryology, physiology and pathology of the one led [him] almost inevitably into an investigation of the natural history of the other." When he had completed *Treatise on the Gods*, it was but natural that he should turn to a study of morality. The result was *Treatise on Right and Wrong*, published in 1934.

It is generally considered to be a less successful work than its predecessor, and he was pretty much convinced of this himself. He was dissatisfied, for one thing, with the title, but could think of nothing better. Within him, he confessed, was a deep-lying conviction that ethics was only a delusion anyway and hence scarcely worth writing about, and he swore that once he got the book off his hands he would never go back to the subject again. He began it in 1931, but there were numerous and prolonged interruptions caused by the heavy demands of the *Mercury* and by his wife Sara's precarious health and frequent illnesses. It was not until he had divested himself of all responsibility for the magazine that he was really able to buckle down to work on it. The final page of the typescript bears the notation in his handwriting: "Finished 11:45 A.M. January 17, 1934."

Despite his own misgivings and the generally hostile or derisive reviews, any failure of the book should really be measured only in commercial terms. It did not sell nearly as well as *Treatise on the Gods* (though the times undoubtedly had a lot to do with this), and there was never any call for a second printing. Actually, it contains some of his most typical and vigorous writing; it would be wrong to claim that there is any appreciable letdown from its companion work. The scheme and format of the two books are identical, even to the chapter headings, and on many pages they cover pretty much the same ground. One cannot help feeling that a lot that went into the second *Treatise* could have fit just as easily into the first, and vice versa. Perhaps, in the final analysis, this only serves to disprove his own thesis that there is no real connection between them.

If there are any dull stretches at all, it may be laid to the fact that it is absolutely impossible to write about ethics without some consideration of the issue of free will vs. determinism, and not even an H. L. Mencken could make this interesting and lively. As might be expected, it was the toughest part of the book to write; he struggled with it endlessly in the manuscript, treating it first from the standpoint of theology with Augustine, Aquinas, Duns Scotus, and the Molinists as his examples, and then covering it again from a purely philosophical point of view and showing how it had been handled by thinkers from Socrates to Bergson. "The Free Will controversy," he wrote to Harry Leon Wilson, "is endless and maddening. I have had to write a couple of thousand words about it for my new book. The job took me weeks, and reduced me to a frazzle."[60]

He himself was inclined heavily toward determinism. "There is not," he observed to Wilson in the same letter, "the slightest evidence that man has any actual free will, but his illusion that he has is so powerful that he simply couldn't live without it." In an early work entitled *Damn! A Book of Calumny,* published by his friend Philip Goodman in 1918, he wrote that "I can scarcely remember performing a wholly voluntary act. My whole life, as I look back upon it, seems to be a long series of inexplicable accidents, not only quite unavoidable, but even quite unintelligible. Its history is the history of the reactions of my personality to my environment, of my behavior before external stimuli. I have been no more responsible for that personality than I have been for that environment. . . . The more the matter is examined the more the residuum of free will shrinks and shrinks, until in the end it is almost impossible to find it."[61]

But by the time he came to write the *Treatise,* some fifteen years later, he was apparently not so sure. After studying the writings of the theologians and philosophers just mentioned, he speaks of the issue as one still unresolved, and adds that it may be ultimately unresolvable. It still seemed to him that all the available scientific evidence —particularly the evidence put forward most recently by those Freudians of whom he otherwise took such a dim view—tended to narrow the field of freedom ever more sharply; man might be free up to a point, but beyond that point he was in very large degree at the mercy of his passions and his unconscious mind, to say nothing of hostile forces impinging upon him from without. Yet the "illusion" of freedom was undeniably there, and even the staunchest determinist, in his ordinary day-to-day living, acted in accordance with it.

He considered the matter for twenty-five pages (considerably more than the "couple of thousand words" that he mentioned to Wilson) and at the end concluded:

> As a practical matter, we have to assume that [the will] is more or less free—if not quite as free as the mind, then at least sufficiently so to support the work of priest and hangman. This pragmatic doctrine of its freedom, though large doubts may linger, yet undoubtedly works better than determinism. For determinism, if it is to have any genuine validity, must exclude free will absolutely, whereas even the most radical libertarianism has room in it for plenty of determinism.[62]

As a practical matter, too, he might have added, any system of ethics must necessarily assume that the will is free or there is no point in its assuming anything else at all. Such concepts as good and bad, right and wrong, reward and punishment—those very things, in short, that Mencken calls "the work of priest and hangman"—become meaningless otherwise.

All moral codes, he remarks—those of savages whose religious ideas are very primitive, those of the major civilized religions, and those of rational systems that do not depend in any way on a revelation—condemn certain acts. He singles out murder, theft, adultery, trespass, and false witness as examples. These are specifically prohibited in the Ten Commandments that lie at the base of the Judaeo-Christian tradition, but the prohibitions against them were already hoary with age when that document came into being. The repugnance felt for them is universal in mankind, and those guilty of them are subjected to penalties more or less drastic.* There must, therefore, be something in their nature that makes them wrong objectively and under all conditions—that makes them, in other words, in the language of religion, "sinful."

And it is precisely at this point that Mencken parts company with all religious approaches to human conduct. He is perfectly willing to admit, of course, that these things are wrong and that no decent person

---

*Mencken was perfectly well aware, of course, that, as he put it, this "does not mean that they are observed with anything properly describable as pedantic strictness; on the contrary, they are evaded on occasion, both by savages and by civilized men, and some of them are evaded very often." (*Treatise on Right and Wrong,* p. 7.) But such evasion, no matter how general, has no bearing upon their wrongness.

will engage in them, but the notion of sin meant nothing whatever to him and the cognate notion of immorality meant hardly any more. For him, the "moral" man is the one who abstains from such acts because his religion holds out promises of the most glowing rewards if he does not commit them and, much more important, threatens him with the most gruesome punishments if he does. Such motivation is beneath contempt. "My own private code of ethics, I like to think," he declared, "is superior to that of most Christians, but there is no more religion in it than there is in my *principia* of aesthetics."[63]

What animated that private code was not any concept of the moral but rather the concept of honor, and the word "honor" plays a very important part in his writings on the subject. In a letter of February 20, 1921, to Fanny Butcher, literary critic for the Chicago *Tribune,* he complained in good-natured fashion that the reviewers of his books had never shown the slightest sign of understanding, or even suspecting, his feelings. "Many of them," he said, "actually set up the doctrine that I have none, which is an imbecility. Every man has feelings. Mine chiefly revolve around a concept of honor. This concept is incomprehensible to most Americans. They are a very moral people, but almost anaesthetic to honor."[64] The common man, he wrote in another place, "is extremely and even excessively moral, but the concept of what is called honor is beyond him."[65]

The differences between the two, to his way of thinking, were plain enough. The moral man refrained from a given act because he was afraid that somebody might be looking; the man of honor refrained from the same act for the simple reason that it was beneath his ideas of what constituted human dignity. The moral man set great store by the opinion that others held of him, regardless of whether that opinion was right or wrong; the man of honor cared not a whit for what others might think—he was guided only by his own innate sense of what was and was not decent. The moral man would lie just as readily as he would tell the truth, depending upon which was necessary to save his skin; the man of honor told the truth instinctively but would not hesitate to lie if a lie were necessary to save the good name and happiness of someone else. Nor was this to say that the man of honor did not now and then slip; he did, but he usually recognized the fact honestly and made peace with himself, whereas the moral man made every effort to conceal his weakness, to deny it both to himself and to others, and to evade it by trying to pass the blame off onto someone else.

Honor, Mencken concluded in a sharp definition, is "simply the morality of superior men."[66]

And superiority was precisely that quality which the Anglo-Saxon Christian did not have. As we shall see later, he wrote about many races—the Greeks, the Romans, the French, the Italians, the Spaniards—and he usually managed to find something unkind to say about each of them. In spite of the commonly accepted notion that he was strongly pro-German during the First World War and even, to some extent, during the Second, he could be realistic and critical about the Germans too. But upon no race did his strictures fall more ferociously than upon the Anglo-Saxon, which is to say the dominant English-speaking stock that had settled in the New World and brought over with it its centuries-old tradition of Christian teachings and values. In describing it, he would frequently use the first person plural: "A mongrel and inferior people," he maintained, "incapable of any spiritual aspiration above that of second-rate English colonials, we seek refuge inevitably in the one sort of superiority that the lower castes of men can authentically boast, to wit, superiority in docility, in credulity, in resignation, in morals. We are the most moral race in the world."[67]

This intransigent morality, as he went on in the very next breath, carried with it a conviction that as a nation "our confessed aim and destiny . . . is to inoculate [all other nations] with our incomparable rectitude." In other words, the American Anglo-Saxon Christian moralist is, first of all, the man who believes that he has some special advantage or insight in knowing what acts are moral and what are immoral, and who believes further that anyone whose ideas about such acts differ from his own must be of the devil's party. Such a one is not moral as the Christian is moral; ergo, he is immoral and his beliefs must be put down, if necessary by the police. He is, secondly, the man whose opinion of human nature and conduct is a very dim one anyway: "A moralist," Mencken wrote to Dreiser, "is one who holds that every human act must be either right or wrong, and that 99 percent of them are wrong."[68]*

---

*Mencken must have been particularly fond of this aphorism; the letter to Dreiser is neither the first place nor the last in which he used it. Its earliest appearance was in *A Little Book in C Major* (New York: John Lane Co., 1916), p. 19; it was carried over from there into the second edition of *A Book of Burlesques* (New York: Alfred A. Knopf, Inc., 1920), p. 206; and given a final embalming in the *Chrestomathy*, p. 617.

Finally, the moral man is the one who, since he is without courage to do certain things himself, is grimly determined that no one else will do them either. He is, in other words, the Puritan, beset by the haunting fear that somebody, somewhere, may be having a good time. And this determination to inoculate all others with his own rectitude leads naturally and inevitably enough to that movement which was such a curious phenomenon of American life in the early years of this century and which Mencken, with his gift for the precisely right term, referred to again and again as "the uplift."

The "uplift" manifested itself in a variety of forms. It was Comstockery, the suppression of literature, including even the best and truest literature, by self-constituted censors who had taken offense at certain words or descriptions in books and thereupon decided that they were going to protect other people from being offended in the same way. It was Prohibition, the conviction that the drinking of alcoholic beverages was an evil because certain country hinds had never taken a decent drink and would not have known how to handle it if they had. It was vice-crusading, and laws against blasphemy, and a ban by Tennessee backwoodsmen against the dissemination of scientific knowledge because its facts were in apparent violation of the teaching of Genesis. It was, in brief, a whole outlook upon life convinced not only of its own innate superiority but of its duty to enforce that superiority on those unhappy enough to lack it.

That Mencken was opposed to all of these things goes without saying. His opinions on censorship are widely enough known and, in practice, altered the course of American literature. His writings on Prohibition could be assembled into a small and very entertaining volume if the subject were important and timely enough to make it worth publishing. On the matter of vice-crusading, of which he had taken a dim view ever since his days as a reporter on the *Herald,* he simply held that "the average prostitute is decenter than the average reformer."[69] Nor had he anything personal against those who held to such ideas; he was convinced that they were idiots, of course, and wanted no part of their company, but they were perfectly welcome to cling to their idiocies; what he objected to so vehemently was their effort to foist them onto others.

In this he was being wholly consistent with himself. Like any man, and perhaps more than most, he had a firm belief in the rightness of his own position—"in all my life," he once said, "I don't recall ever writing a line that, at the moment, I didn't believe to be true."[70] But he had no slightest wish to bring anyone else around to his own way of thinking and, as a matter of fact, detested converts from and to anything. "I do not make converts," he declared in an unpublished note; "on the contrary, I dislike them, and have no respect for them."[71] This included former Communists who suddenly started expounding on the Red Menace, former Catholics who attacked the Church as false and evil, and former almost anything else; such a man, in his opinion, was simply carrying his right to make an ass of himself too far.

What gave the uplift its unparalleled virulence, he held, was the belief of its adherents that the moral system of Christianity was superior to that of any other religion ever heard of on earth, and that it thus had to be spread abroad as widely and forcefully as possible. Yet actually no genuine advance in moral ideas had ever come from religion. He cites slavery as an example. It was accepted, as everyone knows, in both the Old Testament and the New; even Paul, who stoutly upheld the equality of all men before God, had no difficulty in living with it, and neither, following him, did the great Christian theologians of the Middle Ages. When the institution finally broke down, it was not so much because of the moral objections to it as because it had turned out to be economically unworkable, and most European nations had passed laws against it long before the Church got around to denouncing it as sinful. So with the emancipation of women, which Mencken thought was "the most revolutionary social event of modern times."[72] Here there could be no doubt that Christianity had done much to improve upon the ancient idea of them as in a class with children, cattle, and property, but it was only natural that a priesthood committed to an ideal of celibacy should back off from women as temptresses and an incitement to evil, and thus make every effort to keep them in their place. The first efforts to provide any moral, social, and legal equality for them, he points out, came not from believers but from skeptics and agnostics like Condorcet, Robert Owen, and John Stuart Mill. Even laws against cruelty to animals were inspired more by infidels than by Christian teaching, which held that the dumb brutes, not having any duties or responsibilities, also had no rights.

What Mencken called his "own private code of ethics" was extremely practical and even commonplace, and on the surface hardly seems like anything as formal as a code at all. On the same surface, too, it seems in flat contradiction to the public figure: the critic who sat down at his typewriter and, peering over the top of his horn-rimmed glasses, began pecking away with two fingers at the keyboard, and attacked Christianity, democracy, Americanism, conventional morality, and every other idea that the ordinary person held sacred; he poured ridicule on politicians, ecclesiastics, and reformers with a violence that left his poor victims literally gasping for breath. Yet it is a well-known fact that he was personally one of the kindest of men, with an unfailing courtesy and consideration for all with whom he came in contact. "He is a foe of democracy," George Jean Nathan once wrote, "and politely sees every person, however asinine, who comes to call on him." It was not at all unusual, when he actually met the men whom he attacked, for him to end up by liking them, and often by going out of his way to do them favors.

His day-to-day routine was meticulous and exacting, and gives some idea of the stern demands which he made upon himself. No one knows, and probably no one ever will know, how many letters Mencken wrote in the course of his life; one estimate runs as high as a quarter of a million; yet it was his invariable habit to answer every letter addressed to him on the day that it was received, and he stubbornly maintained that this was nothing more than a courtesy owed to the writer. He claimed to be "ombibulous," meaning that he enjoyed every known alcoholic drink;* his writings bristle with almost as many references to beer, wine, and liquor as they do to music; but he actually drank very temperately and here again it was his ironclad rule never to touch anything as long as there was work to be done. "The intelligent layman," he believed, "no longer resorts to the jug when he has important business before him, whether intellectual or manual; he resorts to it after his business is done, and he desires to release his taut nerves and reduce the steam-pressure in his spleen. . . . The harsh, useful things of the world, from pulling teeth to digging potatoes, are best done by men who are as starkly sober as so many convicts in the death-house, but the lovely and useless things, the charming and exhilarating things, are best done by men with, as the phrase is, a few sheets in the wind. *Pithecanthropus erectus* was a teetotaler, but the angels, you may be sure, know what is proper at 5 P.M."[73]

Mention has already been made of how he felt about Baltimore and the house on Hollins Street, but it should hardly be necessary to

---

*He admitted, of course, that he liked some better than others.

add that this love—and really, "love" is the only word to use here—
extended to all the members of his family as well. We have seen his
closeness to August, Sr., and his devotion to his long-widowed mother;
he and his brother Charlie went through boyhood together not just as
brothers but as chums too, though when Charlie's job as an engineer
with the Pennsylvania Railroad took him away from Baltimore, this
relationship naturally tended to become less close. Virtually his entire
adult life was lived with his younger brother August, with whom he had
an almost perfect affinity. And this sense of family ties extended also to
the next couple of generations: childless himself, he lavished all the
doting affection of a bachelor uncle on his niece Virginia, Charlie's
daughter, and the record shows that he helped put her through college. In the Pratt Library's Mencken collection there are hundreds of
letters which he wrote to her at all stages of her life, and when Virginia
married and had a family of her own, many of these letters are concerned with choosing the precisely right birthday or Christmas present
for his young grandnephew.

No relative, friend, or acquaintance could be in the hospital without a cheering visit and a gift. He prided himself on never being late for
an engagement, on never missing a train, on the orderly neatness of his
rooms, his personal effects, and his records. He was generous, and yet
at the same time very prudent in money matters: "[I] never have debts,"
he told Isaac Goldberg. "If I want something, and can't pay cash for it,
I do without it."[74]

These are homely virtues, and there is nothing particularly
"Christian" about them. Certainly they seem to have only a very loose
connection with the science of ethics. Yet singly and collectively they
guided him through seventy-five years of life with a consistency that it
would be hard to match in any other man. If, as it turned out, he did
stand before the Twelve Apostles and apologize humbly for having
been wrong about them, one hopes that they took these things into
consideration in what must have been the extremely difficult matter of
deciding how to handle his case.

5 CHARLES ANGOFF, in *H. L. Mencken: A Portrait
from Memory*, has given us a picture of his former employer as a disgustingly lewd and foul-mouthed person whose conver-

sation, whatever the subject of the moment might be, was sprinkled with constant reference to sexual and excretory functions and tales of his accomplishments in bed. In Angoff's pages Mencken tells of having slept with thirty-five different French girls but, being offended by their smell, turning for more refined partners to the women of Holland and Belgium. He modestly grants that on such matters George Jean Nathan was a greater authority than he was. He discusses Queen Mary's seven pairs of "drawers" and the cotton panties of the girls of Brooklyn, and speaks throughout of women—all women, including even the wives of his own close friends—in such terms as "whore," "bitch," and "slut."

It can only be said that no one else who knew Mencken agrees that he talked this way, and that when the book came out practically everybody who was in a position to do so indignantly denied that he did.* His conversation, according to these people, was free and uninhibited, but it was not vulgar. As a young reporter covering the streets and police stations of Baltimore, he undoubtedly had every opportunity to pick up a full range of what used to be called "the language of the gutter," and hearing it in after years would not be likely to shock him; but there is no indication that he himself commonly used it in places or circumstances where it might offend others. A number of passages in his writings make clear that he detested the usual type of "dirty joke," and his dislike of it is certainly to be explained more on grounds of taste than of prudery.

Much the same thing may be said of his feelings about pornography. When the Comstocks attacked Dreiser's *The "Genius"* and Cabell's *Jurgen* and he came vigorously to their defense, it was not because he thought that Dreiser, or Cabell, or anybody else, should be free to turn out smut; it was because the Comstocks were treating the books as if they were smut, and he was convinced that they were works of serious literature with a high degree of artistic merit. As an "extreme libertarian" who believed in "absolute free speech,"[75] he was willing to admit, of course, that such freedom inevitably carried with it the right of any man either to publish pornography or to buy and read it, and he would not deprive them of this right; he was absolutely opposed to censorship in any form. But he himself had no interest in such stuff, and he did not believe that any normal man did.

---

*Sometimes one gets the impression that Mencken went out of his way to scandalize Angoff, who seems by his own account to have been a remarkably humorless person.

In his general attitude toward sex and sexual matters he was, as has already been observed, conventional to the point of being straitlaced. Admittedly, one does not get quite this impression either from his written work or from the occasional public utterances with which he delighted to shock people; when he treated of the subject in *The Smart Set* or the *Mercury* (which really was not all that often), he did so with a frankness rare in the 1920's, even if it would not so much as flutter an eyelash today.* Setting aside Angoff's stories, it is true that he liked to enthuse to friends about the charms of some blonde waitress of Wagnerian proportions in one of his favorite German restaurants, or tell of how he was being pursued by the slightly moldy widow of a rich brewer in Hoboken, New Jersey; but the record shows that the women to whom he was attracted—and over the years he was attracted to quite a few of them—were neither as opulent in figure, nor as far gone in years, nor as generous in giving of their persons, as he always claimed. Usually they were trim, petite, young enough, highly respectable, and more often than not they had literary interests or ambitions.

Certainly there was nothing of the Puritan about him; the fact that he did not marry until the quite late age of fifty is hardly a reason to assume that he was without knowledge or experience until that time. Isaac Goldberg is authority for the statement that while he was a student at the Baltimore Polytechnic, between the ages of twelve and sixteen, he "was being initiated into the cruder biological realities of sex."[76]† It was his belief that the whole elaborate system of taboos surrounding sex and its expression was nonsensical; he held that "most of the professional proponents of 'moral' legislation are plain rogues preying on fools,"[77] and he opposed any kind of law, such as the Mann Act, that sought to regulate private morality. What happened when a man and a woman went into a hotel room together and locked the door, he maintained with fervor, was strictly nobody else's business.

But it should be obvious enough by now that Mencken the public figure was one person, and Mencken the private man was another and very different one. The contradictions between them may have been more apparent than real; yet it remains a fact that the liberties he

---

*In the columns of the *Sunpapers* he had, of course, to be a bit more circumspect.

†This must be something that Mencken told Goldberg in private conversation; there is no basis for it in the manuscript that he prepared for his biographer's use.

demanded for others he almost totally eschewed himself. In his own life he practiced a code of sexual behavior that was as rigid in its way as that of the Puritans whom he denounced, and while he would never try to tell his friends how they ought to conduct themselves, this code inevitably had some effect on his relations with them. When, during the years of his marriage to Sara, Scott and Zelda Fitzgerald lived in Baltimore, he did not want her to have anything to do with them, not only because of Scott's heavy drinking but also because of what he considered to be their loose and irregular way of life. For several decades he and Dreiser had a close relationship, but he could never quite stomach Dreiser's endless succession of mistresses, and when the novelist asked in one of his books whether the average strong and successful man ever limited himself to one woman, Mencken had back at him with a list of examples ranging from Johann Sebastian Bach and Bismarck to Thomas Henry Huxley and John D. Rockefeller. He told James T. Farrell (and many another young writer too) that if he wanted to develop as an artist he would have to stay away from three things— "booze, women and politics."

It might be possible, indeed, to build up a solid enough case to show that Mencken undervalued sex rather than the other way around. He may even have been a bit afraid of it, in the sense at least that he was reluctant to let himself be ensnared in its clutches; "sex," he declared, "would be unimportant if it were not for its capacity to produce an overwhelming ecstasy."[78] He was, after all, a highly cerebral man whose whole life was "devoted to the pursuit, anatomizing and embalming of ideas,"[79] and the point hardly needs belaboring that a man caught up in the throes of sexual passion is not exactly in the best possible state to engage in abstract speculation. Somewhat naïvely, perhaps, he thought that the way he felt about it was also the way that most other men felt too: "I do not believe," he wrote,

> that the lives of normal men are much colored or conditioned, either directly or indirectly, by purely sexual considerations. I believe that nine-tenths of them would carry on all the activities which engage them now, and with precisely the same humorless diligence, if there were not a woman in the world. . . . sex, at bottom, belongs to comedy and the cool of the evening and not to the sober business that goes on in the heat of the day. That sober business, as I have said, would still go on if women were abolished and heirs and assigns were manufactured in rolling-mills.[80]

In the same vein, he criticized the Catholic Church for attaching much too great an importance to it in its ethical code; the Church, he felt, "overlooks the capital fact that there is immensely more to sex, at least among civilized adults, than mere animal passion. Of all that lies above the belt it refuses to take practical cognizance; it is too busy policing the horrors below."[81]

But if sex as the physical coming together of a man's body and a woman's had less than average attraction for him, sex as romance and mystery had a very great appeal indeed. In the profession of book reviewer at which he engaged, month in and month out, for exactly twenty-five years, he naturally felt obliged every now and then to draw attention to what he termed "the vast literature of so-called sex hygiene," and almost every time he did so he expressed two principal objections to it. Both were founded on aesthetic rather than moral grounds. The first was that all such books were pedagogically dishonest and inconsistent—that after describing the phenomenon of reproduction among dahlias, herring, and frogs as a beautiful and God-given thing, they went on to describe precisely the same phenomenon among human beings as something disgusting and shameful, bound to lead eventually to the gutter and the fires of hell. The second was even more basic: "they are all founded upon an attempt to explain a romantic mystery in terms of an exact science. Nothing could be more absurd: as well attempt to interpret Beethoven in terms of mathematical physics."[82]*

The result, he claimed, was that the American "flapper" was no longer naïve and charming: "she goes to the altar of God with a

---

*Almost every year since his death in 1956, one or another columnist has been moved to paraphrase Wordsworth and exclaim "Mencken! thou shouldst be living at this hour," when some new cultural or political imbecility seemed to be of the kind that had always called forth his wit. The temptation is especially strong in this area. What would he have thought and said about a subsequent body of literature that has gone to precisely the opposite extreme from the kind that he criticized—such works, in brief, as *Everything You Always Wanted to Know About Sex But Were Afraid to Ask*, the Masters-Johnson report, *The Sensuous Woman*, *The Sensuous Man*, *The Joy of Sex*, and the whole vast proliferation of so-called "sex education manuals" that has glutted the market in the past few years? His essential conservatism in these matters being what it was, it is not hard to guess. We may get a hint of his attitude from a brief paragraph written in 1948 as a footnote added in the *Chrestomathy* to a much earlier piece: "I see nothing in the Kinsey Report to change my conclusions here. All that humorless document really proves is (a) that all men lie when they are asked about their adventures in amour, and (b) that pedagogues are singularly naive and credulous creatures." (P. 36 n.)

learned and even cynical glitter in her eye."[83] The veriest schoolgirl knew as much about sex and its processes as a midwife had known in 1885, and spent a large part of her time disseminating the information. It followed inevitably that innocence had been killed and romance sadly wounded. Here again Mencken sounds naïve, but really he was not; his view of innocence, if not skeptical, was at least realistic, and as an intelligent man who required intelligence in those persons, whether male or female, with whom he came regularly in contact, he hardly expected a woman to be wholly unenlightened in this area. He would have had a very dim opinion of one who was. What he wanted to know was how any woman could continue to believe in the honor, courage, and tenderness of a man after she had learned, perhaps by affidavit, that his hemoglobin count was 117%, that he was free from sugar and albumen, that his blood pressure was 112/79 and his Wasserman reaction negative. He mourned what Agnes Repplier had mourned when she spoke of the "repeal of reticence"; this new frankness, he protested, was "highly embarrassing to the more romantic and ingenuous sort of men, of whom I have the honor to be one. . . . What is neither hidden nor forbidden is seldom very charming."[84]

Possibly it was because he was "romantic and ingenuous" that he could not think of women simply in terms of sex, and this fact in turn may have been the reason for his high opinion of their intelligence. That opinion was so high, in fact, that he wrote a whole book on the subject, and one marvels that today's advocates of "women's liberation" have not resurrected *In Defense of Women*, added it to their canonical scriptures, and spread it abroad in large quantities. In its time, which was of course a bit earlier than *The American Language* and long years before the *Days* books, it was easily the best received and most successful of his works. He wrote it in the early winter of 1918 and allowed it to appear under the imprint of his friend Philip Goodman, "an advertising man who had a hankering for the publishing business"; its initial reception was unpromising, and shortly thereafter Goodman's venture failed. But within a year the book was taken over by Alfred Knopf and embarked at once upon a long and vigorous career. In 1922 Mencken revised and considerably expanded it for Knopf's "Free Lance" series, and all told it went through eleven printings in the United States, to say nothing of English editions and translations into French, German, and Hungarian.

Why, then, has it fallen into such neglect at a time when, as I have indicated, the subject itself has been turned into one of the most burning of contemporary issues? In the introduction which he wrote for the revised edition, Mencken observed that his principal business as a critic of life and letters was that of "manufacturing platitudes for tomorrow, which is to say, ideas so novel that they will be instantly rejected as insane and outrageous by all right-thinking men, and so apposite and sound that they will eventually conquer that instinctive opposition, and force themselves into the traditional wisdom of the race."[85] He was writing, remember, during and immediately after the First World War, more than half a century ago; some of those insane and outrageous ideas have indeed since entered into the "traditional wisdom of the race," and it has to be admitted that a few of the others (for example, his contention that it is to the advantage of women to get married at the earliest possible opportunity) may have been true at the time but are not necessarily true today. In more than one respect, the book does date. In addition, being by Mencken, it is as unsparing of feminine psychology as of masculine. Nevertheless, it can reasonably be called the prototype of the vast literature that has appeared in recent years, and since virtually all of this is by women it might at least be argued that Mencken's was not only the first contribution to the subject but one of the very few to come from a relatively disinterested observer.

His basic premise is that women are not only more intelligent than men but have a virtual monopoly of the more subtle forms of intelligence. What is commonly called "feminine intuition" he dismisses as nonsense:

> Women decide the larger questions of life correctly and quickly, not because they are lucky guessers, not because they are divinely inspired, not because they practice a magic inherited from savagery, but simply and solely because they have sense. They see at a glance what most men could not see with searchlights and telescopes; they are at grips with the essentials of a problem before men have finished debating its mere externals. They are the supreme realists of the race. Apparently illogical, they are the possessors of a rare and subtle super-logic. Apparently whimsical, they hang to the truth with a tenacity which carries them through every phase of its incessant, jelly-like shifting of form. Apparently unobservant and easily deceived, they see with bright and horrible eyes.[86]

Proof of this, he thought, lay in the fact that women simply refused to concern themselves with the mass of shoddy banalities that make up the lives of most men: "the imbecile jargon of the stock market," the ideologies of rival politicians, "the minutiae of some sordid and degrading business or profession," billiards or grouse-shooting or golf. Their finer intelligence makes it impossible for them to take such idiotic pursuits seriously. They profess, of course, to admire the men who are successful at them, but this in itself is only one more proof of that intelligence: knowing quite well the inordinate vanity and hollowness of most men, they also know precisely how to make the most of male weaknesses. They are almost entirely without sentiment, and never permit mere emotion to corrupt their judgments. Men have foisted upon them an artificial character which well conceals their real one, and women have found it profitable to encourage that deception; but actually "a man's women folk, whatever their outward show of respect for his merit and authority, always regard him secretly as an ass, and with something akin to pity."[87]

The inferior position they have held in society goes back hundreds or even thousands of years before Christianity, and Christianity has been of no help to them in overcoming it. The religion preached by Christ, which according to Mencken is wholly extinct, held them in high esteem and lifted them to equality with men before the Lord; but the religion preached by Paul, and after him by the medieval bishops and theologians, has been at all times their natural enemy. On the one hand, and in order to account for the embarrassing but undeniable fact that there were women holy enough to be raised to sainthood, it has glorified them as vestal virgins and so deprived them of practically all normal human attributes; on the other, that the discipline of a celibate clergy might be safeguarded, it has depicted them as temptresses with whom any kind of traffic can only be an incitement to sin. But in the first case as much as in the second, it has clung to the notion of their natural inferiority and joined forces with the state and society to keep them subservient.

That subservience, however, Mencken felt certain, was fast coming to an end. True, women were still enmeshed in a formidable network of man-made taboos and sentimentalities, but progress was visible. In another generation, he declared (and again it may be necessary to remind the reader that he was writing in the early 1920's), they would gain genuine freedom. Once marriage had been the only vocation open to them, and a woman who did not marry was condemned not only to the stigma of spinsterhood but to the most humiliating kind of dependence upon others; now they were entering professions which had hitherto been exclusively male domains and achieving economic freedom thereby. If a woman did not choose to marry, she could still lead an independent, useful, and rewarding life. In the second edition of his book he gloated over the fact that in the presidential election of 1920—the first one in which women had enjoyed the suffrage—the massive Republican victory had constituted a decisive rejection of the "Wilsonian idealism" which he so much despised, and he attributed that victory directly to the feminine vote. Eventually, he felt, the greater intelligence of women would lead them to initiate measures against democracy, "the worst evil of the present-day world."[88]

One of his predictions has come true in a way which, as I indicated earlier, might have shocked even him. He attached little or no value to the concept of virginity, and believed that as women threw off other outmoded and preposterous ideas they would throw off this one too. It was a holdover from the ancient notion of women as property, "one of the hollow conventions of Christianity; nay, of the levantine barbarism that preceded Christianity."[89] The belief that a woman who had abandoned her virginity before marriage was a lost and shameless creature was certain, he declared, to go the way of all the other ridiculous notions that had shackled her, and she would feel under no more obligation to apologize for its absence than men ever had.

Obviously a man holding so high a regard for women would be expected to enjoy their company, and enjoy it he did; mention has already been made of the circle of his feminine friends. *In Defense of Women* comes to a close with a poetic and highly evocative picture of such a fair companion:

> It is the close of a busy and vexatious day—say half past five or six o'clock of a Winter afternoon. I have had a cocktail or two, and am stretched out on a divan in front of a fire, smoking. At the edge of the divan, close enough for me to reach her with my hands, sits a woman not too young, but still good-looking and well-dressed—above all, a woman with a soft, low-pitched, agreeable voice. As I snooze she talks—of anything, everything, all the things that women talk of: books, music, dress, men, other women. No politics. No business. No theology. No metaphysics. Nothing challenging and vexatious—but remember, she is intelligent; what she says is clearly expressed, and often picturesquely. I observe

the fine sheen of her hair, the pretty cut of her frock, the glint of her white teeth, the arch of her eyebrow, the graceful curve of her arm. I listen to the exquisite murmur of her voice. Gradually I fall asleep—but only for an instant. At once, observing it, she raises her voice ever so little, and I am awake. Then to sleep again—slowly and charmingly down that slippery hill of dreams. And then awake again, and then asleep again, and so on.

I ask you seriously: could anything be more unutterably beautiful? The sensation of falling asleep is to me the most delightful in the world. I relish it so much that I even look forward to death itself with a sneaking wonder and desire. Well, here is sleep poetized and made doubly sweet. Here is sleep set to the finest music in the world. I match this situation against any that you can think of. It is not only enchanting; it is also, in a very true sense, ennobling. In the end, when the lady grows prettily miffed and throws me out, I return to my sorrows somehow purged and glorified. I am a better man in my own sight. I have grazed upon the fields of asphodel. I have been genuinely, completely and unregrettably happy.[90]*

The question naturally arises then: why, if this was the way he felt about women and their companionship, did he wait such a long time to marry? Publicly he gloried in his bachelorhood and flaunted it before a nationwide audience; he leveled against the institution of marriage some of the most brilliant witticisms in the language, epigrams on a level with those of an Oscar Wilde or an Ambrose Bierce. He defined love as "the delusion that one woman differs from another."—"The only really happy folk are married women and single men."—"He marries best who puts it off until it is too late." —"Husbands never become good; they merely become proficient."—"Bachelors have consciences; married men have wives."—"Bachelors," he maintained, "know more about women than married men. If they didn't, they'd be married too."[91] "If I ever marry," he said in a letter to Charles Green Shaw, "it will be on a sudden impulse, as a man shoots himself."[92]

Yet when he married Sara Powell Haardt in 1930 it was certainly on no sudden impulse (he had known her for seven years), and they were not yet settled down in their Cathedral Street apartment when he

---

*Marion Bloom believes that Mencken had her in mind when he wrote this piece (which first appeared in *The Smart Set* in 1921), and it is the opinion of Carl Bode that she is right (*Mencken*, p. 154).

modestly proclaimed himself to be an exemplary husband. The formal announcement of their engagement had burst upon a world quite unprepared for such a thing, and the newspapers had made merry with it; editorial writers the length and breadth of the land exclaimed, "Oh, Henry!" and imagined the shades of Schopenhauer and Nietzsche cackling together, and predicted that Sara would make him put on rubbers and take an umbrella when he went out in the rain. The Columbia, Mississippi, *Commercial Dispatch* was pleased that he was marrying a southern girl, since she would be certain to have a refining influence upon him. Mencken, who, as William Manchester correctly observes, was for once in his life on the defensive, insisted that his action was in no way incompatible with anything he had ever written about women and marriage in the past. In this he was perfectly right, as anyone who might have taken the trouble to reread *In Defense of Women* would have seen, but the opportunity was just too good for the public to miss.

Moreover—and this was what no one seemed to realize—when he had written specifically about marriage it had always been in terms lauding its most commonplace and respectable form—namely, ordinary Christian monogamy and family life. In the same letter to Charles Green Shaw from which I have just quoted (and in fact in the same paragraph) he declared: "I believe in marriage, and have whooped it up for years. It is the best solution, not only of the sex question, but also of the living question." He had added, to be sure, that it would probably not be good for him, since his living schedule was too erratic. "As for monogamy," he had said a bit earlier, "I believe that it is one of the few institutions of civilization that stand in accord with the fundamental instincts of Homo sapiens. . . . I have praised and encouraged [it] for long years. . . . The happiest men I know are strict monogamists."[93]

There can be no doubt that Mencken was in love—deeply and romantically in love—with Sara. There can also be no doubt that she was not the first woman he had loved, but at all events she was the one he chose to marry. She was southern, a native of Montgomery, Alabama, eighteen years younger than he was, tall and slender in comparison to his rather chunky figure. Sara Mayfield, who knew her better than any of Mencken's other biographers, describes her thus: "She was tall, slender and willowy, with something of both the *femme savante* and the *femme fatale* about her—a strikingly beautiful woman as well as a charming and intelligent one. She had a fine head, regular, rounded features, and slender, sensitive hands. Her hair was like burnished bronze, curly and crinkled with gold highlights; her eyes were very large and of a soft deep brown; her skin was as fair as the petals of a white japonica. There was both a fragility and a subtle power in her beauty, and it caught and held Mencken's eye."[94]

They met in the spring of 1923, when she was twenty-four and an English instructor at Goucher College and he was already the forty-two-year-old author of a dozen books and the most widely known editor and newspaperman in America. He had recently rejected a short story that she had submitted to *The Smart Set*. Now that their paths had actually crossed, Sara could not make up her mind whether to be attracted to him or offended by his plainspoken and utterly public comments on the subject of women and marriage. For his part, he was at that very moment deeply upset by the fact that his long relationship with Marion Bloom was coming to an end under rather painful circumstances. He consoled himself for the next several years by dating a pretty and vivacious New York girl named Beatrice Wilson. So late as 1926 he met the noted Hollywood actress Aileen Pringle, and their friendship developed to a point where whenever the papers speculated about Mencken getting married, it was always Miss Pringle who was linked with him. He continued to see and correspond with her almost up until the time that his engagement to Sara was announced.

Thus, while he was undoubtedly smitten by Sara at first sight, their romance developed slowly and their courtship, if one could call it that, was neither regular nor smooth. He began by encouraging her in her writing, and used his enormous influence in literary circles to help find a market for her work. Neither had as yet any claim on the other; yet if some news item appeared telling about Mencken being seen with another woman, Sara made known her displeasure, and if she went out with another—and younger—man, Mencken sulked. In 1925 his mother died, and her passing left an immense void not only in the house on Hollins Street but in his own life as well. More and more when he entertained friends at such Baltimore restaurants as Marconi's or Schellhase's, Sara came to be at his side as hostess. In 1928 she researched his shelves of clipping books to pick out the choice bits of invective that would go into *Menckeniana: A Schimpflexikon*. By the following year she was unquestionably the only woman in his life; when he went to London late in 1929 to cover the Naval Conference for the *Evening Sun*, he wrote to tell her how much he missed her, and added that even before embarking he had been tempted to tear up his ticket and come back to Baltimore to be with her. There was a silent understanding now that they were engaged.

It was characteristic of him that, once the news was officially out, he treated the whole thing in his light and deadpan manner. To his speechless friends he announced: "The bride is a lady from Alabama—(white)." He had given her permission to call him by his first name after they were married, and in return for this courtesy she would let him go out five nights a week, not counting the anniversaries of the great German victories. As the date drew nearer, he began to issue a whole series of bulletins describing the complex legal negotiations by which he hoped to get out of it; through his attorney, Otto Pagentecher, he had offered Sara $5,000, but through her attorney, Leon Greenbaum, she had refused to settle for anything less than $350,000. Pagentecher and Greenbaum were attempting to arrive at a compromise, but their discussions fell through and all hope vanished. He besought his friends to pray for him. Yet in an interview which he granted to a United Press correspondent who asked if he was experiencing the usual nervous misgivings of prospective bridegrooms, he replied: "I discern no tremors. Getting married, like getting hanged, is probably a great deal less dreadful than it has been made out to be."

It was indeed. By the accounts of all who knew them, their marriage was idyllically happy. It was also, alas, doomed from the start. Sara's health had never been good; during the period when they had been no more than friends she had had a whole series of debilitating operations, and he had watched anxiously beside her hospital bed. Just before their marriage he was assured by her doctors that she did not have more than three years to live. Yet it would be utterly irrational to imagine that a man like Mencken would uproot himself from the long-familiar routine of Hollins Street and adapt to an entirely new life, knowing that it would be for such a short time, if he had been motivated by nothing more than pity for a sweet and attractive but tragically predestined girl. Something within him must have made him believe, stubbornly and against all reason, that the doctors were wrong and that he could look forward to spending the rest of his days with her.

On the morning that she died, May 31, 1935, he dropped in at the office of Hamilton Owens at the *Sunpapers* and unburdened to this old friend his grief. "When I married Sara," he told Owens, "the doctors said she could not live more than three years. Actually she lived five, so that I had two more years of happiness than I had any right to expect."

Those five years were not without their trials. Sara's frequent hospitalizations must have been enormously expensive at a time—the depths of the Depression—when Mencken's income from his writings had sunk to an unaccustomed low. In addition, they cut deeply into his hitherto sacrosanct working schedule; Betty Adler's bibliography shows that during that whole period only one book—the 1934 *Treatise on Right and Wrong*—was published,* and his trips to New York on *Mercury* business had to be curtailed and in some cases canceled on very short notice. To an ever greater degree, responsibility for getting the magazine out came to rest with Angoff. Yet there is little evidence that Mencken resented these demands, or ever complained about them; when he did have to be out of town for even a few days he would write to Sara constantly and could not wait to be back at her side.

Sara Mayfield, who saw much of them during those years, says that Mencken "had known a few years of requited love of a rare kind with Sara."[95] Louis Cheslock, a member of the Saturday Night Club and a close friend, spoke of him years later as being "tender and loving." An indication of his feelings may be gleaned from what he permitted to biographers like Manchester and Kemler. So far as he was concerned, they could say what they liked; they were free to criticize both him and his ideas, and he would not deny them this freedom. But when it came to Sara they enjoyed no such liberty: their picture of her had to conform in every slightest detail to the memory of her that he still carried in his heart.

6 WHETHER OR NOT THE MAXIMS that governed Mencken's own personal conduct may be dignified by any such stiff and formal term as "code," there is little doubt that they came to him in the nature of an inheritance from his family back-

---

Treatise on the Gods had appeared in 1930, the year of his marriage, but it had been completed on Thanksgiving Day, 1929. *Making a President* was published in 1932, but it consisted simply of "my reports of the two national conventions . . . for the Baltimore *Evening Sun*," and William Manchester says that he put it together with scissors and paste in thirty-six hours.

ground—from a long line of high-principled German ancestors and the sternly Victorian morality of middle-class life in late-nineteenth-century Baltimore. His wide reading as youth and man, the culture he acquired and the experiences he absorbed over the course of his life, may have given them a more solid intellectual foundation, but at bottom they rested on a few very simple convictions learned from his mother and—more particularly—his father. August Mencken, for example, divided all mankind into two groups: "those who paid their bills and those who didn't."[96] The former, whatever faults they might otherwise have, were virtuous in his eyes; the latter, whatever else might be said to their credit, were inherently and incurably scoundrels. His son picked up this idea from him, and a strict probity in money matters was one of his acid tests for an honorable person.

But Mencken had still another way of classifying mankind, and even if it was not, strictly speaking, based upon ethics or standards of conduct, it was at least as clear-cut and absolute as his father's. This was the division of men into that group which he liked to call the "intelligent minority" and those whom he referred to variously as the "booboisie," "*Homo boobiensis*," and the "vast herd of human blanks."

Such a classification raises immediate doubts about the honesty and sincerity of the one who makes it, since it is to be taken for granted that he includes himself in the intelligent minority—which Mencken certainly did. There is more than a hint of snobbery in it, a cold indifference and even callousness toward the average human being, a lofty judgment which really no man is in a position to make about any other. Yet it was the judgment that Mencken made. He held to it from the beginning to the end of his career, he never apologized for it, it was the fundamental postulate on which his whole moral, political, and social philosophy was built. It seemed to him to be the most obvious of all scientifically observable facts.

Whether the idea came to him from Nietzsche or he hit upon it independently in those early days as a reporter for the *Morning Herald*, it would not be easy to say now. Roaming the corridors of Baltimore's City Hall and witnessing the processes of justice in its police courts, coming into daily contact with an array of humanity that began in his own highly respectable household (and the alley behind it) and ran through political bosses and public servants to thieves, prostitutes, and murderers, it did not take him very long to note that intelligence was not exactly distributed evenly in the world and that some people had a more delicate sense of honor than others. With a sharp eye and a quick instinct, he distinguished between men who were genuine and those who were palpable frauds. It struck him, too, that in most cases a very definite correlation could be established between the degree of intelligence and that of honor. Nor was all this based upon abstract theorizing; on the contrary, as he put it years later, he was laying in at this time "the worldly wisdom of a police lieutenant, a bartender, a shyster lawyer, or a midwife."[97]

But even if the division that he then began to make was his own inspiration, it is undeniable that he found powerful support for it in the writings of Nietzsche. He had begun to study him at least as early as 1906, when he himself was only twenty-six years old and much of the philosopher's work had not yet been translated into English; two years later his book about him appeared.

Nietzsche, it will be remembered, had drawn a distinction between two types of human action which he called "master morality" (*Herren-Moral*) and "slave morality" (*Sklaven-Moral*). This distinction occurs for the first time, though not in precisely these terms, in a brief section of *Human, All Too Human* (1878); it is returned to again, but still without being developed to the fullest, in *Beyond Good and Evil* (1886); and then finally it is subjected to exhaustive analysis in the first part of *The Genealogy of Morals* (1887). "Master morality" is the standard of the noble, the strong, the brave, the free; it is essentially a morality of ascending values, one that is "value-creating." "Slave morality," on the other hand, is the standard of the lowly, the weak, the fearful, of those who live in spiritual and intellectual—even if not necessarily in physical—bondage. The former is opposed to the latter as the man rejoicing in his own freedom and strength is opposed to the man wretched in his subjection.

What this leads to—and it was the conclusion that Nietzsche went on to draw—is that master morality is the morality of the superior *individual*, while slave morality characterizes the "herd." The herd, in other words, fearful of its superiors and distrusting them, bands together and creates its own set of values to protect itself against them.*

---

*In one of that huge collection of miscellaneous notes published posthumously as *The Will to Power*, Nietzsche stated the characteristics of the "herd" with his usual incisiveness: "The instinct of the herd considers the middle and the mean as the highest and most valuable: the place where the majority finds itself; the mode and manner in which it finds itself. It is therefore an opponent of all orders of rank, it sees an ascent from beneath to above as a descent from the majority to the

But in his later works Nietzsche went even further. *The Antichrist,* one of the last books written prior to his final collapse in 1888, puts forward the idea that the Judaeo-Christian tradition had accomplished what he called a "transvaluation of values." That is to say, it had stood morality on its head: it had sought to turn the good of master morality into evil or, what was worse yet, into sin. Abject before the justifiable pride of those above it, it condemned pride and made a virtue of humility; helpless before their strength, it called strength an evil and glorified weakness. It was thus a morality of "resentment" *(ressentiment),* that said "no" to "everything representing an *ascending* evolution of life—that is, to well-being, to power, to beauty, to self-approval." Nietzsche's voice becomes positively strident as he declares that "Christianity is a revolt of all creatures that creep on the ground against everything that is *lofty."* "I condemn Christianity," he roars. "I bring against the Christian church the most terrible of all the accusations that an accuser has ever had in his mouth. It is, to me, the greatest of all imaginable corruptions; it seeks to work the ultimate corruption, the worst possible corruption."[98]*

Mencken seized upon all this and absorbed it so thoroughly that, in later years, he was not really conscious of having absorbed it at all. I have already quoted (page 66) from his letter of March 1, 1937, to Edward Stone, a graduate student doing an M.A. thesis entitled *H. L. Mencken's Debt to F. W. Nietzsche,* in which he says that in his own mind his debt to Nietzsche seemed small. A few months later,

---

minority. The herd feels the exception, whether it be below or above it, as something opposed and harmful to it. Its artifice with reference to the exceptions above it, the stronger, more powerful, wiser, and more fruitful, is to persuade them to assume the role of guardians, herdsmen, watchmen—to become its *first servants:* it has therefore transformed a danger into something useful. Fear ceases in the middle; here one is never alone; here there is little room for misunderstanding; here there is equality; here one's own form of being is not felt as a reproach but as the right form of being; here contentment rules. Mistrust is felt toward the exceptions; to be an exception is experienced as guilt." See *The Will to Power,* #280, translated with commentary by Walter Kaufmann (New York: Random House, 1967), p. 159.

   Nietzsche recognized, of course, that master morality and slave morality may exist side by side and interpenetrate each other—"even in the same human being." It is a point that is frequently overlooked by commentators on his philosophy, with resultant tragic misunderstanding of what he actually meant. See *Beyond Good and Evil,* #260, also translated and edited by Walter Kaufmann (New York: The Modern Library, 1968), p. 204.

*It is perhaps worth emphasizing that the steps in Nietzsche's argument have to be studied with the greatest care before one either accepts or rejects his conclusions.

having received a copy of Stone's work and read it, he admitted that he may have been mistaken. "As you know," he said, "I was under the impression that my debt to Nietzsche was very slight. I must say now that your argument rather shakes me. Such influences are exerted, it appears, very insidiously. I was picking up Nietzscheisms without being aware of them, and they undoubtedly got into my own stuff."[99] It would hardly be accurate, of course, just to set him down as a Nietzschean and let it go at that; he was much too vigorous and independent a personality in his own right to be nothing more than the disciple of another man, however much he might be in agreement with that other man's thought. But as he remarked to Stone, influences are insidious, and in the course of his study of the German philosopher he picked up much that was to form him into the man he became.

More than one biographer and critic has observed that *The Philosophy of Friedrich Nietzsche* is as much Mencken as it is Nietzsche. This is true, and of course the reason it is true is that Mencken is adopting and joyously developing ideas which in Nietzsche were perhaps still only implicit. When he says, for example, that "it is only a small minority of human beings who may be said, with any truth, to be capable of thought,"[100] he is being entirely faithful to his expressed purpose—namely, expounding Nietzsche's philosophy—but at the same time he is pushing forward on his own. When he adds a few pages later that "It is only doubt that creates. It is only the minority that counts," he is not just echoing Nietzschean aphorisms but stating two basic Menckenian premises that will be repeated in countless variations over the next forty years.

To record every one of those variations would be all but impossible and would really serve no useful purpose; they are buried in a dozen books, in hundreds of the *Sunpapers'* "Monday Articles," in innumerable reviews in *The Smart Set* and editorials in *The American Mercury*. But I select a few as evidence of how his opinions on these matters, once fixed, never underwent any significant change. The Nietzsche volume, remember, was published in 1908. In 1924, in an essay entitled "Bugaboo" included in *Prejudices: Fourth Series*, he declared:

> The fact is that the safeguarding and development of civilization are and always have been in the exclusive care of a very small minority of human beings of each generation, and that the rest of the human race consists wholly of deadheads. Consider, for example, the telephone, a very

characteristic agent of Christian advancement. It has been invented, perfected, organized and brought to every door in our own time by less than 20 men—nay, by less than 10 men. All the others who have made it, financed and installed it have been simply trailers. All the rest of the human race has taken a free ride.[101]

Two pages later, he adds in the clearest possible terms:

I believe fully that the first-rate men of the world constitute a distinct and separate species—that they have little, if anything, in common with the lower orders of men.

Notes on Democracy, which appeared in 1926, restates this premise:

. . . men differ inside their heads as they differ outside. There are men who are naturally intelligent and can learn, and there are men who are naturally stupid and cannot.[102]

The point is hammered home again within a few paragraphs:

Men are *not* alike, and very little can be learned about the mental processes of a congressman, an ice-wagon driver or a cinema star by studying the mental processes of a genuinely superior man. The difference is not only qualitative; it is also, in important ways, quantitative.

Insofar as Mencken's career is divisible into "periods" (and as I shall try to show later, this is at least true of his style even if not of his ideas), *The Philosophy of Friedrich Nietzsche* obviously belongs to his early period, while the *Prejudices* and *Notes on Democracy* may be called "middle." The brief paragraphs and aphorisms making up *Minority Report* are undated in the book itself, but an examination of the manuscript material shows that most of them were written in the very late thirties and the early forties—that is to say, in the final active decade of his life. A single example from here re-echoes the 1924 "Bugaboo":

All the great enterprises of the world are run by a few smart men: their aids and associates run down by rapid stages to the level of sheer morons. Everyone knows that this is true of government, but we often forget that it is equally true of private undertakings. In the average great bank, or railroad, or other corporation the burden of management lies upon a small group. The rest are ciphers.[103]

What did Mencken mean by "morons," "ciphers," "human blanks"? Plainly enough, he meant exactly what Nietzsche meant when he spoke contemptuously of the "herd," and for both men this accounted for 95 percent or more of the human race. As I have already indicated, it constitutes a very harsh and cavalier dismissal, and one is justified in asking on what grounds anybody can arrogate to himself the right to make it. After all, not everyone can be an Aristotle or a Leonardo or a Goethe—or, for that matter, a Nietzsche or a Mencken. (Both, incidentally, would readily have admitted that this is just as well.) Some men have to be hewers of wood and drawers of water, but is that any reason to dismiss them out of hand and hold that they contribute nothing whatever to humanity's development? Mencken, I believe, would be the first to admit that it is not, and in order to understand his position here it is very important to know just what he meant by an "inferior man." Fortunately, he stated it as often and as clearly as he stated his fundamental distinction between the two types.

That distinction, it should be said at once (and I really apologize for making so obvious a point), had in the first place nothing whatever to do with wealth or financial position. As Carl Bode has noted in his biography, Mencken was that rarest of all specimens, a financially successful author; at no time in his life did he ever have to worry about money, and at his death he left an estate valued at approximately $300,000. He enjoyed to the fullest the independence and the comforts that these resources made available to him. But one has only to read his estimates of such men as John D. Rockefeller, Sr., Jay Gould, or Judge Elbert Gary, then chairman of the United States Steel Corporation, to realize how little value he placed upon their possessions. "The fact . . . ," he once wrote, "that John D. Rockefeller had more money than I have is as uninteresting to me as the fact that he believed in total immersion and wore detachable cuffs."[104]

He had made the point abundantly clear almost as soon as he originally distinguished between inferior and superior men. In 1909, only one year after the appearance of the Nietzsche book, he became involved in a debate with an "intellectual Socialist" named Robert

Rives La Monte. At that time Mencken, the scion of a typical respectable bourgeois family, was editor of the *Sunday Sun* but could reasonably be described as a "wage slave" in the employ of wealthy capitalists. La Monte, who just happened at the same time to be working for the *News*, a rival paper, came from a very well-to-do background (one of his relatives was Thomas W. Lamont, a partner in the firm of J. P. Morgan & Co.), but he had been attracted some years earlier to Socialism and proposed to devote his money, time, and energies to defending the rights of the "common man." The debate took place in the form of a series of letters, with Mencken, the wage slave, defending the rights of capitalism and extreme individualism, and La Monte, the rich dilettante, calling for the overthrow of capitalism and the establishment of a socialist economy.*

In his reply to La Monte's first letter, Mencken reiterated quite forcibly the point he had already made two years earlier when writing of Nietzsche:

> The mob is inert and moves ahead only when it is dragged or driven. It clings to its delusions with a pertinacity that is appalling. A geological epoch is required to rid it of a single error, and it is so helpless and cowardly that every fresh boon it receives, every lift upon its slow journey upward, must come to it as a free gift from its betters—as a gift not only free, but also forced.[105]

But in his third letter he made it abundantly clear that by the "mob" he did not mean the "poor":

> It is possible, you will note, for a man to amass billions, and yet lend no hand in [human] progress; and it is possible, again, for a man to live in poverty, and yet set the clock ahead a thousand years. . . . And so, to sum up, it is possible for a poor man to belong to the highest caste of men, and for a rich man to belong to the lowest.[106]

---

*H. L. Mencken and Robert Rives La Monte, *Men versus the Man* (New York: Henry Holt & Co., 1910). The book was commercially unsuccessful and very quickly remaindered; ten years later Mencken wrote that it was "as completely forgotten as Baxter's 'Saint's Rest' or the Constitution of the United States." ("Professor Veblen and the Cow," *Smart Set*, LIX, 1, [May 1919], p. 138; *Prejudices: First Series*, p. 60; *Chrestomathy*, p. 266.) Another five years after that he told Isaac Goldberg that "the book seems somewhat archaic today, but it at least shows one thing clearly, that my politics were firmly formulated so early as 1909. I'd change the essential doctrine very little if I had it to rewrite today." (Autobiographical notes supplied to Goldberg, p. 128.)

Neither, in the second place, did it have anything to do with learning or cultural attainments. Save for politicians and bishops, no class of men ever had to bear more heavily the scourge of Menckenian rhetoric than pedagogues, and this was especially true of that branch of the profession which taught English: "Not one in ten of them," he claimed, "has any sort of grasp of the difficult subject he professes, or shows any desire to master it."[107] In this, to be sure, personal feeling may have had some effect upon impartial judgment: Mencken was writing original and important criticism at a quite early stage in his career, but the professionals—the men, in short, with the appropriate letters behind their names, like William Crary Brownell, Paul Elmer More, and Stuart Pratt Sherman—either ignored him because he lacked the proper academic credentials or else tried to pretend that he was much too vulgar to be admitted to their circle. He would have been less than human had he not been nettled now and then by this attitude on the part of what he called "the faculty."

What made them "inferior" in his eyes was not just a lack of ability to teach—for some of them, perhaps, may have had it—but their almost total preoccupation with the past and indifference to what was going on around them. Those who professed literature truend out their dreary papers on the "A," "B," and "C" texts of *Piers Plowman* and the metaphysical subtleties of Wordsworth's *Prelude*, and sublimely ignored men like Theodore Dreiser, Sherwood Anderson, and James Branch Cabell; the more enlightened among them were just coming to be aware that Mark Twain had a place in American letters. Those who taught the language itself were so busy investigating the decay of inflectional endings in Middle English that they could give no time to the living speech of the 120 million people around them. He had to write *The American Language*, Mencken always claimed, not because he was competent to do so—from the first edition in 1919 to Supplement II in 1948 he kept insisting over and over again that he was not—but because all those who in theory should have been competent to do it regarded the task as beneath their dignity.

No, it was not lack of money or lack of education that, in themselves, made a man inferior. Rather, the inferior man was simply the one who knew nothing that was not common knowledge to every adult and could do nothing that had not already been done by someone else. He meanly admired mean things. His outstanding characteristic was his readiness to believe what was palpably not true. He was an eager

customer of any and all forms of quackery: Socialism, the New
Thought, anti-vivisectionism, chiropractic, Prohibition, the latest
utopia dangled by some brummagem aspirant for public office. The
more nonsensical a proposition, the more unquestioningly he swallowed it. He ferociously resisted every step in human progress, and
looked upon those who did contribute something to that progress—a
Darwin, a Huxley, a Pasteur—as immoral and enemies of God.

Fearing anything that was different, anything or anybody not in
conformity with his own very limited ideas, he had a natural tendency
to flock together with the rest of the "herd"—that is to say, with those
whose minds were on a level with his. This explained the "joiner"—the
member of Kiwanis, Rotary, the Elks, the Knights of Pythias, the
Knights of Columbus. In such an environment no upsetting intellectual demands were made upon him; he encountered nothing that
would be likely to disturb his narrow convictions. In Mencken's view:

> The one permanent emotion of the inferior man, as of all the simpler
> mammals, is fear—fear of the unknown, the complex, the inexplicable.
> What he wants beyond everything else is safety. His instincts incline
> him toward a society so organized that it will protect him at all hazards,
> and not only against perils to his hide but also against assaults upon his
> mind—against the need to grapple with unaccustomed problems, to
> weigh ideas, to think things out for himself, to scrutinize the platitudes
> upon which his everyday thinking is based.[108]

What the inferior man dreaded above all else was liberty. Liberty,
in fact, would have been of scant use to him; his conception of it was
"to quit work, stretch out in the sun, and scratch himself."[109] He
mouthed platitudes about freedom, but freedom was really the last
thing in the world he wanted; his sole desire was to be safe. And the
ironic thing was that this safety could be guaranteed him only by the
direction and control of his betters, whom he bitterly resented and
strove at all times to bring down to his own cultural level. Most of the
liberties he enjoyed had been thrust upon him, usually to the tune
of his loud complaining, by those above him.

In contrast, the superior individual—he who belonged to "the
more enlightened minority of mankind"—refused to be swept along by
public sentiment or the passing fashions of the day. The mere fact
that everybody else believed something was, for him, sufficient evidence that it was not true. He was skeptical alike of popular taste, the

dogmas of religion, and political shibboleths. He had no objection to the inferior man believing what he pleased, so long as he did not attempt to impose his beliefs on others by taking a vote and then enforcing the outcome by police regulations. His skepticism was even complete and amiable enough for him to admit that his opinions, too, were but opinions, and that the other fellow might after all be right.

He directed his aspirations not to what was cheap and commonplace but rather to the rare and difficult. Contemptuous of obloquy and indifferent to both praise and blame, he usually made some kind of contribution to the improvement of the race; but his motive in doing so had nothing in common with the motives that inspired the "do-gooder" and the "forward-looker." The fact of the matter was that he cared precisely nothing about improving the race; what fascinated him was the challenge presented by a particular problem. That problem might be the composition of a sonata, or the isolation of a bacillus, or the marketing of a better rat trap; but whatever it was, it gave to man something he had not hitherto had and that was of lasting value.

Whatever it was, too, the important thing was that he could do it well, and this, for Mencken, was the supreme virtue—namely, competence. He called it "the most steadily attractive of all human qualities,"[110] and in the final analysis it was the basis on which he judged all men. The English professor who wrote a poor book, one showing little knowledge and less mastery of his subject, was a mountebank and a fraud. The tailor who could measure, cut, and fit a decent suit, or the plumber who could with minimum labor and cost to his customer open up a clogged drain, was deserving of respect. "The only sort of man," he wrote, "who is really worth hell room [is] the man who practices some useful trade in a competent manner, makes a decent living at it, pays his own way, and asks only to be let alone." To which he added at once: "He is now a pariah in all so-called civilized countries."[111]

Finally, just as neither money nor learning was what made a man superior, so, too, such a one did not necessarily have to have what we usually think of as "refinement." The superior man would not be needlessly vulgar or offensive, but this did not mean that he had to conduct himself, in his speech and demeanor, like a member of the House of Lords or a graduate of Harvard. As I have already indicated, there can be no doubt that Mencken thought of himself as belonging to that

"intelligent minority" whose right to exist he so zealously defended;
but he once painted a word portrait of himself in which, perhaps with
less exaggeration than usual, he humorously described his own tastes
and predilections:

> I am by nature a vulgar fellow. I prefer *Tom Jones* to "The Rosary,"
> Rabelais to the Elsie books, the Old Testament to the New, the expur-
> gated parts of *Gulliver's Travels* to those that are left. I delight in beef
> stews, limericks, burlesque shows, New York City and the music of
> Haydn, that beery and delightful old rascal! I swear in the presence of
> ladies and archdeacons. When the mercury is above ninety-five I dine in
> my shirt sleeves and write poetry naked. I associate habitually with
> dramatists, bartenders, medical men and musicians. I once, in early
> youth, kissed a waitress at Dennett's. So don't accuse me of vulgarity. I
> admit it and flout you. Not, of course, that I have no pruderies, no
> fastidious metes and bounds. Far from it. Babies, for example, are too
> vulgar for me; I cannot bring myself to touch them. And actors. And
> evangelists. And the obstetrical anecdotes of ancient dames. But in
> general, as I have said, I joy in vulgarity, whether it take the form of
> divorce proceedings or of *Tristan und Isolde,* of an Odd Fellows'
> funeral or of Munich beer.[112]

7 BUT IF MEN COULD NOT be labeled "superior" or
"inferior" on the basis of wealth or education, or even
of their ordinary manners, there was at least one ground on which
Mencken was quite willing so to categorize them, and that was on the
basis of whether they came from the city or the country. Expressed in
terms of mathematical proportion, the city dweller was to the country
yokel as "superior" is to "inferior." "Even the lowest varieties of city
workmen," he held, "are at least superior to peasants."[113]

Perhaps it should be made clear that Mencken was not, and never
considered himself to be, a sophisticate or cosmopolite—certainly not
in the sense that George Jean Nathan was, or his other colleague in the
early days of *The Smart Set,* Willard Huntington Wright. Despite
what he says in the passage I have just quoted, he admitted to detest-
ing New York and was never really comfortable there. Even Theodore
Dreiser, hardly a model of urban polish himself, thought that he

looked like "Anheuser's own brightest boy out to see the town" when Mencken called upon him in the office of Butterick Publications in 1908. He commuted to the big city at least once a month, and sometimes oftener, for a quarter of a century, but he always claimed that he could not wait to bang his desk shut at 3 P.M. so that he might catch the 3:25 train back to Baltimore; behind him was a place fit only for the gross business of making money, while ahead was a place made for enjoying it.[114] During that period he turned down several highly tempting job offers for no other reason than that they would have required him to live in New York.

Neither was he at all insensitive to the beauties of nature. We have seen how, as a grown man, he would go back to the little country town of Ellicott City, where he had spent boyhood vacations, so that he might revel again in its quiet pastoral loveliness, and in later years he liked, too, to visit his sister's home in the rolling farmlands of central Maryland.

But in spite of all this, his attitude toward rural America and the people who inhabited it was from beginning to end one of devastating contempt and implacable hostility. The "Bible and hookworm belt" where "the cows low through the still night, and the jug of Peruna stands behind the stove, and bathing begins, as at Biarritz, with the vernal equinox," represented for him everything that was cheap, backward, and preposterous in the country's life. It stood for all that made the United States "a buffoon among the great nations."

He began his attacks on it early and came back to them again and again over the years, but they rise to an unsurpassable climax in the *American Mercury* editorial for March 1924, which was subsequently included with a few minor changes in *Prejudices: Fourth Series:*

> Let the farmer, so far as I am concerned, be damned forevermore! To hell with him, and bad luck to him! He is, unless I err, no hero at all, and no priest, and no altruist, but simply a tedious fraud and ignoramus, a cheap rogue and hypocrite, the eternal Jack of the human pack. He deserves all that he suffers under our economic system, and more. Any city man, not insane, who sheds tears for him is shedding tears of the crocodile.

Once launched upon his subject, he proceeded with a fervor from which all his customary good humor had disappeared:

No more grasping, selfish and dishonest mammal . . . is known to students of the Anthropoidea. When the going is good for him he robs the rest of us up to the extreme limit of our endurance; when the going is bad he comes bawling for help out of the public till. . . . Yet we are asked to venerate this prehensile moron as the *Ur*-burgher, the citizen *par excellence*, the foundation-stone of the state! And why? Because he produces something that all of us must have—that we must get somehow on penalty of death. [115]

It was Mencken's unshakable conviction that this "rabble of peasants who sleep in their underclothes" was responsible for all of the idiotic legislation that reigned over the land and oppressed civilized men and women. The farmer had brought about Prohibition, for example, not because he believed that drinking was evil *per se*, but simply because he was limited to guzzling his raw corn liquor while the city man could enjoy vintage wines and quality whiskeys. He had brought about, too, such an obscene statute as the Mann Act, which did not in the least mean that farm lads were not free to drag virgins down into infamy behind barn doors. Nor was it going too far to say that he was behind Comstockian censorship, or at all events willing to give it his support, because the classics and serious modern literature were quite beyond his comprehension and thus to be viewed with suspicion; frank pornography, such as *Confessions of an Ex-nun* and *Adventures on a Pullman Sleeper*, was seldom attacked because the farmer could understand them and drool over them. What inspired all such measures was "no more and no less than the yokel's congenital and incurable hatred of the city man—his simian rage against everyone who, as he sees it, is having a better time than he is."

And in the near future, he predicted, the "hog's theology" of the "rural total immersionists" stood a good chance of becoming the state religion, with disagreement from it constituting a capital offense. "The Wesleyan code of Kansas and Mississippi, Vermont and Minnesota will be forced upon all of us by the full military and naval power of the United States. Civilization will gradually become felonious everywhere in the Republic, as it already is in Arkansas."

Once again it may be asked how much of this murderous attack can stand up under impartial and critical examination. Even if it was not just (which it may very well have been), even if it was not fair (and after all, fairness was the last thing in the world to be expected from

Mencken), yet the question may still be put: Was there any real basis in fact for such unqualified accusations?

It depends, one supposes, on whether the matter is looked at from the vantage point of his time or ours. As I remarked earlier, the gap that separated urban from rural America in the early years of Mencken's activity was a much more real and effective force than it is now. Today there is not a farm anywhere in the land so isolated as to be without access to the instant-news media of television and radio. The farmer no longer needs to pick his appliances out of a Sears, Roebuck catalogue and send for them by mail, and his wife is not limited to choosing her plain wardrobe from the same source. At a complete and modern shopping center, readily accessible in their car, they can find all the luxuries they see on TV commercials. Their sons and daughters, rather than follow them in tilling the soil, are more likely than not to go to college and enter some profession. The very science of agriculture itself has undergone significant development, and the farmer needs a certain amount of technological sophistication to engage in it.

But in the twenties and thirties of this century the gap remained almost as great as it had been in the middle of the last. Distance still created a chasm, and across it travel and communication were slight. A Ford "flivver" might bring the farmer in over dusty roads at least as far as the county seat, but this was still a long way from the big city with its refinements and sins. The mere fact of his isolation from the mainstream of events tended to leave him uninformed and uneducated, and this in turn naturally made him suspicious of what was so far off and unfamiliar. One cannot precisely blame him for this, any more than one can blame the nineteenth-century immigrants for coming over in ships rather than jet planes; but his ignorance did leave him a prey both to mountebank politicians eager for his vote and to the Fundamentalist preachers who swarmed over the land at the time.

Under the circumstances, Mencken's strictures against the "husbandman," while not essentially untrue, were at least harsh, and it may not be going too far to say that they were downright cruel. But doubtless he cannot be blamed either; the situation was what it was, and he was no more inclined to show understanding and forbearance than they were. Perhaps, in today's very different social and cultural conditions, he might exhibit a greater tolerance. Yet somehow one doubts it—such a thing would go against his fundamental principle of never changing his mind on a capital matter.

8 IF THE FARMER was by nature inferior to the city man, there was, among city men, at least one class inferior by nature to all others. This was the humble pedagogue, or teacher. As early as the book on Nietzsche, Mencken laid down this premise clearly and unequivocally: "school teachers, taking them by and large, are probably the most ignorant and stupid class of men in the whole group of mental workers."[116]

When he wrote this, about 1907, he was not really all that far from F. Knapp's Institute and the teachers who had instilled in him there the first rudiments of learning—just far enough, probably, to be convinced that he had an infinitely greater wisdom than they had ever had. Years later his attitude toward them would mellow, and he would speak of them with something almost approaching fondness. Granted that they had been idiots, asses all, preposterous popinjays and numskulls, pathetic imbeciles, yet the fact remained that they had had a genuine love for the subjects they taught and that by virtue of this enthusiasm they had managed, somehow or other, to cram a vestige of it into the minds of their young charges. Their sole technical equipment had been a knowledge that ran just slightly ahead of their pupils', a box of chalk, and a stout rattan; all the rest of the educational process followed normally enough.

They needed, in fact, no more; the best teacher of children, he remained convinced, was one whose mind was essentially childlike: "For even stupidity, it must be plain," he wrote,

> has its uses in the world, and some of them are uses that intelligence cannot meet. One would not tell off a Galileo to drive an ash-cart or an Ignatius Loyola to be a stock-broker, or a Mozart to lead the orchestra in a night-club. By the same token, one would not ask a Duns Scotus to instruct sucklings. Such men would not only be wasted at the job; they would also be incompetent.[117]

But in the intervening years a revolution had taken place in the world of education, and the ghost of Pestalozzi, "once bearing a torch and beckoning toward the heights, now [led] down dark stairways into the black and forbidding dungeons of Teachers College, Columbia."[118] Teaching had become a science in itself, separable from and superior to the thing taught. An esoteric technique was now the all-important thing, and once armed with it the teacher was in theory competent to teach any subject, just as a dentist was competent to pull any tooth. The practitioners of this technique were for the most part frauds, pure and unmitigated; they had little knowledge of the subjects they were assigned to teach, and even less ability to communicate that knowledge to others; they could not think. Pedagogy in the United States had descended to the level of a childish necromancy, and the worst idiots, even among pedagogues, were the teachers of English.

The principal aim of this dreadful hocus-pocus was not to impart knowledge (assuming that knowledge could ever be attained or imparted at all), but rather "to cram the pupils, as rapidly and as painlessly as possible, with the largest conceivable outfit of current axioms, in all departments of human thought." In other words, its aim was not to educate human persons but simply to turn out good citizens—and a good citizen was one whose views and conduct differed as little as possible from those of all other citizens. The job of the university professor, with his administration and its board of trustees observing him closely from behind, was to "manufacture an endless corps of sound Americans. A sound American is simply one who has put out of his mind all doubts and questionings, and who accepts instantly, and as incontrovertible gospel, the whole body of official doctrine of his day, whatever it may be and no matter how often it may change."[119]

That this was a correct enough estimate of higher education in the United States in the years between the two World Wars, and even beyond, few will deny. In some respects the situation has not shown very much improvement; the preoccupation with technique is still there, and the techniques themselves have grown ever more complex and remote from reality, and the language used to describe them is a specialized jargon unintelligible to anyone outside the charmed circle. Yet few will deny, too, that there has been some evidence of a change for the better. Those changes had scarcely gotten under way in Mencken's lifetime, but he noted their first faint beginnings and predicted the outcome when, in *The Smart Set* for May 1923, he reviewed Upton Sinclair's book *The Goose-Step.* "The American university student, in the past," he wrote,

> has been a victim of the same process of leveling that destroyed his teacher. He has been taught conformity, obedience, the social and in-

tellectual goose-step; the ideal held before him has been the ideal of correctness. But that ideal, it must be plain, is not natural to youth. Youth is aspiring, rebellious, inquisitive, iconoclastic, a bit romantic. All over the country the fact is bursting through the chains of repression. In scores of far-flung colleges the students have begun to challenge their professors, often very harshly. After a while, they may begin to challenge the masters of their professors. Not all of them will do it, and not most of them. But it doesn't take a majority to make a rebellion; it takes only a few determined leaders and a sound cause.[120]

When one thinks of the student demonstrations on so many campuses in the late 1960's, it will be seen how chillingly accurate Mencken's prophecy was. This is not to say that he would have fully approved of them, or of the tactics that were so often employed; given his essential conservatism, he probably would not. But he would at least have understood the cause, and he would certainly have had more sympathy for the students than for the professors against whom they revolted.

I I I

THE
POLITICAL THEORIST

I believe that all government is evil, and that trying to improve it is largely a waste of time.

—"The Coolidge Buncombe,"
Baltimore *Evening Sun*, October 6, 1924

◇◇

1 WHEN, IN 1908, MENCKEN accepted the invitation of Fred Splint, managing editor of *The Smart Set*, to become the magazine's book reviewer "with the rank and pay of a sergeant of artillery," he was already the author of the first critical study to appear in either England or America on the plays of Bernard Shaw, and the author, too, of a much bigger and more substantial work on the philosophy of Friedrich Wilhelm Nietzsche. In Baltimore he had achieved some local repute as a drama critic, first on the *Herald* and later on the *Sun*. But this recognition was limited indeed in comparison with what was to come; over the course of the next fifteen years his monthly review articles in *The Smart Set* would bring him national—and to a degree at least even international—fame as the country's foremost arbiter of letters. The publication of *A Book of Prefaces* (1917) and the first two or three volumes of the *Prejudices* series, in which the essays dealt largely with literary subjects, further enhanced this reputation.

True, he was not an academician, and the academicians timidly kept him at arm's length. He was much too vulgar and irreverent for them, and his aesthetic principles were at an opposite pole from theirs. But by the sheer force of an indomitable personality and his utterly unique style he managed to beat them at their own game and, in doing so, literally overthrew their concept of what American literature ought to be.

He is often given credit for having changed the whole course of that literature. This is true, and without going into the matter in any detail here—since it will be the subject of Chapter IV—it may at least be said that he accomplished the task in two complementary ways. First of all, the ridicule that he poured upon the work of "Puritan" authors simply laughed it out of court and cleared the path for a new, fresh, and honest realism. Secondly, and at the same time that he was doing this, he was also encouraging and helping writers who were either little known or who were receiving from the academicians scant recognition and even less encouragement. It is hardly too much to say that there was not a single notable American writer of the twenties and thirties who was unwilling to acknowledge his indebtedness, either directly or indirectly, to H. L. Mencken.

Now and then, to be sure, this influence is exaggerated—if not always by the writers themselves, then by contemporary and later historians. For example, it is sometimes said that he "discovered" Dreiser—which is quite untrue, since *Sister Carrie* had been published as far back as 1900. Yet no man did more than Mencken to advance Dreiser's cause, and to defend him from the attacks of censors even at the cost of outlay from his own pocket. The same thing may be said of his relationship to such figures as Sinclair Lewis, Sherwood Anderson, James Branch Cabell, Willa Cather, and Scott Fitzgerald. Actually, people of this stature are never really "discovered" by anybody; they create themselves by their own genius or talent. But it goes without saying that they can be helped enormously by the intelligent advice and the favorable notice of an influential critic, and it was both of these that Mencken was in a position to give them.

By the time he contributed his last piece to *The Smart Set* in the issue for December 1923, after having written 182 consecutive monthly articles totaling 900,000 words, he was without a doubt the most powerful single force in American criticism.

Yet the curious thing is that during all that time he never really looked upon himself as primarily a literary critic and did not especially want to be one. His work for the magazine may have gained him a national audience and a national reputation, but it was in a field where he had no desire to shine. He brings this point out in an unpublished autobiographical fragment written long afterward, toward the close of his active career:

> For many years I was known principally as a critic of literature, but it was a subject that never really interested me profoundly, and such writings of mine as show any promise of surviving lie in other directions.[1]

As year followed year he became restive. In 1922, almost at the end of his period of "servitude" with *The Smart Set*, he brought out a new and expanded edition of *In Defense of Women* for Knopf's "Free Lance" series, and at that time, as has already been mentioned, he wrote a new preface for it. In the closing pages of that preface he remarked:

> During the same year [i.e., at age twenty-five] I published my first book of criticism. Thereafter, for ten or twelve years, I moved steadily from practical journalism, with its dabblings in politics, economics and so on, toward purely aesthetic concerns, chiefly literature and music, but of late I have felt a strong pull in the other direction, and what interests me today is what may be called public psychology, *i.e.* the nature of the ideas that the larger masses of men hold, and the processes whereby they reach them. If I do any serious writing hereafter, it will be in that field.[2]

It was this pull that, inevitably, led him away from *The Smart Set* and toward the creation of *The American Mercury*. Under his and George Jean Nathan's joint editorship *The Smart Set* had published some of the best fiction and some of the top names of the period, but it had never quite been able to overcome its original rather sleazy reputation and achieve anything properly describable as dignity. Its paper was cheap and its typography uninviting, its cover was (for that time) a bit risqué, and it was primarily a market for short stories and novellas. Mencken dreamed of something more. The magazine that he envisaged would be handsome in appearance, of unquestioned integrity, and would cover a much ampler field—politics, economics, sociology, the sciences, the whole range of American culture and mores. Most important of all, it would reflect, as *The Smart Set* had never been able to, the personality and interests of its editor.

The *Mercury* was and did all of these things. With the financial backing of Alfred Knopf and the somewhat dubious acquiescence of

Nathan, it was launched in January 1924 and within a matter of a few months had become one of the best-known and most influential periodicals in the land. The publisher and editors had dared to hope for a circulation of 12,000; the first issue sold out and required two additional printings, bringing it up to 15,000, and the second climbed from there to almost 22,000. Thereafter it continued to mount steadily: by the end of the first year it was at 42,614, and by December 1925—at the end, in other words, of just two years of existence—it had gone on to 62,323.* Since it sold for 50 cents per copy at the newsstand—a high price for a magazine in those days—such figures were clear evidence of a very broad and powerful appeal; they may also have indicated that that "intelligent minority" for which Mencken wrote was numerically greater than he had himself ever believed.

The editorial in the very first issue, after declaring that it would live up to the adjective in its name by laying chief stress at all times upon American ideas, problems, and personalities, ended by saying:

> There are more political theories on tap in the Republic than anywhere else on earth, and more doctrines in aesthetics, and more religions, and more other schemes for regimenting, harrowing and saving human beings. Our annual production of messiahs is greater than that of all Asia. A single session of Congress produces more utopian legislation than Europe has seen since the first meeting of the English Witenagemot. To explore this great complex of inspirations, to isolate the individual prophets from the herd and examine their proposals, to follow the ponderous revolutions of the mass mind—in brief, to attempt a realistic presentation of the whole gaudy, gorgeous American scene—this will be the principal enterprise of THE AMERICAN MERCURY.[3]

In pursuit of this aim short stories were very definitely subordinated to nonfiction, and poetry was limited to but two or three pages—sometimes not even that. Typical articles treated of such sub-

---

*I take these figures from Marvin K. Singleton, *H. L. Mencken and the* American Mercury *Adventure* (Durham, N.C.: Duke University Press, 1962), pp. 37, 64. The high point of circulation was reached in 1927 with an average of 77,277 copies per issue. Thereafter it began to decline—slowly at first, then with alarming rapidity. For this there were two reasons. The first, and doubtless the most important, was the corresponding decline in popularity and influence of its editor; the second, almost as great but coming a bit later in time, was the advent of the Great Depression. The circulation for the December 1933 issue—the last one under Mencken's editorship—was "probably not much more than 23,000." (*Ibid.*, p. 232.)

jects as "The Senate's Last Leader" (Boies Penrose of Pennsylvania), "The Presidency," "Mr. Munsey" (Frank A. Munsey, newspaper and magazine publisher), and "Fads in Health Legislation"; Mencken's editorials ranged from osteopathy to Prohibition, with journalism, rural religion, federal judges, and government in general coming in between. The 5,000-word monthly article in *The Smart Set* in which he had often reviewed an entire shelf of books was replaced by a department called "The Library" where six, eight, or at the most ten new books were noticed; they were chiefly works on politics, economics, jurisprudence, and the social and natural sciences. Now and then he might deal with one on literary criticism and theory, and he always found room for books about one of his favorite subjects—music—but more and more rarely now did he review novels. In 1925, sending Mencken a copy of his latest work, *The Great Gatsby*, Scott Fitzgerald wrote in the flyleaf: "Dear Menck: I see you don't review fiction any more."*

---

*To be sure, that same editorial in the first issue had stated: "The dramatic reviews will, however, cover the entire range of the New York theatre"—undoubtedly written by, or a concession to, Nathan. Earlier, while the magazine was still in the planning stage, Mencken had insisted to Knopf that he and Nathan must be co-editors of it, as they had been of *The Smart Set*. Before the second issue came out, however, a serious disagreement had erupted between them over Eugene O'Neill's play *All God's Chillun Got Wings*. Nathan wanted it for the magazine and as a matter of fact had contracted with O'Neill for it; Mencken did not believe it had any place in the *Mercury*. Knopf cast the deciding vote in Nathan's favor and the play appeared in the February number, but relations between the two editors were now definitely strained and they continued to get worse. By February 1925 Nathan had ceased to have any editorial control over the magazine or any responsibility for its contents, though he continued to write his monthly article on the drama and contribute to the "Clinical Notes" department. In 1930, after long-drawn-out and painful business negotiations, his connection with the *Mercury* ceased entirely.

The "break" between Mencken and Nathan was perhaps the most famous *cause célèbre* in the literary history of the period. Nathan always insisted that there never was one, but there can be no doubt that for Mencken it was very real indeed. Yet they continued to correspond, and a decade later their friendship, if not their collaboration, was warmly resumed. It was simply a matter of utterly divergent interests; this divergence lay in the very natures of the two men and thus went back long before the *Mercury*, but it was, of course, the founding of the magazine that brought things to a head. Mencken, as I have said, had no really deep interest in literature or the drama but leaned toward politics and the general social scene; for these things Nathan cared precisely nothing. When Mencken complained to Knopf that his partner was not carrying a fair share of the responsibility for getting the magazine out and that this threw an intolerable burden upon him, he was doubtless being truthful enough; but on the other hand it was simply impossible for Nathan to feel any genuine enthusiasm for a project that represented so little of his own interests. William Manchester (*Disturber of the Peace*, pp. 218–21) and Carl Bode (*Mencken*, pp. 211–20) have both treated of the matter in much greater depth than is possible here.

The picture of the college student with an "arsenic green" copy of *The American Mercury* tucked under his arm in order to show off his sophistication has become such a cliché of the period that there seems little need to repeat it once more. Yet the fact remains that subscribing to, or buying, or even just reading, the *Mercury* was something of a hallmark of liberated intelligence during the middle and late twenties. If ever a magazine was a panorama of ten years of a nation's life, this one was—a panorama extremely one-sided, to be sure, since its editor had little tolerance for a point of view that did not coincide with his own; but a virtually complete picture, nonetheless, of all the varied activities that made up the American scene at what was really—though nobody could have known it at the time—the end of an era. They were the years when the United States, having emerged from the First World War as not yet quite a great power but certainly the one with the mightiest potential and promise, vacillated between a policy of isolationism and one of active involvement in world affairs. They were the years, too, of the dizzy Harding-Coolidge "prosperity," when the national wealth soared to undreamed-of heights and each day's trading on Wall Street broke the record set the day before. It was the time of Prohibition, bootleggers, bathtub gin, "law enforcement," and the sudden appearance of a wholly new phenomenon, the "gangster." It was the "Jazz Age," when women bobbed their hair, and began to smoke, and wore dresses that revealed their knees. Radio had its beginnings, Hollywood became a national institution, American life and habits were transformed utterly by the automobile. Sacco and Vanzetti were convicted and (seven years later) executed; John Thomas Scopes willfully and unlawfully taught the public-school pupils of Rhea County, Tennessee, the Darwinian theory of evolution, thereby contradicting the story of creation revealed in Genesis. The national heroes were Babe Ruth and Charles Lindbergh. And at the end came the "crash" that ushered in the Great Depression and seemingly laid everything waste—an event that, for a long time, Mencken stubbornly refused to admit had happened.

In brief, it was a period extraordinarily rich in materials for the student of Americana—there has perhaps never been a comparable one—and he was the last person in the world to pass up the opportunity to make the most of it. "Life in America interests me," he wrote, "not as a moral phenomenon, but simply as a gaudy spectacle,"[4] and his comments on that spectacle made him, in words of *The New York*

Times quoted earlier, "the most powerful private citizen in America," or—if you prefer the viewpoint of the Muskogee (Okla.) *Times-Democrat*—a "national menace."

But the point which I have been building up to at such length—and the passages from his writings quoted a few pages back should surely leave little doubt about it—is that this transition from the literary thrust of *The Smart Set* to the political and sociological one of the *Mercury* in no way represented a change of interest on his part. Rather it represented a return to what had been his original and basic interests. Even this statement is not entirely true if it gives the impression that he had abandoned them for a dozen years or more and was now at last coming back to them. He had never abandoned them at all. During that whole period on *The Smart Set*—from 1908, that is, to 1923—he was really leading two quite separate lives: that of magazine editor and literary critic in New York, and that of active newspaperman in Baltimore. In this latter career he had always been deeply absorbed in the political, social, and cultural issues of the day. While he mingled with authors and publishers in New York, in his own city he was writing about all of the things I have just mentioned: about the First World War and the supposed neutrality of the United States, about the Eighteenth Amendment and the Volstead Act, and on such a wide variety of current problems as taxes, blue laws, vice-crusading, the death penalty, higher education, and the virtues and evils of capitalism. In 1916 he traveled to Germany as a war correspondent, and en route home went out of his way to report on a revolution in Cuba; in 1921 he covered such widely differing events as the Jack Dempsey–Georges Carpentier heavyweight championship bout in Jersey City and the Armaments Limitation Conference in Washington.

The "Free Lance" column, which ran daily in the *Evening Sun* from 1911 to 1915, dealt in very large part with matters of local interest,* and an analysis of the "Monday Articles," which began in 1920 and continued without a break until 1938, shows that a substantial majority of them—perhaps two-thirds—were devoted to party politics, the holders of public office, the aspirants to such offices, their

---

*Cf. Mencken's own retrospective comment on the "Free Lance" in the autobiographical notes he supplied Isaac Goldberg in 1925: "I carried on endless wars against the Anti-Saloon League, the vice crusaders, the town boomers, and other such frauds. I also devoted a great deal of space to politics, particularly to local politics." (P. 95.)

campaigns against each other, and the questions that came before the people in local and national elections.

For above all it was politics, and the men who engaged in it, that fascinated him, and if Philip Wagner is right in saying that he was a newspaperman before anything else, then it was as a commentator on the political scene that he chiefly saw himself. The fascination, indeed, had begun long before—in his days on the *Herald* and his reportorial coverage of Baltimore's public figures in and out of City Hall. The "Untold Tales" which he wrote for the *Sunday Herald* throughout much of 1901 and 1902 may have been laid in ancient Rome, but they dealt with local issues in a farcical manner and the Roman senators and tribunes were thinly disguised caricatures of the city's officeholders and job seekers. If there was, for the time, an unaccustomed irreverence in these stories, there was really no malice in them; writing years later of his first encounter with politicians in the days when he was "an infant at the breast in journalism," he says:

> They shocked me a little at my first intimate contact with them, for I had never suspected, up to then, that frauds so bold and shameless could flourish in a society presumably Christian, and under the eye of a putatively watchful God. But as I came to know them better and better I began to develop a growing admiration, if not for their virtue, then at least for their professional virtuosity, and at the same time I discovered that many of them, in their private character, were delightful fellows, whatever their infamies *ex officio*. This appreciation of them, in the years following, gradually extended itself into a friendly interest in quacks of all sorts, whether theological, economic, military, philanthropic, judicial, literary, musical or sexual, and in the end that interest made me a sort of expert on the science of rooking the confiding, with a large acquaintance among practitioners of every species. But though I thus threw a wide net I never hauled in any fish who seemed to me to be the peers of the quacks political—not, indeed, by many a glittering inch. Even the Freudians when they dawned, and the chiropractors, and the penologists, and the social engineers, and the pedagogical wizards of Teachers College, Columbia, fell a good deal short of many Congressmen and Senators that I knew, not to mention Governors of sovereign American states. The Governors, in fact, were for long my favorites, for they constituted a class of extraordinarily protean rascals, and I remember a year when, of the forty-eight then in office, four were under indictment by grand juries, and one was actually in jail. Of the

rest, seven were active Ku Kluxers, three were unreformed labor leaders, two were dipsomaniacs, five were bogus war heroes, and another was an astrologer.[5]

In 1904, just a few months after the Great Fire that had leveled downtown Baltimore and while the *Herald* was still operating from makeshift quarters, he was sent out to cover his first pair of national conventions—that of the Republicans in Chicago from June 19 to 24, and the Democratic one in St. Louis from July 5 to 11. It was the beginning of a practice that would be a quadrennial highlight not only of his own career but of American journalism as well; one pictures him, still a mere twenty-four years old but with an astonishing background of reportorial experience and responsibility behind him, drinking in with wide-eyed and unabashed delight the cavortings of the assembled politicos. Malcolm Moos is probably not far wrong in comparing it to "the delights of a small boy attending his first circus."[6] The dispatches that he sent home offer a foretaste of what would become his standard method of treatment in after years:

> All day long the original Abraham Lincoln men and other patriarchs bemoaned the lack of excitement. State leaders sat about in the lobbies and sweltered gloomily, senators and bosses sought the cool and calm of their rooms, and the boys who yearned to voice their joy in the fact that they were Republicans and alive had to content themselves with discussing pitifully unimportant state contests and the weather.

If, admittedly, this is not quite yet the mature Mencken, the tone is not greatly different from that of the last convention he covered, forty-four years later, when Henry Wallace's Progressive Party assembled in Philadelphia in July 1948:

> The delegates, taking them one with another, have seemed to me to be of generally low intelligence, but it is easy to overestimate the idiocy of the participants in such mass paranoias. People of genuine sense seldom come to them, and when they do come, they are not much heard from. I believe that the percentage of downright half-wits has been definitely lower than in, say, the Democratic Convention of 1924, and not much higher than in the Democratic Convention of this year. This is not saying, of course, that there were not plenty of psychopaths present.

They rolled in from North, East, South and West, and among them were all of the types listed by Emerson in his description of the Chandos street convention of reformers, in Boston more than a century ago. Such types persist, and they do not improve as year chases year. They were born with believing minds, and when they are cut off by death from believing in a F.D.R., they turn inevitably to such Rosicrucians as poor Henry. The more extreme varieties, I have no doubt, would not have been surprised if a flock of angels had swarmed down from Heaven to help whoop him up, accompanied by the red dragon with seven heads and ten horns described in Revelation xii, 3. Alongside these feebleminded folk were gangs of dubious labor leaders, slick Communists, obfuscators, sore veterans, Bible-belt evangelists, mischievous college students, and such-like old residents of the Cave of Adullum.

In the years between he was to become a familiar figure at these conclaves, seated at a table in the press gallery, wearing a seersucker suit rumpled enough to give the impression that he had slept in it, horn-rimmed glasses perched on the very tip of his nose while he looked out over them with unrestrained glee at the proceedings on the platform, cigar clutched between his teeth, banging away with two fingers at the keyboard of his venerable typewriter as he ground out the copy to go back to the *Sun*. Afterward, "descending into the crypt below" to see what might offer in the way of a drink, he shared information, opinions, and experiences with his fellow newspapermen, most of whom stood in awe of his fearsome reputation and past achievements. Yet it is a matter of record, and there are reporters and columnists living today who will vouch for the fact, that he mingled easily with any and all of them, often perched at a counter in some one-arm restaurant with his legs draped around the stool while he cheerily argued down his peers and helped younger men with names, dates, facts, and figures out of the store of his prodigious memory. More than any other group of men with whom he associated—more than the writers, or the critics, or even the musicians of the Saturday Night Club—these were his colleagues.

He loved the conventions. Each time he would grumble that this was the end, he would never go to another, these all-night sessions were simply getting to be too much for him, he would fold up and have to be carried home on a shutter. Yet more than a year in advance of the next pair, the "Monday Articles" would start speculating on candidates, issues, and the probable direction that each party's platform would take, and when the time rolled around he was ready and impatient to be off. "There is something," he maintained,

> about a national convention that makes it as fascinating as a revival or a hanging. It is vulgar, it is ugly, it is stupid, it is tedious, it is hard upon both the higher cerebral centers and the *gluteus maximus,* and yet it is somehow charming. One sits through long sessions wishing heartily that all the delegates and alternates were dead and in hell—and then suddenly there comes a show so gaudy and hilarious, so melodramatic and obscene, so unimaginably exhilarating and preposterous that one lives a gorgeous year in an hour.[7]

But though it was at the conventions that the eminent statesmen and guides of the national destiny displayed themselves at their most knavish and idiotic, they provided plenty of copy in the intervening four years too, and not even the most intense absorption in matters literary, theological, or linguistic ever turned his attention entirely away from them. It was a rare month that did not bring forth at least one blast from his typewriter, and usually several; beginning in 1924, the editorials in the *Mercury* tended to concentrate very heavily on current issues, and in the last three volumes of the *Prejudices* literature and the other arts all but disappear to make way for political and social commentary.

To the end of his days he remained unalterably convinced that the politician, far from being the servant of the people, was in point of fact their worst possible enemy. His chief aims in life were (*a*) to get a job; (*b*) to hold on to it as long as he possibly could; and (*c*) having gotten it, to augment to the limit the power that it gave him. Nothing that he did was inspired by any other purpose. The art and mystery that he pursued were thus essentially and incurably antisocial. The whole American political system was based on the assumption that politicians could be divided into two groups—good ones and bad ones— and any election campaign was ostensibly an effort to turn the bad ones out of office and put good ones in their place; but to Mencken this was the sheerest nonsense. "If experience teaches us anything at all," he maintained, "it teaches us this: that a good politician, under democracy, is quite as unthinkable as an honest burglar. His very existence, indeed, is a standing subversion of the public good in every rational sense."[8]

Thus the best that could be said about any of them was that there were some who were not quite as bad as others, and even of the ones who started out as relatively decent and honorable men the sad truth was that their failure was ignominious and their success disgraceful. Over a period of more than forty years Mencken had few kind words for any of them, and an anthology of the judgments he made on the public figures of his era would result in a sizable *Schimpflexikon.* I limit myself here only to what he said about those men who occupied the highest office in the land during the period in which he was a newspaperman. After he ceased to be one he wrote: "So far as I can recall, I have never written a single commendatory word of any sitting President of the United States."[9] As I hope to show, this statement is not entirely true; but the exceptions are so rare that for all practical purposes they prove the rule.

Theodore Roosevelt "in a political career of nearly forty years . . . was never even fair to an opponent." He was "blatant, crude, overly confidential, devious, tyrannical, vainglorious, sometimes quite childish." His successor, Taft, was characterized by "native laziness and shiftlessness"; if he had been elected to a second term it might have sufficed to paralyze the government. This language may sound strong, but it is really quite restrained in comparison to what he wrote about the next President, Woodrow Wilson, toward whom he cherished a hatred bordering upon monomania. "The archangel Woodrow" was "a typical Puritan," "a bogus Liberal," "the perfect model of the Christian cad." He did more than any other one man "to break down democratic self-government in America and substitute a Cossack despotism, unintelligent and dishonest." "More money was stolen under Wilson than under all other Presidents put together."

Harding was "the numskull Gamaliel," a "stonehead" and "ignoramus" whose platform resembled "words scrawled on a wall by feeble-minded children." For the literary style of his addresses Mencken coined the word "Gamalielese"; it was "so bad that a sort of grandeur creeps into it." His cabinet was made up of "three highly intelligent men of self-interest, six jackasses and one common crook." Calvin Coolidge was "simply a professional politician, and a very petty, sordid and dull one"; "a cheap and trashy fellow, deficient in sense and almost devoid of any notion of honor—in brief, a dreadful little cad." His record as President was "almost a blank . . . his chief feat during five years and seven months in office was to sleep more than any other

President." Reviewing Coolidge's autobiography in the *Mercury* for January 1930, some two years after he had left office, Mencken wrote: "Having got through his appalling self-revelation, horrified and yet spellbound, I hasten to apologize to the readers of this great family magazine for my writings about him in the past. He was, as President, a great deal worse than I ever made him out—nay, a great deal worse than I ever, in my most despairing moments, suspected."

"Lord Hoover," who followed upon Coolidge, had "a natural instinct for the low, disingenuous, fraudulent manipulations that constitute the art and mystery of politics under democracy." He was "a politician of a highly practical sort, eager for the main chance, and anything but squeamish."

But it remained for Hoover's successor, Franklin Delano Roosevelt, to bring out the ultimate resources in Mencken's vocabulary. It is rather curious that during the campaign of 1932, and even through the first few months that FDR was in office, Mencken wrote of him in mild and—so far as it was possible for him—even in admiring terms. In the "Monday Article" for July 5, 1932, he spoke of him as "one of the most charming of men," and observed that he transcended his physical handicap "in a most gallant manner." With the election out of the way and Roosevelt installed in the White House, he declared in the same place on March 13, 1933, albeit with a certain amount of reservation, that he had "the utmost confidence in his good intentions" and that he had acted so far "with courage, sense and due restraint." He was "a far better man than Wilson, and on all counts." Even so late as the following January (1934) he thought that the plain people recognized the President "to be what is called for a lack of better word, a gentleman," and declared that he was "his own man."

But after that the tune begins to change. As Roosevelt assumed powers that no President, at least since Lincoln, had had, as he launched his programs for social reform and devalued the dollar and sought to pack the Supreme Court, Mencken's face became red with indignation and resentment, and finally with hatred. Thereafter he hurled against him invective that he had not used for any holder of the presidential office since Wilson. He became "Roosevelt II." One of the "Monday Articles" satirically suggested that, under Article V of the Constitution, he proclaim himself king *de jure*, since he already was *de facto*. His premises were "so false as to be absurd," and the conclusions he drew from them were "always dubious and sometimes completely idiotic." "His constant appeals to class envy and hatred," Mencken charged, "and his frequent repudiation of his own categorical pledges have stripped him of every plausible claim to the name of statesman."

The Rooseveltian conception of government was that of a "milch cow with 125,000,000 teats." The Brain Trust was made up exclusively of "quacks," and the New Deal was a "political racket"; in its whole philosophy there was only one genuinely new and original idea, and that was the proposition that "whatever A earns really belongs to B. A is any honest and industrious man or woman; B is any drone or jackass." "A gang of professional politicians," he growled, "advised and abetted by a gang of half-educated pedagogues, non-constitutional lawyers, starry-eyed uplifters and other such sorry wizards, is engaged upon the performance of a series of stupendous bogus miracles, all of them extremely expensive to the taxpayer."

But as the Second World War drew on and the *Sunpapers* allied themselves ever more closely with Roosevelt's foreign policy, Mencken found it increasingly difficult and awkward to say what he thought. His articles appearing on the same page with the *Sun's* editorials simply made no sense. He considered the paper's position to be "insane," but there was no way he could control it and so he did again what he had done a quarter of a century before: he stopped writing for it, though remaining on the staff as a "consultant." Retiring to the house on Hollins Street, he gave himself over to the supplements to *The American Language* and the writing of his autobiography. Thereafter newspaper and magazine readers heard little from him. But his last word on the subject was not yet spoken; so late as 1948, just a few months before his stroke, he was announcing gleefully that "Truman is as transparent a fraud as Roosevelt ever was, and far more of a fool."*

---

*I have omitted William Jennings Bryan from this catalogue for the rather obvious reason that he was never President, but it would be unthinkable to leave him out of any study of Menckenian judgments on public figures. Certainly he ran neck and neck with Wilson and FDR as the politician whom Mencken most thoroughly detested. In the famous obituary which he wrote immediately following Bryan's death in Dayton, Tennessee, just a few days after the end of the Scopes trial, and while other papers were speaking with appropriate respect of the departed statesman, he laid about him with unrestrained ferocity: "He was . . . a charlatan, a mountebank, a zany without sense or dignity. His career brought him into contact with the first men of his time; he preferred the company of rustic ignoramuses. It was hard to believe, watching him at Dayton, that he had travelled, that he had been received in civilized societies, that he had been a high officer of state. He seemed only a poor clod like those around him, deluded by a childish theology,

That many of these judgments were uncharitable is a point that scarcely needs laboring; not quite so obvious, perhaps, is the fact that a lot of them were also untrue. As a political prophet Mencken was anything but reliable, and more than once his predictions were clearly the result of wishful thinking on his part. In 1931 he considered it "highly probable" that Hoover would be re-elected to a second term. In 1935 he had a "suspicion" that the "More Abundant Life" would be dead on the Tuesday following the first Monday in November of the next year; as it turned out, Roosevelt won the most sweeping electoral majority in modern American history, carrying every state but Maine and Vermont, and Mencken took sour comfort in reflecting that while the plain people were obviously with him today, they might very well turn against him tomorrow. The error for which he was chiefly famous was one that, in fact, he never really made: writing of the same campaign in the *Mercury* for March 1936, he declared that if Roosevelt could be beaten at all he could be beaten "with a Chinaman, or even a Republican." Somehow this got distorted into the statement that even a Chinaman could beat Roosevelt, and it took him a long time to live it down.

Perhaps the most amusing tale about his mistakes in judgment concerns the Democratic Convention of 1924 in New York—the one that ran from June 24 to July 29 and required 103 ballots to nominate John W. Davis as the party's candidate for President. As the interminable politicking ran down toward its end, Mencken left the press box to send off to the *Sun* a dispatch that began:

> Everything is uncertain in this convention but one thing: John W. Davis will never be nominated.

---

full of an almost pathological hatred of all learning, all human dignity, all beauty, all fine and noble things. He was a peasant come home to the barnyard. Imagine a gentleman, and you have imagined everything that he was not." ("In Memoriam: W.J.B.": *Chrestomathy*, p. 245.)

As far back as 1918 he had written in *Damn! A Book of Calumny* (p. 68): "As for William Jennings Bryan . . . the whole of his political philosophy may be reduced to two propositions, neither of which is true. The first is the proposition that the common people are wise and honest, and the second is the proposition that all persons who refuse to believe it are scoundrels. Take away the two, and all that would remain of Jennings would be a somewhat greasy bald-headed man with his mouth open." So late as 1943, in *Heathen Days* (p. 286), he reaffirmed that "Bryan was essentially and incurably a yap."

Returning a few minutes later, he was informed by one of his colleagues that Davis had just been nominated. For a moment he was too stunned to speak; then, recovering himself, he snapped: "I hope those idiots in Baltimore will have sense enough to strike out the negative!"*

2 HIS OPPOSITION TO ROOSEVELT and the whole New Deal scheme of social reform, coming relatively late in his career, points up an attitude that had characterized him from the beginning and only hardened as time went on. In brief, his political views were those of a dyed-in-the-wool conservative. Recognition of this fact surprised many of those who read him in his own lifetime, and it still does even today; large numbers of people have come to Mencken under the impression that he was a radical, or at all events a thoroughgoing liberal, and then been shocked to find out that in politics he was as right-wing as, in the area of sex, he was puritanical. They usually resent it, and feel that he has played a rather shabby trick on them.

But he was himself under no illusions as to where he stood on such matters, and never tried to pass his position off as other than what it was. Writing to his friend Ernest Boyd in 1920, when he was still only forty years old, he admitted that "it is hard for me to think in Liberal terms. I grow more and more reactionary as I grow older."[10] In an article appearing in the Chicago *Tribune* in 1926, after remarking that the usual charge made in those days against any American holding unpopular ideas was that he was a Bolshevik in receipt of Russian gold, he went on to say: "It has been leveled at me so often that probably a majority of the persons who have heard of me at all believe it, and there are even dismal days when I half believe it myself, though I have been denouncing Socialism publicly for twenty years, and am, in fact, an incurable Tory in politics. A short while ago a Boston critic, becoming aware of the latter fact by some miracle, at once proceeded

---

*Thus the legend, which Malcolm Moos credits to one of Mencken's most distinguished colleagues on the *Sun*, Mark S. Watson. However, I can find no basis for it either in Mencken's typed dispatches for the convention or in the *Sun* itself.

to denounce me because my radicalism, as he thought he had discovered, was bogus."11*

Here, if anywhere, his family background and early training account for the direction that his thought would take. There was, first of all, his solid German bourgeois ancestry. There was, secondly, the essential stability and resistance to change typical of middle-class life in a city like Baltimore at the end of the nineteenth century. Finally, August Mencken was, in at least a modest sense of the word, a capitalist, and like capitalists everywhere and at all times, he bristled at the idea that the government had any right to tell him how to run his business. He also took a very dim view of the progressive labor legislation that was getting under way in those years, and would tolerate no union in his shop. His employees were treated well, and perhaps even better than the average, but it simply never occurred to him that he had an obligation to them over and above a just wage for services rendered. The thought that the government might have an obligation to take care of those who could not take care of themselves would have led him to prophesy formally the end of the Republic!

His son, working in the office of August Mencken & Bro. during that brief period between graduation from Poly and becoming a reporter on the *Morning Herald,* may have developed little enthusiasm for the tobacco business, but he at least absorbed thoroughly the philosophy that guided its operations. Very early, too, he noted a clear and basic distinction among men. There were those who, either by native talent or through a fortunate combination of circumstances, got on in the world, and there were those who, lacking natural gifts or because circumstances just went against them, did not. He, like his father, happened to belong to the former class. One might feel a certain pity for those less fortunate, but it would be useless and a waste of time to try to take any measures against what was, after all, an inexorable law of nature.

The distinction, while not precisely the same as that between the "civilized minority" and the "vast herd of human blanks," is at least related to it and has its origin in the same set of premises. The ones who

---

*But almost a score of years later, in one of the unpublished autobiographical notes written about 1941, he said: "It always amuses me to be denounced as a conservative, as happens almost every time I am mentioned at all. I am actually an extreme radical. . . ."

cannot make it constitute for the most part the "herd" and are the dupes and eager followers of any mountebank who promises them the New Jerusalem; by contrast, the chief mark of the independent and superior man is that he pays his own way and asks in return only to be let alone.

It followed, then, that government, insofar as one was called upon to think about it at all, was a distant and rather shadowy thing that seldom intruded itself into the considerations of such a person. The superior man, in fact, made it something of a point of honor to have as little to do with it as possible. It existed, really, for but two purposes: to repel any possible foreign enemy and to protect its citizens from lawless elements in their own midst. Beyond this it had no reason for being. In the absence of any threat from outside and in a society that was peaceable and orderly, it belonged very much in the background of life. "The ideal government of all reflective men," Mencken believed, "from Aristotle to Herbert Spencer, is one which lets the individual alone—one which barely escapes being no government at all."[12]

Unhappily, though, the very fact that this was an ideal meant that it was something never even remotely approximated in practice. In practice, "all government, in its essence, [was] a conspiracy against the superior man: its one permanent object [was] to police him and cripple him."[13] Why? For the simple reason that the superior man, being devoid of any illusions or sentimentalities, could see with unsparing gaze the weaknesses of the government he lived under and so might be moved to propose changing it; and change was the thing that any existing government feared above all else. Change was an invasion of its own prerogatives, and he who advocated such a thing, for whatever reason, was its natural enemy. "Thus one of its primary functions is to regiment men by force, to make them as much alike as possible and as dependent upon one another as possible, to search out and combat originality among them."[14]

As far back as 1908, in the Nietzsche volume, Mencken had argued:

> Knowledge and not government brought us the truth that made us free. Government, in its very essence, is opposed to all increase of knowledge. Its tendency is always toward permanence and against change. It is unthinkable without some accepted scheme of law or morality, and such schemes . . . stand in direct antithesis to every effort to find the absolute truth. Therefore, it is plain that the progress of humanity, far

from being the result of government, has been made entirely without its aid and in the face of its constant and bitter opposition.[15]

In opposing this threat to its own permanence, in holding in check any knowledge or originality among its subjects, it would not stop at any means, however base. And to say this was to say that it was "an agency engaged wholesale, and as a matter of solemn duty, in the performance of acts which all self-respecting individuals refrain from as a matter of common decency."[16]

Again, why should this be so? Because however much one might voice pious platitudes about government by law, the plain truth was that it was exercised by men. There has always been a tendency to think of it as an abstract and impersonal force, almost occult and mystical in nature, distinct from the people and standing above them, and if this were the case then it would indeed let most private individuals alone. In actual fact, of course, it is no such thing. Every form of government, and every law, is man-made, and the kind of man attracted to these things is seldom the one with any genuinely superior gifts and abilities. No other human pursuit carries with it more appeal for the mountebank, the charlatan, the fraud; in no other area of activity does incompetence carry with it such assurance of success.

True, an ordinarily decent and well-meaning man might now and then be tempted to enter the field of politics. He might even come into it with certain ideals of honor and service. But the moment his hat was in the ring the ideals had to be thrown overboard; weighed down with them he could not hope to survive for an instant. In order to make a go of it at all, he either had to kowtow to the mob, promising it all sorts of things which he knew perfectly well he would never be able to deliver, or he had to knuckle under to political bosses whose patronage was indispensable to his success. Failure to do either the one or the other meant the sacrifice of his career; the performance of either meant the sacrifice of his honor. "No other man," Mencken thought, "confronts so hard a choice. It is still possible for a medical man, or even a lawyer, to be completely honorable and yet to make a relatively decent living, but it is virtually impossible for a politician. The minute he makes a serious effort in that direction he loses office, and thus ceases to be a going concern."[17]

Even at best, though, such misguided idealists rarely entered the political arena. The kind of man who did was the one who was attracted to it by the prospect of power that it gave him over others and by the profit to be reaped. "Politicians," Mencken charged,

> . . . are seldom if ever moved by anything rationally describable as public spirit; there is actually no more public spirit among them than among so many burglars or street-walkers. Their purpose, first, last and all the time, is to promote their private advantage, and to that end, and that end alone, they exercise all the vast powers that are in their hands. Sometimes the thing they want is mere security in their jobs; sometimes they want gaudier and more lucrative jobs; sometimes they are content with their jobs and their pay but yearn for more power. Whatever it is they seek, whether security, greater ease, more money or more power, it has to come out of the common stock, and so it diminishes the shares of all other men.[18]

Mencken knew perfectly well that men who could with justice be called great had entered the field of government, and that they had not been moved to do so by any desire for private gain or advantage. In more than one place he speaks in glowing terms of Frederick the Great, whom he regarded as the most enlightened monarch in modern European history. If he had a high opinion of Bismarck, it could be argued that this was because the founder of the modern state of Germany was by way of being a collateral ancestor.* He admired George Washington, "the first, and perhaps also the last, American gentleman," but felt that Washington, who operated a still on his Mount Vernon estate, and swore freely, and lifted his eyebrow at the sight of a pretty ankle, would probably be in jail in the America of the 1920's. He had a similar admiration and respect for Jefferson, but lamented that it was one of "the fine ironies of history that the party which professes to follow him has been led almost exclusively, for a hundred years, by leaders wholly unable to grasp the elements of his political philosophy. It stands as far from him today as the Methodist Board of Temperance, Prohibition and Public Morals stands

---

*Luise Wilhelmine Mencken, a celebrated beauty of the court of Friedrich Wilhelm II at Potsdam, married in 1806 Captain Karl Wilhelm Ferdinand von Bismarck, and nine years later gave birth to a son who was destined to become the famous "Iron Chancellor." She was the daughter of Anastasius Mencken, who was in turn descended from Lüder Mencken, "Das Orakel des Rechtes." (Cf. pp. 34–5.)

from Christ. That is to say, it stands as far off as it is humanly possible to get."[19]

No, it was not men like these who constituted the ordinary run of politicians. These were the colossal exceptions, and the reason they stood so far above the average was that they were superior by their very nature, members of the civilized minority. They were not part of the mob, and would not be swayed by it, and they could not be bought by it. Whatever they had contributed to the progress of government had been the result of their own genius and efforts, and those efforts had usually been met by the fiercest opposition of those beneath them in the scale of humanity. It was the politicians of lesser kidney, with no more qualifications than a shrewd knowledge of mob psychology and a gift for preying upon it in every conceivable form, who got into government in order to use it not for the public good but for their private advantage. They were out for themselves and themselves alone—at best a necessary evil, at worst intolerable nuisances and irreconcilable enemies of the common weal.

Such men have occurred at all times in history and under all forms of government. They are to be found in monarchy, in oligarchy, even in aristocracy. But Mencken firmly believed, and spent a very large part of his life maintaining, that nowhere have they occurred more often or in a more vicious and degrading form than in the United States of America in the twentieth century, for the simple reason that America was the homeland and outstanding example of that "universal murrain" of the Western world, democracy.

3 NOTES ON DEMOCRACY is probably Mencken's least convincing and satisfying work. He himself thought of it as the first volume in a trilogy, of which the other two parts were to be *Treatise on the Gods* and *Treatise on Right and Wrong*, and together the three books would constitute a definitive statement of his *Weltanschauung*, his whole political, religious, and moral philosophy. But the differences are glaring. The *Treatises* were conceived and written as books; they are intimately related to one another, but each has the thematic and artistic unity that comes from a single conception and purpose. They were entirely new, and the advertising

for them made a point of the fact that no part of their contents had previously appeared elsewhere.

The *Notes*, on the other hand, not only lacks any obvious connection with the *Treatises*, but in itself seems disorganized and without central design. He had started accumulating materials for it as far back as 1910, but in a preface which he inserted into the bound typescript that now rests in the Pratt's Mencken Room he says that the actual writing was not begun until the early autumn of 1925. Even then there were interruptions: first his mother's illness and her death in December of that year, followed by the celebrated "Hatrack" case in Boston, which preoccupied him throughout much of the spring of 1926. He completed it that summer, and Knopf brought the book out in October. Worked into much new matter were old pieces from the *Evening Sun*, *The Smart Set*, and, most recently, the *Mercury;* all of this, he says, was rewritten, but there is no getting around the fact that the scissors-and-paste job shows.

The Mencken humor is present, of course, on almost every page, but here, for perhaps the only time in all his writing, it becomes harsh and now and then even strident. His denunciations of the democratic theory of government are so violent that, in the end, he all but defeats his own aim. It will be remembered that he described his attitude toward religion as one of "amiable skepticism"; toward democracy it was apparently impossible for him to be even so much as amiable.

Most of the reviews, he noted in that same typed preface, were "furiously hostile." Those which might be considered at all favorable deplored the content in the same breath with which they paid tribute to the style; Rebecca West, for example, writing in the New York *Herald Tribune*, was sure that none of the English authors whom he had so much maligned over the years would ever have produced "a book so shallow, so slick, so innocent of argument and so empty of everything else," and Walter Lippmann thought that if the typical Menckenian treatment were taken away there would remain "only a collection of trite and somewhat confused ideas." But he was prepared, of course, for this sort of thing; as far back as 1920, in a letter to Burton Rascoe, he had speculated that the ideas contained in the book might be so explosive he would have to have it published abroad.[20]*

---

*In 1930 the Berlin publishing house of Widerstands-Verlag brought out a German translation under the title *Demokratenspiegel*. The former Kaiser Wilhelm II, in exile at Doorn, thought so highly of it that he sent Mencken two autographed portrait photos of himself.

Nevertheless, a bit after the manner of Nietzsche he persuaded himself that its time would come: in a copy that he autographed for Knopf he wrote: "Dear Alfred: In 5 or 6 years this book will begin to be read. In 10 or 12 years it will begin to sell."

The prediction, alas, turned out to be rather wide of the mark. Of all the books of his maturity, it is today the one which is most completely forgotten, and even admiring biographers like Manchester and Bode tend to apologize for it.

Yet in spite of all this, it cannot be omitted from any study of Mencken's thought. However extravagant it may be, however unfair some of its judgments and unreasonable some of its claims, there is not a line in it that is intellectually dishonest or that was written with the mere intent to shock. He really did loathe democracy, and he really did believe, too, that it had reached its *reductio ad absurdum* in the United States. He defined it as "that system of government under which the people, having 60,000,000 native-born adult whites to choose from, including thousands who are handsome and many who are wise, pick out a Coolidge to be head of the state." It was, he averred, "the theory that the common people know what they want, and deserve to get it good and hard." Democracy, he wrote again, "is the art and science of running the circus from the monkey-cage."* Such charges run all through his writings, even in places where the immediate subject matter has only a very indirect connection with politics; there are scores of unpublished notes—quick jottings perhaps never really intended for publication at all—that say the same thing and in more vitriolic language.

Its whole ideology, of course, was reared on a proposition that he simply found it impossible to accept, and his inability to accept it was what distinguished him from practically all other Americans and made their reaction to him so "furiously hostile." That proposition is the one set forth most succinctly in the second paragraph of the Declaration of Independence, in the statement that all men are created equal. Nothing, it seemed to him, could be further from the truth. If the first-rate men of the world did constitute a distinct and separate species having little in common with the lower orders of humanity, if there was a minority that was naturally intelligent and a vast majority that was

---

*These definitions, and more like them, appear at various times and in various places in the Menckenian canon. A few are gathered together in the "Sententiae" section of the *Chrestomathy*, pp. 622–23.

naturally and incurably stupid, then it was idiotic to claim that there was any kind of equality between them. All the available evidence, in fact, ran in precisely the opposite direction.

This notion, Mencken believed, had had its origin not among the inferior classes themselves but amid a group of sentimental idealists belonging on a somewhat higher social level. They were the direct ancestors of today's liberals, with a "stale Christian bilge" yet running through their veins. At the outset their poetic theorizing made relatively little mark on the proletariat, for the latter, then as always, were much less concerned with political philosophies than they were with finding enough to eat and devising ways to get more money for doing less work. Even the two great historical events that are usually thought to have transformed democracy from theory into practice—the American and French revolutions—had little immediate effect: Mencken was convinced that the Founding Fathers had had no belief in democracy whatever and had framed the Constitution "to hold the superior few harmless against the inferior many,"[21] and the only tangible result of the French Revolution, he held, had been to throw out one tyranny in order to make way for another.

It was not until the wars of the nineteenth century had come to an end, leaving Europe drained and exhausted, that the democratic idea began to filter down gradually from the metaphysicians to the mob. The proletarian, contemplating himself, found a new and hitherto unsuspected worth in his image. His condition had plainly improved a great deal: he was no longer a slave or serf but a free man, he had certain rights which he was assured were his by virtue of his human nature and which thus could not be taken away from him, and he was at liberty to criticize those who ruled him without any fear of reprisal. Hence arose this leveling process, this idea of the essential equality of all men.

Now, if democratic man had been satisfied merely to claim this equality and rest his case there, it might have been possible to grant some validity to his argument, for in theory at least all men should be equal before the law, and all should have the same right, too, to give voice to their opinions, however asinine. But he was not: he was really even less interested in the idea of equality than were his betters. Having gone so far, he could not help but go all the way, and accomplish—in Nietzschean terms—a "transvaluation of values"; in other words, he was not only as good as those who ranked above him on the social and economic scale, but on all counts better. And to argue this much was to argue further that "there is a mystical merit, an esoteric and ineradicable rectitude, in the man at the bottom of the scale—that inferiority, by some strange magic, becomes a sort of superiority—nay, the superiority of superiorities."[22]

This, for Mencken, constituted the very essence of democracy—and constituted, likewise, its ultimate and unspeakable obscenity. To hold that "all moral excellence, and with it all pure and unfettered sagacity, reside in the inferior four-fifths of mankind"[23] was to hold, too, that the opinion of some illiterate Tennessee backwoodsman on the theory of evolution deserved as much respect as Huxley's, or more; it was to hold that any ignorant and unprincipled political boss was on a level of statesmanship with Frederick or Bismarck, or that a county crossroads magistrate had as much wisdom in the field of jurisprudence as Justinian. Finally it was to hold, as democracy unquestionably did, that the masses of the plain people were competent to govern themselves—that the only guidance they needed came to them from on high and the decisions they arrived at by the simple process of taking a vote were, after the manner of Rousseau's "general will," always right.

"Perhaps—" Mencken growled with heavy irony, "but on what evidence, by what reasoning, and for what motives!"[24]

What he failed to see, or what for his purposes it might have been self-defeating to admit, is that the theory of democracy enunciated by the Fathers, and before them by such English political philosophers as Locke, does not necessarily make equality an absolute or think of it in mathematical terms. To say that all men are equal is by no means to say that they are all the same. Even the most extreme egalitarian could hardly deny, and presumably no one of them ever has denied, that between one man and another there may be very great differences in the area of physical strength and endurance. They could hardly deny, either, that there are differences just as great in wealth and social position, though here the admission that these inequalities exist is offset by the Socialist or Marxian insistence that they are unnatural and ought to be eliminated. And a sound democratic philosophy must likewise concede that there are enormous gradations in human intelligence, that some men are richly endowed with it and others are not, and that some by their very nature are leaders while others are followers.

Thus the theory of democracy does not really have to maintain that the poor hind in the backwoods of Tennessee is Huxley's intellectual equal, or that the corrupt precinct boss has the same high gifts of statesmanship that an inscrutable Providence saw fit to bestow upon Frederick the Great. On the contrary, it recognizes and admits such diversities. All it presumes to argue is that, regardless of them, the essential nature of all men is the same and that no man has a greater (or lesser) degree of humanity than any other. And this much being granted, it follows that despite any differences in strength or wealth or intellectual acumen, all men have the same human dignity and all possess the same inalienable rights.

But this much, of course, was just what Mencken simply could not grant. We have seen that he was willing to accord all men equality before the law (though on his own principles it is difficult to see how he could consistently do this), and he was just as willing to accord to every man the same absolutely illimitable right of free speech. But if there was really such a thing as an "inferior four-fifths of mankind," then the logical inference had to be that one-fifth was superior. Obviously physical strength could have nothing to do with this superiority, since it was entirely beside the point, and just as obviously wealth and social position could have nothing to do with it either, since the most stupid man could at least be born to these even if he lacked the brains to attain to them by his own effort. The superiority must lie, therefore, in such largely innate qualities as intelligence, breeding, decency, tolerance, honesty, and a sense of honor—the very things, in short, that the inferior four-fifths were without and the presence of which they so deeply resented in their betters.

Resentment, in fact—Nietzsche's *ressentiment*—was the key to the whole absurd business. His distaste for democracy, Mencken admitted, might very well be due to some inner lack in him rather than in the theory itself, and he was inclined to find this lack in his utter incapacity for the feeling of envy. "That emotion," he said, "or weakness, or whatever you choose to call it, is quite absent from my make-up; where it ought to be there is a vacuum. In the face of another man's good fortune I am as inert as a curb broker before Johann Sebastian Bach."[25] Democracy, on the other hand, like its obverse side, Puritanism, had its source in envy, and to pump envy out of it would be to take away its very lifeblood. "There is only one sound argument for democracy," he went on a bit later in the same piece, "and that is the argument that it is a crime for any man to hold himself out as better than other men, and, above all, a most heinous offense for him to prove it." The essential thing about it was that it was "a device for strengthening and heartening the have-nots in their eternal war upon the haves."[26]

This war, then, had but one motivation—the inferior man's envy of his betters—and it was carried on with but one aim in mind—that of bringing them down to his own degraded and miserable level. He waged it in the most ferocious manner and without the slightest concept of fairness or honor. It was a mark of the superior man to view the acts and ideas of others with a certain magnanimity and tolerance; the inferior man's resentment of those who ranked above him on the intellectual or social scale permitted him to display no tolerance whatever. Again, the superior man was perfectly willing to grant that opinions which differed from his own might, after all, have something to be said for them; the inferior man could not for a moment admit that any view other than his own had a right to exist. Finally, it was characteristic of the superior man to be open and receptive to new ideas and at least give them a hearing; on the contrary, new ideas were precisely what the inferior man dreaded most. They were unfamiliar and threatening, they made demands upon his limited mental powers to which he was incapable of responding, they cast doubt on the threadbare clichés by which he had hitherto lived. Therefore he made every possible effort to put them down; those who originated them and those who defended them were, for him, agents of the devil.

But he could not do this alone. In his acute awareness of his own weakness, in his envy of the superior man's quiet and self-assured strength, democratic man simply had to be part of a group. Otherwise he could accomplish nothing, and would be terrified by his own loneliness. The group had to be made up of souls like himself (and here, of course, we get back again to Nietzsche's concept of the "herd"), and it demanded from its members total acquiescence and conformity to its narrow body of ideas. Whoever presumed to doubt was not only a traitor but a heretic. It was one of the shibboleths of the democratic idea that it respected and guaranteed the rights of the minority, but Mencken never ceased to point out that under democracy in practice the minority had no rights at all, for the simple reason that it stood in opposition to what the majority had decreed to be true.

Finally the mob must have its leaders—and this is the origin of that most contemptible of all figures, the democratic politician. Since

"Nature, it must be obvious, is opposed to democracy—and whoso goes counter to nature must expect to pay the penalty,"[27] and since "in democratic nations everything noble and of good account tends to decay and smell badly,"[28] it followed that the political leader in a democracy could not be honest even if he wanted to be, and must inevitably become corrupt even if he started out with the best of intentions. To be a leader at all he had to be as cheap, ignorant, grasping, dishonest, and ignoble as those he led. In Mencken's most often used words, running like a leitmotif through forty years of political writing, he was a "fraud," a "mountebank," and a "charlatan."

He was at once the master of the mob and its abject slave. He knew how to play upon its immemorial fears and prejudices, and toward that end he used every device of his brummagem rhetoric to stir it up for his own purposes. He would promise it anything in return for his job, or for keeping his job, or for augmenting the power which the job gave him. He would offer it the New Jerusalem in a thousand and one preposterous forms, knowing full well that he could never make good but cynically confident that the mob, in its ignorance, would mistake the promise for the gift and continue to follow him blindly.

At the same time he had to grovel ignominiously before it. "One of the greatest defects of democracy is that it forces every candidate for office, even the highest, into frauds and chicaneries that are wholly incompatible with the most elementary decency and honor."[29] It was necessary for him at all times to keep a careful eye on how the mob was blowing and make sure that he blew with it. Did his constituency, inflamed by the demagogues of the Methodist Board of Temperance, Prohibition and Public Morals and the Anti-Saloon League, decide that alcoholic beverages were a great evil and ought to be put down? Then the democratic politician, concealing the flask of corn liquor in his hip pocket, had to bawl for Prohibition too. Did the mob, simply tiring of the whole imposture or swayed by another and opposite group of breast-beaters, call for Repeal? Then he had to hastily unsay today what he had said yesterday and trust that none of those on whose votes he counted would have enough brains to note the inconsistency. His own career was as full of alarms and apprehensions as those he putatively served, since he knew quite well that the instant he misjudged them, they would turn against him and go running after some other mountebank—which would mean that he would be out of a job.

"The average citizen of a democracy," Mencken concluded, "is a goose-stepping ignoramus and poltroon. . . . The average democratic politician, of whatever party, is a scoundrel and a swine."[30]

This was not to say, of course, that there were no sound elements at all in the democratic philosophy; obviously there were. Equality before the law, to repeat, was one of them, and free speech was another, and the limitations that it placed upon government could hardly fail to be a very powerful consideration to a man who believed, as he did, that the ideal form of government was one which came close to being no government at all. These were genuine values, and hence to be cherished. The point was that no "professional whooper-up of democracy" really believed in them, at least not to the extent of being ready to stand up for them at whatever cost or when they happened to run counter to his own personal welfare. In practice, for the most part, they were catchphrases designed to attract the mob and hold it enthralled. Every time democratic enthusiasm had risen to orgiastic heights—as for example in a war—they were usually abandoned very quickly.

Moreover, most such values had not come up from the mob at all, since it was as incapable of originating such highly abstract ideas as it was of appreciating them when they were received from others. They came down, rather, from country gentlemen, from philosophers, from poets, even—on occasion—from kings. They were by-products of a political system which attached far more importance to common decency than it did to equality. "We are dependent for whatever good flows out of democracy," Mencken maintained, "upon men who do not believe in democracy."[31]

These caveats against government of the people, by the people, and for the people applied to it wherever it had raised itself, alike in all places and at all times, but nowhere had democracy become such an offensive and disgusting spectacle as in that country which claimed to be its birthplace in modern times and to embody it in all its perfection—namely, the United States.

Mencken's assaults upon his native land constitute, as everyone must know, a major theme in his writings—perhaps, indeed, *the* major theme—and they are of course not confined by any means to its politics but spread over into its arts, business, education, general culture, and history, as well as its own idea of how that history ought to be told.

They are scored, as he himself once wrote, "in the manner of Berlioz, for ten thousand trombones *fortissimo.*" Again it may be necessary to emphasize that this heavy orchestration was not for mere effect or to draw attention to himself; undoubtedly he enjoyed the reaction it got, and the attacks on him that it inspired simply led in turn to even more vitriolic outbursts in the *Sun* and the *Mercury*, but he would have felt as he did, and would have said so with the same forthrightness, if he had been totally ignored.

He had nothing against patriotism; on the contrary, he insisted that he could both understand it and respect it. But the patriotic man had to have genuine reason to admire and love his country, and the country had to be worthy of his love. For that reason, he could not understand it when it was lavished upon such a land as the United States, "a coward and a hypocrite among nations. . . . I believe," he wrote to Isaac Goldberg, "that the worst curse of life in America is that it is impossible to think of one's self as an American without blushing."[32] From among literally thousands of examples, the famous denunciation at the beginning of the essay "On Being an American" in *Prejudices: Third Series* may be taken as wholly typical. After disposing in turn of the executive, legislative, and judicial branches of government, he directed his gaze toward the nation as a whole and announced that

> it is my fourth (and, to avoid too depressing a bill, final) conviction that the American people, taking one with another, constitute the most timorous, sniveling, poltroonish, ignominious mob of serfs and goose-steppers ever gathered under one flag in Christendom since the end of the Middle Ages, and that they grow more timorous, more sniveling, more poltroonish, more ignominious every day.[33]

The American people, not unnaturally, repaid the compliment. Mencken may have been the most famous newspaperman and magazine editor of his time, and perhaps the most influential one as well, but there can be no doubt whatever that he was also the most hated. A continual torrent of execration was heaped upon him from the beginning almost to the end of his active career, and some of it climbed pretty close to his own heights. When, during the First World War, he wrote fearlessly in his "Free Lance" column against the English and in favor of Germany, he was denounced as an agent of the Wilhelmstrasse, an intimate of "the German monster, Nietzsky" (who had been dead for almost twenty years), and a subverter of the national morals. When, in the postwar era, he criticized the ferocious witch-hunts of Attorney General A. Mitchell Palmer against so-called "Reds" and their blatant disregard of the most elementary civil rights, he was labeled a Bolshevik and invited to "go back" to Russia; this accusation was repeated regularly in the years that followed, to the point where, as we have seen, he confessed that there were times when he half believed it himself.

These onslaughts make up a very sizable portion of the eighty-odd clipping books which he laboriously assembled in his lifetime and bequeathed, along with his manuscripts and other memorabilia, to the Pratt Library. It was from them that, under his direction, Sara Haardt culled the examples published in *Menckeniana: A Schimpflexikon.* This incredible anthology of abuse could not, in the very nature of things, be exhaustive, but a real effort was made to keep it "representative." The temptation is strong to quote from page after page, but I limit myself here to just a few of the entries which express a certain amount of doubt about Mencken's 100% Americanism.

Thus the Boston *Transcript* declared that he was "fully 90% Prussian in all his utterances, and proud of it," while on the other hand the Lowell (Mass.) *Sun* dismissed him as simply "a British toady." The Richmond (Va.) *Times-Dispatch* accused him of being "an outstanding example of what constitutes a poor American." A Mr. Harold N. Coriell, writing in the New York *Herald Tribune*, called him "an offense in the nostrils of all Americans who love the ideals and best traditions of their country. He seems to love the putrid, the sinful, the low, and uses any occasion to air his antipathy to the customs and beliefs of the average American citizen." The *Arkansas Democrat* announced that he was "a former subject of the German Kaiser," and Mr. Cobb Hall, writing in the Chicago *Tribune*, wanted to know if he might timidly ask "why Mr. Mencken chooses to remain in this country."*

---

*Menckeniana: A Schimpflexikon (New York: Alfred A. Knopf, Inc., 1928). I hope it will be clear that these few examples give only a very imperfect idea of the riches to be found in this little volume—now, alas, out of print and obtainable only from rare-book dealers. Among the less imaginative epithets are those which characterize Mencken as "a pole-cat," "a howling hyena," "a parasite," "a mangy mongrel," "an affected ass," "an unsavory creature, putrid of soul," "a public nuisance," and "a literary stink-pot." The President-General of the Daughters of the American Revolution averred that "one Calvin Coolidge is worth ten thousand times ten thousand of this Mencken and his kind." "In the legitimate literary world," thought the Jackson (Miss.) *News,*

But though Mencken, like any artist who took pride in his work, might occasionally experience disappointment at the cool reception given to one of his books, he delighted in this sort of thing and went out of his way to invite more of it. Nothing gave him greater pleasure than to "stir up the animals." Their yapping at him, after all, only proved his point.

That point, "boiled down," amounted to this: "that the United States is essentially a commonwealth of third-rate men—that distinction is easy here because the general level of culture, of information, of taste and judgment, of ordinary competence is so low. . . . Third-rate men," he went on, "exist in all countries, but it is only here that they are in full control of the state, and with it of all the national standards."[34]

The remote explanation for this was to be found in the fact that the New World had originally been peopled not by bold adventurers, as the history books liked to make out, but by incompetents who had fled to it for no other reason than that they were unable to get on at home. They were not the superior men of their native lands, but rather the botched and the unfit. The typical American prides himself on being of pure Anglo-Saxon descent, but this is quite untrue because there is probably as much Celtic blood in him as Teutonic, and it was precisely this admixture, Mencken felt, that was responsible not only for his physical appearance but for much of the common stock of his ideas as well. The Celts (which is to say, the Scotch, Irish, and Welsh) are a very gloomy race and "far more given [than the English] to moral obsessions and religious fanaticism."[35] It is characteristic of them to exhibit a narrow conformity to a very narrow body of ideas, so that 95

"Mencken is a mountebank, a perpetual and preposterous pageant, a rantipole, a vain hysteric raging to and fro. He is a pariah, an outcast, a literary renegade." The Toronto *Star* described his style as "that of a trained elephant," while a writer in the St. Louis *Times* termed it "a mixture of cheap sarcasm and bombastic drivel." "His writing," according to the Mason City (Iowa) *Gazette*, "is the gibberish of an imbecile." The Tampa (Fla.) *Tribune* observed that "it would be a reflection on all the liars who ever lived to say that Mencken is a liar." One Donald Allen Farr, writing in *Public Relations*, asked, "Did Mencken ever write, as does the *Rotarian Magazine*, in love and kindliness toward mankind?" He was "the editor of perhaps the worst magazine in the United States." The *Idaho Statesman* accused him of holding nothing sacred, "from the character of George Washington to the divine form of beautiful woman." A writer in the Asheville (N.C.) *Citizen* complained that he had insulted not only Christian believers in the doctrine of the Virgin Birth "but the beautiful and kindly State of old Tennessee as well."

out of 100 of them will hold exactly the same opinion on a given subject and resent the five who believe differently. Plainly inferior to most other races, they are almost invariably worsted whenever they come into any kind of conflict with men of other—and hence better —stocks.*

Moreover, as the first settlers or their immediate descendants had moved away from the coastlands and on into the Midwest, they had tended to deteriorate still further. In the Appalachian highlands stretching down from Vermont to Georgia they had been cut off from every amenity of life and from anything that even remotely approximated culture. They were without resources for education, and would have been fearful of it if it had been offered to them. Their moral code

---

*At this point it is no longer possible to evade the question: "Was Mencken a racist?" Let it be said first of all that in the sense in which the term is commonly used today he scarcely knew it; it does not occur anywhere in *The American Language*, and neither is it in the *Oxford Dictionary* or the *Dictionary of American English*. The "Addenda" to the *Shorter Oxford* traces it only as far back as 1942, which clearly indicates that it was coined to refer to the Nazi concept of the *Herrenvolk* and the policy of Hitler's Germany toward the Jews, Poles, and other peoples whom they sought to exterminate. If the question means to ask, "Did he believe that some men are superior by nature to others?" then obviously the answer, in view of all that he wrote about the "enlightened minority" and the "vast herd of human blanks," must be an unqualified "yes." The record is there, and it would be futile to deny his position or try to get around it with any lame arguments that he did not really mean what he said. But this is not precisely the same thing as being a racist. If the question is put: "Did he believe that certain whole races of men are naturally superior to other races and thus have a right to rule and exploit them?" the answer is much less absolute. Rather naturally, in view of his own background, he had a high opinion of the Germans *(but not of Hitlerism)*; plainly, in view of what has just been said, he took a dim view of people of Celtic origin. In more than one place he makes clear that he thought Western European civilization was infinitely superior to anything that the countries of the East had to offer. But despite his very strong opinions on most subjects he was remarkably free of any kind of prejudice, and no man who believed in civil liberties as passionately as he did could ever have countenanced the denial of those liberties to whole groups on the basis of their race, color, or beliefs. On numerous occasions during the thirties he was accused of being sympathetic toward the Nazi regime, and certainly he failed for a long time to take Hitler at all seriously, but in a letter of May 2, 1936, to Upton Sinclair (Forgue, *Letters*, p. 403) he says very sharply: "I am against the violation of civil rights by Hitler and Mussolini as much as you are, and well you know it." He has been accused, too, of anti-Semitism, but in a letter which he wrote to a Unitarian clergyman, L. M. Birkhead, on January 31, 1941 (Forgue, *Letters*, p. 455), after speaking of efforts by Jewish groups in New York to put down criticism of themselves, he adds simply, "I don't share the common prejudice against them." His attitude and feelings toward Negroes will be treated in a later section; here it may simply be remarked that he constantly encouraged black writers and published them as often as possible in the *Mercury*. The very last thing he ever wrote ("Equal Rights in Parks," Baltimore *Evening Sun*, Nov. 9, 1948) was a scathing attack on racial segregation in Baltimore's parks and on its golf courses; "it is high time," he declared, "that all such relics of Ku Kluxry be wiped out in Maryland."

was a fanatical and constricting Puritanism, and their religious beliefs but little distinguishable from the practice of voodoo. Inbred and degenerate, superstitious and ignorant, they shrank from all that lay outside the bounds of their own incredibly limited experience, and regarded those whose experience was wider or different as their natural enemies.

Such, according to Mencken, was the *Ur*-American—the progenitor of all the debased Presbyterians and Baptists, Kiwanians and Rotarians, dirt farmers and investment security brokers who, taking one with another, made up the national culture in the early years of the twentieth century. There had been exceptions to the rule, of course, at all times: in the South a genuine aristocracy had flourished for a while, characterized by hospitality to ideas and an appreciation of fine living, but its last salient figures had been Washington and Jefferson and it had vanished utterly in the holocaust of the Civil War. Even in the gloomy theocracy of New England men like Emerson and Hawthorne had represented a strain at least of individualism, if not of actual revolt against the oppressive climate of Puritanism.

The later waves of immigrants, he held—those coming over from, say, the 1850's on—were a much superior stock. To be sure, they still included large numbers of Anglo-Celts (one has only to recall the influx of the Irish in the wake of the great potato famine), but against these were Germans, Italians, Jews, Scandinavians, and Slavic peoples from the countries of Central Europe. They had settled for the most part in the larger cities, and once located there had tended to move up very rapidly in the social and economic scale. Their names, often startlingly un-American, became a veritable roll call of achievement in the arts and sciences, in industry and business, in education and the higher branches of learning—even in the roster of Congress! Wherever they had come in competition with the older bloodstream, the defeat of the latter had been overwhelming and unmistakable.

The "pure" Anglo-Saxons had resented these newcomers, of course. After all, they did not speak English, or spoke it only haltingly and in barbarous accents; they did not look like good Americans were supposed to look; they brought over with them cultures and customs quite at variance with those which the "natives" regarded as proper. In a word, they were different. And because they were different, because their life-style did not conform to the accepted ideas of what constituted decency and decorum, they were regarded with suspicion and looked upon as foreigners who were somehow a threat to the American way of life.

Happily, however, the Anglo-Saxons had one advantage on their side—that of sheer numbers; and in a democracy nothing else is necessary. They could always triumph at the polls. They could establish the truth by taking a vote, and then enforce its observance by such engines as the Department of Justice, the American Legion, the Anti-Saloon League, and the Ku Klux Klan. Thus dangerous ideas and people who insisted on thinking for themselves could be brought safely under control. Thus, with "envy turned into law, cowardice sanctified, stupidity made noble, Puritanism,"[36] the majority was free to make America in its own image—which was to say, to make it a buffoon among the nations.

Yet all the while they were doing this they could not get away from the uncomfortable sense of their own essential inferiority. They knew how far down in the scale of human enlightenment they were, and so—by a protective mechanism easily explainable in terms of the "Freudian necromancy"—they compensated for it by a native arrogance and braggadocio designed to shield their true character from themselves, even if from no one else. Thus America became "the land of the free," though the lives of its citizens were hemmed about by a thousand-and-one idiotic prohibitions, and "the home of the brave," though its armies had never won a war fairly or against an evenly matched antagonist. Particularly after the First World War it became the fashion to boast that America had "won the war," though by the time it entered the conflict the Central Powers were already worn out by almost three years of fighting, and outnumbered by odds of eight to one, and (in those days at least) could not have struck back at the United States without the aid of divine intervention.

But chiefly Americans were convinced that their form of government was the envy and despair of all other and hence lesser states, and that they were called upon by Providence to spread it abroad among those less fortunate than themselves. Any country that failed to take advantage of this generous offer, or that appeared skeptical of the usufructs of democracy, was by that token backward, or an enemy, or both. It was America's duty, solemnly proclaimed by Presidents from Theodore to Franklin Delano Roosevelt, to "lead the world"—and in Mencken's eyes all that this meant was reducing the rest of the world to America's own ignominious level of culture.

4 TO THE QUESTION, so frequently put to him, "Why, if you find so much that is unworthy of reverence in the United States, do you continue to live here?" Mencken usually replied with a counter-question: "Why do people visit zoos?"

His animadversions against democracy, he was always at pains to make clear, were those of a pathologist, not those of a therapist. To him had fallen the role of pointing out its ills, but this did not mean that he was also required to prescribe any remedies and he had little patience with those who complained that his criticisms were not "constructive." "This great pox of civilization . . . ," he declared,

> I believe to be incurable, and so I propose no new quackery for its treatment. I am against dosing it, and I am against killing it. All I presume to argue is that something would be accomplished by viewing it more realistically—by ceasing to let its necessary and perhaps useful functions blind us to its ever-increasing crimes against the ordinary rights of the free citizen and the common decencies of the world. The fact that it is generally respected—that it possesses effective machinery for propagating and safeguarding that respect—is the main shield of the rogues and vagabonds who use it to exploit the great masses of diligent and credulous men.[37]

Moreover, his generally dim view of democracy did not necessarily blind him to the fact that it also had certain charms. He could not bring himself to believe in it, but he was "perfectly willing to admit that it provides the only really amusing form of government ever endured by mankind."[38] It was based, of course, on propositions that were palpably untrue, but what is untrue is always immensely more soothing and fascinating to the great masses of mankind than the truth. In this case, it gave to the common man a feeling that he had a hand in running things, that the progress of the world somehow depended upon him, that his very commonness bestowed on him a vast and transcendent power. Such a feeling made him happy, and was thus an important factor in promoting domestic peace and tranquillity.

Finally, over and above all this, there was its unique value as a show for connoisseurs of the higher mountebankery. Its hugest delights, in fact, were reserved not for the participant but for the spectator. "Has the art and mystery of politics no apparent utility?" he wanted to know. "Does it appear to be unqualifiedly ratty, raffish, sordid, obscene and low down, and its salient virtuosi a gang of unmitigated scoundrels? Then let us not forget its high capacity to soothe and tickle the midriff, its incomparable services as a maker of entertainment."[39] However painful and unedifying it might be to watch such frauds going up in the world, this pain was always balanced by the joy of seeing them come down with a thump.

Publicly, in his writings, he excoriated democracy as the government of jackasses by jackals. Privately he admitted that he could suggest nothing better.

For what, after all, was one to offer in its place? Obviously, Socialism was not the answer. In these days we hear very little of Socialism—it has ceased to play any role on the American political scene; and so it is rather hard for us to realize that throughout much of the period when Mencken was doing his most important newspaper work it was a kind of bugaboo, conjuring up visions of bearded anarchists seeking to overthrow the government by planting bombs in out-of-the-way spots. Nevertheless and despite this image, as a party it usually ran third—a poor third, to be sure, pretty far down the field—to the Democrats and Republicans. Eugene Debs was the Socialist candidate for the presidency of the United States in every campaign save one from 1900 to 1920, and the last of these campaigns he waged from jail, whither he had been thrown by the Wilson administration for alleged violation of the Espionage Act. When, late in 1921, he was grudgingly released by Warren G. Harding, Mencken sneered at the way the government had conducted itself in the whole sorry farce and wrote that Debs was "independent and brave . . . honest and a gentleman." "Is the old fellow," he demanded, "disliked by right-thinkers and 100-percenters? Is his release denounced by the New York *Times*, the Rotary Clubs, and the idiots who seem to run the American Legion? Then it is precisely because he is fair, polite, independent, brave, honest and a gentleman."[40]

Debs's place as the perennial Socialist candidate was taken over by Norman Thomas, who ran for the presidency (among numerous other public offices) in the campaigns of 1928, 1932, 1936, 1940, and 1944. By that time the party, hopelessly split by internal schisms, had ceased to amount to very much. There is curiously little about Thomas in the whole canon of Mencken's writings—less, indeed, than about any other American political figure of the time—and yet one somehow has the impression that he always felt a grudging respect and affection for him. Perhaps, given the typical Menckenian method of treatment, he may have decided that the kindest way to handle him was simply to say nothing at all.

For however much he might admire as individuals some of the "principal gladiators" of the movement, Socialism itself was to his way of thinking only one more form of quackery. Robert Rives La Monte had tried very hard to bring him over to its gospel as far back as 1909, but their epistolary debate had failed utterly to convince him and he never saw any reason, in the years that followed, to change his conviction that it was simply "a species of insanity." "[I] shrink from Socialists," he once said, "as I shrink from Methodists,"[41] and he maintained that his last word on the gallows would be "a hoot at Socialism."[42] In the very article in which he had written in such lofty terms of Debs, he had added at once that the old man was "unquestionably wrong, both in his naive belief in the Marxian rumble-bumble and in his sentimental opposition to war," and then gone on to say that the Socialists' "fundamental ideas are all hollow and feeble—that Socialism is a delusion, and its advocates boozy dreamers."

The trouble with them, in a word, was that they were men with "believing minds." It was impossible for them to distinguish between what was subjectively pleasant and desirable and what was objectively a fact. "A Socialist," Mencken held, "is simply a man suffering from an overwhelming compulsion to believe what is not true. He yearns for it as a cow yearns for the milkman, lowing in the cool of the evening. He pines for it as a dry congressman pines for a drink."[43] He could not take seriously the concern which they professed to feel for the poor and the downtrodden, and even less seriously could he take the strictures they put forth against the capitalist system. "Even the Socialists, who profess to scorn money," he wrote, "really worship it. Socialism, indeed, is simply the degenerate capitalism of bankrupt capitalists."[44]

No, Socialism was no more a cure for the ills that beset the country than democracy was, and quite possibly it was even less so.* What ailed

---

*Considering the fact that the Russian Revolution and the establishment of the Communist Party as a major political force in many countries took place entirely within his own mature lifetime, Mencken wrote surprisingly little on the subject of Communism. Most of what he did write was, needless to say, highly unfavorable. His opinion of Marx was on a level with his opinion of Freud, and the Marxian evangel, like Freud's, was "rumble-bumble." It consisted "in large part of very palpable nonsense" (*Minority Report*, p. 237). The Communist leaders of the Russian people were "blind leaders of the blind." "It is characteristic of the stupidity of American capitalists," he wrote in 1932, "that they fear Bolshevism on the same ground that the Southern latifundists feared Abolition—that is, on the ground that it is a colossal conspiracy, hatched in Hell, for the liberation

it, in fact, was nothing more or less than the complete absence of a
civilized aristocracy. In making this charge, Mencken knew perfectly
well that he was leaving himself open to serious misunderstanding: to
the American, nurtured all his life long on the democratic "fustian"
about everybody being equal, the very word "aristocracy" was offensive. It conjured up pictures of decadent English lords riding to the fox
hunt (Oscar Wilde's "unspeakable in pursuit of the uneatable"), or of
Wall Street bankers and their bejeweled wives occupying boxes in the
"Diamond Horseshoe" of the Metropolitan Opera House, or of
haughty dowagers enthroned in their palatial summer homes at New-
port. But it goes without saying that this was not what Mencken was
speaking of at all. What he had in mind was an aristocracy not of family
or blood or money, but one of nature.

Every other civilized country on earth, past and present, had had
such a thing. Its chief characteristics were a quiet assurance of its own
worth and a total interior security. It was educated and enlightened,
animated by an intelligent curiosity, skeptical in its habits of mind,
open to new ideas but adamant against crazes and fads. The born
aristocrat was free to do as he liked—but his own ingrained sense of
decorum and ordinary common decency meant that he would never
disturb the public peace or show any lack of consideration for the rights
of others. He was free, too, to think as he pleased and to make mistakes
doing it, but he did not have to account to anyone else for his thoughts
and his mistakes would not bring down upon him the scorn and obloquy of his peers. He was his own man. His class was "the custodian of
the qualities that make for change and experiment; it is the class that
organizes danger to the service of the race; it pays for its high prerogatives by standing in the forefront of the fray."[45]

Such a class was, quite obviously, beyond any responsibility to the
general masses of men and stood above their degraded longings, aver-
sions, and fears. Where the lower orders were "inert, timid, inhospita-
ble to ideas, hostile to change, faithful to a few maudlin supersti-

---

of slaves. It is, of course, almost precisely the opposite. If it manages to survive, as now begins to
seem likely, the Russian masses will be such slaves as not even Judge Gary ever dreamed of. For
not only will they be enslaved beyond hope of redemption; they will also be convinced that their
slavery is an heroic and even swell estate; they will be slaves by conviction as well as in fact." ("The
Moscow Nietzsches," Baltimore *Evening Sun*, Jan. 18, 1932.) His unsparing criticisms of American democracy led, naturally enough, to frequent accusations that he was himself a Communist,
and this always amused him greatly.

tions,"[46] the aristocracy was active, courageous, open, and clear-eyed. If the mob eagerly acclaimed some new jitney messiah, it remained aloof and skeptical and waited for proof of his *bona fides;* when, inevitably, he was exposed as a fraud it permitted itself only a slight smile. Never did it allow logic to be polluted by emotion. If humanity had made any progress at all across the ages, it was this born aristocracy that had brought it about.

But here in the United States, democracy—the craze, that is, for reducing everybody to the lowest common denominator of mankind—had left only a vacuum where such an aristocracy ought to be. The makings of one had flowered for a brief moment in the South, principally in Virginia, but it had not long survived the Revolutionary Era and by the time of the Civil War and the rise of the industrial system the very memory of it had perished. In its place, not only in the South but throughout the rest of the country as well, there had sprung up a plutocracy—a gentry, in other words, built solely on the power of money. It had risen from the mob and now looked down upon it, but though it had come so far, those natural endowments that marked the genuine aristocrat were forever beyond its grasp. Its sorry fate was to "remain in a sort of half-world, midway between the gutter and the stars."[47]

This plutocracy—culturally indistinguishable from the masses, full of the same low-caste superstitions and indignations, badly educated, stupid, inherently swinish, lacking in both courage and honor—was responsible for making the United States "the first great empire in the history of the world to ground its whole national philosophy upon business."[48] Its earls and dukes were the Vanderbilts, the Astors, the Morgans, the Judge Garys—dynasties and men with the aspirations of so many pawnbrokers. But though it controlled the national wealth, it enjoyed nothing that could be described as security; quite the contrary, it was beset by all kinds of doubts and fears. For money, after all, is a rather uncertain thing; one may have it today and be without it tomorrow, and its loss naturally means the loss, too, of whatever hollow dignity and honor goes with it.

Mencken's concept of the natural aristocrat is set forth most explicitly in the essay "The National Letters" in *Prejudices: Second Series,* and the context there, of course, is one of literary values and appreciations. But the idea fits with equal or even greater appropriateness into his political and social philosophy, and in these areas he did not fail to draw from it its fullest implications. The year in which the second *Prejudices* appeared (1920) was one of the most prolific in his entire career. He would write better things later on, but for sheer incredible volume it is unlikely that anything would ever again approach this. The year before, he had published the first edition of *The American Language,* and already he was hard at work preparing a second. But not even the monumental labors that this involved, combined with the necessity each month of writing a 5,000-word book-review article and other miscellaneous pieces for *The Smart Set,* could exhaust his fantastic energies. He began the "Monday Articles," which would run weekly in the *Evening Sun* for the next eighteen years. He put together the *Prejudices* volume, in some cases expanding to very great length the original brief essays. He translated Nietzsche's *Antichrist* and wrote a thirty-page introduction to it. He collaborated with Nathan on *The American Credo,* and here again he wrote an enormously long preface. Finally—though this has no real connection with the matters that concern us here—he also collaborated with Nathan on the farcical play *Heliogabalus.*

The idea of the aristocrat runs like a leitmotif through much of these writings of 1920, indicating that it was a subject which much preoccupied him at the time. It appears not only in the *Prejudices* but also in the Nietzsche introduction and, most especially, in the preface to *The American Credo,* which its co-authors regarded as "a contribution toward the interpretation of the national mind."* In these latter works he approaches it, so to speak, from the opposite direction, and for that reason they deserve to be read in careful conjunction with "The National Letters." (Unhappily, neither book is easily obtainable today.) As always, his thought is perfectly consistent and of a piece, unmarred by any internal contradictions.

The inferior man, like a good democrat, believed and loudly maintained that nobody was any better than he was. But democracy, remember, has its origin in envy, and precisely from the fact that he was a democrat it followed that he was incurably envious of all those who

---

*Nathan was primarily responsible for assembling the 869 articles that made up the *Credo* (and also for some others, unprintable in that day, which were circulated privately as an addendum to the published book), but there can be no doubt that Mencken contributed a great many of them. The typescript of his 100-page preface is contained in one of the bound volumes in the Pratt Library entitled "Contributions to Books—1920–1936."

ranked above him on the economic and social scale. His whole life, therefore, was marked by a dominant passion—"a passion to improve his position, to break down some shadowy barrier of caste, to achieve the countenance of what, for all his talk of equality, he recognizes and accepts as his betters. The American [was] a pusher. His eyes [were] ever fixed upon some round of the ladder . . . just beyond his reach, and all his secret ambitions, all his extraordinary energies, group themselves about the yearning to grasp it."[49] Despite his professed scorn of an aristocracy, he was forever trying to lift himself up to what he conceived it to be.

But—to repeat a point already made—there was no aristocracy. In its absence he naturally tended to mistake the plutocracy for it, and thus to believe that the mere acquisition of wealth would suffice to admit him to its exclusive position and high prerogatives. Money, in other words, automatically carried with it intrinsic worth and excellence.

He soon found, alas, that getting into the plutocracy was not easy (even though making money might be), and that the requirements for membership, once he had arrived, were onerous. Those already a part of it did not exactly greet newcomers with open arms, since the latter could, after all, pose a threat to their own security. The candidate, in order to make the grade at all, had to abase himself in a most humiliating manner and sacrifice any shred of independence and integrity he might have. Once in, he had to submit to a regimentation more despotic than that of any of the hierarchical societies of Europe. His home had to be in the right neighborhood. He and his wife had to have the right circle of friends, and belong to the right clubs, and attend the right church, and be interested in the approved shows and sports. It was important, regardless of the party to which he professed allegiance, that he harbor acceptable political views. His children must go to the right schools. And the slightest deviation from any of these norms—the harboring, say, of too liberal political beliefs no less than using the wrong spoon for his soup—could bring down on him the ridicule and contumely of that whole society he had struggled so long and hard to enter.*

---

*Mencken develops his arguments on these social phenomena at considerable length in *The American Credo*, pp. 28–37. The same points are made in very similar language in "The National Letters" (*Prejudices: Second Series*, pp. 67–69): "One gets into it [i.e., the bugaboo aristocracy] only onerously, but out of it very easily. Entrance is effected by dint of a long and bitter struggle,

But, of course, most of those who made it would be fortunate enough to escape such a fate. At a high level or a low one they would be absorbed into the life of the plutocracy, accepting its standards without question, living by its brummagem code, mouthing its platitudes, defending it against the attacks of its enemies. They would prudently cover up their own humble origins and trust that in another generation their sons and daughters would be accepted as to the manner born. But though they might cover up that origin they could never quite forget it, and the result was that they were never wholly secure. Always there was a haunting uneasiness, a feeling of uncertainty even in the presence of one's peers. Always, too, there was a fear that the wealth that had brought them into this society might suddenly be gone and take position and pretensions with it.

Those who failed to gain entrance sank back down into the masses, still filled with their corroding envy. Some of them might join one or another of the tin-pot fraternal orders, which admitted anyone not a downright felon, go through its spooky initiation ceremonies, don its regalia, and march in its parades. Such a thing gave them at least some sense of importance. Others, in whom envy was now reinforced by hate, might clamor for the overthrow of the order they could not be a part of; these were the ones who became Socialists, or radicals, or

---

and the chief incidents of that struggle are almost intolerable humiliations. The aspirant must school and steel himself to sniffs and sneers; he must see the door slammed upon him a hundred times before ever it is thrown open to him. To get in at all he must show a talent for abasement—and abasement makes him timorous. Worse, that timorousness is not cured when he succeeds at last. On the contrary, it is made even more tremulous, for what he faces within the gates is a scheme of things made up almost wholly of harsh and often unintelligible taboos, and the penalty for violating even the least of them is swift and disastrous. He must exhibit exactly the right social habits, appetites and prejudices, public and private. He must harbor exactly the right political enthusiasms and indignations. He must have a hearty taste for exactly the right sports. His attitude toward the fine arts must be properly tolerant and yet not a shade too eager. He must read and like exactly the right books, pamphlets and public journals. He must put up at the right hotels when he travels. His wife must patronize the right milliners. He himself must stick to the right haberdashery. He must live in the right neighborhood. He must even embrace the right doctrines of religion. It would ruin him, for all opera box and society column purposes, to set up a plea for justice to the Bolsheviki, or even for ordinary decency. It would ruin him equally to wear celluloid collars, or to move to Union Hill, N.J., or to serve ham and cabbage at his table. And it would ruin him, too, to drink coffee from his saucer, or to marry a chambermaid with a gold tooth, or to join the Seventh Day Adventists. Within the boundaries of his curious order he is worse fettered than a monk in a cell. Its obscure conception of propriety, its nebulous notion that this or that is honorable, hampers him in every direction, and very narrowly. What he resigns when he enters, even when he makes his first deprecating knock at the door, is every right to attack the ideas that happen to prevail within. Such as they are, he must accept them without question."

single-taxers, or Prohibitionists, or went in for some other and equally preposterous form of quackery.

This, for Mencken, was the last and most damning indictment of democracy. By obliterating the old aristocracy, it had done away with that class which alone could have introduced intelligence, order, and common decency into the affairs of government. All that it had been able to set up in its place was a plutocracy characterized by inherent stupidity and swinishness. It had failed utterly to lift up that mob in which, according to its own principles, all wisdom resided. The result was a chaos where everything noble and good had been destroyed, and everything cheap and base ruled in its stead.

5 IN THE WHOLE VAST BULK of Mencken's political writings there are only occasional references to the Constitution, and their burden is invariably the same: the document is plain proof that the Founding Fathers had no belief at all in democracy, and in any case its force and authority have long been extinct. He made the latter charge at least as far back as 1919, in his famous *Smart Set* article on the sociological ideas of Thorstein Veblen entitled "Professor Veblen and the Cow." In *Heathen Days*, which was published in 1943, he tells an amusing story of how he was groomed surreptitiously to be Democratic candidate for Vice-President when that party held its national convention in Baltimore in 1912; as it turned out, he explains, he would not have been eligible because Article II, Section 1, of the Constitution provides that "no person shall be eligible to the office of president [and thus to that of vice-president] who shall not have attained to the age of thirty-five years"—and on the day of the balloting he was precisely 31 years, 10 months, and 23 days old. "The Constitution," he adds with his characteristic gravity, "was still in force."

The inevitable corollary of this, one can only suppose, is that it ceased to be in force on March 4 of the following year when his arch-enemy, Woodrow Wilson, took the oath of office as President.

But if he has little to say about the Constitution as such, he has a great deal to say about the Bill of Rights—to the point where one almost gets the impression that if he regarded anything on earth as worthy of veneration, this was it. Those first ten amendments to the basic document were for him a charter of the individual's inalienable liberties and privileges; they set up clear lines of demarcation across which no government, whatever its form, had any right to trespass— and for a man who believed, as he did, that the ideal government was that which came close to being none at all, those lines were sacred indeed. It comes as no surprise, therefore, to find him protesting angrily, and in his most violent language, at any attempt to cross them.

For example, there is the guarantee of freedom of speech and the press contained in the very first of the amendments. Obviously a man who believed the things that Mencken did, and who said and wrote them with such uncompromising forthrightness, had to require the utmost freedom of speech for himself. But requiring it for oneself is not exactly the same thing as believing in it for others, and there have been all too many cases in history of men who claimed the right to express their own ideas but tried to deny that right to those who differed from them. Mencken was guilty of no such inconsistency. "I know of no other man," he told Isaac Goldberg, "who believes in liberty more than I do. . . . I am against Socialism in all its forms, but I have always done all I could to help the Socialists when their rights were denied them."[50] "Almost the only thing I believe in with a childlike and un-questioning faith," he wrote in another place, "in this world of doubts and delusions, is free speech."[51]

He believed in it, indeed, "up to the last limits of the endurable." These words occur in the recorded interview which Donald Kirkley, the *Sun*'s drama critic, did with him for the Library of Congress, and immediately afterward he goes on to say:

> I think there is a limit beyond which free speech can't go, but it's a limit that's very seldom mentioned; it's the point where free speech begins to collide with the right to privacy. I don't think there are any other conditions to free speech. I have got a right to say and believe anything I please, but I haven't got a right to press it on anybody else. Take for instance the Catholic Church, which I am on good terms with personally but have no belief in whatsoever. I have got a right to print my dissent from its doctrines—utterly. I have exercised that right for many years. But I have no right to go on the cathedral steps on Sunday morning when the Catholics are coming out of High Mass and make a speech denouncing them. I don't think there is any such right. Nobody's got a right to be a nuisance to his neighbors.

The interview with Kirkley was done in the summer of 1948, just a few months before the stroke that ended his activities, but the philosophy expressed in it was hardly a late development in his thought. It went back, in precisely that form, to the very beginning of his newspaper career, and in the years that followed it guided all his work as editor, critic, and spokesman on public affairs. When he was writing his "Free Lance" column in the *Evening Sun* from 1911 to 1915, he attacked, at one time or another, virtually every idea, every institution, and every person that Baltimoreans held in reverence, and the result, not unnaturally, was a steady stream of letters to the editor denouncing him, reviling him, and not infrequently demanding that he be shut up or even run out of town. But though Mencken firmly believed, as he also told Kirkley, that "most people who write letters to newspapers are fools," he controlled the two columns of space next to his own and never failed to see to it that a fair sampling of these letters got printed.* Much the same policy was followed during the twenties and thirties in relation to the "Monday Articles."

Fortunately for him, he always received unqualified support from the paper, which jealously demanded the right to full freedom of expression not only for itself but for anyone else (and, indeed, continues to do so to this day). Mencken was of course the most famous figure on the *Sun*, and was responsible in large part for its national reputation, but one cannot escape the conclusion that very often he was a thorn in its flesh. Like any great metropolitan daily its staff was made up of a broad spectrum of men, having different backgrounds and holding very different convictions, and it would be the worst kind of understatement to say that not all of them saw eye to eye with him on every issue. His blunt manner of expression could offend readers, which no newspaper likes to do, and, even more important, it could at times threaten advertising revenues, which no paper can afford to do. Yet with two colossal exceptions there is no record that it ever shrank from his side to look after its own interests. In 1931 a "Monday Article" denounced in unusually scathing terms a lynching on Maryland's Eastern Shore, and the inhabitants of that region were so incensed that they attacked some of the *Sun*'s delivery trucks, beat up their drivers, and threatened a

---

*He admitted to Goldberg that this "was partly mere bombast and braggadocio, but also partly genuine belief in free speech." (Autobiographical notes, 1925, p. 190.)

boycott of the city unless an apology were forthcoming. The Baltimore Chamber of Commerce duly apologized; the *Sun* did not.

The exceptions, of course, were the two World Wars. Even here, both times, his highly personal and unpopular views continued to appear down to the moment when it was no longer possible to print them, and when, at his volition as much as theirs, he withdrew and became silent, it had little effect on his relationship with either the business management or his editorial colleagues. From the very outset of the First World War, Mencken made no secret of his pro-German sympathies. He defended the invasion of Belgium on the ground that it was nothing more than inescapable military necessity; the sinking of British merchant ships by German U-boats, he argued, was carried on with strict regard for the international laws governing naval warfare, while on the other hand the English blockade was a cruel and illegitimate measure which had the effect of starving innocent civilians. Almost day in and day out, in the columns of the "Free Lance," he derided the English, ridiculed their clumsy propaganda, and openly looked forward to the day when Germany dominated all of Europe. Wilson, he maintained, under cover of a hypocritical pretense of neutrality was actually planning to horn in at the first convenient moment.

These views were contrary not only to the overwhelmingly pro-Allied feeling of the American people but to the official position of the *Sun* itself, and the time came when they were so isolated and discordant that it simply made no sense to let them appear on the editorial page. Abruptly on October 23, 1915, a year and a half before America entered the war, the "Free Lance" ceased. Throughout 1916 he continued to write for the paper, but his columns dealt for the most part with literature, music, and local events. Feeling more and more cut off from any platform where he could give free voice to his opinions, he busied himself with the linguistic studies that would eventually result in the first edition of *The American Language* and with his writing for *The Smart Set*, where he and Nathan made it a kind of standing policy to pretend that the war was not really happening.

Once the United States was an active belligerent, things became far worse than even he had dared to prophesy. One expects that in wartime there will be strong feeling against the enemy, but Mencken, at least, had not supposed that the thousands upon thousands of

German-American citizens who, after some three generations, were far more American than they were German, would be regarded as enemies too. Neither had he supposed that they would be spied upon and subjected to every conceivable humiliation. In his own Baltimore the name of German Street had to be changed to Redwood Street. "Sauerkraut" seemed much too Germanic a word for the dish of that name, and an effort (on the whole unsuccessful) was made to turn it into "liberty cabbage." In New York, Wagner's operas could not be performed at the Metropolitan, and Beethoven and Brahms virtually disappeared from concert programs. When Dreiser's The "Genius" was attacked by the Comstocks for alleged obscenity and blasphemy, his German name was regarded as clear proof that the novel ought not to be read by patriotic Americans, and when Mencken came to the book's defense the same charge was leveled against him.

Somehow he managed to restrain himself through it all, but a few years later he wrote with a bitterness unaccustomed even for him of the government's "colossal waste of public money, the savage persecution of all opponents and critics of the war, the open bribery of labor, the half-insane reviling of the enemy, the manufacture of false news, the knavish robbery of enemy civilians, the incessant spy hunts, the floating of public loans by a process of blackmail, the degradation of the Red Cross to partisan uses, the complete abandonment of all decency, decorum and self-respect."[52] He had kept, he said, an exhaustive record of this unprecedented swinishness and promised that someday he would publish it "in twenty volumes folio," but he never did.

One expects, too, that with the return of peace such extravagances will die down. In this case they did not. For in the midst of the war an old ally turned into a new enemy, and by the time Germany had been defeated the Communist government established in the wake of the Russian Revolution appeared as an equally dangerous threat. There followed, in the postwar years, a "Red scare" of unimaginable magnitude and ferocity. Under the direction of A. Mitchell Palmer, Wilson's Attorney General and thus head of the Department of Justice, a savage campaign of repression was carried out against "Bolsheviks," whatever vague meaning might attach to that term. Anyone who was suspected of harboring sympathies for the new regime in Russia, anyone thought to have doubts about the perfect wisdom and rectitude of the government of the United States—all such persons were liable to be seized and thrown into jail without warrant or recourse, sentenced to long prison terms on the most farcical of charges, and in some cases were deported willy-nilly to the Soviet Union.

Following the end of the war there had been long-drawn-out and, at least in the beginning, somewhat cautious negotiations between Mencken and the *Sun* with a view to his resuming a position on the staff. These maneuvers, concluded in 1919, resulted in his being named "general editorial adviser," with the understanding that he would have to devote no more than a few hours a month to his duties; he would thus be able to give *The Smart Set* all the time and attention that it required, and would be able, too, to pursue his other literary interests. On February 9, 1920, there appeared on the editorial page "A Carnival of Buncombe," the first of the "Monday Articles," and for the next eighteen years he was free to disport himself on any topic or issue of his choosing and to talk about it in whatever language he wished to use. It was a freedom of which he availed himself to the fullest. "In the columns of the *Evening Sun*," he wrote to Goldberg some five years later, "I can say anything I please. I tackle subjects that are never mentioned in other newspapers." [53]

From the outset, he attacked Palmer and the Justice Department in language so strong that one marvels he was not caught up himself in the general sweep. "Government by Blackleg," later that year, may be taken as typical:

Here is a department which, for two and a half years past, has maintained a system of espionage altogether without precedent in American history, and not often matched in the history of Russia, Austria and Italy. It has, as a matter of daily routine, hounded men and women in cynical violation of their constitutional rights, invaded the sanctuary of domicile, manufactured evidence against the innocent, flooded the land with *agents provocateurs*, raised neighbor against neighbor, filled the public press with inflammatory lies, and fostered all the worst poltrooneries of sneaking and malicious wretches. [54]

The federal courts, he charged, had become mere complaisant dupes of the executive branch of government, and as a result "the old rights of the free American, so carefully laid down by the Bill of Rights, are now worth nothing. Bit by bit, Congress and the State Legislatures have invaded and nullified them, and today they are so flimsy that no lawyer not insane would attempt to defend his client by bringing them up."[55] Socialists like Debs, and some poor young Russians in New York who had protested in mere academic terms the American attitude toward their country, had been thrown into prison for no crime more serious than holding an opinion which differed from that of the majority: by the same logic the present Congress, which was predominantly Republican, could vote to deny the use of the mails to all Democrats, or to all Catholics, or to all single-taxers or violoncellists, and there would be no power on earth to say them nay. The very Supreme Court itself had gradually established the doctrine that a minority in the Republic had no rights whatever.

Palmer personally was the object of some of his choicest epithets. He had "probably done more than any other one man, save only Mr. Wilson himself, to break down democratic self-government in America and substitute a Cossack despotism, unintelligent and dishonest"—in brief, "a hollow charlatan."[56] He was "perhaps the most eminent living exponent of cruelty, dishonesty and injustice."[57]

Eventually, of course, the Red scare wore itself out by its own sheer excess, as the like practices of the "McCarthy era" after the Second World War would wear themselves out, and Palmer, after an unsuccessful attempt to win the Democratic nomination for the presidency in 1920, disappeared into obscurity. The nation settled down to a long period of what Warren Gamaliel Harding would call "normalcy." Through three administrations—those of Harding, Coolidge, and Hoover—Mencken could content himself with proclaiming that the President of the United States was a "cipher" or "some half-anonymous ass." There was, to be sure, one colossal infringement of his personal rights in those days which he bitterly resented and to which he devoted some of his most impassioned prose—the one represented by the Eighteenth Amendment and the Volstead Act; but of that, more in the next section. Otherwise, save for the quadrennial conventions and campaigns, politics was almost too tame for him to write about; when he did his famous obituary of William Jennings Bryan in 1925, the very heart of the Coolidge era, he complained that "dullness has got into the White House, and the smell of cabbage boiling."

Of course, this is by no means to say that he was idle during those years, or lacked opportunity to make himself heard. Quite the contrary. As almost everyone who has ever written about him has observed, this period of the twenties was peculiarly *his* decade, the time when he really emerged upon the national scene, the high-water mark of his fame and influence. It was then that he became, to quote once more the words of *The New York Times*, "the most powerful private citizen in America." He busied himself on a score of fronts, gleefully exposing quackery and fraud wherever they showed themselves, ridiculing Puritanism, the "Bible Belt," democracy, and "100% Americanism," defending rights that no one else would dare to speak up for, and in the process making himself more hated than probably any other American had ever been.

For example, at Dayton, Tennessee, in 1925 the Fundamentalists sought to overthrow the laws of biological science, and Mencken came promptly to the defense of "the infidel Scopes." Not only that: he got the *Evening Sun* to put up Scopes's bond, and persuaded the eminent and controversial trial lawyer Clarence Darrow to head the young teacher's defense counsel.* The outcome, though legally a victory for the state of Tennessee, was in reality a mortal blow at the narrow theological system Mencken so despised. A year later, in Boston, the Comstocks tried to bar *The American Mercury* from the mails for alleged obscenity, and he met them on their own ground and defeated them in the courts. Puritanism began to follow its old ally, Fundamentalism, into an outmoded past.

Naturally he did not win all his battles—at least not right away. But he was alert to every threat against his rights and those of all other citizens, and he called attention to them ceaselessly. "The yokels out in Iowa," he growled,

> neglecting their horned cattle, have a right, it appears—nay, a sacred duty!—to peek into my home in Baltimore, and tell me what I may and may not drink with my meals. An out-at-elbow Methodist preacher in Boston sets himself up to decide what I may read. An obscure and unintelligent job-holder in Washington, inspired by God, determines what I may receive in the mails. I must not buy lottery tickets because it offends the moral sentiment of Kansas. I must keep Sunday as the Sabbath, which is in conflict with Genesis, because it is ordered by persons who believe that Genesis can't be wrong. Such are the laws of the greatest free nation ever seen on earth.[58]

---

*It is possible that his motives were not entirely unmixed. "Nobody gives a damn about that yap schoolteacher," he told Darrow. "The thing to do is to make a fool out of Bryan."

Indeed, there was plenty to keep him busy. But on the political front a Republican President had declared that "the business of America is business," and that business was prospering mightily, and from the conduct of it Washington stayed pretty much aloof.

And then suddenly—almost overnight, it seemed—everything was changed. That dizzy prosperity vanished, and America found itself in the midst of the most terrible economic crisis it had ever known. One year the trading on Wall Street reached heights that had never been seen before; the next year stocks were worth nothing. Thousands— eventually millions—of people were unemployed, and standing in breadlines, and facing the threat of literal starvation. Mortgages were foreclosed, and banks shut their doors. Whether justly or not, Hoover was blamed for the general collapse and went down to ignominious defeat in the 1932 election. An entirely new philosophy of government came upon the scene in the person of his successor, Franklin Delano Roosevelt.

Mencken had been born and brought up in an era when govern- ment was a distant and, on the whole, rather benign thing that intruded itself only seldom into the lives of ordinary citizens. There were as yet few reformers, uplifters, and world-savers; no vast army of bureaucrats had come into existence to mulct the taxpayer and regulate the minutest details of his life with a host of insane laws. "People could spend weeks, months and even years without being badgered, bilked or alarmed." [59] August Mencken, for one, not only believed that this was the way things should be, but could not imagine them being otherwise, and his son inherited this philosophy and held to it through- out his entire life. The nicest thing he could find to say about Coolidge, when it came time to write his obituary in 1933, was: "There were no thrills when he reigned, but neither were there any headaches. He had no ideas, and he was not a nuisance." [60]

But now he—and the country as a whole—was faced with a totally new concept of the role and function of government. As we have seen, Mencken had at first welcomed Roosevelt, and written of him with untypical civility and even praise. Hoover, he charged, had ignored the Depression and tried to pretend that it was not there (an accusation which could have been made with equal truth and justice against Mencken himself), and Roosevelt was at least trying to do something about it. The honeymoon, however, was destined to be short-lived. In a prompt effort to reduce unemployment and turn the economy back toward something approaching normal, Roosevelt launched a program of social reform surpassing anything that had been dreamed of in the past. The new Social Security system collected taxes to provide for people in their old age, and a welfare system was set up to help those who were without work and means of subsistence. Government agencies sprang into being with bewildering profusion, each having its own alphabetical designation—the NRA, the WPA, the CWA, the CCC, the NLRB—and these very quickly spawned a huge federal bureaucracy. Businesses had to display "voluntarily" the NRA eagle proclaiming: "We do our part"; if they failed to show it in their windows, the inevitable implication was that they were not doing it.

Obviously someone who believed that the only kind of man really worth hell room was the one who paid his own way could not be expected to look with sympathy on the Rooseveltian "dole." "Old age insurance" did little more than offer a means for prolonging the needless survival of the unfit. In addition, Mencken had always been suspicious of any increase in governmental authority and power, since every such addition to it inevitably meant a diminution of the power of the rest of us. He watched the "New Deal" at first with uneasiness, and then with alarm, and then finally with unrestrained fury.

"So far," he wrote on March 27, 1933, when the new administration had been in office less than a month, "no one has paused to figure out what the whole Roosevelt program will cost us, but it will be a plenty, you may be sure."[61] "How long," he cried out a year later, "the American people will submit to this colossal tomfoolery remains to be seen."[62] Roosevelt was king in fact, and might as well be made king in name—a process which Mencken claimed could be accomplished very easily and with complete legality under Article V of the Constitution. Congress, like the Roman Senate, had become a mere battery of rubber stamps. But it remains a fact that during those first couple of years most of his criticisms were directed not so much at the President himself as at the "Brain Trust" —those "sorry wizards" like Raymond Moley, Rexford Guy Tugwell, Harry Hopkins, and Adolf Berle, whom Roosevelt had gathered around him and who, it appeared, were chiefly responsible for the New Deal's social legislation. It was they, Mencken firmly believed, who were bringing the country to the verge of bankruptcy. His belief in Roosevelt had speedily evaporated, but on the whole he treated him with restraint until an event that took place toward the very end of 1934.

The story of Mencken's talk at the Gridiron Club dinner on December 8 of that year has been told so often that there would be little point in repeating it here, were it not for the fact that the episode apparently had a great deal to do with his subsequent attitude toward the President. Heretofore his opposition had been a purely ideological one: the man's politics were at an opposite pole from his, he could see no logic or sense in them, and with his characteristic forthrightness he did not hesitate to say so in the baldest terms. But over the years Mencken had attacked many people, not only in politics but in literature and religion as well, and it is an undeniable truth that a lot of those who were the objects of his most biting wit—men like Upton Sinclair, and Bishop James Cannon, and his fellow townsman Dr. Howard Kelly—were also people for whom he also had a certain humorous affection. Up to now there had been no reason for him to feel any personal animosity toward Roosevelt, but what happened that night apparently caused him to hate him, and it was something that he never forgot.*

The Gridiron Club is, to explain, an association of members of the Washington press corps who, once a year, hold a dinner at which the "honored" guest is the President of the United States. It is the sort of thing that, in recent years on television, has come to be known as a "roast." There is a great deal of lampooning, and the principal speaker usually delivers a blistering but essentially humorous attack on the chief executive, his administration, and his policies and programs. Afterward the President has an opportunity to respond in kind.

That year Mencken had been invited to be the speaker. Following dinner and a number of satirical skits, he was introduced by James Wright, president of the club, and rose to deliver his talk. "Mr. President," he began in his gravelly voice, "Mr. Wright, and fellow subjects of the Reich." He speculated on how long it would take for the New Deal to bring the country to absolute ruin, and expressed gratitude for the fact that there was at least one article in the Bill of Rights which had not yet been violated: so far no soldier had been quartered in anyone's house without the consent of the owner. The brief talk, while sharply critical, was in general good-natured and certainly without anything

---

*The boxes of brief miscellaneous notes in the Mencken Room marked *Minority Report II* and *III*, most of which appear to have been written in the mid-forties, are made up in large part of attacks on Roosevelt so incredibly bitter that one feels that even today they would be unprintable.

like the invective of his articles and columns. He sat down to a round of applause.

A little later it was the President's turn to speak. Flashing his famous smile, he acknowledged "my old friend, Henry Mencken." He made a few humorous introductory remarks. But after that all pleasantry vanished: within a few minutes he was launched upon a diatribe against journalism and newspapermen so all-embracing and vicious that cold chills began to run up and down the spines of his listeners. "The majority of [reporters]," Roosevelt declared, "in almost every American city, are still ignoramuses, and proud of it. All the knowledge that they pack into their brains is, in every reasonable cultural sense, useless; it is the sort of knowledge that belongs, not to a professional man, but to a police captain, a railway mail-clerk, or a board-boy in a brokerage house. . . . There are managing editors in the United States, and scores of them, who have never heard of Kant or Johannes Müller and never read the Constitution of the United States; there are city editors who do not know what a symphony is, or a streptococcus, or the Statute of Frauds; there are reporters by the thousand who could not pass the entrance examinations for Harvard or Tuskegee, or even Yale."

Gradually it began to dawn upon his audience that the President was not really making a speech at all; he was simply quoting an extremely long excerpt from "Journalism in America," which had appeared as an editorial in the October 1924 issue of *The American Mercury* and subsequently been included in *Prejudices: Sixth Series.* Every eye in the room focused upon Mencken, who, as Sara Mayfield was later to write, had turned the color of "oxblood porcelain." What Roosevelt had done was, by any kind of standard at all, unfair; Mencken's talk, of course, had had to be submitted in advance to the White House and cleared there, but neither he nor anyone else had had any way of knowing what the President would say. "I'll get the son of a bitch," Mencken whispered to Governor Ritchie of Maryland, who was sitting next to him. "I'll dig the skeletons out of his closet." But any response right there was naturally out of the question, and as Roosevelt was wheeled out of the hall he paused at Mencken's table for a genial handshake.

It was a public humiliation for Mencken, and it never ceased to rankle within him. He assured colleagues at the *Sun* that he would even the score, but there was really no way that he could. No way, that is, except to make his assaults on Roosevelt and the New Deal even more virulent than they had already been. In the next few months the "Monday Articles" definitely assumed a sharper and more personal tone. He spoke of "the idiotic Roosevelt *cultus*,"[63] and declared that "not a single one of the problems that confronted Dr. Roosevelt and his necromancers on March 4, 1933, has been solved. They have got rid of more than $8,000,000,000 of the taxpayers' money to date, and are preparing to grab and waste at least $8,000,000,000 more, but the state of the nation is worse than it was when they began."[64]

The American Mercury, from which he had resigned at the end of 1933, had been pretty much closed to him during Charles Angoff's tenure as its editor; but in a little over a year Knopf had let Angoff go and sold the magazine to Paul Palmer, who turned it once more into a journal of conservative opinion. Mencken was thus able to come back into its columns as a contributor, and in the issue for March 1936 appears one of his bitterest assaults—so bitter, indeed, that *The New York Times* complained of his "gross disrespect" for the President:

> The blame for this dreadful burlesque of civilized government is to be laid at the door of the Hon. Mr. Roosevelt, and at his door alone. He is directly and solely responsible for every dollar that has been wasted, for every piece of highfalutin rubbish that has been put upon the statute books, and for the operations of every mountebank on the public payroll, from the highest to the lowest. He was elected to the Presidency on his solemn promise to carry on the government in a careful and sensible manner, and to put only competent men in office. He has repudiated that promise openly, deliberately, and in the most cynical manner. Instead of safeguarding the hard-earned money of the people and relieving them from their appalling burden of taxation, he has thrown away billions to no useful end or purpose, and has piled up a debt that it will take generations to discharge. And instead of appointing conscientious and intelligent officials, he has saddled the country with a camorra of quarreling crackpots, each bent only upon prospering his own brand of quackery and augmenting his own power. There has never been a moment when he showed any serious regard for the high obligations lying upon him. The greatest President since Hoover has carried on his job with an ingratiating grin upon his face, like that of a snake-oil vendor at a village carnival, and he has exhibited precisely the same sense of responsibility in morals and honor; no more.[65]

When, later that same year, Roosevelt campaigned for a second term and Governor Alf Landon of Kansas opposed him as the Republican candidate, a "Monday Article" declared:

> Whatever the result of the plebiscite of November 3, we are in for four more years of grief and melancholy. If the Hon. Mr. Landon is elected it will take him the whole of his first term to clean up the mess that Dr. Roosevelt hands on to him, and if Dr. Roosevelt is reelected we may expect it to be made much worse before any honest effort is undertaken to make it better.[66]

And when November 3 came and Roosevelt won by the greatest popular majority that had yet been seen in American history, still another article proclaimed that he

> now carrie[s] all the burdens of omnipotence. There is no one to say him nay—that is, no one he is bound to heed. He has in his hands a blank check from and upon the American people, authorizing him to dispose of all their goods and liberties precisely as he listeth. The Congress that was elected with him will no more dare to challenge him than a pussy cat would dare to challenge a royal Bengal tiger, and even the nine old metaphysicians on Capitol Hill may be trusted to recall, if only subconsciously, that it is imprudent to spit too often into Caesar's eye.[67]

Early in 1938 a thorough reorganization of the three *Sunpapers* left the *Evening Sun* temporarily without an editor. Philip Wagner, who was to assume the post, could not be released from his current duties for three months, and Mencken agreed, somewhat reluctantly, to take over during that time. (Afterward he referred to it as a "brief and unhappy interlude.") On February 10 the editorial page astounded all of Baltimore, and most of Maryland, by appearing to the naked eye to be blank. Apart from the masthead and a few brief paragraphs in the unmistakable style, it was made up of a vast mass of tiny dots—1,000,075 of them to be exact, 3,500 to the square inch—done by what is known to printers as the Benday screen process. Its purpose was to show the number of federal jobholders as of that day; in the accompanying editorial Mencken advised that "the chart is too large for the taxpayer to paste in his hat. Let him hang it, instead, on his parlor wall, between 'The American's Creed' and the portrait of Mr. Roosevelt. . . .

"If there were no jobholders at all," he went on, "every tax-payer's income would be increased twenty-seven per cent. Such is the bill for being saved from revolution and ruin by Wonder Men."

But his criticisms, though they might be ever more vehement, were also becoming increasingly less relevant. A new shadow had loomed upon the scene, infinitely more dangerous than the Depression, and it came closer and grew darker with each passing month. The rise of Adolf Hitler and his Nazis to power in Germany brought with it the frightful possibility of another World War. Mencken's refusal to recognize the threat of Hitler was baffling to his friends and associates, and it remains today the least creditable aspect of his long career; he persisted in treating him as a clown, a kind of comic-opera villain who could be safely laughed at, and when he used him as a mere convenient peg upon which to hang further attacks on Roosevelt he was somewhat less than convincing. In the summer of 1938 he toured Germany and sent back dispatches to the effect that Hitler's "New Deal" seemed far more successful than FDR's; picture post-cards from him were apt to have a message scrawled on the back saying "This proves that *Der Führer* loves children." Some of his comments were not meant to be taken seriously, of course, but inevitably they were; he infuriated Philip Goodman and hurt Alfred Knopf by the seemingly lighthearted way in which he brushed off Nazi treatment of the Jews.

When war finally did come in September 1939, it was a repetition of twenty-five years before. This time he did not defend the Germans quite as outspokenly, but his denunciations of England were every bit as violent as they had been in the First World War. Above all, he was sure that Roosevelt, like Wilson, was eagerly awaiting the first possible opportunity to lead the country into a war in which it had no business whatever: "That the Hon. Mr. Roosevelt and his associated wizards are itching to horn into the great crusade to save humanity must be plain by now to the meanest understanding."[68] In June 1940, less than two weeks before the *Blitzkrieg* that would crush France and leave England standing alone before the Nazi terror, he wrote: "Such are the net results of seven years of government by charlatans, the most impudent and shameless ever seen on earth. The country is led into war wholly unprepared for war, and the job of getting it ready is cynically handed over to the same incompetents who have already almost wrecked it."[69]

Later that summer, as he had done every four years for a generation, he covered the national conventions. The Democrats renominated Roosevelt for a third term, and when the "obscene" proceedings were over, Mencken packed up his typewriter, put on his coat, and went around for a farewell handshake with his colleagues. "Goodbye, goodbye," he kept saying to them. "No, we won't see each other in 1944. This is the last political convention that will ever be held in this country." On February 2, 1941, he wrote his final column for the *Evening Sun* and retired a second time to Hollins Street; his by-line would not appear in the paper again for seven years. The kind of life and the form of government that he had known and cherished were gone irretrievably, wiped out by a "preposterous mountebank," and all the rights and freedoms he had struggled so long to defend seemed gone with them.

6 ONE THING, THOUGH, Roosevelt had done: it was early in his first administration that the "noble experiment" of Prohibition had come to its inglorious end. To be sure, Mencken gave him little credit for it: according to his accounts, FDR, completely mistaken as to which way the wind was blowing, had originally sent to the 1932 Democratic National Convention in Chicago a platform even drier than that of the Republicans under the unfortunate Hoover. But when it turned out that the contest was not really between "wets" and "drys" at all but rather between "wet wets" and "damp wets," and when it further turned out that the "wet wets" routed the "damp wets" by odds of four to one, Roosevelt suddenly saw a great light and began to bawl for Repeal. He took office on March 4, 1933, and on March 22 Congress legalized the sale of beverages containing no more than 3.2 percent of alcohol. Even before that, in mid-February, the Twenty-first Amendment to the Constitution, annulling the Eighteenth, had been submitted to the states; by the following December 5 the requisite three-quarters of them had ratified it, and Prohibition was only an "evil memory."

Thus ended what some historians have since called the "thirteen awful years." Mencken, more precise in such matters, pointed out that the actual time was 12 years, 10 months, and 19 days. While it lasted, he said, it seemed almost like a geological epoch, "and the human suffering that it entailed must have been a fair match for that of the Black Death or the Thirty Years' War," but he added at once that his own share of the blood, sweat, and tears had been extremely meager.[70] On March 20, 1933, with 3.2 beer about to become legal, he informed readers of the *Sun* that "during all the thirteen years of so-called Prohibition I can't recall a single occasion when I wished for a drink and could not get it."[71] In this, of course, he was hardly alone, but he also laid claim to being the first man south of the Mason-Dixon Line to brew a drinkable home brew—a claim for which there were never very many substantiating witnesses.

Prohibition was, for Mencken, the ultimate and grossest violation of those individual liberties which he so cherished. He argued against it years before it actually came, and when it was at last on the books as law he turned upon it the full force of his incomparable rhetoric. Betty Adler, in her bibliography, notes forty-two "Monday Articles" on the subject between 1920, when the series began, and 1933, when the law was repealed. But it has to be remembered that these are only the ones which treat of it specifically and *ex professo*; the figure does not include unnumbered others, dealing with the political and social scene, which refer to it at greater or lesser length in passing, and neither does it include pieces in *The Smart Set*, *The American Mercury*, and other magazines and newspapers. He fought it, indeed, without any real hope of ever winning his war: "As for me," he wrote in 1923 in a moment of discouragement and false prophecy, "I can find no reason whatever for believing that, within the lifetime of men now living, the voluptuous consumption of alcohol will be countenanced by law in the Republic, and neither do I see any reason for believing that it will ever be stopped, nor, indeed, any reason for believing that any serious effort will be made to stop it."[72]

As the catastrophe loomed he began to make all necessary preparations for meeting it. In 1917 he had proposed to Ellery Sedgwick, then editor of *The Atlantic Monthly*, that he do an article for the magazine that would be "a last, sad caveat to prohibition . . . a serious, melancholy article, not protesting against national prohibition (which is certain to come shortly), but shedding a few philosophical tears over it." In a letter of April 20, 1918, he told Ernest Boyd that "I drink all I can hold while the going is good," and in a subsequent letter dated January 18, 1919, he announced to Boyd that "All is lost, including honor." Thereafter he began to issue quite contradictory reports as to how much stuff he had on hand to see him through the drought. In the second of those letters to Boyd he claimed that "I have enough good whiskey, fair wine and prime beer secreted to last me two solid years," and added that by that time he hoped to be "far from these Wesleyan scenes." A bit later he told Dr. Louise Pound that he had "750 bottles of prime ale in [his] cellar," and in a letter of December 24, 1921, to Sinclair Lewis he stated that "in my own cellar are bottles enough to keep me stewed for 15 years." According to William Manchester, a visit from this same Lewis just one month later left his stock virtually devastated, but so late as February 3, 1925, he was assuring Percy Marks that "My cellar is still holding out."*

In Baltimore the Saturday Night Club had of course to move out of its headquarters in the Rennert Hotel and start meeting in the members' homes, where they dipped into each other's stock and tried out various melancholy attempts at home brew. On his regular trips to New York, Mencken had little difficulty getting whatever he wanted, but he soon found that the stuff to be had on the actual island of Manhattan was bad to the point of being poisonous, and he established contact with reliable sources in Hoboken and Union Hill, New Jersey. So far as the national conventions were concerned, they offered—as one might have expected—few insurmountable obstacles to the art of drinking: the Democratic one in San Francisco in 1920 was, Mencken thought, "the most charming in American annals," chiefly because the mayor of the town, James Rolph, Jr., had had the foresight to provide "a carload of Bourbon whiskey, old, mellow and full of pungent but delicate tangs." On the other hand, the Republican conclave in Cleveland four years later remained a horror in his memory for years afterward; like everyone else, he had assumed that "the prohibition agents would lay off while the job was put through, if only as a mark of respect to their commander-in-chief," but they actually clamped down on the city with the utmost ferocity, and Mencken had to get in touch with some Christian friends in Detroit and beseech them to start out across Lake Erie with ten cases of bottled beer and ale. Unhappily, the "goons" in charge of the expedition consumed half of the stock en route, and then, fearing that they would have nothing left for the return

---

*A very full and quite amusing account of Mencken as a drinker, replete with quotations on the subject from his writings, is to be found in Bud Johns, *The Ombibulous Mr. Mencken* (San Francisco: Synergistic Press, 1968).

trip, turned around and went back with what was left. In his memoirs Mencken called that particular convention "the worst adventure of my whole life, though I have been shot at four times and my travels have taken me to Albania, Trans-Jordan and Arkansas."[73]

Actually his implacable hostility to the whole idea of Prohibition stemmed only in part from his own love of drinking—though it would be idle to deny that that had a great deal to do with it. He considered alcohol "the greatest of human inventions" (greater by far than hell, the radio, or the bichloride tablet), and was "prepared to admit some merit in every alcoholic beverage ever devised by the incomparable brain of man."[74] In brief, as has already been mentioned, he was "ombibulous." But when he referred to himself as a "somewhat cagey drinker" he was speaking the simple truth. He had certain very definite rules about its consumption, rules which he hardly ever violated throughout his entire life, and he explained them at some length to Donald Kirkley in their recorded interview. He would not drink alone, and he would never take a drink before the sun went down. Finally and most important of all, he would not touch a drop as long as there was work to be done. "If I've got a job of work to do at 10 o'clock at night," he told Kirkley, "I wouldn't take a drink up to that time." He employed it only to relax his faculties, never to stimulate them. Despite his friendships with men like Sinclair Lewis and Scott Fitzgerald, he thought that they had done inestimable harm to their talents by excessive drinking.

The point was that whether he drank or not—and if so, what—was simply nobody else's business. In particular it was not the business of the Methodist Board of Temperance, Prohibition and Public Morals, an organization dedicated by its very name and bylaws to harassing people and making a concerted effort to prevent them from having a good time. The whole movement, he was convinced, had had its origin among the primitive inhabitants of the "cow states," who resented the fact that they had to swill raw corn liquor while men in the big cities could enjoy good whiskeys and vintage wines; it "had little behind it, philosophically speaking, save the envy of the country lout for the city man, who has a much better time of it in this world."[75]

The effects that, both before and after, he predicted would follow the adoption of Prohibition were quite horrendous. In the first place, it would gradually empty the United States of its small minority of civilized men, since no civilized man would submit to living under such barbarous conditions. Secondly, it would scare off the better sort of immigrants. Thirdly, it would have an inevitable effect on the marriage rate. In the beginning, and for a while, it would tend to cut it down, since a man cold sober was obviously in much better condition to fend off the advances of some designing female than he would be if his guard were lowered by a few cocktails. But afterward it would send the rate back up, and for a very plain reason: under Prohibition the life of a bachelor would become simply intolerable. In the past a man had gone to his club for an evening's entertainment, but "a club without a bar is as hideously unattractive as a beautiful girl without hair or teeth." Thus, with nothing better to do, he would inevitably cast about for a charming girl to ease his agonies and so be led unresisting to the altar.

These predictions, and others like them, were no doubt written with tongue in cheek. But some of the things that happened when the blight did actually settle down on the land were anything but funny, and on them he turned humor of a different sort. As a huge corps of "Prohibition agents" came into being to enforce the unenforceable law, as bootlegging developed into a major national industry, as tens of thousands of perfectly respectable and otherwise law-abiding citizens made no secret of their contempt for the Volstead Act or the means by which they circumvented it—as all of these things gathered momentum, so, too, did the force of Mencken's prose. He had at his disposal two major regular forums, a local one (the *Sun*) and a national one (the *Mercury*), and in addition he contributed regularly to other magazines and newspapers; in all of them he poured forth a ceaseless stream of vituperative ridicule upon the Methodist Church, the Anti-Saloon League, the "hinds" of the Bible Belt, the "dry" congressmen who managed somehow to reconcile their need for Christian votes with their love of liquor, and the whole foul machinery by which the federal government tried to keep *him* from having a drink when he wanted one.

On the Prohibition agent in particular he turned language that heretofore he had held in reserve for politicians and bishops. The agents had entered their infamous trade for one reason and one only —to get as much out of it as they could; and in pursuit of that end they engaged in the most cynical violations of the Bill of Rights that had ever been seen in the nation's history. Four-fifths or more of them were irremediably corrupt. It cost the government $50 million a year to maintain this staff of "spies and *agents provocateurs*," and the only persons whom they hauled into court for violating the law were those who simply refused to pay them the bribes they demanded.

Openly he expressed his admiration for the bootlegger and thought he belonged in the line of succession to such figures as the Revolutionary War heroes and the cowboy—"not, of course, the abject scoundrel who peddles bogus Scotch in clubs and office buildings, but the dashing, romantic, defiant fellow who brings the stuff up from the Spanish Main. He is, indeed, almost an ideal hero. . . . Think of him creeping in in his motor-boat on Christmas Eve, risking his life that the greatest of Christian festivals may be celebrated in a Christian and respectable manner!"[76]

But over and above the huge illicit traffic in liquor, above too the corruption in the executive branch of the government, was the effect that the whole machinery of enforcement would have upon the judicial system. Mencken believed that in the long run the chief victims of Prohibition might turn out to be the federal judges. They were sworn to uphold a law that none of them believed in, save those who owed their appointments to the Anti-Saloon League, and to administer penalties for its violation that contravened the most elementary decencies. Nine times out of ten the people hailed before them in court were ordinary citizens guilty of nothing more nefarious than buying a jug of inferior whiskey from some clandestine dealer and transporting it to their homes for private consumption, but their act had to be treated precisely as if it were on a level with arson or piracy. The injunction process, which made it possible to restrain a person by court order from the performance of a given act whether or not that act had been determined to be illegal by a jury of his peers, was for Mencken an assault upon individual liberties that made a travesty of the whole American system of justice.

And what was the net effect of the whole thing? He described the workings of Prohibition for the readers of the Sydney (Australia) *Bulletin* in an article appearing in that paper on July 20, 1922, and after telling them about the bootleggers, the agents, and the corruption, he assured them that "in every American city, and in nine-tenths of the American towns, every known alcoholic beverage is still obtainable—

at prices ranging from 100% to 500% above those of pre-Prohibition days—and even in the most remote country districts there is absolutely no place in which any man who desires to drink alcohol cannot get it."[77]

In brief, "the enforcement of Prohibition entails a host of oppressions and injustices—[it] puts a premium upon the lowest sort of spying, affords an easy livelihood to hordes of professional scoundrels, subjects thousands of decent men to the worst sort of blackmail, and makes for bitter and relentless enmities."[78]

When Repeal finally came in 1933 he hailed it as joyously as any man—since no man had worked harder to bring it about—and precisely at midnight on April 6 he was standing at the bar of the Rennert Hotel to get down his first legal glass of beer since the horror had descended more than a dozen years before. He set the glass down and pontifically announced that it was "pretty good—not bad at all!" though Hamilton Owens, alongside him, declared that it was awful. From there he, Owens, Harry Black, and Paul Patterson embarked upon a tour of Baltimore's resurrected drinking spots that would last for hours. Later that week the Saturday Night Club came up from underground and began meeting in public once more, but its members soon found that the Rennert was not what it had been and took up headquarters at Schellhase's German restaurant on Howard Street, where they would continue to hold forth until the club's final dissolution in 1950.

In a sense, though, Mencken's victory was his own undoing. It left him, temporarily at least, without an enemy, and Mencken without an enemy was simply unable to function. For a while he continued to beat the dead horse. Roosevelt's New Deal was to claim all his energies within a short time, of course, but the effect would not be exactly the same. If Prohibition had been a symbol of the twenties, and if Mencken was the twenties' foremost intellectual spokesman, then his war against it had helped to make him something of a national celebrity. The thirties, however, ushered in an entirely different atmosphere, symbolized not by Prohibition but by the Great Depression, and Mencken's commentaries on the times did not seem very funny to jobless men standing in breadlines and waiting for Franklin Roosevelt to do something to help them. It was the beginning of a decline in his popularity and influence that would last for many years, and when he regained it at last, it would be in a very different form.

7 ALTHOUGH MENCKEN WAS in disagreement with most of the political, social, and cultural ideas of his time, and expressed that disagreement in the sharpest possible language, he was nevertheless a product of the time and very many of its fundamental assumptions and postulates formed part of his own intellectual stock in trade. There is nothing unusual or surprising about this: precisely the same statement could be made about Aristotle, or St. Paul, or Voltaire, or Nietzsche. Every man is conditioned by the society in which he is born and brought up, and this applies as much to the original thinker and the iconoclast as it does to the more conventional citizen.

Such a thing may constitute a limitation, but it is a limitation that is both inevitable and forgivable. Mencken spent a very large part of his life battling for the rights and liberties of the individual, including many people for whose ideas he had no sympathy whatever, but within the context of his time and place in history it does not seem to have occurred to him to do battle for that group which was most cruelly deprived of both liberties and rights—American Negroes.

This is not to say that he was unaware of the problem—he may, indeed, have been more aware of it than most of his contemporaries. In the September 1917 issue of *The Smart Set* he reviewed two books, one a novel and the other nonfiction, treating of racial matters, and as so often with his reviews he used the books as a mere jumping-off point for his own reflections. The picture that he painted of the emerging black man is eerily prophetic: "Emerging he is," he declared,

> both quantitatively and qualitatively, and there will come a morn, believe me or not, when those with ears to hear and hides to feel will discover that he is to be boohed and put off no longer—that he has at last got the power to exact a square answer, and that the days of his docile service as minstrel, torch and goat are done. When that morn dawns, I pray upon both knees, I shall be safe in the Alps, and not below the Potomac River, hurriedly disguised with burnt cork and trying to get out on the high gear. Soon or late . . . it will come to rough work—and perhaps sooner than most of us fancy. [79]

Three years later, again in *The Smart Set*, he spoke of the "almost unbearable injustices" that black people had to endure. [80] A "Monday Article" entitled "Changing Baltimore," appearing in the *Evening Sun* for December 17, 1928, disputes the idea that a Negro "invasion" was responsible for the decay of a large part of northwest Baltimore; they could hardly be blamed, Mencken argued, for wanting to come out of the alleys to which they had been restricted for so long and find decent dwellings, and the fact of the matter was that the more prosperous among them kept up their homes quite as well as the whites who had migrated to the suburbs. In 1935 a young Baltimore Negro named Donald G. Murray, who had graduated with honors from Amherst College, was denied admission to the University of Maryland Law School purely and simply because he was black, and the incident drew forth Mencken's most unsparing vocabulary; the place, he pointed out, was supported by the taxpayers of the state, including the young man's parents, and to refuse him on no other ground than that of his color, despite his obvious qualifications, was to show the most intolerable bigotry. He dismissed the Law School as a "fifth-rate pedagogical dump."

When he described himself as being entirely without prejudice, he was speaking the simple truth. He corresponded with black authors, journalists, and public figures like James Weldon Johnson, Walter White, and George S. Schuyler on precisely the same terms that he used in writing to, say, Ernest Boyd, or Ellery Sedgwick, or Alfred Knopf. When Johnson, who had been a poet, educator, diplomat, and leading figure in the NAACP, was writing his memoirs, Mencken recommended the book to Knopf and published excerpts from it in *The American Mercury*. In Supplement I of *The American Language* he informed his readers in a footnote that Schuyler "is the most competent journalist that his race has produced in America. There are few white columnists, in fact, who can match him for information, intelligence, independence and courage."[81]*

Yet it cannot be denied that he was himself bound to a degree, even if unconsciously, by the prevailing sociological mores of the era. Throughout his writings, from beginning to end, whenever he has occasion to refer to black people he uses one or another of a half-dozen standard terms: "blackamoor," "Aframerican," "the colored brother," "darkey," "Ethiop," "coon," "niggero." They are used, of course, humorously, and certainly with nothing like the offensive intent of the language he applied to Socialists or Methodists, but it would be understandable if black readers of his work failed to appreciate the humor or

---

*The passage occurs in the midst of a truly exhaustive discussion, running to twenty pages, of all the terms that have been applied in America to black people over a period of two centuries.

found in the terms themselves a certain insensitivity. In "The Sahara of the Bozart," which first appeared in 1917 and which he reprinted without change in the *Chrestomathy* so late as 1948, he makes the astounding statement that "it is a commonplace that nearly all Negroes who rise above the general are of mixed blood, usually with the white predominating"[82]—a rather cruel generalization for which it is fair to assume he had no kind of documentation whatever.

He thought that two-thirds of the social disabilities of blacks, even in the South, stemmed from their economic inferiority, and that when they called for rights what they were really after was privileges —privileges which, he pointed out, large numbers of whites had to do without as well. The moment any Negro became well enough off to enjoy such privileges, he would immediately try to deny them to those members of the race who had not made it up to his own level. Meantime, he felt, the best they could do was to make their immediate situation as tolerable as possible. These observations, and more like them, are to be found among the brief undated notes in *Minority Report*, and in one of them, which must be quite late, he again speaks in the voice of prophecy:

> The more noisy Negro leaders, by depicting all whites as natural and implacable enemies to their race, have done it a great disservice. Large numbers of whites who were formerly very friendly to it, and willing to go to great lengths to help it, are now resentful and suspicious. The effort to purge the movies, the stage, the radio and the comic-strips of the old-time Negro types has worked the same evil. The Negro comic character may have engendered a certain amount of amiable disdain among whites, but he certainly did not produce dislike. We do not hate people we laugh at and with. His chief effect upon white thinking, in fact, was to spread the idea that Negroes as a class are very amiable folk, with a great deal of pawky shrewdness. This was to their advantage in race relations. But when the last Amos 'n' Andy programme is suppressed, the Negro, ceasing to be a charming clown, will become a menacing stranger, and his lot will be a good deal less comfortable than it used to be.[83]

The historic 1954 decision of the Supreme Court in *Brown* v. *Board of Education* came at a time when he was no longer active or capable of commenting on public affairs, and less than two years later he was dead. It is tempting, even if it is also quite useless, to speculate on what his reaction would have been to the civil rights movement launched then and carried on, through the fifties and sixties, right down to the present time. Certainly he would have been horrified by the excesses, on both sides, of Watts and Detroit and Newark; he would probably have been skeptical of the demonstrations of Montgomery and Selma, and indeed of public "demonstrations" anywhere. One plays in the imagination with "Monday Articles" on white liberals, no less than on "black power" advocates claiming that violence was the only means of obtaining rights. But he would have been the last person on earth to deny those rights, and he could have pointed to many places in his own work that admitted the appalling injustice of the white man to the black and to the fact that a day of retribution must inevitably come.

§ SO FOR ALMOST HALF A CENTURY he damned America, its people, its government, its laws, its ideas, its culture, its arts and entertainment and customs. It was, he stoutly maintained, inferior on all counts to any one of the civilized nations of Western Europe. Its legislative and executive arms were "ignorant, incompetent, corrupt, and disgusting," and its administration of justice was "stupid, dishonest and against all reason and equity." In its relations with other countries, whether friend or foe, it was "hypocritical, disingenuous, knavish and dishonorable." "Here," he wrote, "the general average of intelligence, of knowledge, of competence, of integrity, of self-respect, of honor is so low that any man who knows his trade, does not fear ghosts, has read fifty good books, and practices the common decencies stands out as brilliantly as a wart on a bald head, and is thrown willy-nilly into a meager and exclusive aristocracy."[84] Clearly, one could not think of being an American without blushing.

Yet he remained on the dock, wrapped in the flag, when the Young Intellectuals set sail. He could never understand the expatriates—the Henry Jameses, the Ezra Pounds, the T. S. Eliots—who thought the first table of the Americans so crude and tacky that they were content to sit at the second table of the English. Whenever their voices were raised in animadversions against their native land he responded only with a polite but feeble "Hear, hear!" He paid his taxes uncomplainingly (at least until Roosevelt came along), obeyed all laws that were physiologically obeyable, accepted without protest the searching duties and responsibilities of citizenship, avoided all commerce with men sworn to overthrow the government, and did his modest best to enrich the national arts and letters.

Nor did anything anger him quite as much as that American subservience to the ideas and culture of the "Motherland" which characterized so much of the nineteenth century and survived to some degree into his own time—nothing, that is, except possibly the patronizing and even contemptuous air with which the English looked on things American. His attitude in the World Wars was not so much pro-German as anti-British. It was true, he believed, that the United States, as a nation, was inferior to England, but the only reason for this was that Americans were willing to let it be so. Once they got over the shock of discovering that the English were actually incompetents and "deadbeats," superior only in impudence, shamelessness, and hypocrisy, their attitude would very quickly change. One of the principal theses of *The American Language,* in all its editions, was that the English spoken in this country infinitely surpassed, in life and vividness and capacity for change and development, the English spoken in England.

Why did he stay here? Why did he consistently spurn all lures (and even all invitations) to get out and stay out? He gave his reason on numerous occasions, and it was always the same: no intelligent man could be as happy, or even one-half as happy, elsewhere. It was as impossible for him to live in these free and independent states and not be happy as it would be for a boy to weep when his schoolhouse burned down. The show was simply too good, too hilarious, too unimaginably gaudy and obscene; where else could one get better entertainment for his money? In its final form this statement occurs in one of the very last things he ever wrote, the 1948 preface to the *Chrestomathy*:

> Those who explore the ensuing pages will find them marked by a certain ribaldry, even when they discuss topics commonly regarded as grave. I do not apologize for this, for life in the Republic has always seemed to me to be far more comic than serious. We live in a land of abounding quackeries, and if we do not learn how to laugh we succumb to the melancholy disease which afflicts the race of viewers-with-alarm. I have had too good a time of it in this world to go down that chute. I have witnessed, in my day, the discovery, enthronement and subsequent

collapse of a vast army of uplifters and world-savers, and am firmly convinced that all of them were mountebanks. We produce such mountebanks in greater number than any other country, and they climb to heights seldom equalled elsewhere. Nevertheless, we survive, and not only survive but also flourish. In no other country known to me is life as safe and agreeable, taking one day with another, as it is in These States. Even in a great Depression few if any starve, and even in a great war the number who suffer by it is vastly surpassed by the number who fatten on it and enjoy it. Thus my view of my country is predominantly tolerant and amiable.[85]

He encountered very little tolerance and amiability in return, but of course that only proved his point.

I V

THE CRITIC

This, as I conceive it, is what criticism is for: to find out what an author is trying to do, and to beat a drum for him when it is worth doing and he does it well.

—*A Book of Prefaces*

◇◇

1 IF MENCKEN DID NOT REALLY think of himself as a literary critic, he was certainly not alone in his opinion. There were large numbers of people, including very many critics, who did not think he was either, and who resolutely opposed admitting him to the faculty. Stuart Pratt Sherman, over a period of years perhaps his bitterest antagonist, saw his work as "not criticism at all, but mere scurrility and blackguardism." Paul Elmer More spoke of the "malignity" of his critical writing as displayed in the *Prejudices,* and termed him a "brawling vulgarian." George Goetz, a fellow Baltimorean who under the pen name of V. F. Calverton wrote from a Marxist standpoint, dismissed him as a "prophet of the tawdry run of anti-bourgeois liberals." Louis Bromfield, the novelist, considered him "far more a politician." Even so late as 1950 Edgar Kemler, in his biography, made the point that "Mencken was a cynic, and no cynic has ever qualified as a truly professional critic."

At the very kindest, it would have to be said that the authors of these remarks did not understand him. But even those with somewhat more insight into his work, and a greater sympathy for what he was trying to do, appear to have had reservations about whether he was a critic in the usual sense of the word. Thus John Farrar of *The Book-*

man claimed that he could not "by any stretch of the imagination be called a critic. He is purely and simply a mustard plaster." Benjamin De Casseres wrote a whole book entitled *Mencken and Shaw*, in which his comparisons of the two men were overwhelmingly in Mencken's favor, but even he held that "he is not a critic at all. He is an advocate, a prosecuting attorney." Edmund Wilson, who followed after him and survived into a later period, but whose career spanned on the whole much the same era that Mencken's did, was always perceptive and kind toward his colleague, but he, too, thought that he was "perhaps a prophet rather than a critic."[1]

Without doubt, there was some basis for all of these judgments, both friendly and unfriendly. Carl Dolmetsch is probably right when he says that "by the standards of our day [Mencken] was abysmally untrained and ill-equipped to run the critical department of a national magazine"—though he may go a bit too far when he adds immediately that "he knew no more of literature than one could then acquire with a city high school education and a passion (unsystematic and idiosyncratic) for leisure reading."[2] It is perfectly true that when Mencken assumed the post of book editor of *The Smart Set* in November 1908 he was venturing out onto a field dominated by professionals, and that he had little of their training and equipment. He was without a degree and, as a matter of fact, had never spent a day in any college or university; he knew some German but no other modern European language; his knowledge of criticism, as distinct from the literature on which it bore, had gaps in it and in some areas was undoubtedly at second hand.

Yet it is also true that in those years from 1908 to 1923 he became the most widely known critic in the nation, and that no other one, then, before, or since, has ever wielded anything like his enormous power and influence. He quite literally changed the course of American literature, bringing one period of it to an end and inaugurating another, and in the process of doing so he helped some of the most important and salient figures in the new generation of writers to achieve prominence. The objection could be raised that the old era was due to end anyway, and the new one to come forth, and this is of course true; but Mencken, by the sheer force of his critical work, accelerated these developments and gave a sense of direction to them.

The most astonishing thing about all this is that he did what he did from a vantage point that could not possibly have been more ill-suited and unpromising. At no time did *The Smart Set* ever have anything properly describable as "mass circulation." Moreover, not all of his and Nathan's efforts to make it "The Aristocrat Among Magazines" and "A Magazine of Cleverness" ever quite succeeded in ridding it of its earlier dubious reputation, and so the audience that it did reach was far from being the same one that read such dignified periodicals as *The Atlantic Monthly*, the *Century*, and *Harper's*. Mencken's books on Shaw and Nietzsche had attracted some attention, and without question he had made a name for himself in newspaper circles, but the fact still remains that here he was starting out not just as a virtual unknown, but from a position hardly calculated to put him on an immediate level with those whose critical opinions carried weight.

Thus his influence would have to be slow in growing, and it was perhaps only natural that it would take root at first among young people—those too irreverent to be awed by the older and stodgier journals, and rebellious enough to delight in the iconoclasm that he and Nathan made a kind of official editorial policy.

It is difficult for us now, at a distance of well over half a century, to realize the excitement that *The Smart Set* generated in its day among youthful aspirants to immortality in literature. The noted playwright S. N. Behrman, in the introductory "Reminiscence" which he wrote for Dolmetsch's anthology, conveys some idea of it: "*The Smart Set* magazine," he says, "edited by H. L. Mencken and George Jean Nathan, had had an electrifying effect. It was an influence. Along with *The New Machiavelli* and *The New Republic*, we swallowed *The Smart Set* as part of our literary nourishment. Its editors had already [he is speaking of his undergraduate years at Harvard, 1912–16] become legendary."[3] Charles Angoff, whose feelings would undergo rather marked change some two decades later, describes much the same thing: "The stories in *The Smart Set*," he tells us in his *Portrait from Memory*, "seemed like no stories in any other magazine. The same was true of the articles and poems, but it was H. L. Mencken's book reviews and George Jean Nathan's drama reviews that attracted most of the young people I knew. They were dazzlingly written, and they expressed the rebellion that we all felt. Groups of us would discuss these reviews—always enthusiastically. Some of us could recite by heart paragraph upon paragraph of certain reviews by Mencken and Nathan."[4] By 1924 Carl Van Doren could write that "no other contemporary critic is so well known in the colleges. No other is so influential amongst the latest generation of boys and girls of letters."[5]

But Mencken, though he was at all times willing to recognize new talent and give it encouragement, had no desire whatever to be a hero to "sophomores." He was after much bigger game. It would take a while to bring it down, but his efforts never flagged and the results were not for a moment in doubt. Ernest Boyd says that the publication of *A Book of Prefaces* in 1917 "marks the beginning of his rise to popular fame,"[6] and this is probably true; the appearance two years later of the first volume of *Prejudices*, where he gathered some of the best of his *Smart Set* pieces, further consolidated his reputation. By that time he was a national figure, and for the most part he had made himself so by those monthly 5,000-word review-articles which he wrote for 182 successive issues of the magazine. When he left it at the end of 1923 to establish *The American Mercury*, he was, in the words of Huntington Cairns, "the closest embodiment of the Johnsonian type of literary dictatorship the United States had known."[7]

Thus Boyd, immediately following the passage I have just quoted, added that "his main indictment against American literature and its critics, that they are wholly indifferent to esthetics, has not been seriously questioned. The specific battles waged by him on behalf of writers victimized or neglected because of the puritan obsession have resulted in victories." It was the belief of Frank Harris that "to say that Mencken is the best critic in the United States is less than his due; he is one of the best critics in English"; and of Vincent O'Sullivan that "a criticism by him is as absorbing as a well-planned short story. Just as much art goes into it."[8] Isaac Goldberg thought that "after you strip Mencken of such externalities as sociological, political and philosophical wrappings, you find in him essentially the creative critic."[9] And I have already quoted Walter Lippmann's estimate, in a 1926 review of *Notes on Democracy*, that Mencken was "the most powerful personal influence on this whole generation of educated people."

But even more significant than testimonials like these (for there were cases, too, where their authors were only grudgingly admitting the undeniable) were the tributes paid to him by the men and women whose work he had helped to place in the forefront of the new literature. Again it may be necessary to emphasize that Mencken did not really "discover" any of these people—they would have been important in their own right even if he had never lived. But he published many of them in *The Smart Set*, and showed an intuitive understanding of what they were trying to do, and encouraged them to keep on, and never lost an opportunity to "beat a drum" for them. Their gratitude speaks out eloquently in scores or hundreds of the volumes from his personal library that now line the shelves of the Pratt's Mencken Room.

Sherwood Anderson, autographing a copy of *The Triumph of the Egg,* saluted him as the "champion of men who need champions." Among the innumerable signed volumes from Theodore Dreiser, *Twelve Men* acknowledges "many courtesies and services." The poet Joseph Auslander wrote in a presentation copy of his collection *Cyclops' Eye:* "For H. L. Mencken . . . because, this side idolatry, I am in admiration as much as any." James Branch Cabell sent *Preface to the Past* "in admiration and gratitude." Eugene O'Neill wrote in the flyleaf of *The Moon of the Caribbees* that "*the* first letter of genuine critical appreciation I ever received" was from Mencken. Sinclair Lewis dedicated *Elmer Gantry* to him "with profound admiration," and in a letter tipped into Mencken's copy of the German translation of *Main Street (Die Hauptstrasse)* he wrote, apropos of his forthcoming *Arrowsmith:* "I'm more interested in your review than in that of anyone else." Scott Fitzgerald wrote him about *The Great Gatsby:* "As you know I'd rather have you like a book of mine than anyone in America." Nor was this sort of thing confined to American authors by any means; Aldous Huxley, for example, sent him a copy of his novel *Crome Yellow* "with homages," and Hugh Walpole forwarded a copy of *The Cathedral* simply to "my friend."

Such lines must have paid Mencken many times over for all the ninth- and tenth-rate stuff he had to plow through in order to dredge up a few pearls, and for the vituperation he had to endure from the entrenched critics who viewed him as a threat to polite letters. His admirers understood him as he understood them, and it may even be that they did as much to enhance his reputation as he did for theirs. Despite all their differences, they were comrades-in-arms in the same great battle—and with hardly an exception they acknowledged him as their leader in the fray.

2 IN ORDER TO UNDERSTAND just what it was that Mencken accomplished during those years when he was functioning as a professional critic, it is desirable to go back and exam-

ine in greater depth the state of "the national letters" at the end of the nineteenth century and on into the first two decades of the twentieth.

It was his own belief that, "despite several false starts that promised much," American literature had long since settled down into a condition of "respectable mediocrity."[10] The false starts were at least three in number. To begin with, there was Poe—not, of course, the Poe of the doggerel verse and the horror stories but Poe the critic, who had written such capital things as "The Poetic Principle" and "The Philosophy of Composition" and thus made himself the first (at least in point of time) of the nation's literary theoreticians. But his countrymen, seeing in him only a drunkard and wastrel, had allowed him to die up an alley like a stray dog; and it remained for the French to recognize his genius, make the most of it, and then export him back into the United States at second hand. There was Whitman, whose poetry shocked the national sensibilities to such a degree that he was incontinently kicked out of his job and narrowly escaped going to jail as a public nuisance. And finally there was Mark Twain, who turned out two or three indubitable masterpieces but then sank back into a puerile romanticism simply because he feared that the public (and his wife) would disapprove of the ideas that he really held. He was looked upon (and half looked upon himself) as a professional after-dinner comedian, a clown on the same level with Artemus Ward, Bill Nye, and Petroleum V. Nasby.*

---

*Mencken consistently overlooked, I think, one figure of towering greatness who arose in the post-Civil War era and survived virtually into his own time—namely, Henry James. Despite Dreiser, Fitzgerald, Hemingway, Faulkner, and all the rest, it is unlikely that the American novel has ever seen a more accomplished artist than James, but Mencken's attitude toward him was curiously ambivalent. In a letter of September 4, 1911, to Harry Leon Wilson (Forgue, *Letters*, p. 17) he confessed that *What Maisie Knew* was the only novel of James's that he could read ("*The Golden Bowl*—ye Gods!"), but added: "Still, the artist is there, and on the whole I believe that his influence has been for the good." He acknowledged that James was a "superb technician" and that the "makings of a genuinely first-rate artist" were in him, but felt that in fleeing to Europe he had made the mistake of going in the wrong direction. He "would have been vastly improved as a novelist by a few whiffs from the Chicago stockyards." (*Smart Set*, LXIII, 3, Nov. 1920, p. 141; *Chrestomathy*, p. 500.) In the essay on "Puritanism as a Literary Force" in *A Book of Prefaces* he singles him out, along with Howells, Mark Twain, and Bret Harte, as one of "four writers who at least deserved respectful consideration as literary artists," but thought that along with Howells he quickly showed "that timorousness and reticence which are the distinguishing marks of the Puritan" (pp. 217–18). In the very first article which he wrote for *The Smart Set* in November 1908, he dismissed James's *Views and Reviews* in one line: "Early essays by Henry James—some in the English language."

He also neglected, I think, Melville. In the whole vast canon of his critical writing I can find no mention of *Moby Dick*.

But save for these three lonely and Himalayan exceptions, the nation's literature was characterized by "a sort of timorous flaccidity, an amiable hollowness." Its typical great man in one generation had been Washington Irving, and in the next one James Russell Lowell, and in the generation after that William Dean Howells—all competent, conscientious craftsmen, no doubt, but in intellectual content as empty as a jug. "When one turns," Mencken held,

> to any other national literature—to Russian literature, say, or French, or German or Scandinavian—one is conscious immediately of a definite attitude toward the primary mysteries of existence, the unsolved and ever-fascinating problems at the bottom of human life, and of a definite preoccupation with some of them, and a definite way of translating their challenge into drama. These attitudes and preoccupations raise a literature above mere poetizing and tale-telling; they give it dignity and importance; above all, they give it national character. But it is precisely here that the literature of America, and especially the later literature, is most colorless and inconsequential. As if paralyzed by the national fear of ideas, the democratic distrust of whatever strikes beneath the prevailing platitudes, it evades all resolute and honest dealing with what, after all, must be every healthy literature's elementary materials. One is conscious of no brave and noble earnestness in it, of no generalized passion for intellectual and spiritual adventure, of no organized determination to think things out. What is there is a highly self-conscious and insipid correctness, a bloodless respectability, a submergence of matter in manner.[11]

This literature existed in three layers, "each inordinately doughy and uninspiring—each almost without flavor or savor." It was not easy to say which one deserved to be called the upper, but for decorum's sake the honor could be given to that which enjoyed the approval of the reigning and accepted critics. It consisted of such things as the novels of Howells, Robert Grant, Alice Brown, "and the rest of the dwindling survivors of New England *Kultur*"; the academic poetry of George Woodberry and Robert Underwood Johnson; the "tea-party" essays of Samuel Crothers and Agnes Repplier; and—of course—the "solemn, highly judicial, coroner's-inquest criticism" of More, Brownell, Irving Babbitt, and their followers, to whom we shall return. This layer was always correctly done; it was never crude or gross; there was in it a faint perfume of college-town society. But "one never remembers a character in the novels of these aloof and de-Americanized Americans; one never encounters an idea in their essays; one never carries away a line out of their poetry. It is literature as an academic exercise for talented grammarians, almost as a genteel recreation for ladies and gentlemen of fashion."

The bottom layer was given over to the literature of Greenwich Village—and "Greenwich Village" was not so much a precise geographical location in New York City as it was an artistic state of mind, an attitude of revolt against the academicians, the literature of bohemianism and the avant-garde. "Miss Amy Lowell is herself a fully equipped and automobile Greenwich Village, domiciled in Boston amid the crumbling gravestones of the New England *intelligentsia*, but often in waspish joy-ride through the hinterland." It was concerned for the most part with technique; its practitioners, having no intelligible ideas to offer, tried to make the most out of mere form and so descended into meaningless gibberish. Most of them were frauds and all of them wrote alike, so that not even an expert could tell the work of one from another. But despite the low quality of its output, it had at least the merit of challenging the accepted canons and canon lawyers of literature, and there was always the faint chance that something halfway decent might come out of it.*

The layer in between was made up of the books that most people actually read. It was, in other words, the popular literature, even more commonplace and uninspiring then than it is now. The list of those who confected it was a long one: to call off only a few, there were Richard Harding Davis, Rex Beach, Emerson Hough, Augustus Thomas, Robert W. Chambers, Henry Sydnor Harrison, George Barr McCutcheon, Harold MacGrath, F. Hopkinson Smith, Mary Roberts Rinehart, Gene Stratton-Porter, Harold Bell Wright, John Fox, Jr., Eleanor H. Porter . . . such names, as Mencken was to write in a slightly different context, are as meaningless today as a roll call of

---

*In a review of Alfred Kreymborg's *Troubadour*, appearing in the Baltimore *Evening Sun*, April 4, 1925, and included in *Prejudices: Fifth Series*, pp. 214–17, Mencken showed a mellower attitude toward the inhabitants of the Village. "As one who poked many heavy jocosities at it while it lasted," he said, "I hope I may now say with good grace that I believe Greenwich Village did a good service to all the fine arts in this great land, and left a valuable legacy behind it. True enough, its own heroes were nearly all duds, and most of them have been forgotten, but it at least broke ground, it at least stirred up the animals. . . . All that excess did no harm. The false prophets changed from day to day. The real ones remained."

Sumerian kings. In the novels and tales ground out by these people, the heroes were always 100% red-blooded American males; the heroines were always antiseptically pure; the villains were very incarnations of evil—but in the end, after incredible vicissitudes, virtue always triumphed, and the hero and heroine were united chastely, and very often he won not only her but the management of her father's business as well.

This literature filled the magazines first of all, and then eventually the book counters of the department stores. In remote villages and on farms it was ordered out of Sears, Roebuck and Montgomery Ward catalogues. The stuff paid "like a bucket-shop or a soap-factory," and at bottom it touched "such depths of banality that it would be difficult to match it in any other country." It had "a native quality that is as unmistakable as Mother's Day, Billy-Sundayism or the Junior Order of United American Mechanics. It [was] the natural outpouring of a naive and yet half barbarous people, full of delight in a few childish and inaccurate ideas."

This is not to say, of course, that the men and women responsible for it were all totally inept and third-rate. Some of them wrote very well, and in the work of a few—Mrs. Rinehart, for example, and O. Henry—there was an unmistakable technical excellence. Booth Tarkington, Ring Lardner, and Montague Glass had graduated from this school as, forty years earlier, had Mark Twain. But the power of money, and no less the power of acclaim, were constantly exerting their downward pull, and many who could have done better and more serious work yielded supinely to temptation and went on grinding out the sort of thing that would assure them a bank account, and a suburban home, and the dignity of being considered important.

If Mencken's judgment of this layer seems unnecessarily harsh, a glance at the "best-seller list" for the year in which he started his career as a book reviewer should bear out his estimate of the national taste. These were the books that, in 1908, outstripped all others in popularity and sales:*

---

*I take this from *70 Years of Best Sellers: 1895–1965* by Alice Payne Hackett (New York: R. R. Bowker Co., 1967). It should be borne in mind, of course, that "best-seller lists" are not, and have never pretended to be, an index of the best that is being written; as the term indicates, they simply report what books are having the best sales. They reflect very faithfully the popular taste, but not a discriminating one.

Mr. Crewe's Career, Winston Churchill
The Barrier, Rex Beach
The Trail of the Lonesome Pine, John Fox, Jr.
The Lure of the Mask, Harold MacGrath
The Shuttle, Frances Hodgson Burnett
Peter, F. Hopkinson Smith
Lewis Rand, Mary Johnston
The Black Flag, Louis J. Vance
The Man from Brodney's, George Barr McCutcheon
The Weavers, Gilbert Parker

Obviously one could not blame the established critics of the land for paying scant attention to work like this, for in all of it, from end to end, there was nothing to engage the critical faculty. On the other hand, one might very well blame them for their failure to appraise it for what it really was, or to give encouragement to a more honest and realistic literature. One of Mencken's chief complaints against them was that they lived entirely in the past: they studiously investigated the influence of German romanticism on Coleridge and compared Sterne with Smollett; they wrote their precious essays on Milton and Shakespeare and Chaucer; they went back further yet and knelt at the altars of Dante, Virgil, and Homer. They turned out authoritative but essentially pedestrian textbooks on the history of English or American literature which always stopped at least a generation short of their own time. And it simply would not have occurred to them to look at the work which was coming into being around them, or to imagine for one moment that it deserved their attention.

There can be no doubt that Mencken was cruelly unfair to these men. There is a difference, which he seems never to have been aware of or which he chose to ignore, between literary criticism and literary scholarship, and the latter, after all, has its high uses. Almost without exception, they were scholars. William Crary Brownell (1851–1928) was an authority on French literature and served for forty years as an editorial adviser to Charles Scribner's Sons, then as now one of the largest and most respected publishing houses in the United States. Irving Babbitt (1865–1933), usually regarded as the leader of the "New Humanist" movement in American letters, was professor of French language and literature at Harvard for two generations, and students flocked to his classes. Paul Elmer More (1864–1937) taught Sanskrit and the classics, edited *The Nation*, and wrote an enormous number of books, including the fourteen volumes of the *Shelburne*

Essays and several works on Plato which remain today on the shelf of standard studies of the great Greek philosopher. Stuart Sherman (1881–1926), a disciple of More and Babbitt, and Mencken's arch-enemy, hardened during the war years into a rigid American and Puritan chauvinism that bordered on the fanatical; but toward the end of his relatively short life he became much more open to new developments in writing, and admitted that he might have been mistaken—something which Mencken never did! All of them were respected by their peers, and all still have a place in histories and dictionaries of American literature.

The point was that, individually and collectively, they stood for everything he was against, and were opposed to all that he admired and fought for. Actually we are anticipating here, for the New Humanism that they represented did not really reach its peak as a formal intellectual movement until the years between, say, 1915 and 1925, when Mencken had passed the high point of his own critical activity and was pretty much ready to abandon the field for other interests. It was during that time that the famous "Battle of the Books" was waged with unrestrained ferocity on both sides. But the aesthetic principles of the New Humanism had been at least implicit in much of the criticism of an earlier date, and Brownell, the movement's founder and prophet, had expounded them in books written as early as the 1890's. Babbitt and More, influenced by Brownell, did little more than develop and formalize his ideas in the decades that followed.

None of them, it should be made clear, were literary critics—at least not in the sense that Mencken was, or Van Wyck Brooks, or Edmund Wilson, or Howard Mumford Jones. One sometimes gets the impression, in fact—particularly with Babbitt—that they had very little knowledge of what was being written and published around them, and could not possibly have cared less. They were theoreticians of criticism—that is to say, their aim was to provide the actual critics with a set of standards that could be used for judging individual works and authors. These standards were iron-clad and absolute, and a literal application of them would leave no doubt in the mind of a critic or reader as to whether a given book was acceptable or not.

Babbitt, in a series of highly erudite volumes of which *The New Laokoön* (1910) and *Rousseau and Romanticism* (1919) were perhaps the most important, gave the New Humanist philosophy its definitive expression—to the extent, that is, that theories so vague could be set forth with anything even approaching clarity. Briefly, he held that all the ills of the modern world were the result of "naturalism" and romanticism, and that the only way to solve them was by a return to humanism. But—and this point should be noted well—humanism for him was not at all the intellectual movement that had sprung out of the Renaissance and whose finest flower is to be found in men like Erasmus and Colet. That humanism had been a reaction against the decadent Scholasticism of the later Middle Ages, and it had sought to find in a return to classical learning some basis for its belief in the natural nobility and dignity of human nature. Babbitt, however, maintained that in correctly separating man from God the Renaissance humanists had fallen into the opposite and equally pernicious error of identifying him with "nature." This had the effect of casting man down from his true place in the universe and making of him only a cog in a subhuman machine.*

His efforts to bring himself back up from this level had resulted in still another error—the "romanticism" of Jean-Jacques Rousseau, which really left him no better off than before. In the philosophy of Rousseau man had developed his feelings rather than his intellect. Sentiment took precedence over reason, and a sickly humanitarianism took the place of genuine humanism.

What Babbitt wanted to do, at least in his own mind, was to restore the balanced belief of the Greeks in a dualistic universe—a universe in which man stood distinct from and over against nature. Only such a view could correct the twin vices of naturalism and romanticism, and only the same sense of balance and moderation that had characterized the ancient Greeks could bring back a proper and genuinely human sense of values.

This sense of values had to manifest itself in literature, of course, as well as in life. Brownell had held that the two were integral with each other, and that no literary aesthetic could be complete that did not stand on the Christian ethic of character, the Platonic doctrine of form, and the Aristotelian reliance upon reason. Echoing Sainte-Beuve, he

---

*It might be worth pointing out that the medieval Scholastics never for a moment fell into the philosophical error of pantheism. If there was one thing they were sure of, it was that the divine and human natures were substantially distinct. God's being is "a se"—that is, He is Being, full and uncreated, and His being is identical with His essence. The being of the entire created universe, including man, is "per se"—that is, it has being which it receives from another source, namely God.

believed that "our liking anything is not enough . . . it is necessary to know further whether we are right in liking it." Babbitt, coming after him, disdained any form of "naturalism" in literature, whether in Frenchmen like Zola and the Goncourts or American writers like Dreiser, Lewis, Eugene O'Neill, and John Dos Passos. In the works of such men human nature was exhibited as nothing more than the slave of degraded passion, and toward them he would show no mercy: "One should not be moderate," he proclaimed, "in dealing with error."

In his writings Babbitt always made it a point to pay tribute to Paul Elmer More, and More, in his *Shelburne Essays*, was always careful to return the compliment. As Van Wyck Brooks was later to put it, "More's hand was against every living writer."[12] More, too, had no patience with naturalism; he thought that Dos Passos' *Manhattan Transfer* was "an explosion in a cesspool," he admitted having been shocked at first by the audacity of some of Robert Frost's poetry, and he believed that Sinclair Lewis was "perhaps the crudest member of the group" of writers coming out of the Midwest. Just as Babbitt upheld the necessity of a "will to refrain," so More upheld the necessity of an "inner check"; both these rather nebulous concepts would lead the good man to espouse the true in life, and the good writer to treat only of the beautiful in literature.

The curious thing about all this is that both of them, along with Sherman and other fellow Humanists, insisted that they had nothing whatever against literary realism: what they were opposed to was naturalism. This is a fine-drawn and subtle distinction not immediately evident to the lay mind, and Mencken disposed of it briefly in an article, "The Dreiser Bugaboo," which he published in *The Seven Arts* magazine for August 1917 and then made a part of the chapter on Dreiser in *A Book of Prefaces*. Sherman, writing in *The Nation* for December 2, 1915, had said that Dreiser lied when he called himself a realist; that by giving Frank Cowperwood, the protagonist of *The Financier* and *The Titan*, a "rapacious appetite" for money and women, he had exposed his "naturalistic philosophy." Dreiser, Mencken rejoined, "in point of fact, is scarcely more the realist or the naturalist, in any true sense, than H. G. Wells or the later George Moore, nor has he ever announced himself in either the one character or the other— if there be, in fact, any difference between them that any one save a pigeon-holing pedagogue can discern." Dreiser's sense of the universal and inexplicable human tragedy, his vision of life as a seeking without a finding, was at an infinite remove from the empty, meretricious nastiness of, say, Zola in *Pot-Bouille*.[13]

With the New Humanists as a group Mencken seldom entered into direct combat; perhaps he was aware that he could not compete with them on the level of scholarship. Toward each one individually he leveled some of his most devastating witticisms, and yet at the same time he treated them, too, with a certain grudging respect. Where Sherman was concerned, his attitude was for a long time uncharacteristically bitter, as a result of the way Sherman had attacked both Dreiser and himself during the First World War on the ground that they had German names; once, when Carl Van Doren tried to introduce them at a luncheon, Mencken refused to cross the room and shake hands on the ground that Sherman was a "dirty fighter." But when Sherman died in 1926 at the age of only forty-five he acknowledged that his passing had cut off a career of great promise. And when More died in 1937 he wrote to Edgar Lee Masters that he was sorry he had never met him, adding that "we had some pleasant enough exchanges ten or twelve years ago"—though *Man of Letters*, Betty Adler's exhaustive census of his correspondence, fails to list any written exchange between them.

One of the very few places in which he attacked the ideological stand of the New Humanism was in the May 1930 issue of the *Mercury*, when he reviewed Norman Foerster's *Humanism in America*—but by that time the movement itself was pretty much spent and Mencken had been for all practical purposes removed from the literary scene for half a dozen years. There he called it "the natural and inevitable refuge of all timorous and third-rate men—of all weaklings for whom the struggle with hard facts is unendurable—of all the nay-sayers of Nietzsche's immortal scorn." "The progress of the human race," he concluded, "is not forwarded by any such vague and witless blather."[14]

I have dealt at such length with the Humanists, even though—as I have indicated—they belong at the end rather than the beginning of Mencken's critical career, because long before they had come upon the scene their philosophy had permeated not only all of American literature and thought but the nation's whole way of life as well. They did little more, in other words, than formalize and set on an intellectual plane the gloomy Calvinism that had characterized that way of life almost from the start. More and Babbitt had no more use for the popular literature of the day than Mencken had; they were intelligent enough men to know how cheap and shoddy it was. But the very principles they espoused made it impossible to turn out anything better. Whenever a genuine artist raised himself above the common level— a Poe, a Whitman, a Henry James—he was put down at once as a naturalist, and hence a threat to the American system of morals. Puritanism held the national letters in an iron grip, and Anthony Comstock's New York Society for the Suppression of Vice stayed keenly alert for so much as a line, in any book, that might "arouse a libidinous passion . . . in the mind of a modest woman." A pamphlet prepared by Comstock himself set forth in its title the whole Puritan approach to the subject: "MORALS, Not Art or Literature."

In 1893 Stephen Crane had to publish *Maggie: A Girl of the Streets* privately, and dared not even acknowledge his authorship of it until a number of years later. Harper's would not dream of publishing Dreiser's *Sister Carrie* in 1900 (mild and harmless as it appears to us today); the firm of Doubleday, Page & Co. accepted it, but after the work was set in type they lost their nerve and, save for a few copies that got out and circulated almost clandestinely, the sheets remained in their basement. It was not until seven years later that another publisher took them over, and even then the book was for all practical purposes under a ban.

> It is on the side of sex [Mencken wrote in 1917] that the appointed virtuosi of virtue exercise their chief repressions, for it is sex that especially fascinates the lubricious Puritan mind; but the conventual reticence that thus becomes the enforced fashion in one field extends itself to all others. Our fiction, in general, is marked by an artificiality as marked as that of Eighteenth Century poetry or the later Georgian drama. The romance in it runs to set forms and stale situations; the revelation, by such a book as *The Titan*, that there may be a glamour as entrancing in the way of a conqueror of men as in the way of a youth with a maid, remains isolated and exotic. We have no first-rate political or religious novel; we have no first-rate war story; despite all our national engrossment in commercial enterprise, we have few second-rate tales of business. Romance, in American fiction, still means only a somewhat childish amorousness and sentimentality—the love affairs of Paul and Virginia, or the pale adulteries of their elders. And on the side of realism there is an almost equal vacuity and lack of veracity. The action of all the novels of the Howells school goes on within four walls of painted canvas; they begin to shock once they describe an attack of asthma or a steak burning below stairs; they never penetrate beneath the

flow of social concealments and urbanities to the passions that actually move men and women in their acts, and the great forces that circumscribe and condition personality. So obvious a piece of reporting as Upton Sinclair's *The Jungle* or Robert Herrick's *Together* makes a sensation; the appearance of a *Jennie Gerhardt* or a *Hagar Revelly* brings forth a growl of astonishment and rage.[15]

This was the world of American literature at the turn of the century. This was the world into which Mencken stepped in the November 1908 issue of *The Smart Set* and which, within little more than a decade, he was to change beyond all recognition.

3 THE OMNIVOROUS READING he had done as a boy and young man, though it may have been unsystematic and undirected, certainly served him well as he embarked on his new career. In *A Book of Prefaces* he speaks familiarly and in an offhand manner of such modern German writers as Gerhart Hauptmann, Ludwig Thoma, Otto Julius Bierbaum, Richard Dehmel, Clara Viebig, and Thomas Mann. He was acquainted with the great Russians: Tolstoi, Dostoievski, Turgenev. Somewhere he speaks of having read the whole of Zola's immense *Rougon-Macquart* cycle—a feat that must have been as heroic then as it would be now. In his own language he had gone as far back as Middle English literature and come forward to contemporary novelists like Thomas Hardy, Joseph Conrad, George Moore, H. G. Wells, Arnold Bennett, and Hugh Walpole. In the field of the drama he had read Pirandello, Strindberg, and Sudermann, and was perfectly at home, of course, with Ibsen and Shaw.

Such a background was invaluable, particularly in the sense that it enabled him to compare writers of such stature with those who were turning out the popular American fiction and theater of the same period.

But there can be no doubt that he was helped too (and this despite the lack of any obvious connection) by his years of experience as a reporter on the *Herald* and *Sun*. For one thing, they had trained him to write a clear, vivid, and expressive prose. For another, it goes without saying that no reasonably alert and intelligent young man can cover the day-in-and-day-out operations of a police court—the routine investigations into squalid murders, the booking of petty thieves and drunks and prostitutes, the handling of such commonplace things as a husband beating up a wife or a child running away from home—without getting some feel for life as it is really lived. If, a bit later, he moves up to covering the doings of the politicians in and around City Hall, he is bound to turn a bit cynical when he hears about virtues like honor and integrity and truthfulness. And if, during this same time, he is making himself familiar with the literature of the day, he will realize immediately how unrelated to real life that literature is.

In a chapter of *Newspaper Days* entitled "Approach to Lovely Letters," he tells of the magazines that he used to get hold of regularly and read with absorption in his late teens and early twenties. Among them were two named *Town Topics* and *M'lle New York.* Both were urbane and highly sophisticated periodicals depicting a world far removed from the complacent bourgeois setting of Hollins Street, and it is doubtful that Mencken, then or later, felt any especial attraction to that world. But the literary critic for *Town Topics* was one Percival Pollard, and in the pages of *M'lle New York* were to be found the writings of a blasé and irreverent commentator on the musical and literary scene named James Gibbons Huneker. These two men would have a substantial influence on Mencken's own critical philosophy, and so the magazines, though they are today as forgotten as *Judge* and *Puck*, have perhaps an importance in the development of American literature that is out of all proportion to their own intrinsic worth.

Pollard (1869–1911) was born in Germany and educated in England, but he came to the United States while still a young man and soon earned a solid reputation as a critic. By virtue of his background he was naturally far more at home with European literature than with its American counterpart, and much of his work consisted of making Continental writers known to American audiences. He was particularly interested in the work of the *Überbrettl'*, a movement toward greater naturalism among modern German dramatists, and his book *Masks and Minstrels of New Germany* described the figures of this movement—Wedekind, Thoma, Hauptmann, Schnitzler, von Hofmannsthal, and others—with sympathy and insight. When it came out in 1911, Mencken reviewed it favorably both in the *Evening Sun* and *The Smart Set.* Somewhat coincidentally, Pollard died that same year in Baltimore, at the Johns Hopkins Hospital, of a brain tumor, and Mencken was called upon to take care of the rather macabre circumstances surrounding his funeral.

Huneker (1860–1921) was not only a far more important writer than Pollard but a much greater influence on Mencken as well. William H. Nolte, in his study of Mencken as critic, says that "there is every reason to believe that he influenced Mencken more than any other of the younger man's contemporaries,"[16] and this judgment is undoubtedly correct. A native of Philadelphia, "that depressing intellectual slum,"[17] Huneker began his career as a music critic and did much to introduce American concert audiences to Brahms, Richard Strauss, and Chopin. For years, as critic for the *Musical Courier* and then later for the New York *Sun*, he covered performances of the Philharmonic and the Metropolitan Opera. But the immense catholicity of his interests soon led him into painting and literature as well; he hymned Manet, Monet, Degas, and Cézanne at a time when the beginnings of modern painting were still an object of ridicule, and he was among the earliest English-speaking critics to write with any understanding of Nietzsche, Maeterlinck, Strindberg, Stirner, and Gorki. Like Pollard, he was far more interested in European than in American literature, but "he was among the first to give a hand to Frank Norris, Theodore Dreiser, Stephen Crane and H. B. Fuller."[18]

He wrote of all these things with an urbane style and a ribald wit that set him very much apart from the academic critics of the day, and the wit spilled over and foamed up in his table talk. He was, in other words, a brilliant and inexhaustible conversationalist. Just when Mencken first met him is not entirely clear; he wrote a long account of it in an article for the June 1921 issue of the *Century Magazine*, shortly after Huneker's death, and included it the following year in *Prejudices: Third Series*, but the date is nowhere given. Mencken says that they met at one o'clock for luncheon at Lüchow's restaurant, and that by the time he had to leave at six the waiter was hauling in Huneker's tenth (or possibly twentieth) *Seidel* of Pilsner and Mencken's own ears were ringing with a "cataract of sublime trivialities: gossip lifted to the plane of the gods, the unmentionable bedizened with an astonishing importance, and even profundity . . . it was, in brief, chaos, and chaos cannot be described."[19] He left, he says, in a sort of fever, and it was days before he could begin to sort out his impressions and formulate a coherent image of the man. The admiration that had begun with the columns of *M'lle New York* and grown with the reading of Huneker's books was solidly confirmed, and though there was a generation's difference in their ages a warm friendship developed between them.

Huneker contributed to *The Smart Set* and Mencken never lost an opportunity to praise him and his work in it.

It was to be a case, though, of the pupil going far beyond the master. Not only was Mencken's critical acumen greater, not only did he develop into a better writer, but the influence he would wield on the whole literary and intellectual scene would be infinitely beyond the older man's. Huneker graciously acknowledged this: when, in 1920, he sent Mencken a copy of his novel *Painted Veils*, he inscribed it: "To my old friend, the Attila of American criticism."

From these two, then—Pollard and Huneker—Mencken was to learn an openness to new ideas, new forms, new figures, that would be an integral part of his equipment throughout all the years of his activity as a critic. He learned from them to keep a watchful eye on the best that was being done abroad. From them, finally, he learned—though really this was only a repetition of what Robert I. Carter, managing editor of the *Herald*, had impressed upon him years before—that the first duty of a critic is to be interesting. Huneker's wit was to become a part of Mencken's stock in trade, and so too, though toned down a bit, was his extraordinary allusiveness. The Menckenian style, in its clarity, richness, and sheer readability, was to surpass Huneker's, but there can be no doubt that Huneker's helped to form it.

His relationship with Dreiser is somewhat easier to date. He told Isaac Goldberg that in 1900 a Baltimore acquaintance named George Bronson Howard gave him a copy of the first edition of *Sister Carrie:* "it made a colossal impression upon me," he said, "and I became a Dreiserista at once."[20] But they apparently did not actually meet until 1908, at which time Mencken was engaged in ghost-writing a series of articles on—of all things!—the care and feeding of babies, in collaboration with a Johns Hopkins physician, Dr. Leonard K. Hirshberg. The articles were to appear in *The Delineator*, one of the chain of magazines owned by Butterick Publications, of which Dreiser was then editor-in-chief; and the novelist, in response to Goldberg's inquiries, described their first encounter in a letter of August 24, 1925: "There appeared in my office," he recalled, "a taut, ruddy, blue-eyed, snub-nosed youth of twenty-eight or nine whose brisk gait and ingratiating smile proved to me at once enormously intriguing and amusing. . . . All thought of the original purpose of the conference was at once dismissed and instead we proceeded to palaver and yoo-hoo anent the more general phases and ridiculosities of life, with the result that an understanding based on a mutual liking was established, and from then on I counted him among those I most prized—temperamentally as well as intellectually. And to this day, despite various disagreements, that mood has never varied."* A bit later that same year Fred Splint, managing editor of *The Smart Set*, asked Dreiser if he knew of anyone who could do a monthly book article for the magazine, and Dreiser immediately suggested Mencken—though Mencken did not know that until more than fifteen years later.

This friendship, too, developed and deepened rapidly. In the summer of 1909 Dreiser left Butterick to assume the editorship of *The Bohemian*, and during his regime Mencken had something in almost every issue: it was here that one of his most perennially popular works, the one-act play *The Artist*, first appeared. Dreiser, meanwhile, was busy with the writing of *Jennie Gerhardt*, and in the spring of 1911 he sent Mencken the manuscript. Mencken offered a few minor suggestions and criticisms, but on the whole his response was overwhelmingly enthusiastic: "The story," he wrote back to its author, "comes upon me with great force; it touches my own experience of life in a hundred places; it preaches (or perhaps I had better say exhibits) a philosophy of life that seems to me to be sound; altogether I get a powerful effect of reality, stark and unashamed." He praised "the great naturalness of the dialogue," and declared that the book was "at once an accurate picture of life and a searching criticism of life. And that is my definition of a good novel."[21] When it was published later that year and he reviewed it in the November issue of *The Smart Set*, he told his readers: "If you miss reading *Jennie Gerhardt*, by Theodore Dreiser, you will miss the best American novel, all things considered, that has reached the book counters in a dozen years."

So it was to go during the two generations of their close but sometimes troubled and always equivocal relationship. Mencken was too honest with himself ever to write a favorable review of a book just because its author happened to be a friend, and he was honest enough with his friends to tell them very frankly and fully what he thought even before publishing his review. He was somewhat less impressed by Dreiser's next novel, *The Financier:* "Frankly," he wrote to him

---

*Despite what Dreiser says in his letter, Goldberg in the text of his book (*The Man Mencken*, p. 114) gives the date of their first meeting as 1904. Either he nodded, or it was one of those typographical errors which elude the most watchful eye.

on October 6, 1912, "there are spots in it that I don't like a bit," but he admitted that the things he criticized were only "minor blemishes on a magnificent piece of work." On the other hand, he thought that *The Titan*, which succeeded *The Financier* as the second volume of "A Trilogy of Desire," was the best thing Dreiser had ever done: "You are not standing still," he told him, "you are moving ahead." Unhappily, Dreiser moved ahead to *The "Genius,"* which Mencken frankly admitted was a "blind spot" for him; in *A Book of Prefaces* he complained that it was "an endless emission of the obvious, with touches of the scandalous to light up its killing monotony. It runs to 736 pages of small type; its reading is an unbearable weariness to the flesh; in the midst of it one has forgotten the beginning and is unconcerned about the end." But when Anthony Comstock and his followers tried to suppress *The "Genius"* for alleged obscenity and blasphemy, Mencken rallied to its defense and enlisted almost every important American and British author to join their names to his in the fight. He explained his position in a letter of November 25, 1916, to Henry Sydnor Harrison, whose "100,000 word Christmas cards" he had often criticized but whose aid he now besought: "Personally," he wrote to Harrison, "I don't care for *The 'Genius.'* I reviewed it very unfavorably, in fact, in *The Smart Set*, and dealt with it so severely in private that Dreiser and I quarreled. I believe that it is stupid, hollow, trifling and vulgar. But I know that, whatever its deficiencies, Dreiser himself is a sincere artist and an honest man, and that he wrote it in absolutely good faith. If we admit the right of arbitrary and disingenuous moralists to attack the work and liberty of such a man, if we put his failure to meet our personal notions of what literature should be above the principle that every bona fide artist should be free, then we plainly hand over letters to a crowd of snooping and abominable Methodists, and say goodbye to all we have struggled for."

Over the years he reviewed each Dreiser book as it came out— short stories, plays, travelogues, memoirs— and though he often complained good-naturedly about the elephantine plodding of the style, the absorption with microscopic detail, the lack of any saving touch of humor, the reviews were always favorable to the point of enthusiasm. There were times when the man infuriated him; he thought Dreiser's political ideas were childish, he was sure he would eventually wind up in the bosom of Holy Church, and his patience almost snapped when, during the *"Genius"* affair, Dreiser persuaded a number of "tenth-rate

Greenwich Village geniuses" to sign the protest about the novel but passed over really important figures who could have helped him. But Mencken never permitted any of these things to interfere with his admiration for the artist, for the one whom he regarded as the greatest living American writer. For his part, Dreiser was deeply grateful for Mencken's encouragement and support, and expressed it frequently in their correspondence.

Then, in 1925, ten years after The "Genius," Dreiser published An American Tragedy, and Mencken found it more than he could take. In his review in the March 1926 issue of the Mercury he called it "dreadful bilge . . . a shapeless and forbidding monster—a heaping cartload of raw materials for a novel, with rubbish of all sorts intermixed . . . a vast, sloppy thing of 385,000 words—at least 250,000 of them unnecessary." Dreiser, understandably enough, was hurt and furious, and it was years before the two men spoke again.

Nathan records, in his Intimate Notebooks, that they first met Sinclair Lewis in 1920, at a gathering in the apartment of their friend T. R. Smith, then managing editor of the Century Magazine. Lewis, who, as one might have expected, was drunk, put an arm around the neck of each of them and proceeded to harangue them at interminable length about a novel that he had coming out shortly and which was "the gottdamn best book of its kind that this here gottdamn country has had." In a cab, after they had managed to extricate themselves from him and get away, Mencken groaned that "of all the idiots I've ever laid eyes on, that fellow is the worst." But three days later he wrote Nathan from Baltimore:

> Dear George: Grab hold of the bar-rail, steady yourself, and prepare yourself for a terrible shock! I've just read the advance sheets of the book of that Lump we met at Schmidt's and, by God, he has done the job! It's a genuinely excellent piece of work. Get it as soon as you can and take a look. I begin to believe that perhaps there isn't a God after all. There is no justice in the world.[22]*

---

*Mark Schorer, in his magistral life of Lewis (New York: McGraw-Hill, 1961; pp. 283–84), suggests that Nathan's account of the incident is "rather questionable." According to Schorer, Mencken was already familiar to some degree with Lewis' previously published work and, having seen an advance copy of Main Street, had written to him to say that it was "the best thing of its sort that has been done so far." He promised to review it in the January Smart Set, "the first issue still open." Nathan, Schorer says, "was a notably unreliable witness in matters of detail, but as a general impression, his anecdote can probably be accepted."

The book was, of course, *Main Street*. In his review in the January 1921 issue of *The Smart Set*, Mencken praised it for presenting characters "that are genuinely human, and not only genuinely human but also authentically American." "The virtue of the book," he went on, "lies in its packed and brilliant detail . . . it would be hard to find a false note in the dialogue. . . . I have read no more genuinely amusing novel for a long while. The man who did it deserves a hearty welcome."

The following year *Babbitt* came out, and his admiration and enthusiasm for Lewis' work doubled. "It avoids," he declared, "all the more obvious faults of [*Main Street*], and shows a number of virtues that are quite new. It is better designed than *Main Street;* the action is more logical and coherent; there is more imagination in it and less bald journalism; above all, there is a better grip upon the characters." He concluded by saying that "I know of no American novel that more accurately presents the real America. It is a social document of a high order."

In all this, as will be evident, Mencken focused upon a book's "realism" (as distinct from any pseudo-scientific "naturalism"), and particularly was he interested in the realism with which it portrayed life in the America of the time. Writing to Dreiser, for example, of the character of old Gerhardt, Jennie's father, he had told the novelist: "His speeches are perfect; nothing could be nearer to truth. I am well aware that certain persons are impatient of this photographic accuracy. Well, let them choose their poison. As for me, I prefer the fact to the fancy. You have tried to depict a German of a given type—a type with which I, by chance, happen to be very familiar. You have made him as thoroughly alive as Huck Finn." Of the character of George F. Babbitt he wrote: "I have personally known him since my earliest days as a newspaper reporter, back in the last century. I have heard him make such speeches as Cicero never dreamed of at banquets of the Chamber of Commerce. I have seen him marching in parades. I have observed him advancing upon his Presbyterian tabernacle of a Sunday morning, his somewhat stoutish lady upon his arms. . . . To me his saga, as Sinclair Lewis has set it down, is fiction only by a sort of courtesy."

So with many another of the authors whose books he would review over the years. In *The Smart Set* for February 1919 he hailed Willa Cather's *My Ántonia* with the statement that "I know of no novel that makes the remote folk of the western prairies more real than *My Án-*

tonia makes them, and I know of none that makes them seem better worth knowing." When a young woman named Ruth Suckow submitted several stories to the magazine he was struck by their fidelity to life, recommended her to Knopf, and when the latter published her novel *Country People* in 1924 he said of it in the *Mercury* that the characters "begin to live on the first few pages, and before the first chapter is ended they seem almost more real than reality itself. . . . Certainly, the American yokel of the Middle West has never had a more sympathetic and understanding interpreter." Of Sherwood Anderson's *Winesburg, Ohio,* he wrote: "Nothing quite like it has ever been done in America. . . . Into its brief pages Anderson not only gets brilliant images of men and women who walk in all the colors of reality; he also gets a profound sense of the obscure, inner drama of their lives."

This preoccupation with realism carried over into works that were in no sense "realistic," as that term is commonly used in literary criticism. The mythical medieval kingdom of Poictesme which James Branch Cabell created in his books is as far from the worlds of Dreiser, Lewis, and Anderson as it would be possible to get; yet Mencken, who admired Cabell enormously and reviewed almost every one of his books as they came out, found it possible to say of him: "In his own sight, perhaps, a romantic, he is really the most acidulous of all the anti-romantics. Even such fantasies as *The Silver Stallion* and *Domnei* and *The High Place* I put among the realistic books. What gives them, as documents, their peculiar tartness is the very fidelity of their realism. Their gaudy heroes, in the last analysis, chase dragons precisely as stockbrokers play golf."[23] He praised humorists for much the same reason: George Ade, for example, "amid a humor so grotesque that it almost tortures the midriff, [offered] a startlingly vivid and accurate evocation of the American scene. Here, under all the labored extravagance, there are brilliant flashlight pictures of the American people, and American ways of thinking, and the whole of American *Kultur.* Here the veritable Americano stands forth, lacking not a waggery, a superstition, a snuffle or a wen." The characters of Ring Lardner were "all as revolting as so many Methodist bishops, and they are all as thoroughly American."

Such examples as these should help to dispel, too, the notion that Mencken was essentially a "destructive" critic. It is probably true that he wrote many more unfavorable reviews than favorable ones; he frankly admitted that he found it much easier to damn a book than to praise it. He told Isaac Goldberg: "A bad writer has no rights whatever. Any mercy shown to him is wasted and mistaken."[24] He was absolutely unsparing toward such "merchants of mush" as Ouida and Marie Corelli, E. Phillips Oppenheim, and Harold Bell Wright. His criticisms of bad or slipshod writing were applied with complete impartiality: they could be leveled just as readily at authors who were his personal friends as at the concocters of cheap romances, a fact which should be sufficiently obvious from what has already been said about his reviews of Dreiser. But he never hesitated, either, to hail good work wherever it came from: the same praise that he lavished on Dreiser, Lewis, Cabell, Hergesheimer, Anderson, Willa Cather, and Scott Fitzgerald was bestowed with equal generosity on lesser figures like Mary MacLane, "the Butte Bashkirtseff," or the poets John McClure and George Sterling, and might go just as readily to a first novel as to the work of established figures.

Meanwhile, and almost in the same breath with which he "whooped up" the new generation of American writers, he battled gaily with opponents on two separate but related fronts. One group was made up of the established critics of the land, men who were—in some sense, at least—his professional colleagues. "The American critic of beautiful letters," he charged,

> in his common incarnation, is no more than a talented sophomore, or, at best, a somewhat absurd professor. He suffers from a palpable lack of solid preparation; he has no background of moving and illuminating experience behind him; his soul has not sufficiently adventured among masterpieces, nor among men. Imagine a Taine or a Sainte-Beuve or a Macaulay—man of the world, veteran of philosophies, "lord of life"—and you imagine his complete antithesis. Even on the side of mere professional knowledge, the primary material of his craft, he always appears incompletely outfitted. The grand sweep and direction of the literary currents elude him; he is eternally on the surface, chasing bits of driftwood. The literature he knows is the fossil literature taught in colleges—worse, in high schools. It must be dead before he is aware of it. And in particular he appears ignorant of what is going forward in other lands. An exotic idea, to penetrate his consciousness, must first become stale, and even then he is apt to purge it of all its remaining validity and significance before adopting it.[25]

The other group was the professors who wrote so solemnly about that same fossil literature. "I am not one . . . ," he insisted, to deny the usefulness of the learned Ph.D. in the palace of beautiful letters, or, at all events, in the ante-chambers thereof. He, too, is one of God's creatures, and he has his high utilities. It is his business, *imprimis,* to ground unwilling schoolboys in the rudiments of knowledge and taste, that they may comprehend the superiority of Ralph Waldo Emerson to Old Cap Collier, and know wherein the poems of Crabbe transcend "Only a Boy." It is his business, *secondamente,* to do the shovel and broom work of literary exploration—to count up the weak and strong endings in *Paradise Lost,* to guess at the meaning of the typographical errors in Shakespeare, to bowdlerize Hannah More for sucklings, to establish the date of *Tamburlaine,* to prove that Edgar Allan Poe was a teetotaler and a Presbyterian. . . . But it is not his business to sit in judgment upon the literature that is in being, for that job requires, above all things, an eager intellectual curiosity, a quick hospitality to ideas, a delight in novelty and heresy—and these are the very qualities which, if he had them, would get a professor cashiered in ten days. He is hired by the God-fearing and excessively solvent old gentlemen who sit on college boards, not to go scouting for what is new in the world, but to concentrate his mind the defense of what is old and safe. It is not his job to inflame his pupils to the pursuit and testing of ideas, but to make them accept docilely the ideas that have been approved as harmless, and his security and eminence in the academic grove run in direct proportion to his fidelity to that programme.[26]

Then, somewhat inconsistently, he belabored the professors when they stuck to the "shovel and broom" work he had outlined for them and failed to show a proper appreciation for new books and new ideas. Hell might bubble over, the Goths and the Huns might be at the gate, but Paul Elmer More would sit aloof and serene in his ivory tower and continue to do his part in a literary war whose outcome had been decided a century ago. Stuart Sherman (his prophecy here turned out to be a bit in error) would hold to his maxim that Puritanism is the official philosophy of America, and that all who dispute it are enemy aliens who should be deported. Gleefully he pounced upon Professor Fred Lewis Pattee, "the Pennsylvania Silurian," for writing *A History of American Literature Since 1870* in which nice things were said about Robert W. Chambers, Marion Harland, R. K. Munkittrick, Gelett Burgess, Carolyn Wells, and John Kendrick Bangs, but in which there was not the faintest indication of Dreiser's very existence. He hailed it as a marvel when William Lyon Phelps, professor of English literature at Yale, published a book in 1910 in which, "imperiling his salary and the honor of his craft," he admitted that Mark Twain was a greater artist than Oliver Wendell Holmes; seven years later he ate his words when a new book by Phelps, *The Advance of the English Novel*, turned out to be "a flat reboiling of old respectabilities . . . hollow and uninspired," and in which, again, Dreiser was utterly passed over.*

The professors, though they would never admit it, took Mencken quite seriously—and the reason they did, of course, was that he did not take them seriously at all. He infuriated them—of that I have already given sufficient evidence. They tried at first to ignore him; then, when that proved impossible and he did not go away, they sought to strike back at him with his own weapons. But the Menckenian rhetoric, so rich and effective in his hands, was feeble and useless in theirs. They tried, too, to hit at him by attacking the authors whose works he trumpeted; Dreiser was "crude," Lewis was "vulgar," Cabell's delicate satire was interlaced with rank obscenity. But the cause for which they fought was a hopeless one, and particularly after the First World War an entirely new spirit dawned, a spirit which brought with it a literature more free, more honest, more realistic— and also, for that matter, better written—than almost anything that had been done up until that time.

In his last article for *The Smart Set*, entitled "Fifteen Years" and published in the issue for December 1923, in which he and Nathan bade their official farewell to the magazine, Mencken surveyed the scene as it was then as against what it had been when he first mounted his "pulpit" in 1908. At that time, he noted, "the old tradition was still powerful, and the young man or woman who came to New York with a manuscript which violated in any way the pruderies and prejudices of the professors had a very hard time getting it printed. It was a day of complacency and conformity." The reigning dramatists were Augustus Thomas, David Belasco, and Clyde Fitch; the most popular novelists Richard Harding Davis, Robert W. Chambers, and James Lane Allen; the chief critical organ the "Literary Supplement" of *The New York Times*. "It is hard, indeed, in retrospect," he went on, "to picture those remote days just as they were. They seem almost fabulous. . . . No novel that told the truth about life as Americans were living it, no

---

*It should perhaps be noted that the relations between Mencken and Phelps were for the most part quite cordial. In later years Phelps invited him to lecture at Yale, and Mencken's letters to him were addressed "Dear Billy."

poem that departed from the old patterns, no play that had the merest
ghost of an idea in it had a chance."

But now "the American imaginative writer, whether he be novelist, poet or dramatist, is quite as free as he deserves to be. He is
free to depict the life about him precisely as he sees it, and to interpret
it in any manner he pleases." Though he did not specifically mention all
of them, he might have added that among the works of those fifteen
years giving evidence of that freedom were Dreiser's *Jennie Gerhardt*, *The Financier*, and *The Titan;* Lewis' *Main Street* and *Babbitt;*
Anderson's *Winesburg, Ohio, Poor White*, and *The Triumph of the
Egg;* Dos Passos' *Three Soldiers;* Willa Cather's *O Pioneers!, The
Song of the Lark*, and *My Ántonia;* and Scott Fitzgerald's *This Side of
Paradise*. Eugene O'Neill was already the foremost American playwright, and such men as Robert Frost, Edgar Lee Masters, and T. S.
Eliot were, each in his own way, breaking through the constraints of
the old (and now old-fashioned) poetry.

Whether the new generation of writers was making the best possible use of the freedom that had been won for them was another matter,
and here he had some doubts. There was a whole group that talked a
great deal and accomplished nothing, and yet another group which
talked more and accomplished even less. But there was a group, too,
which said little and sawed wood, and though those who made it up had
little in common and in no way constituted an organized movement, he
believed that out of them something would come. "Its members," he
said,

> are those who are free from the two great delusions which, from the
> beginning, have always cursed American letters: the delusion that a
> work of art is primarily a moral document, that its purpose is to make
> men better Christians and more docile cannon-fodder, and the delusion
> that it is an exercise in logic, that its purpose is to prove something.
> These delusions, lingering beyond their time, are responsible for most
> of the disasters visible in the national literature today—the disasters of
> the radicals as well as those of the 100 per cent dunderheads. The writers
> of the future, I hope and believe, will carefully avoid both of them.[27]

It was to the destruction of these twin errors and the establishment of a decent freedom in letters that he had devoted a very large
part of his incredible energies for the past decade and a half. In order to
accomplish his ends, he had had to attack the entrenched orthodoxies

and align himself for the most part with young men and women whose courage and faith, he believed, alone gave reason to have confidence in the future. It was something for which he hoped to receive a modest amount of credit. Exactly one year before his final leave-taking he had written: ". . . my critical labors, in the main, have been on the side of the younger generation. I have protested *sforzando* against the schoolmastering of letters—against setting the artist in bondage to his inferiors. For this service, I am convinced, I shall be rewarded by a just and intelligent God when I have been translated from these sordid scenes. If it turns out that I am in error about it, then I confess frankly that I shall be very greatly disappointed."[28]

4 BUT EVEN WHILE HE was still performing this service with an apparently boundless zeal, he had in reality become very weary of the magazine. He was unhappy with its cheap format, and dissatisfied, too, with what he considered to be the essentially trivial nature of most of its contents. For him personally, as for Nathan, it had never been in any way a profitable enterprise; there were long periods, indeed—particularly during the war years— when they worked without any kind of compensation whatever. In the autobiographical notes which he prepared to assist Isaac Goldberg in the writing of *The Man Mencken* he told him, "After 1918 I took but little interest in *The Smart Set*."[29]

Neither did he especially care for the company—the writers, editors, critics, and agents—which his association with it virtually forced upon him. On the trips which he had to make monthly or oftener to New York, he always put up at the Algonquin Hotel, but he never became a part of its famed literary coterie and all but went out of his way to avoid those who were. Most of them he held in ill-disguised contempt. "Literary society . . . ," he said, "is not to my taste. Save for Hergesheimer, Dreiser, Boyd and a few others, I never associate with authors."[30] He made friends in New York, of course, but looking back later it seemed to him that relatively few of these friendships had really lasted, while the ones formed in Baltimore had a tendency to endure for a lifetime. These latter were, in the main, with newspapermen, musicians, and doctors.

In 1919, after the long break occasioned by the war, he had re-sumed his connection with the *Sunpapers*, and the beginning of the

"Monday Articles" in February of the following year finally gave him an opportunity to write again about the things that really interested him—politics, political figures, the doings of the national parties, the whole preposterous and obscene spectacle of American life, beliefs, and ways. He reveled in his new freedom. Before very long the articles came to represent his best and most typical writing, his shrewdest observations and most pungent wit; at the same time the monthly book reviews in *The Smart Set* became more and more forced, and the humor in them more and more artificial.

As far back as 1914, he, Nathan, and Willard Huntington Wright had dreamed of a handsome and prestigious journal, tentatively named *"The Blue Review"* and modeled in broad outline on the London *Mercury* and the famed *Mercure de France.* Wright had even had a dummy issue of it made up, thereby precipitating a crisis that cost him his job as editor of *The Smart Set.* Nothing more had come of the idea then. In the intervening years, however, Mencken had entered into his long and rewarding association with Alfred Knopf and given him all of his books to bring out, and Knopf was very interested in becoming the publisher of a national magazine. The result, of course, was *The American Mercury.*

Negotiations proceeded slowly and carefully over a long period of time. There was even some thought of the Knopfs, father and son, buying out *The Smart Set,* and remaking it to their own (or rather Mencken's) specifications; but Eltinge F. Warner, its principal stockholder, refused to sell, and it became increasingly apparent that a wholly new magazine was the only solution. Mencken and Knopf were both enthusiastic about the idea; Nathan had grave reservations, but in the end went along. Throughout much of 1923 Mencken was writing to Dreiser, Upton Sinclair, Ellery Sedgwick, Sara Haardt, and others, telling them of his plans, and from his literary friends and acquaintances he besought contributions. As I noted at the end of the preceding section, he and Nathan announced their departure from *The Smart Set* in the issue for December 1923, and the following month the first issue of the *Mercury* was launched.

It was everything that *The Smart Set* was not. Designed by the famous typographer Elmer Adler, it had a dignified, attractive cover and a handsome typeface, and it was printed on the finest paper. A "quality" magazine in every respect, it took a position instantly beside such venerable competitors as *The Atlantic Monthly* and *Harper's.* But these differences were only the superficial ones. Mencken had planned it, as he himself made abundantly clear, to cover a much wider range than *The Smart Set* ever had: politics, economics, sociology, the natural sciences, the whole gamut of the American scene. It is probable that, at least in deference to Nathan, he had not deliberately intended to make literature and the arts such a minor part of it; but in the event, that was how it turned out. Each issue had but one or two short stories and a token bit of poetry, and four-fifths of "The Library" department in which he now reviewed books was given over to nonfiction.

"*The Blue Review*" had been envisioned as a mouthpiece of "enlightened Toryism"; the *Mercury*, from the very outset, was unequivocally Tory in its viewpoint. In politics and in commentary on the social scene this was not inconsistent with what Mencken had always stood for, as anyone familiar with his work would have known; but in literature it seemed such a reversal of his former positions that many old friends and admirers felt betrayed. His critical labors in the past may have been, as he said, on the side of the younger generation; now, however, he made the elementary mistake of forgetting that in literature, as in life, a new generation is always coming up. For the work of the writers who emerged out of the First World War he cared little, and apparently understood it even less.

His loss of interest in creative writing seemed, indeed, to be absolute. He continued to review new books by Dreiser, Lewis, Hergesheimer, Cabell, and Fitzgerald simply because they were friends, but all too often his notices were perfunctory and showed little real enthusiasm; he would lump half a dozen novels together on one page of "The Library" and devote a short paragraph to each. The new writers he scarcely deigned even to notice, and the judgments that he expressed of them in conversation with friends and colleagues ran vociferously counter to all the critical thinking of the time.

Thus Hemingway, for example, was simply trying to prove in much of his writing that he was a "naughty fellow." Steinbeck's *The Grapes of Wrath* was "a very poor job . . . full of pink hooey." He could not understand Faulkner; there was no more sense in him, he complained, than in "the wop boob, Dante," and he had not the slightest concept of sentence structure and paragraphing.[31] Angoff (at least according to his own account) tried heroically to persuade him to publish "That Evening Sun," which was later to be one of Faulkner's best-known stories, but Mencken stubbornly refused; finally Angoff got him to agree that if Sara Haardt liked it, it could go in. Mencken was sure that Sara would confirm his own judgment, but it turned out that she liked it very much and he grumblingly gave Angoff permission to print it.

After he and Sara were married, one of the very few quarrels they ever had was over Thomas Wolfe. She admired him tremendously; Mencken tried to read him but was "driven away." Madeleine Boyd, the wife of Ernest and an active literary agent in her own right, had become Wolfe's agent, and it was she who interested Maxwell Perkins of Scribner's in *Look Homeward, Angel* after it had been turned down by a number of other publishers. Writing to her on January 15, 1929, Mencken expressed the hope that if Wolfe had anything that would fit into the *Mercury* he might have a chance to see it, but Manchester relates that when a manuscript arrived in the office it was written on grease-speckled butcher paper and Mencken was so horrified that he refused even to pick it up. "Get that thing out of here!" he ordered Angoff. "It isn't even sanitary!"

Yet at the time of Wolfe's tragic and untimely death in 1938 he wrote to Edward Stone that if he had lived another five years he would have gotten rid of many of his defects. "I met him only a few times," he said, "but had a great liking for him. There was something charmingly boyish about him." Then he added, with a characteristically Mencken-ian touch: "Next to Sinclair Lewis, he was the most modest author I ever encountered."[32]

These erratic judgments were by no means confined to the new generation of American writers. They extended, too, to some of the leading and most acclaimed figures of Europe. According to Bode, it was Mencken who, in 1921, had recommended to Knopf that he get hold of Thomas Mann's *Buddenbrooks* and bring it out in an English translation, since it was "the solidest novel done in Germany for years."* Knopf had done so, and thus established himself as the American publisher of the man who would be known for long years as "the greatest living man of letters." Nevertheless, in 1938 Mencken wrote to Albert G. Keller of Yale: "The Thomas Mann stuff simply eludes me. I certainly do not share Knopf's idea that it is magnificent. I have tried to read it at various times, but always fail to get any distance."[33]

---

*Bode credits this to "Knopf's recollections." Actually, Knopf had brought out Mann's *Royal Highness (Königliche Hoheit)* five years earlier, in 1916. *Buddenbrooks*, though it was written some years before *Royal Highness*, did not appear in English translation until 1924.

In that same year he confessed that as he grew older he read fiction with "decreasing interest." About the only novelist with whom he maintained any kind of relationship toward the end of his life was James T. Farrell, the Chicago-born author of *Studs Lonigan* and the "Danny O'Neill" cycle, whose "naturalism" may have struck a responsive chord in him because it was so reminiscent of Dreiser's. They corresponded regularly over a long period of time; Farrell sent Mencken copies of his books, and the latter always praised them and encouraged him to keep on. But he never reviewed any of them.

5 IN THAT ARTICLE ENTITLED "Fifteen Years" with which he made his final bow to the readers of *The Smart Set*, Mencken tried to estimate the number of books he had reviewed during his period of "servitude" and came to the conclusion that it must have been about 2,000. (He went on to ask rhetorically how many he had actually read and guessed that it was closer to 4,000.) But this figure does not include (naturally) the ones reviewed over the next ten years in *The American Mercury*, and neither does it include a substantial number appearing irregularly in such places as the Baltimore *Evening Sun*, the New York *Evening Mail*, the Chicago *Tribune*, *Town Topics*, and *The Nation*. The "Book Review" section in Betty Adler's *H.L.M.: The Mencken Bibliography* runs to 105 pages of small type.

But it should be unnecessary to say that mere reviewing, even on such a staggering scale, does not of itself turn the reviewer into a literary critic. The two professions, while they may belong to the same genus, are nevertheless specifically distinct. Mencken himself took a very dim view of most reviewers and looked upon them in somewhat the same light that Dr. Johnson looked upon lexicographers—that is to say, as "harmless drudges." "Mere reviewing," he wrote,

> however conscientiously and competently it is done, is plainly a much inferior business [to criticism]. Like writing poetry, it is chiefly a function of intellectual immaturity. The young literatus just out of the university, having as yet no capacity for grappling with the fundamental mysteries of existence, is put to writing reviews of books, or plays, or music, or painting. Very often he does it extremely well; it is, in fact, not hard to do well, for even decayed pedagogues often do it, as such graves

of the intellect as the New York *Times* bear witness. But if he continues to do it, whether well or ill, it is a sign to all the world that his growth ceased when they made him *Artium Baccalaureus*. Gradually he becomes, whether in or out of the academic grove, a professor, which is to say, a man devoted to diluting and retailing the ideas of his superiors—not an artist, not even a bad artist, but almost the antithesis of an artist. He is learned, he is sober, he is painstaking and accurate—but he is as hollow as a jug.[34]

This judgment, while unkind, is probably not untrue, but it should be added at once that some of Mencken's profoundest insights into the nature of criticism lie buried in the reviews of those 2,000 or more books.

The point to be made here is, in other words, simply this: that what it pleased him to call his "*principia* of aesthetics" was not something originated in a vacuum. In this respect it differed very greatly from that of Babbitt and More, who elaborated a critical theory that had no real reference to any living literature. Mencken's, quite the contrary, developed out of the most intimate possible knowledge of the American writing of his own era. The very nature of his job was such that he had to read an enormous number of *current* books—a few good ones and whole shelves full of bad ones—and this reading enabled him first of all to see with clear gaze what virtues made a given work outstanding and what faults made another one inferior. It enabled him, secondly, to see that body of current writing, both the good and the bad, as a whole reflecting its time and place. From here it was a simple enough matter to weigh it against the literature of other times and places, and to derive from this a unified, consistent theory of criticism. It was but another simple step to transpose that theory from literature to other arts, most notably music.

But the theory, however sound and cogent it might be, could not stand as the last word on its subject, and Mencken was of course the last person on earth to devise and put forward a unified, consistent "theory" about anything. He never tired of insisting that criticism was not an exact science—"it is a fine art, or nothing." The best it could do was to pronounce verdicts valid here and now, in the light of current tastes and prejudices. As tastes changed, the verdicts would necessarily have to change with them (and he was fond of pointing out the critical ups and downs of Shakespeare's reputation over the centuries).

"The best critic," he argued, "is not that fool who tries to resist the process—by setting up artificial standards, by prattling of laws and principles that do not exist, by going into the dead past for criticism of the present—but that more prudent fellow who submits himself frankly to the flow of his time, and rejoices in its aliveness."[35] This latter, as I trust I have made clear, is precisely what Mencken did: he may not always have rejoiced in the aliveness of the literature he was reviewing, he may have complained much more often and vehemently of its deadness, but no one can ever argue that he was unaware of the flow of his time.

What, then, was the critic's role? What function did he perform as a kind of middleman between the artist and the artist's public?

Perhaps the best way to answer this question is to make clear first of all what his role was not. To begin with, it was not pedagogical. It was not his task to explain the biblical and classical allusions in *Paradise Lost,* or to count the number of scenes in Shakespeare's plays that end with a rhymed couplet, or to trace the influence of medieval French and Italian romances upon the composition of Chaucer's *Canterbury Tales.* There were more than enough men in the world to undertake such dismal studies and publish their findings in quarterly learned journals—but their work was to criticism as the police regulations of Abilene, Kansas, were to the Ten Commandments.

Neither was his job a constabulary one—or, as Mencken would put it, "to police the fine arts and so hold them in tune with the moral order of the world." If the reader be moved to object that legitimate criticism attempts no such thing, he perhaps needs to be reminded that in the Puritan atmosphere of American life and letters at the turn of the century it did that more often than not. Hamilton Wright Mabie had published a "White List" of respectable books, and Irving Babbitt held firmly that there are tastes "that deserve the cudgel." Poe and Whitman could not be accepted into the world of polite letters because each, in his own way, had violated the accepted standards of morality; ergo, their work must be immoral too. The fact that Dreiser's *Sister Carrie* created vivid and unforgettable characters and told their story with dignity and sustained interest was beside the point; the point was that one of those characters was a young girl who had run away from home and become a man's mistress, and this was precisely the sort of thing that no conscientious Christian critic could recommend to his readers.

Of all the theories of criticism this was the one that Mencken rejected most decisively and fought most vigorously. The true critic, he maintained, was no more concerned with the morality of a book than he was with the morality of the Fifth Symphony or the Parthenon. His sole concern was with what the author had set out to do and with how well he had done it—in short, with whether the book, or story, or play, or poem was successful as a work of art.

These are some negative answers to the question; they tell us, in other words, what the critic is not. But on the positive side, what is he? There is little evidence that Mencken even concerned himself with the matter, at least prior to 1917.

In that year a professor of comparative literature at Columbia University named Joel E. Spingarn published a little volume—a collection of essays, really—entitled *Creative Criticism*. In it he put forth the proposition that "the critic's first and foremost duty is to make plain to himself 'what the poet's aim really and truly was, how the task he had to do stood before his eye, and how far, with such materials as were afforded him, he has fulfilled it.'" This idea was not new with Spingarn, of course, and he did not pretend that it was; the quoted passage, in fact, is from Thomas Carlyle's essay on Goethe, and Spingarn had taken it from the Italian philosopher Benedetto Croce, who had borrowed it earlier from Goethe and made it one of the elements of his own system of aesthetics. Spingarn, adopting it in turn, used it as an axe with which to hew down those schools of criticism that sought to explain a work in terms of fixed standards, or adherence to form, or agreement with conventional ideas of right and wrong, good and evil.

Mencken reviewed the book in the August issue of *The Smart Set*, in an article which he called "Criticism of Criticism of Criticism." He marveled at the spectacle of a professor, formerly of Harvard and now at Columbia, expounding such "magnificently unprofessorial" notions, and called attention gleefully to the way they toppled most of the critical theories then generally accepted. "Dr. Spingarn, in truth," he said,

> here performs a treason most horrible, and having achieved it, he performs another and then another. That is to say, he tackles all the varying camorras of campus-pump critics seriatim, and knocks them out unanimously—first the aforesaid burblers for the sweet and pious; then the advocates of unities, meters, all rigid formulas; then the historical dust-snufflers; then the experts in bogus psychology; then the

metaphysicians; finally, the spinners of aesthetic balderdash. One and all, they take their places on his chopping-block; one and all, they are stripped, vivisected and put away in cans. . . .[36]

Of Spingarn's own proposition—which he dubbed the "Spingarn-Croce-Carlyle-Goethe theory," pointing out that it was anything but new in the world, even in Goethe's time—he said that "obviously, it is a better theory than those cherished by the other professors, for it demands that the critic have comprehension, whereas the others only demand that he have learning, and accept as learning anything that has been sonorously said before." Even if there were nothing else to say for it, it at least cleared off a lot of moldy rubbish and went farther toward establishing the real nature of the critical process than any of the other systems currently on the market.

At the same time it seemed to him that Spingarn, having stated his theory, spoiled it immediately by claiming too much for it. It left the work of art *in vacuo,* so to speak; it demanded of the critic (to say nothing of the audience) that he get within the mind of the artist at the precise moment of his creative intuition—a process manifestly impossible. As between the two positions—Spingarn's and that of the other professors—the safe ground probably lay somewhere between them, but closer to Spingarn. Beauty, Mencken pointed out, does not simply exist in and of itself; it has social, political, even moral implications, and its springs are often to be found not just in the work but in things outside it—those things which influenced the artist in his creation. "To admire the work of Shakespeare is to be interested in his handling of blank verse, his social aspirations, his shot-gun marriage and his frequent concessions to the bombastic frenzy of his actors, and to have some curiosity about Mr. W. H. The really competent critic must be an empiricist."

(Here, although he seems not to have been aware of it, he was really being inconsistent with his own principles. For if, the better to understand and appreciate Shakespeare, it is desirable to know something about his handling of blank verse, and his marriage, and the actors with whom he had to deal, and the identity of Mr. W. H., this knowledge can be had only from the work of literary *scholarship*— from precisely the kind of thing, in other words, done by those "literary pedagogues" whom he professed to hold in such utter contempt.)

That review, like so many he had done over the past nine years, might have put an end to the matter, but apparently the problems that Spingarn's book raised continued to intrigue him and he returned to it again in a brief article written for the New York *Evening Mail* of July 1, 1918, which he called "Critics and Their Ways." Once more he discussed the nature of criticism and the admirable way in which the professor had disposed of most of the current theories—and then, at the very end, he added a couple of paragraphs in which he proposed a theory of his own. Spingarn's use of the word "creative" in the title of his book, he thought, was a bit too flamboyant, and he suggested replacing it with another—namely, "catalytic." A "catalyzer," he pointed out,* is in the vocabulary of chemistry a substance that causes two other substances to interact without itself being changed, and this was exactly the function of the critic.

It was his business, in brief, to provoke a reaction between the work of art and the spectator. The untutored spectator stands before the work more or less inert; he sees it (or reads or hears it) but it fails to make any intelligible impression upon him. ("If he were spontaneously sensitive to it, there would be no need for criticism.") But now the critic, coming between the spectator and the work as a catalyst, makes it live for him; he brings about understanding, appreciation, intelligent enjoyment—which were precisely the things that the artist wanted for his work.

Still another year later, in 1919, he prepared the pieces that were to go into the first volume of *Prejudices*. Retaining his original title, "Criticism of Criticism of Criticism," he considerably revised the *Smart Set* review and to it he joined those paragraphs in the *Evening Mail* article in which he had ventured his theory of the critic as "catalyzer." Spingarn, meanwhile, had entered the U.S. Army with the rank of major, and it delighted Mencken to refer to him throughout by his military title, calling him the "anarchistic ex-professor" and insisting that he still thought of him "not as a soldier extraordinarily literate, but as a professor in rebellion." He placed the piece, now a fairly lengthy essay, at the very forefront of the book, and there it stands not only as a statement of his own critical theory at the moment but as an introduction to the treatment of Wells, Bennett, Howells, Sudermann, Shaw, and many another in the pages that follow.

---

*"Catalyst" is the more usual term. "Catalyzer," the word used by Mencken, is in neither the *Shorter Oxford* nor the *Random House Unabridged Dictionary*—nor, for that matter, in *The American Language*.

Yet despite this obvious preoccupation with the nature of criticism over a period of at least two years, he seems not to have held to his "catalyzer" idea for very long. When, almost thirty years later, he made a selection of his out-of-print writings for the *Chrestomathy*, it is significant that he did not include "Criticism of Criticism of Criticism." Instead he turned to another work that had followed it only two years afterward, entitled "The Motive of the Critic" and appearing in *The New Republic* for October 26, 1921. This piece, again very considerably revised and expanded, was included in *Prejudices: Third Series* in 1922,* and it is this rather than the other which has to be taken as the definitive expression of his theory of criticism.

Here he dismisses at once, as he had before, the notion that the critic's motive is to propagate any particular aesthetic, psychological, or moral idea. Such a thing is true only of bad critics, and its degree of truth increases in direct ratio to their badness. "The motive of the critic who is really worth reading," he holds,

> —the only critic of whom, indeed, it may be said truthfully that it is at all possible to read him, save as an act of mental discipline—is something quite different. That motive is not the motive of the pedagogue, but the motive of the artist. It is no more and no less than the simple desire to function freely and beautifully, to give outward and objective form to ideas that bubble inwardly and have a fascinating lure in them, to get rid of them dramatically and make an articulate noise in the world. It was for this reason that Plato wrote the *Republic*, and for this reason that Beethoven wrote the Ninth Symphony, and it is for this reason, to drop a million miles, that I am writing the present essay. Everything else is afterthought, mock-modesty, messianic delusion—in brief, affectation and folly.[37]

Then he proceeded to submit himself as an example of his own theory. For years, he said, he had been writing critical pieces on the works of Theodore Dreiser, and practically everybody who had taken any notice of them at all had assumed that he was inspired by one or the other of two motives: (*a*) a fanatical devotion to Dreiser's ideas and a desire to propagate them, or (*b*) a yearning to uplift American literature. Both assumptions, he assured his readers, were false. He had

---

*In *Prejudices: Third Series* it is entitled "Footnote on Criticism." In the *Chrestomathy* it becomes "The Critical Process."

very little interest in Dreiser's ideas (when they met, in fact, they usually quarreled about them), and he had no desire whatever to improve the nation's literature: if it ever came to what he regarded as perfection, his job would be gone. His sole motive in writing about Dreiser had been to sort out and give coherence to the ideas of H. L. Mencken, to put them in "suave and ingratiating terms," and to discharge them with a flourish into the dense fog blanketing the Republic. Dreiser's books served as a mere point of departure for this activity.

So, too, with Goethe, Sainte-Beuve, Hazlitt, Macaulay, Carlyle, Matthew Arnold—all of whom he offered as additional examples. Each was a man in whom the critic had been swallowed up by the creative artist. Each, at one time or another, had set out to review a book, or play, or some other work of art, and what he had produced instead was a fresh work of art. It was independent of its ostensible subject, and related to it only indirectly, and might even be superior to it. The original work had been nothing more than a springboard for the critic's own ideas.

"Every critic who is worth reading," he went on,

> falls inevitably into the same habit. He cannot stick to his task: what is before him is always infinitely less interesting to him than what is within him. If he is genuinely first-rate—if what is within him stands the test of type, and wins an audience, and produces the reactions that every artist craves—then he usually ends by abandoning the criticism of specific works of art altogether, and setting up shop as a merchant in general ideas, *i.e.*, as an artist working in the materials of life itself.

That this is a pretty accurate description of Mencken's own critical work (and perhaps even a brief history of his intellectual career), few who are familiar with him will deny. I remarked earlier that in his book reviews it was not at all unusual for him to lose sight of the book entirely after the first couple of paragraphs and proceed to an exposition of his own ideas on the subject with which it happened to deal. Perhaps such a charge is really unjust: when he reviewed a book he invariably managed to say about it everything that seemed to him worth saying, and by the time he came to the end his audience would have no doubt as to whether (in Mencken's terms at least) it was worth reading. As with all reviewers, he sometimes found the author's subject important but his treatment of it inadequate, or he found the treatment well done even though the author's views were—to his way of thinking—all wrong. But whether the review was favorable or unfavorable, the book always had to be seen through the prism of his own highly personal and forthright opinions.

In brief, and to use his own words, it was impossible for him to stick to his task: what was before him was always infinitely less interesting than what was within him. What was within him had a fascinating lure, and he had to get rid of it dramatically and make an articulate noise in the world. In the process of making it there is no doubt that he did produce genuine works of art that are superior in many cases to the ones he was writing about. Huneker, sound critic though he may have been, is much less interesting to us today than Mencken's three pieces about him. The whole collected works of Thorstein Veblen are probably of less importance—and are certainly less readable—than the great essay "Professor Veblen and the Cow." In the later volumes of *Prejudices* he usually included a section entitled "From the Files of a Book Reviewer," in which, one can only assume, he tried to preserve those reviews with which he was himself particularly pleased; in almost all cases the books have been utterly forgotten, but Mencken's reviews of them still make delightful reading.

Finally, it is true beyond any cavil that he began as a critic of specific works of art—in his case, books—and eventually abandoned that profession to set up shop as a merchant in general ideas. If any man was an artist working in the materials of life itself, he was. The very date of "Footnote on Criticism" (1921) is surely significant in this regard: it was the period of his greatest unhappiness with the limitations imposed on him by *The Smart Set,* the time when he was beginning to give serious thought to a new magazine where he could venture out onto a much broader field and function more "freely and beautifully."

The essay stands, then, as a statement of the kind of criticism that he wanted to write (and as a matter of fact was already writing on the editorial page of the *Evening Sun*). This much having been said, it remains to ask whether it can be considered a "theory" of criticism in general. One may venture to suggest that it cannot. As in the earlier piece on Spingarn's book, it clears the ground by disposing seriatim of a number of things that criticism is not. But there, at least, he had come forward in the end with an idea of what it is. Here he specifically repudiates that idea, and then sets up nothing to take its place.

For one thing, it appears to rule out criticism of music, or painting, or any other nonverbal art form. It might be possible to write a critical study of the B Minor Mass or the Fifth Symphony or *Tristan*, the "Mona Lisa" or "Guernica," that would itself be a highly original and profound piece of work; but it would be pointless to argue about whether it was superior to the original with which it dealt, since there is simply no way that an article or a book can be compared to a symphony or an opera or a painting. The man who seized upon one of them as a means of elaborating his own general ideas and philosophy could be well worth reading, but not as a music or art critic. Moreover, there are a few critics in both fields who do genuinely illumine such works for the benefit of the listener or spectator without technical training— who perform, in other words, the role of "catalyst" in Mencken's discarded theory and bring about understanding, appreciation, and intelligent enjoyment. Some of his own pieces on Beethoven, Schubert, and Brahms fit quite well into this category.

For another, the theory plainly demands of the critic that in order to be a critic at all he likewise be an artist—which not one critic in a thousand is. It may be perfectly true that the very greatest critics have been artists in their own right, and that their work has a permanent place in literature. But of how many can this be said? Those whom he specifically mentions—Goethe, Sainte-Beuve, Hazlitt, Macaulay, Carlyle, Arnold—undoubtedly belong in this rarefied company. Probably Dr. Johnson does—but Mencken could not stand Johnson, despite the fact that the two of them have often been compared. Perhaps Coleridge belongs there. Mencken does himself. But are there many others? At least among those writing in English the only ones who come readily to mind are Henry James and T. S. Eliot—but both of them, of course, would have been great creative artists even if they had never written a line of criticism. And there the roll call seems to come pretty much to an end.

In brief, the theory disposes utterly and without appeal of a whole host of "literary" critics—Cleanth Brooks, R. P. Blackmur, Lionel Trilling, Yvor Winters, and John Crowe Ransom among Americans, I. A. Richards, William Empson, and F. R. Leavis, to name but a handful of Englishmen. All were (or are) men with a profound knowledge of literature and an ability to illumine it for the understanding and enjoyment of their readers. All have been influential—perhaps not quite in the same way that Mencken was, but nevertheless each has left his mark on the history of criticism. But none, it seems fair to say, have been artists in the supreme sense of the word. On the other hand, it seems equally unfair to dismiss them as mere "pedagogues" for that reason.

No, the theory is too individualistic to serve as a general proposition on the nature of criticism. It is Mencken's justification for the particular kind of criticism that *he* wanted to write—and as such it is as narrowly personal as his opinion of Methodists, or Prohibition agents, or chiropractors.

This is not to say, of course, that it does not constitute a legitimate challenge to other critics and to the practice of criticism. Neither is it to say that, once disposed of, it leaves him without any kind of critical platform. After all, a man who spent twenty-five years of his life reviewing books, from slim volumes of obscure verse to weighty tomes on science and theology, could hardly fail to have some ideas on the nature of the critical process and on its application to various forms of writing. Mencken had a clear-cut approach to the novel and to novelists, and very definite ideas on poetry, and hardly less definite ones on the drama. These ideas may themselves be subject to criticism in turn, but they are at least of a piece—they fit perfectly with each other and with the whole body of his thought. Let us proceed now to examine each of them in turn.

VERY EARLY IN HIS CAREER as book editor of *The Smart Set*—just two months, in fact, after his maiden article—Mencken ventured upon a definition of the novel form. "A novel," he wrote,

> is an imaginative, artistic and undialectic composition in prose, not less than 20,000 nor more than 500,000 words in length, and divided into chapters, sections, books or other symmetrical parts, in which certain interesting, significant and probable (though fictitious) human transactions are described both in cause and effect, with particular reference to the influence exerted upon the ideals, opinions, morals, temperament and overt acts of some specified person or persons by the laws, institutions, superstitions, traditions and customs of such portions of the human race and the natural phenomena of such portions of the earth as may come under his, her or their observation or cognizance, and by the

ideals, opinions, morals, temperament and overt acts of such person or
persons as may come into contact, either momentarily or for longer
periods, with him, her or them, either by actual, social or business
intercourse, or through the medium of books, newspapers, the church,
the theater or some other person or persons.[38]

This definition represented "the toil of several days" and he
granted that it made "severe demands upon both eye and attention,"
but he went on to claim modestly that "it is well worth the time spent
upon it and the effort necessary to assimilate it, for it is entirely without
loophole, blowhole or other blemish. It describes, with scientific accuracy, every real novel ever written, and by the same token, it bars out
every last near-novel, pseudo-novel and quasi-novel, however colorable, and every romance, rhapsody, epic, saga, stuffed short story, tract
and best-seller known to bibliographers."

No doubt, and despite these guarantees, it is possible to find fault
with the definition and to maintain that it does have some blowholes.
One may question what is meant by "undialectic." One may point out
that a work of only 20,000 words is hardly a novel in the classical sense
of the term; it is more what is usually styled a "novella." As a whole, the
thing reads like the small print in an insurance policy. Yet even after
these reservations—and bearing in mind, too, the obvious fact that it is
written tongue in cheek and not meant to be taken with complete
seriousness—the definition really holds up very well.

The key words occur near the beginning: "certain interesting,
significant and probable (though fictitious) human transactions are described both in cause and effect." A novel (the occasional popular and
even well-written animal story to the contrary notwithstanding) must
be about human beings, and it must describe interesting and significant transactions of these human beings in both cause and effect.
Any work which fails to meet these requirements may be fiction, but it
falls short of being a novel—i.e., a work of art.

Mencken was the first to admit that "the thing we call the story is
the raw material of prose fiction," just as melody is the raw material of
music. Occasionally (he cited Mark Twain's "The Celebrated Jumping
Frog of Calaveras County" as an example) the story is itself so perfect
both in substance and in pattern that nothing more is needed. But this
sort of thing is rare. It is a critical commonplace to say that the really
great stories are few in number and have all been told long since, and

that writers of fiction today can only devote themselves to infinite variations on these limited and hackneyed themes. Sometimes an author may take an inherently banal story thread and envelop it with such ornaments of style, wit, philosophical observation, and human sympathy that its banality goes unnoticed—just as Beethoven took two plain notes of the diatonic scale, one of them twice repeated, and constructed on this unpromising foundation the colossal first movement of the Fifth Symphony.

Story, then, is the essential element in a novel, and any work which does not tell a story can hardly qualify for inclusion in the novel form—but story just in itself is not quite enough. Here, remember, Mencken was engaged in unremitting warfare upon the popular fiction of his day, which carried banality to its *reductio ad absurdum.* "I describe," he wrote elsewhere,

> the optimistic, the inspirational, the Authors' League, the popular magazine, the peculiarly American school. In character creation its masterpiece is the advertising agent who, by devising some new and super-imbecile boob-trap, puts his hook-and-eye factory "on the map," ruins all other factories, marries the daughter of his boss, and so ends as an eminent man. Obviously, the drama underlying such fiction . . . is false drama, Sunday-school drama, puerile and disgusting drama. It is the sort of thing that awakens a response only in men who are essentially unimaginative, timorous and degraded—in brief, in democrats, bagmen, yahoos. The man of reflective habit cannot conceivably take any passionate interest in the conflicts it deals with. He doesn't want to marry the daughter of the owner of the hook-and-eye factory; he would probably burn down the factory itself if it ever came into his hands. . . . A superior man's struggle in the world is not with exterior lions, trusts, margraves, policemen, rivals in love, German spies, radicals and tornadoes, but with the obscure, atavistic impulses within him—the impulses, weaknesses and limitations that war with his notion of what life should be.[39]

The typical masters of this form of writing, he suggested, were "such cheese-mongers as [Richard Harding] Davis, with his servant-girl romanticism, and O. Henry, with his smoke-room and variety show smartness." True, many of those who practiced it showed an admirable technical skill—they had mastered the externals of the form and knew how to get their effects—but their work was totally devoid of substance.

Finally, the interesting and significant human actions had to be described "both in cause and effect." It was not enough for an author to tell *what* his characters did; he must afford a plausible explanation of *why* they did it—that is to say, he must set forth the external circumstances bearing upon their actions, and must show, too, the effect that these actions had upon other men and women in the miniature universe in which they lived, moved, and had their being. When this was not done the work was not really a novel at all, but a mere anecdote. At least twice in his years on *The Smart Set* Mencken took prominent novelists sharply to task for their failures in this regard. Once was when he reviewed Gertrude Atherton's *Julia France and Her Times* in the issue for September 1912; the trouble with the book, he complained, was that

> it describes [the characters] too much and explains them too little. She shows them doing all sorts of amazing things, and in the showing she is infallibly brisk and entertaining, but she seldom gets into their acts that appearance of inevitability which makes for reality.[40]

The second time, five years later, was when he did a review of a new novel by William Dean Howells, *The Leatherwood God*—the last, as it turned out, in "the Dean's" prodigious output. He wrote about it in January 1917, saying:

> An examination of it shows nothing but a suave piling up of words, a vast accumulation of nothings. The central character, one Dylks, is a backwoods evangelist who acquires a belief in his own buncombe, and ends by announcing that he is God. The job before the author was obviously that of tracing the psychological steps whereby this mountebank proceeds to that conclusion; the fact, indeed, is recognized in the canned review, which says that the book is "a study of American religious psychology." But an inspection of the text shows that no such thing is really in it. Dr. Howells does not *show* how Dylks came to believe himself God; he merely *says* that he did so. The whole discussion of the process, indeed, is confined to two pages—172 and 173—and is quite infantile in its inadequacy.[41]

A novelist, then—to go back to and expand upon the semi-serious definition—must create real and recognizable human beings, he must describe transactions among them that are interesting and significant, and he must place them in a rational universe where such transactions, both in cause and effect, can be logically accounted for. To put it in a phrase, his work must have meaning.

And it is just here that we run into a seemingly irreconcilable contradiction in Mencken's critical theory. For he was unalterably convinced, at every stage of his life from earliest youth to old age, that the real universe had no meaning or purpose whatever. No will had brought it forth into being and no intelligence guided it along its way. The end toward which it moved—assuming that it moved toward any logical final end at all—was as much beyond human knowledge as beyond human control, and only the most preposterous egoism and optimism could persuade man that he was himself the end for which all else had been created. The universe was a gigantic flywheel making 10,000 revolutions a minute, and man was a sick fly taking a dizzy ride on it; religion was the theory that the wheel had been designed and set spinning to give him the ride. In the chapter on Dreiser in *A Book of Prefaces* he had quoted the lines of Sophocles in *Oedipus Rex:*

> Races of mortal man
> Whose life is but a span,
> I count ye but the shadows of a shade!*

and this gloomy view of a Greek tragic poet dead 2,400 years summed up perfectly his own philosophy. Sometime in the 1940's he wrote: "It is a folly to try to beat death. One second after my heart stops thumping I shall not know or care what becomes of all my books and articles."[42]

But if life has no meaning, how can the artist portray it and yet give it meaning in his portrayal? The question, indeed, is not so much "*How* can he?" as "*Can* he?" Mencken, for all his intellectual nihilism, firmly believed that he could. Not only that—he believed, too, that this conviction of life's essential meaninglessness typified the very greatest works of creative art, and that failure to reflect it made a given work inferior. "It is obviously the final message, if any message is genuinely to be found there, of the nine symphonies of Ludwig van Beethoven." Mark Twain, superficially a humorist, was haunted by it in secret. In Shakespeare it amounted to a veritable obsession. It was to be found in

---

*As a matter of fact, he even quotes it in the original Greek, and there is no evidence whatever that Mencken knew a word of Greek.

Balzac, Goethe, Swift, Molière, Turgenev, Ibsen, Dostoevski, Romain Rolland, Anatole France. And especially was it to be found in the work of the two novelists whom he admired above all others and about whom, over the years, he wrote at every conceivable opportunity— Joseph Conrad and Theodore Dreiser.

His earliest piece on Conrad appears to be in the Baltimore *Evening Sun* for April 26, 1910, and one gets the impression there that he had encountered the Anglo-Polish novelist only in recent weeks and was filled with all the excitement and enthusiasm of a fresh discovery. "Who," he asks,

> is the greatest living English novelist? Henry James? George Moore? Thomas Hardy? There are many candidates for the bays. Let the reader who would weigh their fine gold upon delicate scales busy himself at that seductive task. As for me, I cast my vote at once. A few weeks ago it would have gone to Samuel Langhorne Clemens, and I should have submitted "Huckleberry Finn" as its sufficient excuse and justification. Today it goes to Joseph Conrad Korzeniowski, and the evidence supporting it consists, not of one book, nor even of two or three, but of a round half-dozen.

If that brief piece was the beginning, it was very far from being the end. His first actual review of a Conrad book came later that year, when he wrote about *The Point of Honor* in the December *Smart Set*. Thereafter he missed none of them as they appeared over the next decade and a half. In 1916, when the First World War made it impossible for him to discuss public affairs and he was using his space on the *Sun*'s editorial page to write mostly about literature and music, he did a series of four articles on Conrad which surveyed all of his work to date, compared him to his contemporaries, and weighed his place in modern English literature; these articles, much revised, embellished, and expanded, eventually became the opening chapter of *A Book of Prefaces*. The personal library which he bequeathed to the Pratt contains thirty-one volumes by Conrad—more than by any other single author except Dreiser.

The most astonishing thing about this long preoccupation with the man's work is the consistently high level of his praise. There were some books, of course, that he liked better than others, and one or two short minor things he dismissed impatiently: *The Return* was "a second-rate magazine story" and *The Inheritors* "a flaccid artificiality and bore"; but these very trifling exceptions aside, he never did a review of a Conrad work that could be called unfavorable. He termed him "a supreme artist in fiction," and said that his "figure stands out from the field like the Alps from the Piedmont plain. He not only has no masters in the novel; he has scarcely a colorable peer." Of Conrad's very first novel, *Almayer's Folly,* he wrote that "if it is not a work of genius then no work of genius exists on this earth." *Lord Jim* was his particular favorite, and he maintained that "as human document and as work of art [it] is worth all the works produced by all the Benaventes and Gjellerups since the time of Rameses II."* The contrast with Dreiser is very striking: Mencken knew Dreiser for years and they were good friends, and yet he never hesitated to be mercilessly frank about Dreiser's weaknesses as an artist; he never even met Conrad and knew the man only through his books, but he was without question his most enthusiastic press agent in the United States.

The narrative element in Conrad's works—the "story"—was, taken in itself, the baldest kind of melodrama. His setting was usually the romantic islands of the South Seas, or if not that, then some Latin American country torn by revolution or the intrigue-ridden Russia of the Czars. His characters were sailors, adventurers, soldiers of fortune, *agents provocateurs.* In every Conrad novel there was sure to be a storm at sea, or a shipwreck, or a volcanic eruption, or some other terrible disaster, whether natural or man-made. But what a difference between his handling of these things and the treatment given them by the "shock-mongers"! "Conrad's materials," Mencken observed,

> at bottom, are almost identical with those of the artisans. He, too, has his chariot races, his castaways, his carnivals of blood in the arena. He, too, takes us through shipwrecks, revolutions, assassinations, gaudy heroisms, abominable treacheries. But always he illuminates the nude and amazing event with shafts of light which reveal not only the last detail of its workings, but also the complex of origins and inducements behind it. Always, he throws about it a probability which, in the end, becomes almost inevitability.[43]

---

*At this point it may be helpful to insert a footnote fulfilling the precise purpose for which footnotes were invented. Karl A. Gjellerup, of Denmark, was co-winner of the Nobel Prize for Literature in 1917 (the other recipient being Henrik Pontoppidan), and Jacinto Benavente y Martínez, of Spain, received it in 1922. Mencken often waxed indignant over the failure of the Nobel Committee to award the prize to Conrad.

The difference, in brief, between him and the shock-mongers is that in the latter the hero always triumphs gloriously over such terrible odds, and marries the girl, and they live happily ever after. Conrad has few women in his books, and nothing that could be called sexual interest, and he really has no men properly describable as heroes. Moreover, they seldom if ever triumph; rather, the forces of a blind and implacable universe usually triumph over them. "His stories are not chronicles of men who conquer fate, nor of men who are unbent and undaunted by fate, but of men who are conquered and undone. Each protagonist is a new Prometheus, with a sardonic ignominy piled upon his helplessness. Each goes down a Greek route to defeat and disaster, leaving nothing behind him save an unanswered question."[44] The point of all his stories is that life is pointless.

But though he might be fascinated by this "immense indifference of things," he was much too fine an artist ever to criticize it or complain about it. He did not moralize; he made war on nothing; he would not even criticize God. "My task," he once wrote, "is, by the power of the written word, to make you hear, to make you feel—it is, before all, to make you see. That—and no more, and it is everything." What he saw, and made others see by the power of an overwhelming artistry, was life as a seeking without a finding, a question without an answer, a striving to no purpose or end. Over all his books there hung a kind of "tempered melancholy," along with irony and a quiet humor. Almost always he ends "upon an unresolved dissonance, a half-heard chord of the ninth." His characters, like Lord Jim, "pass away under a cloud, inscrutable at heart, forgotten, unforgiven, and excessively romantic."

"A very great man, this Mr. Conrad," Mencken concluded. "As yet, I believe, decidedly underestimated, even by many of his post-mortem advocates. . . . At all events, he is vastly less read and esteemed than he ought to be."

As with Conrad, so with Dreiser—even if the differences between the two men were as great as, or greater than, the resemblances. Conrad was a finished artist, a master of narrative technique; Dreiser wrote in a plodding and turgid style that made reading him an experience at times downright painful. Conrad maintained an attitude of aloof detachment from his characters; Dreiser was very much involved with his—"the sorrows of the world become the sorrows of Dreiser himself, and then the sorrows of his reader." The Pole was an aristocrat by birth as well as by nature; the American was an "Indiana peasant," coming

out of one of the most typical of Midwestern towns in the late years of
the nineteenth century. "Dreiser," Mencken pointed out, "is a product of far different forces and traditions [than Conrad]. . . . Struggle
as he may, and fume and protest as he may, he can no more shake off
the chains of his intellectual and cultural heritage than he can change
the shape of his nose. . . . The truth about Dreiser is that he is still in
the transition stage between Christian Endeavor and civilization, between Warsaw, Indiana, and the Socratic grove, between being a
good American and being a free man."[45]

This halfway position in Dreiser's intellectual development led to
still another difference between him and Conrad, and though it may
not have been reflected in the art of either one of them, it represented a
basic conflict in their respective philosophies. Conrad not only saw no
design in the universe, but his aristocratic skepticism was so complete
that it would not have occurred to him even to look for one. Dreiser
the artist viewed the universe in much the same way that Conrad did;
Dreiser the man was forever in search of both an explanation for it and a
panacea for all its ills, and more than once in his life he was convinced
that he had found them. At various stages he sought refuge in a facile
mysticism and supernaturalism, and toward the end, as everyone
knows, he was a ready convert to Communism.

And yet despite these fundamental divergences it seemed to
Mencken that the two men touched each other in a hundred ways, and
it was rare for him to write about one of them without bringing in at
least some mention of the other. Each was alien to his time and place,
as he was; each was a rebel against the current sentimentalities and
assurances, as—again—he was; each was a worker in the elemental
emotions, which he very definitely was not. Both saw human life as
without point or purpose, and this was a position he had arrived at on
his own long before he became acquainted with the work of either one
of them. Here, indeed, he felt that Dreiser may have gone a step
beyond Conrad, and perhaps that was why, with all of Dreiser's
shortcomings as an artist, he felt closer to him. If Conrad saw no order
in life, Dreiser saw in it only a profound and inexplicable *dis*order.
Man's voyage was without chart, compass, sun, or stars; to look into the
blackness ahead was almost beyond his endurance. He was "not only
doomed to defeat, but denied any glimpse or understanding of his
antagonist. Here we come upon an agnosticism that has almost got
beyond curiosity. What good would it do us, asks Dreiser, to know?"

So his characters—his kept women like Carrie Meeber and Jennie Gerhardt, his swashbucklers of finance like Cowperwood, his irresolute artists like Eugene Witla—are basically at one with those of his distant and so different colleague—with Lord Jim, and Razumov, and Kurtz, and Captain MacWhirr. All aspire to some nameless and indefinable goal; all engage in the same agonizing struggle; and in the end "one and all they are destroyed and made a mock of by the blind, incomprehensible forces that beset them."

But—and here is the essential point, here is what matters to the critic of literature rather than to the observer of life—no novelist could ever possibly tell a story that had no meaning, that portrayed mere chaos. A work of art without form or meaning would be a contradiction in terms; the very notion of art implies form. Mencken brought this out in a number of places, thereby clearing himself of a charge of inconsistency which very probably did not worry him anyway, but nowhere did he do it more clearly and forcibly than in a study of the novels of Arnold Bennett. Somewhat in the manner of a Scholastic philosopher, he states the objection ("Life itself is meaningless; therefore, the discussion of life is meaningless; therefore, why try futilely to get a meaning into it?"), and then goes on to give his reply:

> The reasoning, unluckily, has holes in it. It may be sound logically, but it is psychologically unworkable. One goes to novels, not for the bald scientific fact, but for a romantic amelioration of it. When they carry that amelioration to the point of uncritical certainty, when they are full of "ideas" that click and whirl like machines, then the mind revolts against the childish naivete of the thing. But when there is no organization of the spectacle at all, when it is presented as a mere formless panorama, when to the sense of its unintelligibility is added the suggestion of its inherent chaos, then the mind revolts no less. Art can never be simple representation. It cannot deal solely with precisely what is. It must, at the least, present the real in the light of some recognizable ideal; it must give to the eternal farce, if not some moral, then at all events some direction. For without that formulation there can be no clear-cut separation of the individual will from the general stew and turmoil of things, and without that separation there can be no coherent drama, and without that drama there can be no evocation of emotion, and without that emotion art is unimaginable.[46]

What made Conrad and Dreiser artists, then—the first a very great one, the second at least a genuine and sincere one despite all his elephantine plodding and his maddening obsession with irrelevant detail—was precisely this capacity to organize the spectacle, to impart some sense of direction to the "eternal farce." It was the power to evoke emotion. In those words of Conrad, it was the ability to make the reader "hear, and feel, and *see*."

But this did not mean, of course, that all novelists had to be like them, or share their view of the universe and of human life. The field of the novel was after all a very wide one, and Mencken's own tastes were catholic enough to embrace authors who had nothing in common with these two favorites or with each other. The very range of his admirations should be enough to substantiate this: Dreiser and Cabell, Anatole France and Sinclair Lewis, George Moore and Ruth Suckow, *Vanity Fair* and *Huckleberry Finn.* In general, it may be said that he was much more open to experimentation and new developments, to variations in style, and even to otherwise unacceptable philosophies, in the novel than he was in any other form. All he required was that the novelist be also an artist, and that the novel be capable of being judged as a work of art.

This last was the source of his quarrel with H. G. Wells, to whom he devoted a great deal of attention and thought, and it is possible to say that his affair with Wells was analogous in some ways to his original enthusiasm and subsequent disillusionment with George Bernard Shaw. In the beginning he thought that Wells was "easily the most brilliant, if not always the most profound, of contemporary English novelists. There were in him all of the requisites for the business and most of them very abundantly. He had a lively and charming imagination, he wrote with the utmost fluency and address, he had humor and eloquence, he had a sharp eye for the odd and intriguing in human character, and, most of all, he was full of feeling and could transmit it to the reader. That high day of his lasted, say, from 1908 to 1912."[47] During that high day Mencken gave to each successive work in the Wellsian canon the highest praise of which he was capable: he thought that nothing could exceed the sheer radiance of *Tono-Bungay,* that it was "a work that glows with reality"; a year later he praised *Ann Veronica;* and in his review of *The History of Mr. Polly* he expressed the belief that Wells was the successor of Dickens as portraitist of the English middle class.

But then *Marriage* brought with it "the first faint signs of something wrong." Into *The Passionate Friends* "there crept the first downright dullness." And after that Wells's collapse was rapid. In *Mr. Brit-ling Sees It Through* there was "a great hollowness"; *The Soul of a Bishop* was "perhaps the worst novel ever written by a serious novelist since novel-writing began"; and then finally there came *Joan and Peter*, which Mencken confessed "lingers in my memory as unpleasantly as a summer cold. . . . I would not look into it again for gold and frankin-cense." He thought that "the book is a botch from end to end, and in that botch there is not even the palliation of an arduous enterprise gallantly attempted. . . . Its badness lies wholly in the fact that the author made a mess of the writing."

What, he wondered for a time, had happened? Here was "a master of brilliant and life-like representation, an evoker of unaccustomed but nonetheless deep-seated emotions, a dramatist of fine imagination and highly resourceful execution"—and here, less than half a dozen years later, was one of the dullest, most inept, most flatulent writers engaged in the business of concocting novels in the English language. Then gradually it dawned upon him: Wells had made the unhappy but all-too-common mistake of taking himself too seriously. He had portrayed human nature brilliantly and successfully in the novels of that brief period; but "like some foul miasma, there arose the old, fatuous yearn-ing to change it, to improve it, to set it right where it was wrong, to make it over according to some pattern superior to the one followed by the Lord God Jehovah." He had become, in other words, a "jitney messiah," a tin-pot reformer, a professional wise man—and as soon as he donned those robes his days as an artist were at an end.

"What has slowly crippled him and perhaps disposed of him," Mencken explained to his readers,

> is his gradual acceptance of the theory, corrupting to the artist and scarcely less so to the man, that he is one of the Great Thinkers of his era, charged with a pregnant Message to the Younger Generation— that his ideas, rammed into enough skulls, will Save the Empire, not only from the satanic Nietzscheism of the Hindenburgs and post-Hindenburgs, but also from all those inner Weaknesses that taint and flabbergast its vitals, as the tapeworm with nineteen heads devoured Atharippus of Macedon. In brief, he suffers from a messianic delusion —and once a man begins to suffer from a messianic delusion his days as a serious artist are ended. He may yet serve the state with laudable de-votion; he may yet enchant his millions; he may yet posture and gyrate before the world as a man of mark. But not in the character of artist.

Not as a creator of sound books. Not in the separate place of one who observes the eternal tragedy of man with full sympathy and understanding, and yet with a touch of god-like remoteness. Not as Homer saw it, smiting the while his blooming lyre.[48]*

At the same time he would take back nothing of what he had said about the novels of that "high day." On one side of them was a long row of "extravagant romances in the manner of Jules Verne, and on the other . . . an even longer row of puerile tracts." But in between was "some of the liveliest, most original, most amusing, and withal most respectable fiction that England has produced in our time. In that fiction there is a sufficient memorial to a man who, between two debauches of claptrap, had his day as an artist."

Bennett, whom he also admired greatly, was without the messianic delusion that had brought Wells to ruin, and no man had ever described better the social anatomy and physiology of the masses of average, everyday, unimaginative Englishmen. His characters were often vividly real and thoroughly accounted for. The trouble with him, though, was that "he cannot feel with [them], that he never involves himself emotionally in their struggles against destiny, that the drama of their lives never thrills or dismays him—and the result is that he is unable to arouse in the reader that penetrating sense of kinship, that profound and instinctive sympathy, which in its net effect is almost indistinguishable from the understanding born of experiences actually endured and emotions actually shared." He thought that Bennett (and coming from Mencken this is an odd criticism indeed!) "carries skepticism so far that it often takes on the appearance of a mere peasant-like suspicion of ideas, bellicose and unintelligent."[49]

In the mid-twenties, when his days as literary critic for *The Smart Set* were over and he was launched upon the much broader and more demanding job of editing the *Mercury*, he published two articles in the Chicago *Tribune* entitled "Hints for Novelists" and "Yet More Hints for Novelists"; and these pieces, considerably reworked and expanded,

---

*It is interesting to note that in this essay Mencken repeats the point made elsewhere that the novel must give some semblance of order to the apparent chaos of life. "A novelist," he says, "must view life from some secure rock, drawing it into a definite perspective, interpreting it upon an ordered plan. Even if he hold (as Conrad does, and Dreiser, and Hardy, and Anatole France) that it is essentially meaningless, he must at least display that meaninglessness with reasonable clarity and consistency. Wells shows no such solid and intelligible attitude." (*Prejudices: First Series*, p. 34.)

appeared subsequently in *Prejudices: Fifth Series* as "Essay in Pedagogy." The American novel, he argued there, had made very great progress on the purely technical side; in general it was adeptly constructed, and not infrequently it was also well written. The newer novelists had given much study to form. The trouble was that in concentrating upon it they had unhappily overlooked something else just as important—namely, the observation of character. They failed on the whole to evoke memorable images of human beings. "In brief," he said, "a first-rate novel is always a character-sketch. It may be more than that, but at bottom it is always a character-sketch, or, if the author is genuinely of the imperial line, a whole series of them."[50] Who remembered the story of *Vanity Fair*, but who could forget Becky Sharp? Who could summarize the events in *Babbitt*, but had not the character become a part of American culture and the American language?

Into this breach he stepped with a whole list of suggestions to the massed novelists of the Federal Union, pointing out types for whom they might do what Lewis had done for Babbitt. "How long," he demanded to know, "will they gape at the American politician? At the American university president? At the American policeman? At the American lawyer? At the American insurance man? At the Prohibition fanatic? At the revival evangelist? At the bootlegger? At the Y. M. C. A. secretary? At the butter-and-egg man? At the journalist?" All these were salient and arresting American types, but they had never found historians and seemed doomed to perish and be forgotten along with the Bill of Rights.

No novelist, for example, had ever really successfully portrayed the political life of Washington; the closest that anybody had come was in Harvey Fergusson's *Capitol Hill*, but that, despite its merits, was little more than a series of casual sketches. No one had limned the modern American university president: "the new six-cylinder, air-cooled, four-wheel-brake model—half the quack, half the visionary, and wholly the go-getter—the brisk, business-like, confidential, button-holing, regular fellow who harangues Rotary and Kiwanis, extracts millions from usurers by alarming them about Bolshevism, and so builds his colossal pedagogical slaughter-house, with its tens of thousands of students, its professors of cheese-making, investment securities and cheer-leading, its galaxy of football stars, and its general air of Barnum's circus." "Why," he wanted to know, "has this astounding mountebank not got into a book?" And then there was "the most American of all Americans, the very *Ur-Amerikaner*—to wit, the malignant moralist, the Christian turned cannibal, the snouting and preposterous Puritan."

A number of the types he listed have, of course, pretty much passed from the American scene—the butter-and-egg man, the bootlegger, possibly even the revival evangelist. One or two, perhaps, did make it into books that had their brief day. Some—the American policeman is certainly the outstanding example—eventually became a part of television culture rather than of literature. But somehow, half a century later, one cannot escape the feeling that most of the novels Mencken called for in that series of helpful hints never did get themselves written.

7 IN POETRY HE IS much less reliable—in fact, it would not be going too far to say that in poetry he is not reliable at all. He had begun his own literary career as a poet, and his first published book, it will be remembered, was a collection of verse; but he gave it up by the time he was twenty and never felt the slightest desire to go back to it. "One always associates poetry," he maintained, "with youth, for it deals chiefly with the ideas that are peculiar to youth, and its terminology is quite as youthful as its content. When one hears of a poet past thirty-five, he seems somehow unnatural and even a trifle obscene"[51]—a statement which, if true, would, in the most cavalier fashion, dispose of Robert Frost, Carl Sandburg, Wallace Stevens, William Carlos Williams, Marianne Moore, T. S. Eliot, and John Crowe Ransom among American moderns, to say nothing of Virgil, Dante, Chaucer, Shakespeare, Milton, and Goethe.

What he had against it, put quite briefly, was that it was nothing more than "a sweet denial of the harsh facts that confront all of us." Its task was "to lie sonorously and reassuringly." This idea runs through his work from end to end like a leitmotif: "The poet, imagining him to be sincere, is simply one who disposes of all the horrors of life on this earth . . . by the childish device of denying them." "Poetry is one device for defeating God. Its aim is to escape some of the pains of reality by denying boldly that they exist." The point, in more or less similar words, is made in his writings on religion and ethics; it occurs in his discussions of that most unpoetical of all subjects, politics; it is to be found in fragmentary notes that never got published at all. It even spills over into *The American Language,* as when, apropos of the factual basis of Lincoln's Gettysburg Address, he observes: "Poetry is not to be judged by the laws of evidence. It is always, at bottom, a sonorous statement of the obviously *not* true."[52]

Now Mencken, as I trust the foregoing pages have made sufficiently clear, was not an unemotional person. Neither in his life nor in his work does he appear as the cold, analytical thinker. He fell in love with a number of women, married one of them, and grieved when she died. He enjoyed friendship and the pleasure of good company. He liked to relax and let down his faculties by judicious drinking. He was sensitive to the beauties of nature—a landscape, or a cow in some field, or the inviting display of a fried egg. Strong feelings run through the whole gamut of his books, articles, reviews, and columns.

But if he was not unemotional, he had a deep-seated distrust of emotion. He claimed to have been born that way: "I appear," he said, "to have come into the world with a highly literal mind, geared well enough to take in overt (and usually unpleasant) facts, but very ill adapted to engulfing the pearls of the imagination."[53] He devoted his whole life to the pursuit, anatomizing, and embalming of ideas. And this was precisely what poetry did not, and by its very nature could not, do. This was what it implacably opposed. "Poetry can never be concocted by any purely intellectual process. It has nothing to do with the intellect; it is, in fact, a violent and irreconcilable enemy to the intellect."[54]

At the same time, though, no man could be as self-conscious a stylist as he was without being aware that words have an intrinsic value of their own. He knew perfectly well that very often their beauty as pure sound is independent of their literal meaning—no doubt with tongue again partly in cheek, he gave "cellar-door" and "sarcoma" as instances of words that are musical in themselves. In his essay "The Poet and His Art" he quotes some lines from *Othello:*

> Not poppy, nor mandragora,
> Nor all the drowsy syrups of the world,
> Shall ever medicine thee to that sweet sleep
> Which thou owed'st yesterday;

and then goes on to observe: ". . . the effect is stupendous. The passage assaults and benumbs the faculties like the slow movement of Schumann's Rhenish Symphony; hearing it is a sensuous debauch; the man anesthetic to it could stand unmoved in Sainte-Chapelle." And not only were there hundreds of other passages equally lush in Shake-speare, but in the whole range of poetry from Rossetti and Swinburne, Browning and Kipling, all the way back to that most gorgeous of all collections of poetry, the Hebrew Bible, which King James's trans-lators had turned into one of the great glories of English literature.

No, he was not a poetry-hater, even though once, after plowing through some sixty or seventy volumes of bad verse, he had claimed to be one. Had he hated it, he would not have plowed through them, or been as extraordinarily well read in it as he was. He admired above all its craftsmanship: a sound sonnet seemed to him as pleasing an object as a well-written fugue, and a deftly done lyric had all the technical charm of a fine carving. His whole argument with the so-called New Poetry, in fact, was that its practitioners, first and last, failed to show any such mastery; they had thrown overboard all the traditional forms not because they were above such things but because they lacked the ability to handle them. Their work was "a sort of organized imbecility"; "free verse, at bottom, is nothing but an escape for poets too incom-petent to manage the pentameter."[55]

But if he did not hate it, neither would he let himself be taken in by it. He was suspicious of its sensuous imagery, its almost narcotic capacity to soothe; he rejected its half-truths and outright lies. When he was at the height of his powers and fit for any work or deviltry, he wanted no part of it. He reserved it for a special mood—"the mood, in a few words, of intellectual and spiritual fatigue, the mood of re-volt against the insoluble riddle of existence, the mood of disgust and despair."[56] Then it was a capital medicine. Then it lulled the facul-ties and gave reassurance. Then it was an escape from life and its tor-ments, like religion, like enthusiasm, like the sight of a pretty girl.

8 HIS OPINION OF THE DRAMA was no higher (and in fact may have been lower) than his opinion of po-etry, and here again it has to be remembered that he was involved with it almost from the beginning of his career as a journalist. In *News-*

paper Days he tells how he was made drama critic—or, in humbler but more honest terms, "theater reporter"—for the *Herald* at the beginning of the 1901–2 season, the assignment being not a promotion but simply an addition to his other chores. The managing editor, Robert I. Carter, who was himself a man of considerable culture and a lover of the theater, personally covered all the leading plays, so that Mencken was left with second-choice things, cheap melodramas, musical comedies, vaudeville, and what passed in those days for burlesque. When the *Herald* expired in 1906 and he went over to the *Sun*, he continued to review a great many performances.

The Pratt's Mencken Room contains two bound volumes of clippings—"Editorials, Dramatic Reviews and Other Pieces, Baltimore Morning-Evening Herald, 1904–1906" and "Editorials and Dramatic Reviews, Baltimore Sun, 1906–1910"—which preserve his work in this field. They show him covering a range of plays that begins with Shakespeare's *Cymbeline* (which he thought "dull and a bit wearisome"), Ibsen's *A Doll's House,* and Shaw's *Man and Superman* and runs through *The Three Musketeers* to such now-forgotten pieces as *Clothes,* by Avery Hopwood and Channing Pollock, and *The Parisian Model,* "a musical comedy by Harry B. Smith." He later claimed that during the season of 1905–6 he wrote twenty-three unfavorable reviews in a row, whereupon the owner of Ford's Theater, then and for long thereafter the leading legitimate playhouse in Baltimore, complained bitterly to the publisher of the *Sunpapers,* Walter Abell, that Mencken was ruining his business. He admitted that the plays were awful but insisted that it was not his fault, since he had to take whatever the theatrical syndicate in New York sent out on the road. Mencken found himself in sympathy with the man and forthwith asked to be relieved of his job; "I have never," he said in 1941, "written a line of dramatic criticism since."

Not only did he give up drama criticism—for all practical purposes he abandoned the theater. There is no public record of his ever going again. In 1939 he told Blanche Knopf that his regular price for attending a performance was $1,000 cash in advance (the play she wanted him to see was Clarence Day's *Life with Father*). In the January 8, 1947, issue of *Variety,* in an article entitled "Why I Eschew the Theater," he gave as the principal reason for his avoidance the fact that "the seats in the sweat-shop theaters of today are too narrow for my figure, and I object to being pinched and compressed for hours on end." A secondary reason was that "the new perfumes advertised so lasciviously in *Vogue* and the *New Yorker* are too heady for a man of my years and learning, and fill me with wayward thoughts."

But the real reason, no doubt, was the fact that the drama, as an art form, was too "democratic." One of the things he could never understand about George Jean Nathan was how he could go regularly to the theater from one end of the season to the other, "breathing bad air nightly, gaping at prancing imbeciles, sitting cheek by jowl with cads."[57] All the other arts could be enjoyed alone; even music, though it generally required an audience for its performance, could at least be practiced in solitude; but the drama was not conceivable save as a show for the mob, and so it had to descend to the level of the mob in order to survive. This meant that the ideas it put forth had to be so simple that the average man could grasp them at once, and so banal that he would approve of them as soon as he grasped them.

This was true, Mencken insisted, of all the plays—even the few relatively good ones—of the last several generations. "The younger Dumas' *La Dame aux Camélias*, the first of all the propaganda plays (it raised a stupendous pother in 1852, the echoes of which yet roll), is based upon the sophomoric thesis that a prostitute is a human being like you and me, and suffers the slings and arrows of the same sorrows, and may be potentially quite as worthy of Heaven."[58] Even Ibsen, who had thoroughly revolutionized the modern theater and whom Mencken had once admired so much, based his situations and plots on "tasteless platitudes."[59] And as for Shaw, that "Ulster Polonius," in the entire canon of his work there was not a single original idea: his genius, such as it was, lay in "exhibiting the obvious in unexpected and terrifying lights"; his typical formula was to hand down a mass of platitudes with the air of a peep show.

Following an early instruction of Robert Carter, he made it a point to avoid actors all his life long, although in Baltimore as a critic and later in the literary circles of New York he doubtless had plenty of opportunity to meet them. They were simply men of arrested development, "with the cerebrum of a floor-walker and the vanity of a bishop." They were not to be taken seriously—"there stands Richard Coeur de Lion—and there, plainly enough, also stands a poor ham." Perhaps here, at bottom, we have the secret of Mencken's intense dislike of the stage. The rest of us, going to the theater (and provided, of course, that the performance is not too atrocious), are willing enough to suspend disbelief for a few hours and see Richard Coeur de Lion on the other side of the footlights. Mencken, again with his highly literal mind, could never see anything but the poor ham.

HE HAD NEVER REALLY wanted to be a literary critic, and in later years read fiction with "decreasing interest. He considered poetry, as we have seen, to be no more than "a series of ideas, false in themselves, that offer a means of emotional and imaginative escape from the harsh realities of everyday." The theater remained, at best, "infantile and trivial." But there was one art that filled his life from end to end, from earliest boyhood to the afternoon of the day that he died, and to it he gave not only most of his leisure hours but—at least in the early part of his career—a generous portion of his working time. He considered himself devoid of any talent for it, and yet he had an irresistible impulse to practice it and derived immense pleasure from being a part of it. That art was, of course, music.

He used to boast that he had learned to read it by the age of six—that he was unable to remember, in fact, any time in his childhood when he could not read it. Then, in the course of researching family memorabilia for the writing of *Happy Days*, he was shocked to discover that the Stieff square piano on which he had had his first lessons came into the house at Hollins Street on January 13, 1888, when he was in his eighth year. This trivial detail aside, he certainly got off to an early start and, under a succession of teachers, was soon pounding away at a broad range of waltzes, polkas, schottisches, and mazurkas. August Mencken made good use of his virtuosity to drive unwelcome visitors from the house. He composed a number of juvenile works, mostly in waltz form, and in 1895 wrote the score for a musical comedy put on by the boys at the Baltimore Polytechnic. It was apparently successful, but he later confessed that most of it was "snitched from other composers."

During his apprentice years as a reporter he was much too busy to continue with musical studies; his interest in it did not wane, but opportunities to engage in it were virtually nonexistent. Then, after a while, he made the discovery that a number of his colleagues on the paper loved it as much as he did, and they began to get together to play purely for their own enjoyment.

Enough has been written about the Saturday Night Club in the various biographies of Mencken to make any fresh account of it unnecessary here. But it is perhaps worth noting that it first began to meet in 1904 and that it dissolved, by formal resolution of its surviving membership, in 1950—an elapsed time of forty-six years. It survived Prohibition, that evil era when it had to meet, if not underground, then at least in members' basements. It survived the destruction of the old Rennert Hotel, its long-time headquarters. It even survived Mencken's marriage. Sara, a fastidious young woman, took the same dim view of the rather disreputable cronies of her husband's bachelor days that any other bride would, and when it came Mencken's turn to have the group in their Cathedral Street apartment for the first time she looked on in horror as they draped themselves and their instruments over her carefully chosen furniture.

The one thing that it apparently could not survive was Mencken himself. When he was in the hospital in 1948 following his massive stroke, he sent word that he hoped it would continue and that he looked forward to rejoining it as soon as he was out. But he was never really able to take part in its sessions again, and although he lived for another six years the Club died in only two.

For he was at all times its mind, its heart, and its inspiration. I spoke just now of its "surviving membership," but that only means the ones who happened to be on the rolls in 1950. Over the years there were several complete turnovers in its personnel. Some men joined it relatively young and left it when they died of old age. New members succeeded them, and were succeeded in turn. Only Mencken remained.

His loyalty to it probably surpassed his loyalty to any other person, institution, or custom, with the possible exception of the *Sunpapers*. In those forty-four years he hardly ever missed a meeting if he was in town; it is said that the only time he ever let something else take precedence was when he attended the wedding of his biographer William Manchester. He arranged the programs. He was principally responsible for building up the library, which consisted of some 500 works including most of the standard orchestral and chamber-music repertoire. From his seat at the second piano he pretty much controlled the proceedings. He had an authoritative voice in the matter of who was invited to join and who was not.

The music-making session always began at eight o'clock and continued in grim earnestness for the next two hours. It adjourned at ten, and the time from then until midnight was given over to the equally convivial art of beer drinking and—now and then—to some very unconvivial discussion and argumentation.

In a sense the Club was a separate part of his life, at least to the degree that the friendships he made in it did not usually carry over into his other activities and vice versa. If one or another of his New York associates—Nathan, or Willard Huntington Wright, or Dreiser, or Alfred Knopf—happened to be in Baltimore over a weekend, they might, of course, be invited to sit in on a meeting as guests. The same high honor was occasionally bestowed upon dignitaries from the *Sun*—Paul Patterson or Hamilton Owens. But none of the Club's members—Heinrich Buchholz, Raymond Pearl, William E. Moffett, Max Brödel, Adolph Torovsky, Israel Dorman, Albert Hildebrandt, Theodore Hemberger, Willie Woollcott, to name but a few—were literary figures, and after that first charter group few were newspapermen. Mencken seems to have preferred it that way. It did not make the friendships any the less close, and in fact it may have made them more so.

But if the Saturday Night Club existed in a sort of closed compartment, music itself certainly did not. It not only filled his scant leisure hours; it flowed over abundantly into his professional work. Around 1915 he regularly wrote the program notes for the concerts of the then infant Baltimore Symphony Orchestra, and often discussed the principal work of the evening in his column in the *Sun*. Many of his newspaper pieces over the years dealt with music or with particular composers, and some of them, much expanded, eventually found their way into the *Prejudices*.

There are probably more references to music in the complete body of his work than in that of any other writer outside the specific field of music criticism. One of his early books—a collection of aphorisms—is entitled *A Little Book in C Major*, and to some others he actually gave opus numbers. Many of the "Monday Articles" bear musical titles: e.g., "Overture in C Major" (February 28, 1921), "Da Capo" (September 28, 1925), "Variations upon a Popular Tune" (July 5, 1926), "Götzendämmerung" (March 4, 1935). It was not at all unusual for him to use musical terminology in his criticism; as far back as the Nietzsche volume, in describing the philosopher's *Der Antichrist*, he said: "Beginning *allegro*, it proceeds from *forte*, by an uninterrupted *crescendo* to *allegro con moltissimo molto fortissimo*." He spoke of Dreiser's "dreadful cacophony," and called Cabell's *Jurgen* "a devil's sonata, an infernal *Kindersymphonie*." Of Conrad's *Heart of Darkness* he wrote that it is "as thoroughly *durch componiert* as a fugue," and of a speech by William Jennings Bryan at the Democratic National Convention of 1904 he later said that "it swept up on wave after wave of sound like the *finale* of the first movement of Beethoven's Eroica."

As with poetry and women, his tastes tended on the whole to be conservative.* That is to say, they ran to the great German composers of the classical and Romantic periods ("there are," he held, "only two kinds of music: German music and bad music"), and within that field he would admit no composer later in time than Richard Strauss. He placed Beethoven ("old Ludwig") first, even ahead of Bach—though he admitted that the reason for that may simply have been that he had heard more of Beethoven than of Bach. His favorite among the symphonies, he claimed, was No. 8, but if that is so he seems to have written relatively little about it. On the other hand, the first movement of the *Eroica* fascinated him more than any other work of art in the world and is certainly the one that is mentioned most often in his own writings. "Every line of modern music that is honestly music," he maintained, "bears some sort of relation to that epoch-making first movement." Next to Beethoven he put Brahms, and he would rather have been present at Karlsruhe on November 6, 1876, for the premiere performance of Brahms's First Symphony than at the initiation of General Pershing into the Elks. His unqualified admiration for both composers was based upon their total mastery of their art and the fact that neither ever wrote a line that was cheap or banal.

He could discuss both of them rationally, but it was almost impossible for him to use restrained language when it came to Schubert. The composer of the "Unfinished" Symphony was "scarcely human"—"he

---

*In what follows I have drawn chiefly, though not entirely, on Mencken's letter of May 6, 1925, to Isaac Goldberg, wherein he sets forth his musical likes and dislikes in great detail. It is contained in Goldberg, *The Man Mencken*, pp. 178–83, and reproduced in Louis Cheslock's anthology, *H. L. Mencken on Music* (for which see the next footnote), pp. 197–204.

sweated beauty as naturally as a Christian sweats hate." "He was, to music, its great heart, as Beethoven was its great mind." Mozart, like Schubert, was beyond critical analysis: "he simply happened." He did not care for opera ("it is to music what a bawdy house is to a cathedral"), but considered that Wagner's *Die Meistersinger* was "the greatest single work of art ever produced by man. It took more skill to plan and write it than it took to plan and write the whole canon of Shakespeare." He thought that Puccini was underestimated—"*La Bohème* is surely not a great work, but anyone who fails to get pleasure out of it must be tone-deaf." Verdi was hardly to be listened to sober, but Mencken had long ago made the discovery that three drinks of rye whiskey would double the pleasure to be gotten out of *Il Trovatore.*

It should not be supposed, of course, that his tastes were so austere as to give the impression of being snobbish. Schumann, Mendelssohn, Chopin, and Tchaikovsky all belonged to the second table, but all were men of very great talent and had written many beautiful things. He confessed to enjoying greatly such minor figures as Goldmark and Dvořák. He had an especially deep affection for Johann Strauss, delighted in Gilbert and Sullivan, and cherished nostalgically songs that were already old in his day and are utterly forgotten in ours—"Juanita," "In the Gloaming," "Silver Threads Among the Gold," and "Sweet Genevieve."

But just as he had no interest whatever in modern poetry or the new novelists, so he had little or none in twentieth-century music. He does not even seem to have known anything about Bruckner or Mahler, though of course it has to be remembered that they did not really begin to build up anything like a reputation until after his own tastes were pretty well fixed. Such men as Schönberg, Hindemith, Webern, and Berg were apparently quite unknown to him, and he committed the critical gaffe of dismissing Stravinsky as a "prophet of the new enlightenment" who "never had a musical idea in his life." Jazz he defined curtly as "the sort of music that the persons who go to the opera really like."

The pleasure that he got out of music also brought with it a sense of nagging frustration. For the fact of the matter is that he always had a desire to be a composer, and would far rather have written notes than words. In *Happy Days* he makes the statement that whenever he had anything properly describable as a beautiful idea, it always came to him in the form of music. The real reason he had never pursued it as a profession, he suspected, was simply that he had no talent for it, and according to some members of the Saturday Night Club this may have been true—his playing at the second piano seems to have been marked more by force and gusto than by any actual mastery of either the instrument or the music. "All the same," he went on, "I shall die an inarticulate man, for my best ideas have beset me in a language I know only vaguely and speak only like a child." When that time came, when he mounted the gallows at last, he wanted it to be after having heard a performance of Brahms's First Symphony.*

10 SARA MAYFIELD, in *The Constant Circle*, says that Mencken was slightly color-blind—though he himself, in the very full records which he kept of his anatomy, physiology, and assorted malfunctionings, makes no mention of the fact. He admitted, however, that the world presented itself to him chiefly as a complex of aural sensations rather than of visual ones, and it was to this that he inclined to attribute his defective response to painting. George Jean Nathan termed him "anaesthetic" to it. It seemed to him, in his own words, "half an alien among the fine arts."[60]

The trouble with it was that it lacked movement, the chief function of life. It froze the event and the mood of an instant into eternal stillness. Not only that, it did so from a particular angle and vantage point (and in this respect it was inferior even to sculpture, since one could at least move around and view a statue from an infinite number of positions). For this reason, its content was exhausted very quickly; one might read a great work of literature or listen to a great piece of music innumerable times with undiminished, or indeed with constantly augmented, pleasure, but a painting wore itself out and had nothing more to offer the beholder in just a few minutes.

That this is completely untrue must be obvious to anyone who has ever looked at even a reproduction of, say, Masaccio's "The Tribute

*At this point it is both a duty and a pleasure to draw the reader's attention to Louis Cheslock's anthology, *H. L. Mencken on Music* (New York: Alfred A. Knopf, Inc., 1961). Cheslock, a professional musician and composer, a professor on the faculty of Baltimore's Peabody Institute of Music, and a member of the Saturday Night Club, has here brought together most of Mencken's writings on the subject and added an account of his musical life and a brief history of the Club. Of all the posthumous Mencken collections, it is probably the most readable and delightful.

Money," or the Ghent Altarpiece of Hubert and Jan van Eyck, or Picasso's "Guernica," or any one of a hundred other great paintings. Such works contain a wealth of detail which only the most patient study can absorb, and this detail commonly yields itself only by repeated and renewed acquaintance. The chief difference is that a person reads but one book, or listens to one piece of music, at a time, whereas paintings are ordinarily seen in a museum which may have thousands of them hanging on its walls, and one seldom spends more than a few minutes looking at each.

Because of his lack of interest in the subject he wrote little about it, and there is no point in pretending that his reputation as an aesthetician stands or falls on that little. Some of the things that he says flatly contradict each other; in one place, for example, he makes the quite indefensible statement that "the portrait of an ugly woman, even though the artist tries to ameliorate her ugliness a bit, remains almost as horrible as the ugly woman herself,"[61] while in another, dating from a much later time, he says:

> It seems to be generally assumed that there can be no such thing as an ugly work of art. Indeed, art and beauty are taken to be synonymous. They are, of course, nothing of the sort. A work of really appalling ugliness may show artistic skill of the first order.[62]

He was much more sensitive to line than to color (which perhaps bears out the theory of his color blindness), and some drawings done in his boyhood show a gift for composition which one may regret was never developed. A scene of the Jones Falls, near the Mencken summer home in Mount Washington, hung framed on his office wall for years; it is really a quite creditable performance for a boy of twelve. He confessed in after years that he had often thought of entering it "in some free-for-all exhibition of Modernist Art—with the date and signature, of course, discreetly painted out."[63]

V

THE PHILOLOGIAN

Someone had to bring together the widely scattered field material and try to get some order and coherence into it, and I fell into the job.

—Supplement II,
The American Language

◇◇

IT IS A COMMONPLACE OF Menckenian criticism to say that *The American Language* is his most enduring work, and like many such commonplace statements, it is probably true. Certainly he himself thought so: "You are quite wrong," he told Jim Tully rather sharply in a letter of September 28, 1935, "about *The American Language*. It is worth every moment of time that I put into it. It will long outlast anything else that I have ever written."[1] In an unpublished fragment which must be dated a half dozen or so years later he noted that "I'll be remembered longest, I suppose, as a student of language; indeed, it will be difficult, for a century hence, for anyone to write about American speechways without mentioning me."[2] This is not egotism, it is an honest and clear-sighted appraisal of his own achievement.

He had become interested in the subject, he says, while a reporter in the police courts around the turn of the century, but so far as can be ascertained, his first published work on it was a column in the Baltimore *Evening Sun* for October 10, 1910, entitled "The Two Englishes." Supplement II of *The American Language* came out in 1948. A time span of at least thirty-eight years, then, elapsed between the initial tentative approach and the culmination of his labors; for sheer sustained effort, perhaps the only things that can be set beside it are Goethe's sixty-year preoccupation with *Faust* and the twenty-six years that it took Wagner to compose the *Ring*. To be sure, like Goethe and Wagner, he was not constantly engaged upon it; there were long periods when his attention was diverted by other projects. There is a significant difference too: Goethe completed *Faust* (almost on his deathbed) and Wagner completed the *Ring*, but Mencken very sensibly never did regard *The American Language* as a finished work. In the preface to Supplement II he stated that it was highly improbable that he would ever attempt a third, but added that he had hoped to discuss in an appendix certain matters not hitherto dealt with—"for example, the language of gesture, that of children, the names of political parties, cattle brands, animal calls, and so on." Unhappily, none of these topics ever did get treated; less than three months after the book's appearance his stroke put an end to any further writing.

That first column in the *Sun* sounded one of the two major themes which, subject to some development over the years, would guide him throughout the whole colossal work—namely, that "the English people speak an English which differs enormously, in vocabulary and idiom, from the English spoken by Americans." He then proceeded to give three columns of examples of these differences. Four days later, on October 14, he returned to the subject with an article called "England's English," and five days after that, on October 19, he stated the second theme in "Spoken American." "Why," he wanted to know, "doesn't some painstaking pundit attempt a grammar of the American language—of English, that is, as she is spoken by the great masses of the plain people of this fair land?" He offered some instances of this grammar—*I didn't do nothing, I have saw, He would have went*—and then added, "The argument that they are not worthy of serious investigation because they are mere evidences of ignorance is not a very valid one. Any spoken language, however barbarous, is worthy of investigation."

Two more articles followed—one on October 20 entitled "More American" and one on October 25, "American Pronouns"—and then his interest in the subject seems to have subsided.

But not for very long. In 1913 he planned and wrote for *The Smart Set* a series of fairly lengthy articles on "The American"—"His Morals," "His Language," "His Ideas of Beauty," "His Freedom," and "His New Puritanism." The whole thing was apparently to be published eventually as a book, although nothing ever came of that. The article "The American: His Language" appeared in the August issue,[3] and in it he studied in the greatest depth yet the peculiarities of American speech that differentiated it from the mother tongue. "American is now," he said, "so rich in new words, new phrases and old words transferred to new objects that it is utterly unintelligible to an educated Englishman." He had little good to say about "the American" in any of the other pieces, but here he willingly admitted that "his one desire is to make speech lucid, lively, dramatic, staccato, arresting, clear—and to that end he is willing to sacrifice every purely aesthetic consideration."

There is in the Pratt's Mencken Room a slim bound volume containing a typescript entitled *The American Language*, together with a short preface inserted by him at some later date. "This is," the preface states, "apparently the typescript of the first form of *The American Language*. It was probably written in 1915 or 1916. Part of it was picked up from the typescript of an article, 'The American: His Language,' published in *The Smart Set* for August, 1913." The manuscript runs to only 44 pages; some of it, as he says, is picked up from the earlier magazine article, and some looks forward to the first edition, which still lay three or four years in the future. But in that precise form it does not appear ever to have been used anywhere, and one can only speculate now on the specific purpose he had in mind in writing it.

Then came America's entry into the First World War and his gradual withdrawal from the *Sunpapers* because they simply could not print his views on the Allies vis-à-vis the Germans. For the first time since he had gone to work for the *Herald* in 1899, he was for all practical purposes out of a job. He tried to keep his hand in newspaper work by writing articles for the New York *Evening Mail*, but that arrangement turned out to be more trouble than it was worth and it terminated abruptly when the *Mail* was suppressed on account of its own pro-German sympathies. His duties on *The Smart Set* involved no more than a few days a month. Time hung heavy on his hands, and he amused himself with a variety of projects: he collaborated with Nathan on the collection of American folk beliefs and superstitions that would become *The American Credo*, he wrote *In Defense of Women*, he ventured into the field of scholarship by making a fresh translation of Nietzsche's *Der Antichrist*. But although these undertakings might have been enough for any other man, they could not exhaust Mencken's enormous energies.

More and more now the thought of his earlier language studies began to absorb him. Over the years he had accumulated a "formidable bulk" of materials—he was an early and enthusiastic subscriber to *Dialect Notes*, he had already begun the building up of what would eventually be a huge library on linguistics, and even those early articles in the *Sun*, limited though their audience was, had brought a "pleasant response" from readers. Now he began to organize his material and make an intelligible outline for a book on the subject. Throughout much of 1918 he labored on it in his third-floor study, tensely awaiting his call in the draft and while each day, in the streets below, trucks picked up the bodies of the latest victims of the great "flu epidemic." In March 1919 the first edition of *The American Language* was published.

Both he and Alfred Knopf had expected that the interest in such a work would be relatively limited, and the printing was deliberately held to 1,500 copies. They sold out almost immediately. A year later, writing to Burton Rascoe, Mencken observed that "the reviews of my *American Language* actually made me sick,"[4] but really he had no reason to be unhappy about them. In general it was very well received: the Boston *Transcript* called it "a fascinating book; a labor of love, and hence a joy to read," and the great music critic Lawrence Gilman, writing in the *North American Review*, termed it "deplorably engrossing." Even Brander Matthews, one of those "pedagogues" at whom Mencken had been aiming critical barbs for a decade or more, declared in a 2,500-word review in *The New York Times* that "his book is interesting and useful; it is a book to be taken seriously, it is a book well planned, well proportioned, well documented and well written"—though he could not help adding primly that Mencken was "not always so courteous as he might be toward the predecessors with whom he does not agree."

As one might have anticipated, it was in the professional language journals that it took the heaviest drubbing: a certain J. R. Hulbert, for example, writing in *Modern Philology*, crustily noted the book's errors and observed that "one could fill pages with examples resulting from the author's lack of systematic training." But Mencken had been prepared for this sort of thing; in the preface that he typed on New Year's

Day he had made the first of those modest disclaimers that would characterize every fresh edition down through the years. "It is anything," he said there,

> but an exhaustive treatise upon the subject; it is not even an exhaustive examination of the materials. All it pretends to do is to articulate some of those materials—to get some approach to order and coherence into them, and so pave the way for a better work by some more competent man. That work calls for the equipment of a first-rate philologist, which I am surely not. All I have done here is to stake out the field, sometimes borrowing suggestions from other inquirers and sometimes, as in the case of popular American grammar, attempting to run the lines myself.[5]

To be sure, he made another point in that same preface which would also be hammered home again and again—namely, that in his researches for the book he had found that "the whole literature of the subject was astonishingly meagre and unsatisfactory . . . a fugitive and inconsequential literature—an almost useless mass of notes and essays, chiefly by the minor sort of pedagogue, seldom illuminating, save in small details, and often incredibly ignorant and inaccurate." On the subject of American pronunciation he had found nothing save a few casual essays. On American spelling there had been little more. On American grammar there had been absolutely nothing whatever. "Worse," he went on, "an important part of the poor literature that I unearthed was devoted to absurd efforts to prove that no such thing as an American variety of English existed—that the differences I constantly encountered in English and that my English friends encountered in American were chiefly imaginary, and to be explained away by denying them." Accusations like these were not exactly calculated to endear him to the "minor pedagogues" who had turned out that trifling literature, and whose field he was now invading with a brilliance and style that none of them could even begin to muster.

But more important than the reviews, favorable or unfavorable, were the letters that the book itself began to bring into him—the first wave of that never-ending and constantly accelerating flood which, as the years went by, would all but inundate the house on Hollins Street and make his correspondence virtually unique in modern American writing and scholarship. They came, as he said later, from "generals and admirals, privates and seamen . . . presidents of universities and country schoolma'ams . . . high ecclesiastical dignitaries and lifers in prison." They offered a wealth of additional materials, directed his attention to sources he had overlooked, here and there corrected errors. Sometimes they were beautifully typed on engraved stationery and sometimes they were written in a scarcely literate hand with blunt pencil on cheap tablet paper. One of them, he noted, was "no less than 10,000 words long." With hardly an exception he answered each one on the day that the mailman delivered it at his door and then carefully filed it away for future use; if it happened to deal with two or more words or subjects, he cut it up with a pair of scissors and filed each part in its appropriate place. The Mencken Room in the Pratt Library has long been known to his admirers and to scholars in a number of fields, but what is not generally known, even to Baltimoreans and the Pratt's own patrons, is that right next door to it there is a second room containing, so to speak, the overflow—the 32 file drawers which hold this colossal exchange, along with an additional 54 containers for the magazine articles, pamphlets, booklets, and press clippings that were needful or helpful to him in his researches.

The first onslaught of letters, with their criticisms, corrections, and further examples, led him to undertake a revision almost at once, and in 1921 the second edition—"greatly enlarged and thoroughly rewritten"—appeared; it was longer than its predecessor by more than a hundred pages. Another two years went by, and in 1923 there was a third edition, in which, he said, "I have added new material to nearly every chapter, and all of them have been diligently scrutinized for errors." But he added in his preface that he did not propose to make any further changes in it for several years: "the time and labor that I have put into it have kept me from other tasks that now press for execution." He had other irons in the fire: it was during that year that he and Nathan wound up their affairs on *The Smart Set*, and in December the first issue of *The American Mercury* appeared on the newsstands. It would be a long while before he could give his attention to philology again.

He did not return to it, in fact, for ten years, and then only when he had resigned his editorship of the magazine. But during much of that time the "mounting deficiencies" of the third edition had been haunting him, the flow of mail had never really stopped, and the professional literature on the subject was now increasing by geometrical progression. The accumulation of materials that faced him was "really enormous"—the task ahead, he confessed, "turned out to be so formidable as to be almost appalling."[6] Nevertheless, as soon as the *Mercury* was off his hands he began to make plans for rewriting it. The circumstances under which he worked were quite different now from what they had been in the past: he was married, he and Sara were living in the attractive and cheerful Cathedral Street apartment, and, though both of them tried to hold it to a minimum, they were naturally caught up in a much more active social life than he had ever known in his days as a bachelor. On top of all that, her frequent illnesses cut deeply into his energies and his working time. He had made only minimal progress when she died on May 31, 1935.

The event left him, as William Manchester says, "temporarily an emotional cripple." He was "utterly dashed and dismayed"; all incentive to work, and all desire for it, seemed gone. He wrote his gentle thank-you notes to the enormous number of friends who had expressed their sympathy, but for a long time he wrote nothing else. He decided to remain in the apartment, and August moved in with him so he would not be alone; after a while the two brothers decided that a trip to England would be good for both of them. They put in several delightful weeks in London and at Oxford; Paul Patterson of the *Sun* was there at the same time, and a journalist friend of many years' standing, the Manchester *Guardian*'s James Bone, took on many of the duties of host. By the time they disembarked in New York on July 12 the shock of Sara's death was beginning to wear off, his grief was turning into a tender memory, and he was once more feeling the urge to work.

The uncompleted first draft of the fourth edition lay before him, and he fell upon it with an energy that, if possible, even surpassed that of former days. Happily, there were few other things to claim his attention: it was no longer necessary to go up to New York monthly or oftener to get out an issue of a magazine, the weekly "Monday Article" could be polished off in a relatively short time, he was alone in the apartment save for Hester the cook, and he worked away at it sometimes from nine in the morning until ten at night. By midwinter Rosalind Lohrfinck had typed the fair copy and it had gone off to Knopf; when the page proofs started coming back he had to settle down to the extremely tedious and time-consuming job of compiling the 12,000-word "List of Words and Phrases." He cursed God and regretted that he had ever left his father's cigar business, but in April

The American Language: Fourth Edition, corrected, enlarged and re-written reached the bookstores, and Mencken, whose reputation since 1930 had dropped so low that he seemed at times to have been almost forgotten, suddenly found himself with a new and entirely different fame on his hands.

The reviews exhausted their superlatives. They called it "a great book," "a valuable book," "a splendid piece of scholarship," "fascinating," "learned," "entertaining," "superb reading," "a phenomenal achievement." "Anyone who doesn't buy and read it from cover to cover," said *The New Yorker*, "will miss not only a classic, but one of the most unfailingly entertaining books ever produced." The New York *Herald Tribune* observed that "Mencken is exhaustive but never exhausting. Our language delights him." Even the stodgy *Saturday Review of Literature*, which under Henry Seidel Canby had never been particularly sympathetic toward Mencken and the things he stood for, declared that it "tempts the reader who opens it timorously to skip joyfully from one page to another." The Book-of-the-Month Club took it as a dividend, thereby adding another 90,000 copies to the sales and bringing Mencken to the attention of an audience which, for the most part, he had not hitherto reached.

All in all, it was his most successful and best-received work to date, and in a very real sense it marked the beginning of his critical rehabilitation. To this day it remains on sale in any respectable bookstore, it has been reprinted twenty-one times, there has been an English edition, a fourteen-volume edition in Braille, and it has even been translated into Japanese.

What he had done, in effect, was to produce not so much a new edition as a new book. The editions of 1921 and 1923, as in most such cases, had merely been expansions of the original text, correcting errors and adding new material, but this fourth edition was for all practical purposes a new work on its subject. As he put it in his title, it was "rewritten" and bore only a loose resemblance to its predecessors. The very thesis of the work—as we shall see a bit later—was modified, and the arrangement of chapters and sections was different. Instead of putting his bibliographical references in the back, where they had taken up 32 pages of small type in the third edition, he kept them in step with the text, thereby necessitating an enormous number of footnotes in double columns on every page. The general public delighted in it for the sheer fascination of its account and the unsurpassed readability of the style; scholars, and those professionally interested in English, could use it as a mine of valuable information and source material; both kinds of readers found it, in the words of Dr. Louise Pound, editor of *American Speech*, "an independent and original treatment of the subject, the most comprehensive and arresting yet made."

The story of the two "Supplements" may be told more briefly. The mail, of course, never stopped coming, and in the years following 1936 there were a number of large and important philological works—for example, the *Dictionary of American English* and the *Linguistic Atlas of the United States and Canada*—that added substantially to the professional literature on the subject. His first thought was to bring out a fifth edition, but it soon appeared that such a project would result in a volume of impossible bulk—"probably running," he said, "to 2,000 pages." Under the circumstances he decided to resort to a Supplement—"only to discover that even a Supplement of the same size as the fourth edition would not contain the whole of [his] accumulations." Thus he had almost perforce to break it up into two installments. The arrangement of chapters and subsections would be the same as in the parent volume and he would simply add the new material under each appropriate heading. But the new material was hardly in any case a mere repetition of the old, and so once again he was traversing the familiar ground to write what amounted to a wholly new work.

Supplement I, which appeared in 1945, covers the ground of the first six chapters of the fourth edition; it maintains the same high standard and if possible even surpasses it. The treatment is in even greater depth; the style has never been more brilliant; he has never had greater mastery over his material. It is a work of the most impressive scholarship, and yet at the same time it is thoroughly Menckenian—certainly no other writer on the subject could have included so many delightful side comments on drinks and drinking in a learned discussion of the names of cocktails and the technical vocabulary of bartenders!

Supplement II, published in 1948 and paralleling Chapters VII to XI, was the biggest one of them all in sheer number of pages, but one cannot help feeling that it represents something of a letdown. The organization is not quite as successful and the style is less sparkling;

much of it, especially toward the end, is given over to mere word lists from various professions, activities, and walks of life. He seems tired; he was complaining during this time to friends that both his vision and his memory were failing; he had already had two slight strokes. "At my age," he observed drily in his preface, "a man encounters frequent reminders, some of them disconcerting, that his body is no more than a highly unstable congeries of the compounds of carbon." These "reminders" could hardly fail to have their effect on his work, but it has to be remembered, too, that in any event the mere accumulation of material was now becoming almost too much for him to handle.

The great work ends—or perhaps it would be better to say that it simply stops—with an account of Franklin Roosevelt coming to the door of Winston Churchill's bathroom in the White House and calling through to him to suggest the name *United Nations* for the new world organization. There is nothing in the nature of a recapitulation or coda, no hint that there will be no more. The halt is so abrupt that, somehow, one simply wants to turn the page and go on.*

---

*A series of "Postscripts to The American Language" appeared in *The New Yorker* at irregular intervals between September 1948 and October 1949; they were brief articles treating of one or another specific subject, written between the completion of Supplement II and his final disabling stroke. Huntington Cairns included two of them, "Hell and Its Outskirts" and "The Vocabulary of the Drinking Chamber," in his anthology, *The American Scene*, pp. 327–41.

Dr. Raven I. McDavid, Jr., professor of English at the University of Chicago, performed an invaluable service both for Menckenophiles and for students of language in his one-volume abridgment, *The American Language: The Fourth Edition and the Two Supplements, abridged, with annotations and new material* (New York: Alfred A. Knopf, Inc., 1963). Professor McDavid did here what Mencken himself must have seen would eventually be necessary—namely, combining each chapter of the fourth edition with its corresponding chapter in the Supplements. While unavoidably omitting much, he thus made the three separate volumes into a single unified work—and at the same time, without intruding himself or doing the slightest violence to Mencken's own text, he inserted new material and references where it seemed interesting and helpful.

Finally, it might be added that in 1945 Mencken contributed a chapter, also entitled "The American Language," to "a cooperative history . . . projected by a posse of super-pedagogues," *A Literary History of the United States*, edited by Robert E. Spiller et al. (New York: The Macmillan Company, 1946; 3d ed. rev. 1963). "This last," he wrote Nathan on February 8 of that year, "almost broke my back. It was difficult indeed to get a coherent account of the subject into small space" (Forgue, *Letters*, p. 485). Naturally this short article (it runs to but thirteen pages) is in no sense a condensation of its immense namesake, but in spite of his complaints he did manage to cram an astonishing amount into it, and it is probably the best brief treatment of the subject ever done.

2 THE SHIFT IN EMPHASIS as it moved through its successive editions has been noted both by Mencken's biographers and by students of language. In the first three editions (which, remember, followed rapidly upon one another at only two-year intervals) he argued with an overpowering wealth of example that the English of the United States had diverged so sharply from the English of England that they were, for all practical purposes, mutually unintelligible. After that there was a hiatus of thirteen years. Then in the fourth edition (and of course the Supplements) he changed his position and argued that the influence of American English had become so strong that it was pulling English English along in its wake. This was having two effects: on the one hand, some of the differences he had noted earlier were now tending to disappear; on the other, it was entirely possible that in some not-too-remote future the English of England would become a mere dialect of the standard form spoken in America.

Each thesis, it goes without saying, was true at the time he put it forward. That the two main bodies of people speaking the language would develop different usages was doubtless inevitable so long as they were separated by an ocean and had a relative minimum of social and cultural contact. The ocean might remain, but it was likewise inevitable that as contacts broadened to the point where they became constant and commonplace, one branch would exert an influence upon the other. And American English, with its youthful strength and picturesqueness, with the greater demands made upon it by a new life and new conditions, with its marvelous capacity to coin new words and alter the meanings of old ones, could hardly fail to develop in a way that the older branch was not called upon to do.

The growth, both in quantity and in quality, of American literature during the latter part of the nineteenth century and the early years of the twentieth caused it to be exported overseas, where it had a natural effect upon British audiences. The guardians of linguistic purity in the motherland might deplore this effect, but there was little that they could do to stem it, particularly when English writers of fiction were attempting, not always too happily, to incorporate American idioms and turns of expression into their own work. This sort of thing, however, would make an impression only on that small minority in either country who read books. Two events of vastly greater importance gradually deflected the path of the "King's English." The first was the invention of the "talking picture" and the export of Hollywood's products to English theaters. The second was the presence of huge forces of American soldiers—*doughboys* in the First World War, *GI's* in the Second—who would bring with them their own characteristic way of speaking, and leave much of it behind when they departed.

But while all this may be very true, the point, once made, can hardly be overstressed. Mencken himself was not even responsible for it (though some of his critics seemed to believe that he was); like a good reporter, he was doing no more than calling attention to the facts.

Much more important in any consideration of *The American Language*, it seems to me, is the enormous influence that it has had on the whole subsequent development of philology in this country. I have already quoted his remarks that when he embarked on his original researches he found little material upon which to draw, and that what little there was, was of a uniformly low quality. Many—in fact most—professors of English in the United States denied the obvious truth that there were differences in the way the two peoples spoke the same language; yet more, they regarded the way in which the majority of Americans spoke it as being too impossibly vulgar to deserve their scholarly notice. "In no department," Mencken claimed at the outset, "are American universities weaker than in the department of English. The aesthetic opinion that they disseminate is flabby and childish, and their philological work in the national language is extraordinarily lacking in enterprise."[7]

Again, this was true when he wrote it, but the situation was to change drastically over the years. "It is . . . ," says Dr. Raven I. McDavid, Jr., "something more than a coincidence that linguistic science in North America, and particularly the study of the varieties of English spoken in the Western Hemisphere, has developed remarkably since the first publication of *The American Language* in 1919."[8] He goes on to affirm that much of this development has been a response to the challenge which Mencken flung down: "a list of those whose concern with linguistics was stimulated by correspondence about *The American Language*, or whose research was furthered directly by Mencken himself, would include most of those who have made the study of American English a respectable discipline in its own right." His own career, McDavid admits, was diverted from the literature of the English Renaissance to the language of the United States by a reading of Mencken's work, and by "the prompt and heartening encouragement that Mencken always gave beginners."*

The point made in those earlier editions had been that the American user of English had to be virtually bilingual. On the one hand, there was the formal literary language, showing "a sonority and a stateliness that you must go to the Latin of the Golden Age to match"; it was based on such models as Dr. Johnson and Macaulay, was highly ornate and artificial, and was the language approved and inculcated by schoolma'ams, "whether in panties or in pantaloons." But to the average American it was almost a foreign tongue, vague and remote; once out of school, he never used it and seldom heard it used, and only one in thousands ever learned to write it. On the other hand, there was the language that this average American did speak: one impatient of grammatical and syntactical rules, tending to strip away all superfluities and circumlocutions, characterized by a rich freedom and inventiveness, and often hospitable to novelty just for the sake of novelty.

This latter was the language that Mencken set out to study—and because nobody else ever had, he had to do all the work of a pioneer.† He was interested not only in what was the case but why; it was relatively easy, for example, to determine just when Americans had begun

---

*It is interesting to compare this evaluation by a professional philologian like McDavid with the one offered by Charles Angoff in his *Portrait from Memory*. There (p. 151) he quotes "one of the most eminent lexicographers in the English-speaking world" (who remains utterly anonymous) to the effect that "among philologists Mencken is merely smiled at." The eminent lexicographer then goes on to quote in turn "a certain truly great lexicographer" who once told him that he had discovered that "Mencken's knowledge was at times second-hand and even third-hand." Angoff himself professes shock at being described, in Supplement II, as "something of an authority on railroad slang"—though the passage to which he is referring (p. 581), dealing with the names given to trains, simply draws upon an article he had once written for the *Mercury* and makes no claim whatever that he was an "authority." There is an extensive section on railroad slang (pp. 713–18), but Angoff is not mentioned in it.

†This statement is not entirely true. Richard H. Thornton (1845–1925), an Englishman who emigrated to Canada in 1871 and thence to the United States in 1874, spent years of his life compiling an *American Glossary*, in which he listed some 3,700 Americanisms and endeavored to date the earliest use of each of them. "Nothing on so comprehensive a scale or following so scientific a method," says Mencken (Supplement I, p. 99), "had been undertaken before, and Thornton's first two volumes, issued in 1912, remain indispensable to this day. Indeed, the [*Dictionary of American English*] would have been impossible without them, and it shows its debt to them on almost every page." Unhappily, Thornton could interest no American publisher in his work, and it was eventually brought out by a London firm in an edition of only 2,000 copies. He continued to accumulate materials for a third volume, but could find neither a

to drop the "u" in -*our* words, so that *honour* became *honor* and *colour* was simplified into *color*, but what tendencies or what authority (if any) had led to such a thing? How had the -*re* come to be reversed in words like *centre, theatre, calibre,* and *fibre?* What had turned *gaol* into *jail,* and—reversing the process of simplification somewhat—*whisky* into *whiskey?* Why, despite regional differences in pronunciation, is American so notably free from dialects? What is the provenance of the southern *you-all,* and why should there be any objection to forms like *it's me* or *more better?*

These were some of the questions he asked and the hitherto un-explored fields into which he ventured. But he went further yet, be-yond the vagaries of American spelling and pronunciation and even beyond the vulgar grammar. He dared to investigate and write about areas of the language that the professors had not only ignored but which they preferred to think did not exist: slang, the argot of crimi-nals, the forbidden words associated with excretion and sex and the often preposterous euphemisms by which polite usage tried to get around them.* At the time he began his studies the great age of im-migration was still not very far in the past, and in every American city there were large ethnic groups who clung stubbornly to their native speechways and spoke English haltingly if at all; consequently he de-voted much space to non-English languages in the United States—German, French, Italian, Spanish, Portuguese, Polish, Czech, Slo-vak, Yiddish, even such exotic specimens as Gaelic, Finnish, and Ar-menian—tracing any influence they might have had upon the En-glish around them and the far greater extent to which English had in turn affected them.

Thus while the professional philologians busied themselves with Hittite, Goidelic, Old Church Slavonic, and various obscure Indian

---

publisher nor a backer, and it began to appear only serially in *Dialect Notes* in 1931, six years after his death. Even then the installments were highly irregular, and it was not finally com-pleted until 1939. In the fourth edition and the two Supplements there are almost a hundred references to Thornton.

*There were, of course, limits beyond which—at that time at least—even he could not go. So late as 1948, in Supplement II (p. 778), discussing the use of the immemorial four-letter words by the GI's of the Second World War, he said that "one of them, beginning with *f*, became an almost universal verb, and with -*ing* added, a universal adjective"; but he could not—or at all events did not—actually print it. Today it is a rare work of fiction that does not use the term at least once every three or four pages.

tongues, and played around with such semantic subtleties as phonemes, morphemes, and enthymemes, Mencken was concentrating his attention on the language that 120,000,000 people actually spoke. It goes without saying that he knew as well as they did that there was a formal literary language too: he himself used it with incomparable facility. What he could not stomach was their pretension that the formal language was the only one there was, that anybody who did not conform to its highly artificial rules was an ignoramus, and that the everyday speech of living men and women deserved no serious study precisely because it violated those rules.

After a while, of course, the philologians could hardly deny that there was some value to his work; grudgingly they admitted it; but what gave them unease was his contention that the "American language" had become something distinct from the mother tongue, no longer bound by the same constraints. If that were the case, what was to become of English form and style, and how would the textbooks on the subject cope with such barbarisms? When, in the second edition, he offered his "translation" of the Declaration of Independence in "American," it was "denounced as seditious by various patriotic Americans, and in England it was accepted gravely and deplored sadly as a specimen of current Standard American."[9] The trap they fell into, in other words, was that of supposing that the "vulgar" American which he was unearthing and recording with such high relish was what he was solemnly proposing the language should be!

Very gradually, however, the tide began to turn. No doubt it would be going too far to claim that works like the *Dictionary of American English* and the *Linguistic Atlas* owed their inspiration directly to Mencken (though both of them must have profited from the research that he had already done). But they were certainly an indication that at the highest levels of scholarship the study of the language spoken in the United States had become a respectable academic discipline in its own right. And they were only the tip of the iceberg. In 1925 Dr. Louise Pound launched *American Speech* at the University of Nebraska, and for long thereafter she and her pupils eagerly hunted down peculiarities of spelling, pronunciation, syntax, and dialect all over the land. In that same year, and working independently of Mencken, Dr. George Philip Krapp of Columbia published the two-volume *The English Language in America*. When it became apparent that the *Dictionary of American English*, despite its unarguable merits, also had some serious weaknesses (it stopped at 1900, and was notably poor on slang), Dr. Mitford M. Mathews stepped into the breach and issued a *Dictionary of Americanisms*, smaller in physical size but far more authoritative. Scores and even hundreds of lesser figures investigated the speech of individual states and local regions, carefully noting differences in vocabulary, pronunciation, and dialectal usage. Eventually there came a day when even the great standard dictionaries relented and admitted into their columns terms that they would once have dismissed as slang, nonce words, or vulgarisms.

There is no sign even now that the flood is abating. Some indication of how the subject has grown in size and scope may be gleaned from two independent but related statements. The first is from Mencken, in the preface to Supplement I:

> The literature of the subject was so meagre at the time I published my first edition in 1919 that I got a comprehensive bibliography of it into less than seventeen pages.*

The second is from the "Editor's Introduction" which Raven I. McDavid wrote in 1962 for his one-volume abridgment:

> A simple bibliography of linguistic publications since World War II would make a volume as fat as the 1919 edition.

It is quite possible, of course, that many of the men and women working in the field today are only dimly aware of H. L. Mencken, or at least were not directly influenced by him. But it nevertheless remains a fact that they could not do what they are doing, that the very academic discipline in which they specialize would not be what it is, had he not cleared the ground before them.

3 ALL THIS BEING ADMITTED, it is still relevant to pose the question alluded to at the beginning of this chapter—namely, is *The American Language* likely to endure? Certainly it is Mencken's biggest and most important work; into it he poured an immense amount of his fantastic energies; it was the one subject on which he himself liked to think that he was something of an authority. But throughout much of his life, from one edition to the

---

*Why he used *meagre* instead of *meager* is something about which one can only guess.

next, he had to struggle to keep it up to date, and when he wrote the final pages of Supplement II in 1948 he was very far from thinking that everything had been said. Many matters that he still wanted to treat had to remain forever untouched.

For language, remember (unless it be a dead one like classical Greek or Latin), is in a state of perpetual flux. It changes from generation to generation, and the farther it recedes into the past the more strange and difficult it comes to seem. Chaucer could not have read *Beowulf*—assuming he had known that such a work existed, and he did not—and few of us are comfortable with Shakespeare in the text of the quartos or the First Folio. In cases like these we need glossaries and scholarly notes to help us along. Style changes too: any tolerably educated person can read, say, Dr. Johnson today and be perfectly at home with both his vocabulary and his syntax, but the eighteenth century's ponderous and ornate manner of expression has gone out of favor and would be employed now only if one wanted to be consciously artificial.

There was a time when this development moved along at a fairly leisurely pace—when the usage of one generation would not differ significantly from that of the one preceding it. But the thirty-odd years since the appearance of Supplement II have seen an incredible revolution in knowledge, technology, life-style, and culture, so that a person who reached maturity before 1945 lives now in an era as different from that of his childhood as the Middle Ages differed from classical Rome. And the language has had to struggle to keep up with these changes.

When, in 1963, Raven I. McDavid brought out his one-volume abridgment of the fourth edition and its Supplements, he had to insert a considerable amount of new material simply to keep it timely. Today, less than fifteen years later, even McDavid's abridgment is out of date.

Consider, for example, the contributions to American speechways made by the one thing that has changed our way of life more than any other—namely, television. In addition to *TV* itself, there come to mind at once *audio, video, channel, taped, rating, newscast, anchorman, prerecorded, instant replay,* and *situation comedy* (or *sit-com*). *Commercial* is hardly a new word, but it certainly has a meaning different now from what it had in the days before television, or at all events before radio. Similarly the conquest of space has brought into being a whole new lexicon that did not even exist prior to the launching of the first *Sputnik* by the Russians in 1957—e.g., *astronaut, cosmonaut, spacecraft, satellite* (in the sense of an artificial one), *module, count-*

down, blast-off. In both cases these are terms familiar to and used by the ordinary layman; they do not, of course, take into consideration the highly technical vocabulary of the industries themselves.

The field of education and the social and behavioral sciences have given birth to a rich, bewildering jargon, at least some of which has filtered down into common usage. Schoolchildren are no longer simply graded in their academic subjects; they are put in *peer groups*, engage in *role-playing*, are entertained with *audio-visual* or *multi-media* presentations, and *evaluated* on the basis of their *interpersonal relationships*. *Planners* distinguish carefully between *goals* and *objectives*, and *prioritize* among them. Not many people in Mencken's day suffered from an *identity crisis*, or if they did, sought relief for it in a *sensitivity session*. Religion, which had gotten along with pretty much the same standard vocabulary for four or five hundred years, suddenly burst forth with an entirely new jargon at the time of the Second Vatican Council, and in a spirit of *ecumenism* the Protestant Churches quickly hopped onto the bandwagon of the Roman Catholic; henceforth religious people had to be *involved,* they had to have a sense of *commitment*, they had to be sure that what they were engaged in was *meaningful* and *relevant*. Today few Catholic priests *say Mass;* instead they *have a liturgy,* and the faithful, save for die-hards, no longer go into a dark *confessional* but visit a *reconciliation room.*

Perhaps the most conscious and deliberate assault on the language has come from the Women's Liberation Movement, which has struggled heroically to expunge all traces of *male chauvinism* from the way we speak. *Sexism* and *sexist* have established themselves as perfectly good words (the latter, of course, to be distinguished carefully from *sexual*), but in the main the group's efforts seem to have been concentrated on the suffix *-man* as an occupational sign and have resulted in such unimaginative and awkward neologisms as *chairperson, spokesperson*, and even *policeperson* and *mailperson.* Black culture and the *counter-culture* of youth and drugs have, as everyone knows, made heavy contributions. Finally there is the undoubted fact that, as Edwin Newman has said,* Washington, precisely because it is the nation's capital, is also the place where the language is most thoroughly debased, and from it we have had over the years an endless supply of

---

*It is a pleasure to call attention to Newman's two books, *Strictly Speaking* and *A Civil Tongue* (New York: Bobbs-Merrill Co., Inc., 1974 and 1976 respectively). Few works have shown more

instructive specimens—one selects *brinksmanship, détente, presence* (in the sense of military force), *adversary relationship,* and *depoliticization* as typical examples. The high point here was unquestionably reached when the press secretary of the President of the United States made a statement announcing that an earlier statement was *inoperative.*

Now if Mencken had lived to bring out a Supplement III, and IV, and V, there can be no doubt that he would have carefully noted all of these additions, changes, and developments, and would have wrought into the factual report his own characteristic acid comments. But since he did not, *The American Language* is permanently frozen in the form in which he left it to us in 1948. This raises the possibility that it may survive only as a fossil, or indeed that it already is one.

I venture to suggest that it is not and is unlikely to become one. Philip Wagner, for many years a colleague of Mencken's on the *Sun*, has predicted that it will "live as a period piece, a monumental work of scholarship fixing the language as of its time, like a still shot from a movie,"[10] but even this seems to me to be going too far. Granted that it fixes the language of its time as nothing else did or could; granted, too, as I have just tried briefly to indicate, that since that time the language has changed—the fact still remains that there is a very great difference between a "period piece" and a seminal work of scholarship. Biologists of today know more about the processes of organic evolution than Charles Darwin ever dreamed of, but that does not make *The Origin of Species* any less great. Newton's physics have pretty much been replaced by those of Einstein, but the *Mathematical Principles of Natural Philosophy* is still one of the most important books ever written. There are certain works so influential in the development of their subject, so indispensable to its subsequent study, that no advances in knowledge can ever really make them obsolete. *The American Language* is such a work.

Its value lies not just in the fact that it records the living speech of Mencken's own era—though that may be the principal reason why so many of us cherish it. It was the living speech around him, in the streets of Baltimore, in its police courts and its City Hall, that first evoked his interest, as language at any level always fascinates for its own sake the

---

thoroughly or wittily how the language has been debased and barbarized in recent years. Mencken would have thoroughly approved of them—and used them.

person with a gift for setting thoughts on paper; only a bit later, as a result of extensive reading and personal contact with British subjects, did he come to realize that this speech around him was something quite different from the English of England. And this was the fact that he seized upon: What accounted for these differences? What social, cultural, and intellectual forces had set them in motion? When had they started? By what processes had they gained momentum? The subtitle which he used for every edition of the work (and which more often than not is overlooked) surely has a very real significance here: "An Inquiry into the Development of English in the United States." The key word is certainly "development" and it highlights Mencken's whole approach.

He was not simply concerned, in other words, with fixing the language of his time—if that were the case, then it would indeed be a period piece. But because he was eager to know how the language of his time had come to be what it was, he went back to the beginning— if not to the day when the English language landed on these shores with the first English colonists, then at all events to the first occasion when someone noted with alarm the effect that this event was having on the purity of the mother tongue. On the opening page of the fourth edition he quotes an English writer of 1621 who remarked that "*maize* and *canoe* were making their way into English," and one may confidently say that he missed little if anything that was written on the subject, on both sides of the ocean, from that day to his own. The result is a work of massive historical research. The long and thorough sections on "The Two Streams of English," "The Beginnings of American," and "The Period of Growth" chronicle an important facet of the nation's growth, and it is a facet, moreover, that is not brought together anywhere else—at any rate not in such depth, or with such exhaustive documentation.

This part of *The American Language*, at least, is not subject to the ravages of time, and it will be absolutely invaluable to all subsequent researchers for generations to come.

Lastly, there is the fact, noted by everybody who ever reviewed it from 1919 on down or who otherwise wrote about it, that it is probably the most sheerly readable work of scholarship in all history. An easy and graceful style is not, of course, essential to scholarly writing, as everyone knows to his sorrow—but it helps, and *The American Language*, being by Mencken, is unique in this respect. His wit and humor are evident on page after page; they do not desert him in dealing with even the most pedestrian material; and though they are no less effective, they are, too, lighter and gentler on the whole than many of the passages which readers sometimes find objectionable in his political and religious writings. Which of the philologians, calling attention to the horrendous verb *to obituarize* in the London *Times*, would have added in a footnote:

> If I may intrude my private feelings into a learned work I venture to add that seeing a monster so suggestive of American barbarism in the *Times* affected me like seeing an archbishop wink at a loose woman;[11]

or who among them, assuming that he would have so far demeaned himself as to discuss the names of cocktails at all, would have informed his audience that

> William Warren Woollcott and I once employed a mathematician to figure out how many [cocktails] could be fashioned of the *materia bibulica* ordinarily available in a first-rate bar. He reported that the number was 17,864,392,788. We tried 273 at random, and found them all good, though some, of course, were better than others.[12]

Gems like these abound through every one of the six enormous volumes—each reader will have his own favorites. They do not detract in the least from its scholarship or authenticity, and they make the reading of it pure joy. Not many scholarly productions are works of art in their own right; among those written in English one would be hard put to assemble enough to run over the fingers of one hand. But *The American Language* would certainly be on any such list. Though size has no necessary relationship to art, one may reasonably argue that it is a work of art by virtue of its colossal proportions. It is one by virtue of its conception and its superb execution. It is one by its creator's mastery of his subject, both in broad outline and in painstaking detail. Finally it is one by the brilliance of its writing, resulting in a work that is so unflaggingly entertaining that one easily loses sight while reading it of the immense effort, the patience and often elemental drudgery, that went into making it what it is.

And it could well be that, even if everything in it were to become outdated and passé, people would still read it, as they read the rest of Mencken, for its matchless style.

V I

THE STYLE

I believe that a good phrase is better than a Great Truth.

—Letter to Burton Rascoe, 1920

◇◇

FOR IT WAS THE STYLE, after all, that made Mencken what he was and gave him the reputation that he had—far more so than his ideas, which, when you come to think about them, were not really very unusual or radical. Many men have been agnostics, and taken a dim view of organized religion. It is probably safe to say that large numbers of quite patriotic Americans look with skepticism on the whole democratic process and consider most politicians to be frauds. Even in the darkest days of American literature there were critics intelligent enough to know how bad it was, and to know, too, what ought to be done to make it better. In none of these respects was Mencken unique. As I trust the foregoing pages have made clear, his ideas were for the most part conservative and sometimes downright reactionary.

But the way he expressed those ideas was indeed unique. There had never been anybody quite like him before in the national letters, and since his death no one has appeared to succeed him. This is not to say, of course, that he has not had imitators; newspaper columnists by the score have tried to write like him, and unnumbered critics have borrowed his weapons to attack American society, politics, culture, and religion. But somehow the attempt never quite comes off. Neither does he have any real counterpart in the literature of other nations.

It is not easy to describe Mencken's style to somebody who has not read him. One may pick out certain salient characteristics of it and talk about them, but the effect is hardly the same—it is like talking about the Fifth Symphony or the *Meistersinger* Overture or the *Sacre du Printemps* to somebody who has never heard them. And this is to say, really, that in the final analysis it cannot be described—it has to be experienced.

There is, first of all, the absolutely incredible vocabulary—the largest, one may safely venture, of any writer in the English language. In 1920 he estimated to Burton Rascoe that it ran to 25,000 words, but, if anything, this guess must be on the low side. Nor was its use an affectation, employed merely to show off his virtuosity and dazzle the reader; on the contrary, it is often used with almost scientific precision. Gerald Johnson, a *Sunpapers* colleague, tells of having read in a Mencken article about a certain eminent statesman's "chelonian paunch." That, Johnson confessed, sent him to the dictionary, where he learned that "chelonian" means "turtle-like." "I realized," he said, "that it is the only word that describes exactly the gentleman's gently and evenly rounded frontal protuberance. It was not pendulous. It was not circular. It was shaped precisely like the shell of a turtle. It was literally, in a word, chelonian."

Certain words and phrases were used, perhaps unconsciously, over and over again, and were undoubted favorites—"brummagem," "mountebank," the "hon. gentleman," the "rev. clergy," "told off," "to fetch." If some "nascent Ph.D." were ever to undertake the gloomy chore of determining what word occurs more often than any other in Mencken, it would probably turn out to be "palpable": the premises of Marxism "consist in large part of very palpable nonsense," the Protestant Fundamentalists are "palpable idiots," "the most expensive thing on this earth is to believe in something that is palpably not true." As is well known, he coined a number of memorable terms himself— "booboisie" is the best known and survives more or less to this day, but there were also "bootician" ("a high-class bootlegger") and "ecdysiast," a euphemism for "stripteaser" which he invented at the request of a practitioner of the art, Miss Georgia Sothern, in the rather vain hope that a new name might give it more respectable standing.

There is, too, the frankness and absolute fearlessness with which he disposes of somebody or something in a phrase—the designation, for example, of Mary Baker Eddy as "a fraud pure and unadulterated," or of Aimée Semple McPherson as "this commonplace and transparent mountebank," or of Warren G. Harding's prose style as reminding him "of stale bean-soup, of college yells, of dogs barking idiotically through endless nights." There is the sprinkling throughout his work of German terms and honorifics—*Polizei, Kultur, Katzenjammer, Herr Professor-Doktor, zum zweiten, geb.* (instead of *née*) for a woman's maiden name. There is the sly courtesy, especially when he is writing against someone, of including with his opponent's name the full panoply of his academic degrees. There is his habit of placing living people in immediate and startling contrast with illustrious figures of the past—thus Brownell becomes the "Amherst Aristotle," and Paul Elmer More the "St. Louis, Mo., Plotinus," and even such a minor figure of American literature as Mary MacLane is transformed into the "Butte Bashkirtseff."

Above all else, there is the outlandish exaggeration, the inspired similes, and unearthly metaphors which would never occur to anyone else but which seemed to come to him so easily and instantaneously. If Mencken wants to speak of something as being so improbable that there is not a chance in a million that it could ever happen, he does not, of course, put it in such bald language; he says instead that it is "as inconceivable as a Bach festival in Mississippi." An actor acquaintance of his days as drama critic for the *Herald* "knew no more about field sports than a mother superior." Riding on a train through Westmoreland County, Pennsylvania, he blinks at the grotesque architecture of the little country towns "as one blinks before a man with his face shot away." Reviewing in the *Mercury* a book about witchcraft, he observes that its author marshals "an array of proofs that must shake even an atheistic archbishop," and that "if he is wrong, then the whole science of Christian theology is a degraded imposture—something which no right-thinking, law-abiding, home-loving American, I am sure, will want to allege." Viewing a display of modern paintings, they seem to him to have been done "with asphalt and mayonnaise, by a man afflicted with binocular diplopic strabismus."

And finally—or at all events to make an end from among endless examples—there is his constant practice of interjecting not only himself into the matter under discussion but his audience as well. Mencken always takes it for granted that his reader is intelligent enough to be

in the fullest possible agreement with him. He quotes a passage from
Harding's inaugural address and then goes on: "I assume that you have
read it. I also assume that you set it down as idiotic—a series of words
without sense. You are quite right; it is." "You know and I know," he
says of a presidential candidate who had tried to wriggle out of a question about where he stood on Prohibition, "and Dr. Davis well knew
when he emptied his nonsense upon the Clarksburg moonshiners, that
no one had ever solicited him to agree to disregard the Eighteenth
Amendment. . . . Try to imagine Washington skulking up an alley in
any such manner. If you can imagine it, then go out into the street and
give three cheers for Dr. Davis."

No one of these elements in itself, and perhaps not all of them
taken together, necessarily constitutes a great style—and as I have just
indicated, in the hands of Mencken's imitators they usually fall quite
flat. But in his hands they were fused into a master instrument on
which he played with consummate skill for almost half a century, and
which served his purpose in whatever field he chose to put it to work.
It was, by deliberate intent, a style calculated to produce the most
violent reaction. One might stand speechless in admiration before it,
or one might crumple the page in disgust and impotent fury; the one
thing utterly impossible was to remain indifferent to it.

Yet this is not to say that it sprang forth at once and full-born, like
Athena from the head of Zeus, or that he did not have to labor to bring
it to perfection. Though he never went through any "periods" in the
development of his thought, as most men—including very great
ones—do, he did go through certain very definite periods in the
growth of his style.

In *Minority Report*, that collection of late notes published posthumously, he says that his early writing was "pretty bad," and that it
always made him uncomfortable to go back and look at any of it in later
years. "There was," he adds, "a great deal of empty ornament in my
first prose book, *George Bernard Shaw: His Plays.*" In this he really
gives himself less credit than he deserves. The newspaper work for the
Herald is not (of course) mature Mencken, but it certainly stands head
and shoulders above most of the journalism of that period, in the sense
that it is more clearly and vividly written, and it is better, too, than
nine-tenths of today's. The Shaw book, where he not only was free of
the constraints that factual reporting naturally imposes on any man but

was just beginning to find his own métier, is really a genuine enough foretaste of the Mencken who was to come.

He told Isaac Goldberg that his prose style "began to take form after the suppression of the *Herald* in 1906; before that I had written sound journalism, but it was without any character. In 1906 I suddenly developed a style of my own and it was in full flower by the end of that year."

It is possible that, looking back from a distance of almost two decades, he missed by about a year. For the event that brought about the flowering he speaks of was surely his discovery of Nietzsche and the book that he wrote about him, and *The Philosophy of Friedrich Nietzsche* was published in 1908. The little work on Shaw had come out in 1905, and shortly thereafter Harrison Hale Schaff of the firm of John W. Luce & Co. wrote to him suggesting that he do a similar but more ambitious study of the philosopher of the "Superman." Mencken demurred, first on the ground that he knew next to nothing about Nietzsche, and second because at the time his German was much too inadequate. But the more he thought about it, the more attractive the proposition came to seem, and before long he was launched upon it. It took him, he says, about a year; actually he spent about a year reading and studying the complete edition of Nietzsche's works which he found in the Pratt Library, and the actual writing took almost another year beyond that. The latter would have been, more or less roughly, 1907.

At that time Nietzsche was already exerting a powerful influence on the English-speaking world, but little of him had as yet been translated and the library set was in German. This was the edition which Mencken, despite the lack of real proficiency in the language which faced him as he began, had perforce to read. Nietzsche's style, as everyone knows, was unique both in philosophy and in German literature: alive, vivid, incandescent, filled with hyperbole and striking terms of expression. "He became," Mencken was to write of him, "a master of the aphorism and the epigram, and this skill, very naturally, led him to descend, now and then, to mere violence and invective. He called his opponents all sorts of harsh names—liar, swindler, counterfeiter, ox, ass, snake and thief. Whatever he had to say, he hammered in with gigantic blows, and to the accompaniment of fearsome bellowing and grimacing." That description, it should be unnecessary to say, fits his own work almost perfectly; Nietzsche's method, as more than one critic has noted, had perhaps a greater influence on Mencken than he himself ever realized.

In any event, there can be little doubt that by the time he finished the book he had found himself as a writer.

He found himself, too, with a certain amount of fame and reputation on his hands, and so its appearance led quite logically to another event which was infinitely more decisive for his growth as a writer. This was his acceptance, late in 1908, of the post of book editor for *The Smart Set*. Here again he enjoyed the most perfect freedom; he could review whatever books he wished and say about them anything that he pleased. Naturally he made the most of the opportunity. That 5,000-word article, continuing without a break every month for the next fifteen years, did far more than just establish the Menckenian style—it was the style, quite as much as the content, that established him as the leading critic of American letters and ideas.

Nevertheless, I venture the opinion that the writing for *The Smart Set* is not really true and characteristic Mencken. There is about even the best of it an element of smartness, a deliberate attempt to shock and appall, that very often defeats his own purpose and may have justified the reactions of the accepted arbiters of literature. He postures, he makes faces, he thumbs his nose, he uses every trick in the book to cajole the intelligent reader and infuriate the less nimble-witted one. He refers to the article as his "pulpit"; he addresses his audience as "dearly beloved" and calls it "chosen of God." One can picture him sitting down at the battered old Corona typewriter that he used in those days, with a pile of books beside him, searching his mind for things likely to horrify, chuckling at his own cleverness, and delighting in anticipation of the violent reaction that he can be sure will come.

For example, I select as typical an article, "The Troubadours A-Twitter," which appeared in the issue for May 1915, and in which he reviewed a whole collection of volumes of poetry. After listing sixty-five different musical instruments, including some so rare, obsolete, or outside the stream of Western music that only a dictionary like the *Oxford* would even make mention of them, he goes on to discuss the work of one Professor Edwin F. Haworth of Kansas City, Missouri, "the Edgar Allan Poe of those parts." "In his hand," he says, is a copy of his latest work, *Sunshine and Roses;* under his arm is a viola da gamba, gnarled and mellow. He opens fire at once and his choice is a lay of amour. To wit:

> Azmarine! Enchantress, she
> Leads me through the glens,
> Coaxing and beguiling me
> With some power not human's . . .

Hold up, good professor! Let us hear that again. "Through the glens . . . power not human's"? What sort of prosody is this? Hast the effrontery in this high-toned company to rhyme "glens" with "humans," even with "hu*mans*"? The ideer! . . . Out with him, Zarathustra! Down the chute with him! Over the fence with him! To the lions with him! . . . But halt! The rules, it seems, save him, or, at any rate, reprieve him; two chances for every candidate at the bar. Even Shakespeare sometimes slipped, as witness—but no need to offer examples. Let us hear this Prof. Haworth de Kansas City again. . . .

And so on, and so on. This, I submit, is not good writing, or even very humorous writing. It may be granted that Professor Haworth deserved everything that Mencken said about him, and certainly he has not been heard from since; but the weapon with which he was struck down hardly constitutes legitimate criticism, and even he deserved that.

It is surely an indication of Mencken's own dissatisfaction with much of the *Smart Set* writing that he seldom included any of it in the volumes of *Prejudices* without the most thorough and painstaking revision.

At least some of its weaknesses may be due to the fact, already sufficiently emphasized, that he did not really think of himself as a literary critic and that as time went on the monthly review articles became increasingly a chore. For four years they overlapped with what may be considered the next stage in his literary development, the "Monday Articles" for the *Evening Sun.* These began in February 1920, while the *Smart Set* pieces continued until December 1923; yet although he was working at the two of them simultaneously during all this time, the differences are notable. The latter become more and more hollow and strained; in the former there is a sudden new ease and mastery. At no time had Mencken ever lacked assurance; now there is an unlimited confidence both in his powers and in the unarguableness of his positions.

The very first one, "A Carnival of Buncombe," appearing on February 9, strikes the leitmotif that will sound through the majority of them over the next eighteen years. Discussing the candidates for the coming presidential elections, he observes that all of them are "more or less palpable frauds. . . . General Wood is a simple-minded old dodo with a delusion of persecution; Palmer is a political mountebank of the first water; Harding is a second-rate provincial . . . Gerard and the rest are simply bad jokes." For a few weeks he turned his attention to less volatile subjects, like Lizette Woodworth Reese and neglected writers, but returning to the political arena on May 12 with "The Clowns in the Ring," he let his gaze run over the field once more. Hoover had quickly shown himself to be "almost completely destitute of practical political talents"; General Wood was stupid, "but I add at once that he seems to be perfectly honest. In truth, he is the only honest candidate yet heard of—perhaps the only absolutely honest candidate in American history. . . . He is the cavalryman incarnate, all heart and no brains." Hiram Johnson was "almost the ideal candidate—an accomplished boob-bumper, full of the sough and gush of the tin-horn messiah, and yet safely practical. He will give a good show if he is elected."

The vocabulary, it will be seen at once, is the same that he had always used—"palpable," "mountebank," "boob-bumper," "tin-horn messiah"—but the whole tone and treatment are on another level entirely. In the "Monday Articles" there is no straining for effect, no effort, no hollow smartness, no showing off. They are funny, often hilariously so; but beneath the surface humor there is also deadly seriousness. He cares very much about the issues he is discussing, whereas by now the books he was reviewing in *The Smart Set* interested him not at all.

This new style—for that is what, in effect, it was—is carried over, beginning in 1924, into the pages of the *Mercury*. Here again he was free to range over the whole American social, cultural, and political scene; even though he still continued to review books, the approach is different and the books themselves are for the most part not the same ones he would have selected for treatment in *The Smart Set*. Now at last, in both places—the *Mercury* and the *Sun*—we have the mature Mencken: writing with a swift, unerring hand, absolutely sure of himself, fearless and outspoken, playing with a dazzling vocabulary but never using it for mere effect, surveying that bizarre scene with a wit that is always trenchant and biting but never "smart." The two major books of this period, *Treatise on the Gods* and *Treatise on Right and Wrong,* are in this same vein; we have already seen that he regarded the first of these, at least, as the high point of his literary achievement.

Unhappily they appeared at a time when the American scene itself was undergoing drastic change. First came the Depression, and then the Roosevelt era; Mencken's wit lost its appeal, particularly when he exercised it on the problems of the day and the man who seemed to have found their solution. After almost two decades of unparalleled fame, his reputation appeared to be on the point of sinking into obscurity. He would have been less than human if he had not felt a certain chagrin; but if he did, no trace of it ever showed in his work. He went back to his language studies (and it has to be remembered that *The American Language,* despite its own special brilliance, stands somewhat apart from the rest of his writing). And then, in 1940, he published *Happy Days,* and followed it up, within the next couple of years, with the two succeeding volumes of his autobiography. These, and the *Language* books, not only brought back his old admirers but attracted a whole generation of new ones as well.

In these three unique and delightful volumes one encounters the Mencken of the final period. They represent, of course, only the tiniest fraction of his immense output over half a century, and yet they are probably the Mencken that most of today's readers know. It seems somehow trite to say that he had mellowed with age, and yet there is no doubt that he had. He had reached "the perhaps indelicate age of sixty," and that is a time when a man no longer looks forward to combat but turns his gaze back upon his memories. The wars he had carried on against Puritanism, against Comstockery, against Prohibition, had long since been won; the nation's literature, even though he no longer took very much interest in it, was a different thing because of his labors; even the political scene, though he might not have admitted it, had changed. The humor is as brilliant as ever—perhaps more so; the writing is nearly flawless; but the savagery that had once seemed so much a part of him has softened now into a smiling and amiable tolerance of human foibles. Mencken's memoirs, as recorded in the matchless prose of the *Days* books, fixed the way in which readers of later generations will be familiar with him, and perhaps that is how he wanted it to be.

ℒON THE WHOLE, THE STYLE came easily. Malcolm Moos, in the introduction he wrote for A Carnival of Buncombe, tells of Mencken complaining to a fellow reporter on July 25, 1948, as they were walking back to their hotel from one of the sessions of Henry Wallace's Progressive Party convention in Philadelphia, "You know, I don't feel well. When I write, the words don't seem to come as readily as they used to." Moos speculates that this was the first forewarning of the cerebral hemorrhage that would strike him down four months later, and of course it may well have been. But to the very end there was little apparent diminution of his powers; the last thing he ever wrote, "Equal Rights in Parks," which appeared in the Evening Sun for November 9, is as brilliant, forceful, and characteristically Menckenian as anything that ever came from his typewriter.

He was, it should be remembered, a newspaperman before all else, and newspapermen do not ordinarily enjoy the leisure and relaxation that befall other kinds of writers. They may not wait for inspiration to come, or decide to let today go by on the chance that the creative impulse will work better tomorrow. A reporter simply cannot sit back in his chair, stare at the ceiling or look out the window, and weigh carefully in his mind the tone and shading of one adjective as against another; he cannot give much thought to the vexing question of whether to put a comma in or leave it out. Deadlines must be met, and the next edition will shortly go to press; such a man soon learns to write as he thinks, or—perhaps more accurately—to think as he writes.

Mencken's journalistic training was invaluable to him from the very outset of his career and spread over into all the other areas of his far-flung literary activities. Without it, for one thing, he could never have produced the volume that he did. Perhaps the best way to observe him at work is to examine the heavy scrapbooks into which he pasted his dispatches on the national political conventions from 1920 to 1936. These pieces were written, remember, not in his study at Hollins Street but in a crowded and noisy press gallery, jammed cheek by jowl with other reporters and columnists, while on the floor below the candidates for office "bawled" and "heaved" and beat their breasts, and he peered out at them cynically over his horn-rimmed glasses. Alternatively they might be done in his hotel room late at night or early in the morning, after twelve or sixteen hours of grueling sessions. But in either case he would insert one of the long sheets of Western Union copy paper into the old Corona and start pecking away, and the carefully balanced paragraphs, the precisely right words and phrases, the gorgeous witticisms, show no slightest hesitancy and no trace of revisions; they appeared the next day in the *Sun* exactly as they came from his typewriter.

The same is true of the "Monday Articles." There are sixteen thick volumes of these on the shelves of the Mencken Room, and it is rare indeed for a typescript page to give any evidence of changes or afterthoughts.

On the books, of course—such as the two *Treatises*, and *The American Language*, and his memoirs—he was not under any such pressure, and so these do show more leisurely working. He would type the first draft himself, seated at his desk usually in the late afternoon or early evening, and then go over it to insert the changes in pen and ink. He seldom took anything out; for the most part such changes consist of the substitution of a word here, the insertion of a phrase there, lighting up a passage already good with the characteristic touch of his own personality. Mrs. Lohrfinck would then type the fair copy and he might make a few final revisions on that before it went off in the mail to Knopf. But even in the case of these works the total amount of revision is relatively slight; the published text with which the reader is familiar differs by considerably less than 5 percent from the version that Mencken originally set down.

It was the magazine articles that underwent the greatest change —those that he wrote for *The Smart Set* from 1908 to 1923, and to a lesser degree those written for the *Mercury* from 1924 to 1933. These he ceaselessly revised, often coming back after several years to pick them up again and use them in a different place or for another purpose. If they were to go into the *Prejudices* he would touch up the language considerably; if—being after all journalism—the allusions in them had speedily become dated, he would insert new ones. Sometimes he might compress two articles into one, with the end of the first and the beginning of the second omitted and the main bodies of each joined into a new unified piece. Often, in the process of revising, he would expand them greatly, sometimes to four or five times their original length: for example, "The National Letters," which takes up 92 pages in *Prejudices: Second Series*, appeared originally as a 13-page article in the July 1920 issue of the *Yale Review*. Some of the things which he saw fit to preserve in the *Chrestomathy* were revised yet again—"one more embalming," as he said, "before consigning them to statistics and the devil."

It may be of interest to the reader to observe this process of revision at work, and so I have selected a couple of his best-known pieces and present them herewith in their original and revised forms. The first is the famous essay "Professor Veblen and the Cow." Actually, this exists in three versions: it appeared first in *The Smart Set* for May

◇◇

I

Ten or twelve years ago, being engaged in a *fatuous public* discussion with what was then known as an intellectual Socialist *(he has since, observing the proof of the pudding in Russia, renounced the red flag, taken down the wood-cut of Karl Marx from his wall, put up lithographs of Josephus Daniels, Elihu Root and Abraham Lincoln, and bought War Savings Stamps)*, I was *constantly beguiled and assaulted* by his long quotations from a certain Prof. Dr. Thorstein Veblen, then quite unknown to me. My antagonist *seemed to attach* a great deal of importance to these *quotations and urged me to read them well, but* the more I read them the less I could make *out* of them, and so, *growing impatient*, I denounced this Prof. Veblen as a *hawker* of pishposh, refused to waste any more time *on* his *snarling polysyllables*, and applied myself to the other Socialist witnesses in the case, seeking to set fire to their shirts. That old debate, which took place by mail (for the Socialist lived *like a moving-picture actor* on his country estate, and I was a wage-slave attached to a city newspaper), was afterward embalmed in a dull book, and the book is now as completely forgotten as Baxter's "Saint's Rest" or the Constitution of the United States. I myself *have not looked into it for six or eight years*, and *all I remember* of my opponent's argument (beyond the fact that *he* not only failed to convert me to *the embryonic Bolshevism of the time, but*

1919; it was then substantially revised for the first volume of *Preju-dices;* and he put final finishing touches to it years later for the *Chres-tomathy.* Since it would be typographically very difficult to show all three of them, I have chosen to omit the intermediate version; the left-hand pages that follow give it in its original *Smart Set* form, and the pages on the right the form in which he finally left it. At the risk of some visual awkwardness, I have drawn attention to the changes by the use of italics.

◇◇

Back in the year 1909, being engaged in a *bombastic* discussion with what was then known as an intellectual Socialist *(like the rest of the intelli-gentsia, he succumbed to the first fife-corps of World War I, pulled down the red flag, damned Marx as a German spy, and began whooping for Wood-row Wilson and Otto Kahn),* I was *greatly belabored and incommoded* by his long quotations from a certain Prof. Thorstein Veblen, then quite un-known to me. My antagonist *manifestly attached* a great deal of impor-tance to these *borrowed sagacities, for he often heaved them at me in lengths of a column or two, and urged me to read every word of them. I tried hard enough, but found it impossible going.* The more I read them, *in fact,* the less I could make of them, and so *in the end,* growing impa-tient *and impolite,* I denounced this Prof. Veblen as a *geyser* of pishposh, refused to waste any more time *upon* his *incomprehensible syllogisms,* and applied myself to the other Socialist witnesses in the case, seeking to set fire to their shirts.

That old debate, which took place by mail (for the Socialist lived *in levantine luxury* on his country estate and I was a wage-slave attached to a city newspaper), was afterward embalmed in a dull book, *and got the mild notice of a day.* The book, *by name,* "Men vs. the Man," is now as com-pletely forgotten as Baxter's "Saint's Rest" or the Constitution of the United States. I myself *am perhaps the only man who remembers it at all,* and *the only thing I can recall* of my opponent's argument (beyond the fact *even shook my native faith in democracy*) is his curious respect for the aforesaid *Prof. Dr. Thorstein* Veblen, and his delight in the learned gentleman's long, tortuous and (to me, at least) flapdoodlish phrases.

There was, indeed, a time when I forgot even this—when my mind was *purged* of the professor's very name. *This* was, say, from 1909 or thereabout to the middle of 1917. During *that time*, having lost interest in Socialism, even as *an amateur psychiatrist*, I ceased to read its literature, and thus lost track of all its Great Thinkers. The periodicals that I then gave an eye to, setting aside newspapers, were chiefly the familiar American imitations of the English weeklies of opinion, and in these the dominant Great Thinker was, first, the late *Prof.* Dr. William James, and, after his decease, *Prof.* Dr. John Dewey. The reign of James, as the illuminated will recall, was long and glorious. For three or four years running he was mentioned in every one of those *warmed-over Spectators* and *Saturday Reviews* at least once a week, and often a dozen times. Among the less sombre gazettes of the republic, to be sure, there were other heroes: Maeterlinck, Rabindranath Tagore, Judge Ben B. Lindsey, *Arnold Bennett, the late Major-General Roosevelt, Tom Lawson* and so on. Still further down the literary and intellectual scale there were yet others: Hall Caine, *Eugene* Brieux and *Leonard Merrick* among them, with paper-bag cookery and the twilight sleep to dispute their popularity. But on the majestic level of the *Nation*, among the white and lavender peaks of professorial ratiocination, there was scarcely a serious rival to James. Now and then, perhaps, Jane Addams had a month of vogue, and during one winter there was a rage for Bergson, and *for a short space German spies tried to set up Eucken (now damned with Wagner, Nietzsche and Ludendorff)*, but taking one day with another James held his own against the field. His ideas, immediately they were stated, became the ideas of every pedagogue from Harvard to Leland Stanford, and the pedagogues, *laboring furiously at space rates*, rammed them into the skulls of the lesser *intelligentsia. To have called James an ass, during the year 1909, would have been as fatal as to have written a sentence like this one without so many haves. He died a year or so later, but* his ghost went marching on: it took three or four years to interpret and pigeon-hole his philosophical remains and to take down and redact his messages (via Sir Oliver Lodge, Little Brighteyes, Wah-Wah the Indian Chief, and other gifted psychics) from the spirit world. But then, gradually, he achieved the *whole* irrevocable act of death, and there was a vacancy. To it Prof. Dr. Dewey was elected by the acclamation of all right-thinking and forward-looking men. He was an expert in pedagogics, metaphysics, psychology, ethics, logic, politics, pedagogical metaphysics, metaphysical psychology, psychological ethics, ethical logic, logical poli-

that *it* not only failed to convert me to M*arxism*, *but left me a bitter and incurable scoffer at democracy in all its forms*) is his curious respect for the aforesaid Veblen, and his delight in the learned gentleman's long, tortuous and (to me, at least) *intolerably* flapdoodlish phrases.

There was, indeed, a time when I forgot even this—when my mind was *empty* of the professor's very name. *That* was, say, from 1909 or thereabout to the middle of 1917. During *those years*, having lost all *my former* interest in Socialism, even as *a species of insanity*, I ceased to read its literature, and thus lost track of its Great Thinkers. The periodicals that I then gave an eye to, setting aside newspapers, were chiefly the familiar American imitations of the English weeklies of opinion, and in these the dominant Great Thinker was, first, the late Dr. William James, and, after his decease *in 1910*, Dr. John Dewey. The reign of James, as the illuminated will recall, was long and glorious. For three or four years running he was mentioned in every one of those American *Spectators* and *Saturday Reviews* at least once a week, and often a dozen times. Among the less somber gazettes of the republic, to be sure, there were other heroes: Maeterlinck, Rabindranath Tagore, Judge Ben B. Lindsey, and so on, and *still* further down the literary and intellectual scale there were yet others: Hall Caine, Brieux and *Jack Johnson* among them, with paper-bag cookery and the twilight sleep to dispute their popularity. But on the majestic level of the *pre-Villard Nation*, among the white and lavender peaks of professorial ratiocination, there was scarcely a serious rival to James. Now and then, perhaps, Jane Addams had a month of vogue, and during one Winter there was a rage for Bergson, but taking one day with another James held his own against the field.

His ideas, immediately they were stated, became the ideas of every pedagogue from Harvard to Leland Stanford, and the pedagogues rammed them into the skulls of the lesser *cerebelli*. *When he died* his ghost went marching on: it took three or four years to interpret and pigeon hole his philosophical remains and to take down and redact his messages (via Sir Oliver Lodge, Little Brighteyes, Wah Wah the Indian Chief, and other gifted psychics) from the spirit world. But then, gradually, he achieved the *ultimate, stupendous and* irrevocable act of death, and there was a vacancy. To it Prof. Dr. Dewey was elected by the acclamation of all right-thinking and forward-looking men. He was an expert in pedagogics, metaphysics, psychology, ethics, logic, politics, pedagogical metaphysics, metaphysical psychology, psychological ethics, ethical logic, logical politics and political pedagogics. He was *artium magister, philosophiæ doctor* and twice *legum doctor*. He had written a book called "How to Think." *He sat in a professor's chair and caned sophomores for blowing spit-balls. Ergo,*

tics and political pedagogics. He was *Artium Magister, Philosophiae Doctor* and twice *Legum Doctor*. He had written a book called "How to Think." *He was a professor. Ergo*, he was the ideal candidate, and so he was nominated, elected and inaugurated, and for three years, more or less, he enjoyed a *peaceful* reign in the groves of sapience, and the *intelligentsia* venerated him as they had once venerated James.

I myself enjoyed the discourses of this Prof. Dewey and was in hopes that he would last. Born *so recently as 1859* and a man of *sober habits*, he seemed likely to peg along *until 1935 or 1940*, a gentle and charming *geyser* of correct thought. But it was not, alas, to be. Under cover of pragmatism, that serpent's metaphysic, there was unrest beneath the surface. Young *college* professors *who seemed* as harmless as so many convicts in the death-house were secretly flirting with new and red-hot ideas. Whole *regiments and brigades* of them yielded in stealthy privacy to rebellious and often incomprehensible yearnings. Now and then, as if to reveal what was brewing, a hell *fire* blazed and a *Prof*. Dr. Scott Nearing went sky-hooting through its smoke. One heard whispers of strange heresies—economic, sociological, even political. Gossip had it that pedagogy was hatching vipers, nay, was already brought to bed. But not much of this got into the *jitney Saturday Reviews* and *grapejuice Athenæums*—a hint or two, maybe, but no more. In the main they kept to their old resolute demands for a pure civil-service, the budget system in Congress, the abolition of hazing at the Naval Academy, an honest primary and justice to the Filipinos, with *the overthrow of Prussian militarism* added after August, 1914. And Dr. Dewey, on his remote Socratic Alp, pursued the calm reinforcement of the philosophical principles underlying these and all other lofty causes. . . .

Then, of a sudden, Siss! Boom! Ah! Then, overnight, the *rising* of *the* intellectual *Bolsheviki*, the headlong assault upon all the old axioms of pedagogical speculation, the nihilistic dethronement of Prof. Dewey—and rah, rah, rah for Prof. Dr. Thorstein Veblen! Veblen? Could it be—? Aye, it was! My old acquaintance! The *Doctor obscurus* of my half-forgotten bout with the intellectual Socialist! The Great Thinker *redivivus*! Here, indeed, he was again, and in a few months—almost it seemed a few days—he was all over the *Nation*, the *Dial*, the *New Republic* and the rest of them, *and* his books and pamphlets began to pour from the presses, *and* the newspapers reported his every wink and whisper, and everybody who was anybody began gabbling about him. The spectacle, I do not hesitate to say, somewhat distressed me. On the one hand, I was sorry to see so learned and interesting a man as Dr. Dewey sent back to Columbia, there to lecture in imperfect Yiddish to classes of Grand Street

he was the ideal candidate, and so he was nominated, elected and inaugurated, and for three years, more or less, he enjoyed a *glorious* reign in the groves of sapience, and the *inferior umbilicarii* venerated him as they had once venerated James.

I myself *greatly* enjoyed and *profited by* the discourses of this Prof. Dewey and was in hopes that he would last. Born *of indestructible* Vermont *stock* and a man of *the highest bearable sobriety*, he seemed likely to peg along *almost ad infinitum*, a gentle and charming *volcano* of correct thought. But it was not, alas, to be. Under cover of pragmatism, the serpent's metaphysic *that James had left behind him*, there was unrest beneath the surface. Young professors *in remote and obscure universities*, *apparently* as harmless as so many convicts in the death house, were secretly flirting with new and red-hot ideas. Whole *squads* of them yielded in stealthy privacy to rebellious and often incomprehensible yearnings. Now and then, as if to reveal what was brewing, a hell*mouth* blazed and a Dr. Scott Nearing went sky-hooting through its smoke. One heard whispers of strange heresies—economic, sociological, even political. Gossip had it that pedagogy was hatching vipers, nay, was already brought to bed. But not much of this got into the *home made Saturday Reviews* and *Athenæums*—a hint or two maybe, but no more. In the main they kept to their old resolute demands for a pure civil service, the budget system in Congress, the abolition of hazing at the Naval Academy, an honest primary, and justice to the Filipinos, with *extermination of the Prussian monster* added after August, 1914. And Dr. Dewey, on his remote Socratic Alp, pursued the calm reinforcement of the philosophical principles underlying these and all other lofty *and indignant* causes.

Then, of a sudden, Siss! Boom! Ah! Then, overnight, the *upspringing* of intellectual *soviets*, the headlong assault upon all the old axioms of pedagogical speculation, the nihilistic dethronement of Prof. Dewey—and rah, rah, rah for Prof. Dr. Thorstein Veblen! Veblen? Could it be—? Aye, it was! My old acquaintance! The *doctor obscurus* of my half-forgotten bout with the *so-called* intellectual Socialist! The Great Thinker redivivus! Here, indeed, he was again, and in a few months—almost it seemed a few days— he was all over the *Nation*, the *Dial*, the *New Republic* and the rest of them, his books and pamphlets began to pour from the presses, the newspapers reported his every wink and whisper, and everybody who was anybody began gabbling about him. The spectacle, I do not hesitate to say, somewhat *disconcerted me and even* distressed me. On the one hand, I was sorry to see so learned and interesting a man as Dr. Dewey sent back to *the insufferable dungeons of* Columbia, there to lecture in imperfect Yiddish to classes of Grand Street Platos. And on the other hand, I shrunk supinely from

Platos. And on the other hand, I shrunk supinely from the appalling job, newly rearing itself before me, of re-reading the whole canon of the singularly laborious and muggy, the incomparably tangled and unintelligible works of Prof. *Dr. Thorstein* Veblen.

II

Well, I have got through it nevertheless, and, after all, with rather less damage than I looked for. There are, first and last, six volumes on the eminent master's shelf, and I have read the whole half dozen. I rehearse their titles: "The Theory of the Leisure Class," "The Theory of Business Enterprise," "The Instinct of Workmanship," "Imperial Germany and the Industrial Revolution," "The Nature of Peace and the Terms of Its Perpetuation" and "The Higher Learning in America" (all Huebsch). But I do not recommend the complete course; a part will suffice for you, if you are naturally bright. Read the first book and the last, and you will pick up enough of Prof. Veblen's theory to outfit you acceptably. Read the first alone, and you will have a fairly good general acquaintance with his ideas. For those ideas, *save in detail, are* quite simple, and *what is more*, often *very familiar. The only thing that is genuinely new about them is* the astoundingly grandiose and rococo manner of their statement—the almost unbelievable tediousness and flatulence of the *learned schoolmaster's* prose. Tunnel under *those* great *mounds* and stalagmites of words, *dig* down into *that* vast kitchenmidden of discordant and *irritating* polysyllables, *blow* up *that* hard, thick shell of *professorial bombast* and what *you will find is* chiefly a mass of platitudes—the self-evident made *thunderous*, the obvious in terms of the *stupendous*. Marx said a *great* deal of it, and what Marx overlooked *has* been said over and over again by his heirs and assigns. But Marx, at this business, labored under a handicap; he wrote in German, a language he actually understood. Prof. Veblen *suffers* no such disadvantage. Though born, I believe, in These States, and resident here all his life, he achieves the effect, perhaps without employing the means, of thinking in some foreign language—say *Latin*, Sumerian or *Old Church Slavic*—and then painfully clawing his thoughts into English. The result *is* a style that affects the higher cerebral centers like a constant roll of subway expresses. The second result *is* a sort of bewildered numbness of the senses, as before some fabulous and unearthly marvel. And the third result, if I make no mistake, *is* the *present* celebrity of the professor as a Great Thinker. In brief, he *states* his hollow nothings in such high, astounding terms that *they must* inevitably *arrest* and blister the right-thinking mind. He *makes* them mysterious. He *makes* them shocking. He *makes* them portentous. And so he makes them stick and burn.

the appalling job, newly rearing itself before me, of re-reading the whole canon of the singularly laborious and muggy, the incomparably tangled and unintelligible works of Prof. Veblen.

But if a sense of duty tortures a man, it also enables him to achieve prodigies, and so I managed to get through the whole infernal job. I read "The Theory of the Leisure Class" (1899), I read "The Theory of Business Enterprise" (1904), and then I read "The Instinct of Workmanship" (1914). A hiatus followed; I was racked by a severe neuralgia, with delusions of persecution. On recovering I tackled "Imperial Germany and the Industrial Revolution" (1915). Marasmus for a month, and then "The Nature of Peace and the Terms of Its Perpetuation" (1917). What ensued was never diagnosed; probably it was some low infection of the mesentery or spleen. When it passed off, leaving only an asthmatic cough, I read "The Higher Learning in America" (1918), and then went to Mt. Clemens to drink the Glauber's salts. Eureka! the business was done! It had strained me, but now it was over. Alas, a good part of the agony had been needless. What I found myself aware of, coming to the end, was that practically the whole system of Prof. Veblen was in his first book and his last—that is, in "The Theory of the Leisure Class," and "The Higher Learning in America." I pass on the news to literary archeologists. Read these two, and you won't have to read the others. And if even two daunt you, then read the first. Once through it, though you will have missed many a pearl and many a pain, you will have an excellent grasp of the gifted metaphysician's ideas.

For those ideas, in the main, were quite simple, and often *anything but revolutionary in essence. What was genuinely remarkable about them was not their novelty, or their complexity, nor even the fact that a professor should harbor them; it was* the astoundingly grandiose and rococo manner of their statement, the almost unbelievable tediousness and flatulence of the *gifted headmaster's* prose, *his unprecedented talent for saying nothing in an august and heroic manner. There are tales of an actress of the last generation, probably Sarah Bernhardt, who could put pathos and even terror into a recitation of the multiplication table. Something of the same talent, raised to a high power, was in this Prof. Veblen. If one tunneled under his* great *moraines* and stalagmites of words, *dug* down into *his* vast kitchen-midden of discordant and *raucous* polysyllables, *blew* up *the* hard, thick shell of his *almost theological manner,* what *one found in his discourse was* chiefly a mass of platitudes—the self-evident made *horrifying,* the obvious in terms of the *staggering.*

Marx, I daresay, had said a *good* deal of it *long before him,* and what Marx overlooked *had* been said over and over again by his heirs and assigns. But Marx, at this business, labored under a *technical* handicap; he wrote in

No doubt you think that I exaggerate —perhaps even that I lie. If so, then consider this specimen—the first paragraph of Chapter XIII of "The Theory of the Leisure Class":

> In an increasing proportion as time goes on, the anthropomorphic cult, with its code of devout observances, suffers a progressive disintegration through the stress of economic exigencies and the decay of the system of status. As this disintegration proceeds, there come to be associated and blended with the devout attitude certain other motives and impulses that are not always of an anthropomorphic origin, nor traceable to the habit of personal subservience. Not all of these subsidiary impulses that blend with the bait of devoutness in the later devotional life are altogether congruous with the devout attitude or with the anthropomorphic apprehension of sequence of phenomena. Their origin being not the same, their action upon the scheme of devout life is also not in the same direction. In many ways they traverse the underlying norm of subservience or vicarious life to which the code of devout observances and the ecclesiastical and sacerdotal institutions are to be traced as their substantial basis. Through the presence of these alien motives the social and industrial regime of status gradually disintegrates, and the canon of personal subservience loses the support derived from an unbroken tradition. Extraneous habits and proclivities encroach upon the field of action occupied by this canon, and it presently comes about that the ecclesiastical and sacerdotal structures are partially converted to other uses, in some measure alien to the purposes of the scheme of devout life as it stood in the days of the most vigorous and characteristic development of the priesthood.

Well, what have we here? What *do all these harsh, cacophonous sentences mean?* Simply that, in the course of time, the worship of God is corrupted by *extraneous* enterprises, and that the church, ceasing to be *merely a* temple, becomes the headquarters of these enterprises. *In brief, that men try to serve God by serving other men.* This bald platitude, which must be obvious to any child who has ever been to a church bazaar *or a parish house, is* here tortured, worried and run through rollers until it is spread out to 241 words, of which fully 200 *are* unnecessary. The next paragraph *is* even worse. In it the *gifted pundit undertakes* to explain in his peculiar dialect "that non-reverent sense of æsthetic congruity with the environment which is left as a residue of the latter-day act of worship after elimination of its anthropomorphic content." Just what *does* he mean by this "non-reverent sense of aesthetic congruity"? I *have* studied the whole paragraph for three days, halting only for *meals* and sleep, and I *have come* to certain conclusions. I may be wrong, but nevertheless it is the best that I can do. What I *conclude is* this: he *is* trying to say that many people go to church, not because they are afraid of the devil, but because they enjoy the

German, a language he actually understood. Prof. Veblen *submitted him-self to* no such disadvantage. Though born, I believe, in These States, and resident here all his life, he achieved the effect, perhaps without employing the means, of thinking in some *unearthly* foreign language—say *Swahili*, Sumerian or *Old Bulgarian*—and then painfully clawing his thoughts into *a copious but uncertain and book-learned* English. The result *was* a style that affected the higher cerebral centers like a constant roll of subway expresses. The second result *was* a sort of bewildered numbness of the senses, as before some fabulous and unearthly marvel. And the third result, if I make no mistake, *was* the celebrity of the professor as a Great Thinker. In brief he *stated* his hollow nothings in such high, astounding terms that inevitably *arrested* and *blistered* the right-thinking mind. He *made* them mysterious. He *made* them shocking. He *made* them portentous. And so, *flinging them at naïve and believing souls*, he made them stick and burn.

Consider this specimen—the first paragraph of Chapter XIII of "The Theory of the Leisure Class":

> In an increasing proportion as time goes on, the anthropomorphic cult, with its code of devout observances, suffers a progressive disintegration through the stress of economic exigencies and the decay of the system of status. As this disintegration proceeds, there come to be associated and blended with the devout attitude certain other motives and impulses that are not always of an anthropomorphic origin, nor traceable to the habit of personal subservience. Not all of these subsidiary impulses that blend with the bait of devoutness in the later devotional life are altogether congruous with the devout attitude or with the anthropomorphic apprehension of sequence of phenomena. Their origin being not the same, their action upon the scheme of devout life is also not in the same direction. In many ways they traverse the underlying norm of subservience or vicarious life to which the code of devout observances and the ecclesiastical and sacerdotal institutions are to be traced as their substantial basis. Through the presence of these alien motives the social and industrial regime of status gradually disintegrates, and the canon of personal subservience loses the support derived from an unbroken tradition. Extraneous habits and proclivities encroach upon the field of action occupied by this canon, and it presently comes about that the ecclesiastical and sacerdotal structures are partially converted to other uses, in some measure alien to the purpose of the scheme of devout life as it stood in the days of the most vigorous and characteristic development of the priesthood.

Well, what have we here? *What does this appalling salvo of rhetorical artillery signify? What was the sweating professor trying to say?* Simply that in the course of time the worship of God is *commonly* corrupted by *other*

music, and like to look at the stained glass, the potted lilies and the rev. pastor. To get this profound and highly original observation upon paper, he *wastes*, not merely 241, but more than 300 words! To say what *could be* said on a postage stamp he *takes more than a page in his book!*

And so *in the other five* volumes. In "The Higher Learning in America," *the last to be published, the writing reaches its* worst. It *is* as if the practise of *it* were a relentless *and incurable* disease, a sort of progressive intellectual diabetes. Words *are piled* upon words until all *sense* that there must be a meaning in them *is* lost. One *wanders* in a *maze* of nouns, verbs, adjectives, adverbs, prepositions, conjunctions, pronouns and participles, most of them swollen and nearly all of them unable to walk. It *is almost* impossible to imagine worse English, within the limits of *correct* grammar. It is clumsy, affected, *obscure*, bombastic, windy, empty. It *is* without grace or distinction and it *is* often *almost* without *elemental sense. And yet this highfalutin rumble-bumble, with its roots half in platitude and half in nonsense, has been gravely accepted, for a year or two past, as revelation, and the author of it has been put into the front rank of national prophets. Nothing could more horribly reveal the essential childishness of all intellectual speculation in the United States. Nothing could offer a more depressing proof of the extent to which the game of ideas has been divested of all interest and vitality, and reduced to the estate of a formal combat with bladders between platitudinizing pedagogues.*

III

I have said that most of Prof. Veblen's notions are not only flabby, but also stale. This is true. Reading him, one never gets the thrill that goes with sharp and original thinking, dexterously put into words. His fundamental ideas, stripping them of their gaudy investiture, are always seen to be feeble and obvious. The concepts underlying "The Theory of the Leisure Class" *are* simply Socialism-and-water, *and* the concepts underlying "The Higher Learning in America" *are* so *elemental* that even the *editorial writers of newspapers have* often voiced them. *But* now and then, starting from this stock balderdash, the *talented* professor *attempts* flights of a more original character—*and* straightway *comes* tumbling down into absurdity. What the *poor* reader then *has* to struggle with *is* not only intolerably bad writing, but also loose, cocksure and preposterous thinking. *In brief, what he then has to struggle with is stuff so bad that it is almost impossible to imagine it much worse.*

Now for an example or two. The first is from Chapter IV of "The Theory of the Leisure Class." The *specific* problem before the *professor has* to do with the social convention which *frowns* upon the consumption of

enterprises, and that the church, ceasing to be *a mere* temple *of adoration*, becomes the headquarters of these *other* enterprises. *More simply still, that men sometimes vary serving God by serving other men, which means, of course, serving themselves.* This bald platitude, which must be obvious to any child who has ever been to a church bazaar, *was* here tortured, worried and run through rollers until it spread out to 241 words, of which fully 200 *were* unnecessary. The next paragraph *was* even worse. In it the *master undertook* to explain in his peculiar dialect *the meaning of* "that non-reverent sense of aesthetic congruity with the environment which is left as a residue of the latter-day act of worship after elimination of its anthropomorphic content." Just what *did* he mean by this "non-reverent sense of aesthetic congruity"? I studied the whole paragraph for three days, halting only for *prayer* and sleep, and I *came* to certain conclusions. What I *concluded was* this: he *was* trying to say that many people go to church, not because they are afraid of the devil but because they enjoy the music, and like to look at the stained glass, the potted lilies and the rev. pastor. To get this profound and highly original observation upon paper, he *wasted*, not merely 241, but more than 300 words. To say what *might have been* said on a postage stamp he *took* more than a page in his book.

And so *it went, alas, alas, in all his other* volumes—*a cent's worth of information wrapped in a bale of polysyllables.* In "The Higher Learning in America" *the thing perhaps reached its damndest and* worst. It *was* as if the practise of *that incredibly obscure and malodorous style* were a relentless disease, a sort of progressive intellectual diabetes, *a leprosy of the horse sense.* Words *were flung* upon words until all *recollection* that there must be a meaning in them, *a ground and excuse for them, were* lost. One *wandered* in a *labyrinth* of nouns, adjectives, verbs, pronouns, adverbs, prepositions, conjunctions and participles, most of them swollen and nearly all of them unable to walk. It *was, and* is, impossible to imagine worse English, within the limits of *intelligible* grammar. It was clumsy, affected, *opaque*, bombastic, windy, empty. It *was* without grace or distinction and it was often without *the most elementary order. The professor got himself enmeshed in his gnarled sentences like a bull trapped by barbed wire, and his efforts to extricate himself were quite as furious and quite as spectacular. He heaved, he leaped, he writhed; at times he seemed to be at the point of yelling for the police. It was a picture to bemuse the vulgar and to give the judicious grief.*

Worse, *there was nothing at the bottom of all this strident wind-music—the ideas it was designed to set forth were, in the overwhelming main, poor ideas, and often they were ideas that were almost idiotic.* The concepts underlying, *say*, "The Theory of the Leisure Class" *were* simply

alcohol by women, at least to the extent to which men *may* consume it. Well, then, what *is* his explanation of this convention? *In brief*, here *is* his process of reasoning:

> 1. The leisure class, which is the predatory class of feudal times, re- serves all luxuries for itself, and disapproves their use by members of the lower classes, for this use takes away their charm by taking away their exclu- sive possession.
>
> 2. Women are chattels in the possession of the leisure class, and hence subject to the rules made for inferiors. "The patriarchal tradition . . . says that the woman, being a chattel, should consume only what is necessary to her sustenance, except so far as her further consumption contributes to the comfort or the good repute of her master."
>
> 3. The consumption of alcohol contributes nothing to the comfort or good repute of the woman's master, but "detracts sensibly from the comfort or pleasure" of her master. *Ergo*, she is forbidden to drink.

This, I believe, *is* a fair specimen of the *professor's reasoning*. Observe it well, for it *is* typical. That is to say, *it starts* off with a gratuitous and highly dubious assumption, *proceeds* to an equally dubious deduction, and then *ends* with a platitude which *begs* the whole question. What sound reason is there for believing that exclusive possession is the hall- mark of luxury? There *is* none that I can see. It *may* be true of a few luxuries, but it *is* certainly not true of the most familiar ones. *Do* I enjoy a decent bath because I *know* that John Smith *cannot* afford one—or be- cause I *delight* in being clean? *Do* I admire Beethoven's Fifth Symphony because it *is* incomprehensible to *bootblacks* and Methodists—or because I genuinely *love* music? *Do I prefer terrapin a la Maryland to fried liver because plowhands must put up with the liver—or because the terrapin is intrinsically a more charming dose? Do* I prefer kissing a pretty girl to kissing a charwoman because even a janitor may kiss a charwoman—or because the pretty girl *looks* better, *smells* better and *kisses* better? *Now and then, to be sure, the idea of exclusive possession enters into the con- cept of luxury. I may, if I am an idiot, esteem a book because it is a unique first edition. I may, if I am fond, esteem a woman because she smiles on no one else. But even here, save in a very small minority of cases, other attrac- tions plainly enter into the matter. It pleases me to have a unique first edition, but I wouldn't care anything for a unique first edition of Charles Garvice or Old Cap Collier: the author must have my respect, the book must be intrinsically valuable, there must be much more to it than its mere uniqueness. And if, being fond, I glory in the exclusive smiles of a certain Miss — or Mrs. —, then surely my satisfaction depends chiefly upon the lady herself, and not upon my mere monopoly. Would I delight*

Socialism and *well* water; the concepts underlying "The Higher Learning in America" *were so childishly obvious* that *even the poor drudges who wrote editorials for newspapers* often voiced them, *and when*, now and then, *the professor tired of this emission of stale bosh* and *attempted* flights of a more *original character*, he straightway *came* tumbling down into absurdity. What the reader then *had* to struggle with *was* not only intolerably bad writing, but also loose, *flabby*, cocksure and preposterous thinking. . . . *Again I take refuge in an example. It* is from Chapter IV of "The Theory of the Leisure Class." The problem before the *author here had* to do with the social convention which, *in pre-Prohibition 1899, frowned* upon the consumption of alcohol by women—at least to the extent to which men *might* consume it *decorously*. Well, then, what *was* his explanation of this convention? *Here, in brief*, was his process of reasoning:

> 1. The leisure class, which is the predatory class of feudal times, reserves all luxuries for itself, and disapproves their use by members of the lower classes, for this use takes away their charm by taking away their exclusive possession.
> 2. Women are chattels in the possession of the leisure class, and hence subject to the rules made for inferiors. "The patriarchal tradition . . . says that the woman, being a chattel, should consume only what is necessary to her sustenance, except so far as her further consumption contributes to the comfort or the good repute of her master."
> 3. The consumption of alcohol contributes nothing to the comfort or good repute of the woman's master, but "detracts sensibly from the comfort or pleasure" of her master. *Ergo*, she is forbidden to drink.

This, I believe, *was* a fair specimen of the *Veblenian ratiocination*. Observe it well, for it *was* typical. That is to say, *it started* off with a gratuitous and highly dubious assumption, *proceeded* to an equally dubious deduction, and then *ended* with a platitude which *begged* the whole question. What sound reason was there for believing that exclusive possession was the hall-mark of luxury? There *was* none that I could see. It *might* be true of a few luxuries, but it *was* certainly not true of the most familiar ones. *Did* I enjoy a decent bath because I *knew* that John Smith *could not* afford one—or because I *delighted* in being clean? *Did* I admire Beethoven's Fifth Symphony because it *was* incomprehensible to *Congressmen* and Methodists—or because I genuinely *loved* music? *Did* I prefer kissing a pretty girl to kissing a charwoman because even a janitor may kiss a charwoman—or because the pretty girl *looked* better, *smelled* better and *kissed* better?

Confronted by such considerations, it *seemed* to me that *there was little truth left in Prof. Veblen's theory* of conspicuous consumption and

in the fidelity of the charwoman? Would it give me any joy to learn that, through a sense of duty to me, she had ceased to kiss the janitor?

Confronted by such considerations it *seems* to me that *Dr. Veblen is on wobbly ground when he sets up his twin theories* of conspicuous consumption and conspicuous waste, *and that he reduces them to utter absurdity by his long and tedious support of them. Nor is he a bit more persuasive when he deals with the specific position of women. That they are, in a limited sense, chattels is too obvious to need statement.* A rich man *adorns* his wife with expensive clothes and jewels for the same reason, among others, that he *adorns his own head with a plug-hat:* to notify everybody that he can afford it—in brief, to excite the envy of *Socialists.* But he also *does* it, let us hope, for another and far *better and* more powerful reason, to wit, that he *loves* her, and so *wants* to make her happy. This reason *may not appeal to Socialist philosophers. In Russia, I am told, the Bolsheviki have actually repudiated it as insane.* But, nevertheless it *still* appeals very forcibly to the majority of normal men *in civilized countries, and I am convinced that it is a hundred times as potent as any other reason.* The American husband dresses his wife like a circus horse, not primarily because he wants to display his wealth, but because he is a *sentimental* fellow and ever ready to yield to her desires. If any conception of her as a chattel were *really* in him, even unconsciously, he would be less her slave. As it is, her vicarious practise of conspicuous waste commonly reaches such a development that her master himself is forced into renunciations—which *brings* Dr. Veblen's theory to *the verge of* self-destruction.

His final conclusion *is* as unsound as his premisses. All it *comes* to *is* a plain begging of the question. Why does a man forbid his wife to drink all the alcohol that she can hold? Because it "detracts sensibly from his comfort or pleasure." In other words, it detracts from his comfort and pleasure because it detracts from his comfort and pleasure. *Nothing could be feebler.* Meanwhile, the real answer is so plain that even a *college* professor should know it. A man forbids his wife to drink too much because, deep in his secret archives, he has records of the behavior of other women who drank too much, and he is eager to safeguard his wife's *self-respect* and his own dignity against what he knows to be certain invasion. In brief, it is a commonplace of observation, familiar to all males beyond the age of twenty-one, that once a woman is drunk the rest is a mere matter of time and place: the girl is already there. A husband, viewing this prospect, perhaps shrinks from having his chattel damaged. But let us be soft enough to think that he may also shrink from seeing humiliation, *ridicule* and bitter regret inflicted upon one who is under his protection, and one whose

conspicuous waste—*that what remained of it, after it was practically applied a few times, was no more than a wraith of balderdash. What could have been plainer than his failure in the case of the human female? Starting off with a platitude, he ended in absurdity. No one could deny, I was willing to grant, that in a clearly limited sense, women occupied a place in the world—or, more accurately, aspired to a place in the world—that had some resemblance to that of a chattel. Marriage, the goal of their only honest and permanent hopes, invaded their individuality; a married woman (I was thinking, remember, of 1899) became the function of another individuality. Thus the appearance she presented to the world was often the mirror of her husband's egoism.* A rich man *hung* his wife with expensive clothes and jewels for the same reason, among others, that he *drove an expensive car:* to notify everybody that he could afford it—in brief, to excite the envy of Marxians. But he also *did* it, let us hope, for another and far more powerful reason, to wit, that *he delighted in her,* that he *loved* her—and so *wanted* to make her *gaudy and* happy. This reason, *to be sure, was rejected by the Marxians of the time, as it is rejected by those of ours,* but nevertheless, it *continued to* appeal very forcibly, *and so continues in our own day,* to the majority of normal husbands in *the nations of the* West. The American husband, in *particular,* dresses his wife like a circus horse, not primarily because he wants to display his wealth *upon her person,* but because he is a *soft and moony* fellow and ever ready to yield to her desires, *however preposterous.* If any conception of her as a chattel were *actively* in him, even unconsciously, he would be *a good deal* less her slave. As it is, her vicarious practise of conspicuous waste commonly reaches such a development that her master himself is forced into renunciations—which *brought* Prof. Dr. Veblen's theory to self-destruction.

His final conclusion *was* as unsound as his premises. All it *came to was* a plain begging of the question. Why does a man forbid his wife to drink all the alcohol she can hold? Because, *he said,* it "detracts sensibly from his comfort or pleasure." In other words, it detracts from his comfort and pleasure because it detracts from his comfort and pleasure. Meanwhile, the real answer is so plain that even a professor should know it. A man forbids his wife to drink too much because, deep in his secret archives, he has records of the behavior of other women who drank too much, and is eager to safeguard his wife's *connubial rectitude* and his own dignity against what he knows to be certain invasion. In brief, it is a commonplace of observation, familiar to all males beyond the age of twenty-one, that once a woman is drunk the rest is a mere matter of time and place: the girl is already there. A husband, viewing this prospect, perhaps shrinks from having his chattel damaged. But let us be soft enough to

dignity and happiness are precious to him, and one whom he regards with deep and (I surely hope) lasting affection. A man's grandfather is surely not his chattel, even by the terms of the Veblen theory, *and* yet I am sure that no sane man would let the old gentleman go beyond a discreet cocktail or two if a bout of genuine *lushing* were certain to be followed by the complete destruction of his dignity, his chastity and (if a Presbyterian) his immortal soul.

IV

One more example of the *estimable professor's* logic. On page 135 of "The Theory of the Leisure Class" he turns his garish and buzzing searchlight upon a *double* problem. First, why do we have lawns around our country houses? Secondly, why don't we *employ* cows to keep them clipped, instead of *importing sweating* Italians, Croatians, *Alabamans?* The first *is* answered by an appeal to ethnology: we delight in lawns because we are the descendants of "a pastoral people inhabiting a region with a humid climate." *True enough, there is in a well-kept lawn* "an element of sensuous beauty," *but that is secondary: the main thing is that our* dolicho-blond ancestors had flocks, and thus took a keen professional interest in grass. (The Marx *motif!* The economic interpretation of history in E flat.) But why don't *we* keep flocks? Why do we renounce cows and hire Jugo-Slavs? Because "to the average popular apprehension a herd of cattle so pointedly suggests thrift and usefulness that their presence . . . would be intolerably cheap." With the highest respect, Pish! Plowing through a bad book from end to end, I *can* find nothing sillier than this. Here, indeed, the whole "theory of conspicuous waste" *is* exposed for precisely what it *is:* one percent platitude and ninety-nine percent *bosh. Has* the genial professor, pondering his great problems, ever taken a walk in the country? And has he, in the course of that walk, ever crossed a pasture inhabited by a cow (*Bos taurus)?* And *has* he, making that crossing, ever passed astern of the cow herself? And *has* he, thus passing astern, ever stepped carelessly, and—

think that he may also shrink from seeing humiliation and bitter regret inflicted upon one who is under his protection, and one whose dignity and happiness are precious to him, and one whom he regards with deep and (I surely hope) lasting affection. A man's grandfather is surely not his chattel, even by the terms of the Veblen theory, yet I am sure that no sane man would let the old gentleman go beyond a discreet cocktail or two if a bout of genuine *bibbing* were certain to be followed by the complete destruction of his dignity, his chastity and (if a Presbyterian) his immortal soul.

One more example of the V*eblenian* logic *and I must pass on.* On page 135 of "The Theory of the Leisure Class" he turned his garish and buzzing searchlight upon *another* problem *of the domestic hearth, this time a double one.* First, why do we have lawns around our country houses? Secondly, why don't we *use* cows to keep them clipped, instead of *employing* Italians, Croatians and *blackamoors?* The first *question was* answered by an appeal to ethnology: we delight in lawns because we are the descendants of "a pastoral people inhabiting a region with a humid climate"—*because* our dolicho-blond ancestors had flocks, and thus took a keen professional interest in grass. (The Marx *motif!* The economic interpretation of history in E flat.) But why don't *we* keep flocks? Why do we renounce cows and hire Jugo-Slavs? Because "to the average popular apprehension a herd of cattle so pointedly suggests thrift and usefulness that their presence . . . would be intolerably cheap." Plowing through a bad book from end to end, I *could* find nothing sillier than this. Here, indeed, the whole "theory of conspicuous waste" *was* exposed for precisely what it *was:* one per cent. platitude and ninety-nine per cent. *nonsense. Had* the genial professor, pondering his great problems, ever taken a walk in the country? And *had* he, in the course of that walk, ever crossed a pasture inhabited by a cow *(Bos taurus)?* And had he, making that crossing, ever passed astern of the cow herself? And *had* he, thus passing astern, ever stepped carelessly, and—

[There is more to the article, but this is the point at which Mencken chose to break it off in the *Chrestomathy*. The incredible thing about the original *Smart Set* version is that it stops not at the end of a paragraph, or even at the end of a sentence, but in the middle of a word. The last three lines at the bottom of the right-hand column on page 144 of the issue read: "If so much prudence shows itself in a professor admittedly of su-," and the next line, in parentheses and italics, says: "*(More, perhaps, anon.)*." Apparently he had just run out of space, and rather than cut anything in the earlier sections he decided on this quite unorthodox way of breaking off. Naturally, there never was any "anon."]

The second example of his methods of revision is the obituary he wrote on Calvin Coolidge, which appeared originally as a "Monday

◇◇

The brethren who had the job of writing eulogies of the late Dr. Coolidge made very heavy weather of it, and no wonder, for such papers are difficult to do at best, and they become almost maddening when they must be done under pressure. The right hon. gentleman, who had always been more or less baffling to journalists, and hence a source of serious professional concern to them, threw them the hardest of all his hard bones in the end by dying so unexpectedly. I dare say that a poll of the editorial offices of the country would have given him at least thirty years more of life. He seemed, in fact, to be precisely the sort of man who would live to a vast and preposterous age, gradually mummifying in a sort of autogenous vacuum. But he fooled all the amateur actuaries by dying suddenly and melodramatically, and in what for a Vermont highlander was only the beginning of his prime.

I have accumulated a large number of obituaries of him, and examined them with some care. Their general burden seems to be that he was "a typical American." But was he? Alas, the evidence brought forward to support the thesis runs against it instead. For it appears that a typical American, in the view of the journalistic *Todsäufer*, as in that of the au-

Article" in the *Evening Sun* for January 30, 1933. Coolidge had died on January 5, and Mencken waited—as indeed the text itself makes clear—more than three weeks to offer his judgment of the departed statesman. He then rewrote the piece, in a form so substantially altered as to make it a new work, for the April issue of *The American Mercury*, and fifteen years later he reproduced this latter version, with some very minor changes, in the *Chrestomathy*. The differences between the *Sun* and *Mercury* versions are so great, amounting to the deletion of whole paragraphs and the insertion of much new material, that it would be impractical to indicate them by italics; and so I simply set the two of them side by side, cautioning the reader to observe well how they differ.

◇◇◇

The editorial writers who had the job of concocting mortuary tributes to the late Calvin Coolidge, LL.D., made heavy weather of it, and no wonder. Ordinarily, an American public man dies by inches, and there is thus plenty of time to think up beautiful nonsense about him. More often than not, indeed, he threatens to die three or four times before he actually does so, and each threat gives the elegists a chance to mellow and adorn their effusions. But Dr. Coolidge slipped out of life almost as quietly and as unexpectedly as he had originally slipped into public notice, and in consequence the brethren were caught napping and had to do their poetical embalming under desperate pressure. The common legend is that such pressure inflames and inspires a true journalist, and maketh him to sweat masterpieces, but it is not so in fact. Like any other literary man, he functions best when he is at leisure, and can turn from his tablets now and then to run down a quotation, to eat a plate of ham and eggs, or to look out of the window.

The general burden of the Coolidge memoirs was that the right hon. gentleman was a typical American, and some hinted that he was the most typical since Lincoln. As the English say, I find myself quite unable to

thor's school-books, is one who wins his way to high place by heroic endeavors and against desperate odds—and that was certainly not the history of Dr. Coolidge. On the contrary, his path in life was greased for him like that of a royal prince, and there is no evidence that he ever met a single serious obstacle from birth to death, or had to pause even once to get his breath and bind up his wounds.

He came into the world under one of the luckiest stars that ever shined down on mortal man. There was nothing distinguished about his family, but it was at least very respectable, and his father was a man of local importance, and rich for his place and time. If young Cal was ever on short commons no record of the fact survives. He was well fed, he was well schooled, and when the time came for him to launch into life he got a quick and easy start. Going direct from college into a prosperous law office— apparently by the influence of his father—he got into politics almost immediately, and by the time he was 27 he was already on the public pay roll. There he remained continuously for precisely thirty years, advancing step by step, always helped by fortune and never encountering anything properly describable as opposition, until he landed finally in the gaudiest job of them all, and retired from it at 57 with hundreds of thousands in gilt-edged securities.

The typical American, whether in politics or out, is a far different fellow. Whatever his eventual success, his life is normally one of struggle, and he goes through it flogged by a dæmon. If it has its perihelions of triumph and glory, it also has its nadirs of defeat and despair. But no defeat ever stopped Coolidge, and no dæmon gnawed at his liver. His life, for all its blinding lights, was as placid as that of a nun in a convent. The heavenly hierarchy seemed to be in a conspiracy to protect him, and help him along. Asking for nothing, he got everything. In all history there is no minute of a more implacable destiny, or of an easier one.

I recall well the day that he was nominated for the Vice-Presidency in Chicago—a blistering July Saturday in 1920. There had been, as everyone knows, a bitter battle for the Presidential nomination, and it went to the late Dr. Harding by a despairing sort of compromise, and only because he was too obscure to have any serious enemies. The battle over, half the delegates rushed out of the steaming hall and started for home. The nomination of a Vice-President was almost forgotten, and when some one recalled it the only candidates who turned up were fifth-raters. Hiram Johnson, defeated for the Presidential nomination, refused it scornfully, as beneath his dignity. So Henry Cabot Lodge, who was presiding, suggested Coolidge, who came from his own State and was one of his satellites, and Coolidge it was. The balloting took perhaps ten minutes. Then the remaining delegates also rushed out, for the hall was an inferno.

associate myself with that thesis. He was, in truth, almost as unlike the average of his countrymen as if he had been born green. The Americano is an expansive fellow, a back-slapper, full of amiability; Coolidge was reserved and even muriatic. The Americano has a stupendous capacity for believing, and especially for believing in what is palpably not true; Coolidge was, in his fundamental metaphysics, an agnostic. The Americano dreams vast dreams, and is hag-ridden by a demon; Coolidge was not mount but rider, and his steed was a mechanical horse. The Americano, in his normal incarnation, challenges fate at every step and his whole life is a struggle; Coolidge took things as they came.

Some of the more romantic of the funeral bards tried to convert the farmhouse at Plymouth into a log-cabin, but the attempt was as vain as their effort to make a Lincoln of good Cal. His early days, in fact, were anything but pinched. His father was a man of substance, and he was well fed and well schooled. He went to a good college, had the clothes to cut a figure there, and made useful friends. There is no record that he was brilliant, but he took his degree with a respectable mark, proceeded to the law, and entered a prosperous law firm on the day of his admission to the bar. Almost at once he got into politics, and by the time he was twenty-seven he was already on the public payroll. There he remained without a break for exactly thirty years, always moving up. Not once in all those years did he lose an election. When he retired in the end, it was at his own motion, and with three or four hundred thousand dollars of tax money in his tight jeans.

In brief, a darling of the gods. No other American has ever been so fortunate, or even half so fortunate. His career first amazed observers, and then dazzled them. Well do I remember the hot Saturday in Chicago when he was nominated for the Vice-Presidency on the ticket with Harding. Half a dozen other statesmen had to commit political suicide in order to make way for him, but all of them stepped up docilely and bumped themselves off. The business completed, I left the press-stand and went to the crypt below to hunt a drink. There I found a group of colleagues listening to a Boston brother who knew Coolidge well, and had followed him from the start of his career.

To my astonishment I found that this gentleman was offering to lay a bet that Harding, if elected, would be assassinated before he had served half his term. There were murmurs, and someone protested uneasily that such talk was injudicious, for A. Mitchell Palmer was still Attorney-General and his spies were all about. But the speaker stuck to his wager.

"I am simply telling you," he roared, "what I *know*. I know Cal Coolidge inside and out. He is the luckiest goddam ——— ——— in the whole world."

Immediately afterward I retired to the catacombs under the auditorium to soak my head and get a drink. In one of the passages I encountered a colleague from one of the Boston papers, surrounded by a group of politicians, policemen and reporters. He was making a kind of speech, and I paused idly to listen. To my astonishment I found that he was offering to bet all comers that Harding, if elected, would be assassinated before he had served half his term. Some one in the crowd remonstrated gently, saying that any talk of assassination was unwise and might be misunderstood, for the Armistice was less than two years old and the Mitchell Palmer Red hunt was still in full blast. But the Bostonian refused to shut down.

"I don't give a damn," he bawled, "what you say. I am simply telling you what I know. I know Cal Coolidge inside and out. He is the luckiest ——— ——— in the whole world!"

This Bostonian knew a lot, but not all. He was right about the early translation of Harding to bliss eternal, but wrong in assuming that it would have to be effected by human agency. He had not yet learned that Coolidge was under the direct patronage and protection of the Archangels Michael, Raphael and Gabriel, who are to ordinary angels as an archbishop is to an ordinary man, and to archbishops as an archbishop is to a streptococcus. It is quite impossible to account for his career on any other theory. There were massive evidences of celestial intervention at every step of it, and he went through life clothed in immunities that defied and made a mock of all the accepted laws of nature. No man ever came to market with less seductive goods, and no man ever got a better price for what he had to offer.

The achievements of the deceased, in fact, almost always turn out on inspection to have been no achievements at all. Did he actually break up the celebrated Boston police strike? He did not. It was broken up by other men, most of whom were not even in his confidence; all he did was to stand on the side lines until the tumult was over. Did he tackle and settle any of the grave problems that confronted the country during his years in the White House? He tackled few of them and settled none of them. Not a word came out of him on the subject of Prohibition. Not once did he challenge the speculative lunacy that finally brought the nation to bankruptcy. And all he could be induced to do about the foreign debts was to hand the nuisance on to poor Hoover.

His record as President, in fact, is almost a blank. No one remembers anything that he did or anything that he said. His chief feat during five years and seven months in office was to sleep more than any other President—to sleep more and to say less. Wrapped in a magnificent silence, his feet upon his desk, he drowsed away the lazy days. He was no fiddler like Nero; he simply yawned and stretched. And while he yawned and stretched the United States went slam-bang down the hill—and he

It seemed plausible then, and it is certain now. No other President ever slipped into the White House so easily, and none other ever had a softer time of it while there. When, at Rapid City, S.D., on August 2, 1927, he loosed the occult words, "I do not choose to run in 1928," was it prescience or only luck? For one, I am inclined to put it down to luck. Surely there was no prescience in his utterances and maneuvers otherwise. He showed not the slightest sign that he smelt black clouds ahead; on the contrary, he talked and lived only sunshine. There was a volcano boiling under him, but he did not know it, and was not singed. When it burst forth at last, it was Hoover who got its blast, and was fried, boiled, roasted, and fricasseed. How Dr. Coolidge must have chuckled in his retirement, for he was not without humor of a sad, necrotic kind. He knew Hoover well, and could fathom the full depths of the joke.

In what manner he would have performed himself if the holy angels had shoved the Depression forward a couple of years—this we can only guess, and one man's hazard is as good as another's. My own is that he would have responded to bad times precisely as he responded to good ones—that is, by pulling down the blinds, stretching his legs upon his desk, and snoozing away the lazy afternoons. Here, indeed, was his one peculiar *Fach*, his one really notable talent. He slept more than any other President, whether by day or by night. Nero fiddled, but Coolidge only snored. When the crash came at last and Hoover began to smoke and bubble, good Cal was safe in Northampton, and still in the hay.

There is sound reason for believing that this great gift of his for self-induced narcolepsy was at the bottom of such modest popularity as he enjoyed. I mean, of course, popularity among the relatively enlightened. On lower levels he was revered simply because he was so plainly just folks—because what little he said was precisely what was heard in every garage and barbershop. He gave the plain people the kind of esthetic pleasure known as recognition, and in horse-doctor's doses. But what got him customers higher up the scale of humanity was something else, and something quite different. It was the fact that he not only said little, and that little of harmless platitudes all compact, but did even less. The kind of government that he offered the country was government stripped to the buff. It was government that governed hardly at all. Thus the ideal of Jefferson was realized at last, and the Jeffersonians were delighted.

Well, there is surely something to say for that abstinence, and maybe a lot. I can find no relation of cause and effect between the Coolidge somnolence and the Coolidge prosperity, but it is nevertheless reasonable to argue that if the former had been less marked the latter might have blown up sooner. We suffer most, not when the White House is a peaceful dormitory, but when it is a jitney Mars Hill, with a tin-pot Paul bawling from

lived just long enough to see it fetch up with a horrible bump at the bottom.

It was this snoozing, I suspect, that was at the bottom of such moderate popularity as he enjoyed. The American people, though they probably do not know it, really agree with Jefferson: they believe that the least government is the best. Coolidge, whatever his faults otherwise, was at all events the complete antithesis of the bombastic pedagogue, Wilson. The itch to run things did not afflict him; he was content to let them run themselves. Nor did he yearn to teach, for he was plainly convinced that there was nothing worth teaching. So the normalcy that everyone longed for began to come back in his time, and if he deserved no credit for bringing it in, he at least deserved credit for not upsetting it.

That this normalcy was itself full of dangers did not occur to anyone. The people generally believed that simple peace was all that was needed to cure the bruises and blisters of war time, and simple peace was what Dr. Coolidge gave them. He never made inflammatory speeches. He engaged in no public debates with other statesmen. He had no ideas for the overhauling of the government. He read neither the *Nation* nor the *New Republic*, and even in the New York *Times* he apparently read only the weather report. Wall Street got no lecturing from him. No bughouse professors, sweating fourth-dimensional economics, were received at the White House. The President's chosen associates were prosperous storekeepers, professional politicians, and the proprietors of fifth-rate newspapers. When his mind slid downhill toward the fine arts, he sent for a couple of movie actors.

Is anything to be said for this *Weltanschauung?* Perhaps a lot. The worst fodder for a President is not poppy and mandragora, but strychnine and adrenalin. We suffer most when the White House busts with ideas. With a World Saver preceding him (I count out Harding as a mere hallucination) and a Wonder Boy following him, he begins to seem, in retrospect, an extremely comfortable and even praiseworthy citizen. His failings are forgotten; the country remembers only the grateful fact that he let it alone. Well, there are worse epitaphs for a statesman. If the day ever comes when Jefferson's warnings are heeded at last, and we reduce government to its simplest terms, it may very well happen that Cal's bones now resting inconspicuously in the Vermont granite will come to be revered as those of a man who really did the nation some service.

the roof. Counting out Harding as a cipher only, Dr. Coolidge was preceded by one World Saver and followed by two more. What enlightened American, having to choose between any of them and another Coolidge, would hesitate for an instant? There were no thrills while he reigned, but neither were there any headaches. He had no ideas, and he was not a nuisance.

◇◇◇

As I have said, the changes he made in the *Mercury* version when he placed it in the *Chrestomathy* were extremely slight, amounting to little more than the substitution of a word here and there. But at least one of them shows the care and deliberation with which he approached this sort of thing. In the *Mercury* the final sentence reads: "He had no ideas, *but* he was not a nuisance." For the *Chrestomathy* he changed it to: "He had no ideas, *and* he was not a nuisance." Nothing could seem more minor—it is but the removal of one conjunction and the insertion of another, the substitution of one three-letter word for another three-letter word. Yet the effect is magical. That change of "but" to "and" makes all the difference in the world.

3 HE WAS, THEN, NOT JUST a "critic of ideas" (which was the way he always thought of himself), or even a scholar in one fairly specialized field (which was the way he thought of himself least of all), but an artist who brought to his work the most infinite care and pains. He repudiated all systems of aesthetics, yet when it came to the use of words he had the keenest aesthetic sense. As much as any novelist or poet he sought the precisely right term, the felicitous phrase, that would say exactly what he wanted to say in the most effective possible manner. The circumstances of his background and training combined with an innate gift to make this relatively easy for him, but he had, too, that striving for perfection which is part of the equipment of any artist in any field, and he knew the haunting sense of dissatisfaction which tells such a man, even while the public is acclaiming his work, that it is not really as good as he wanted it to be.

His forte was humor, and he must unquestionably be ranked among the great American comic writers. The only other one who can stand comparison with him, despite the very great differences between them, is Mark Twain. If nothing else in the foregoing pages had done so, then the two complete examples of his work reproduced in the preceding section, whether in original or revised form, must surely have established one thing—namely, that Mencken is side-splittingly funny. It is often difficult to read him without tears of laughter streaming down one's face, and since this can be embarrassing in public Mencken buffs usually make it a point to settle down with him in the quiet of their studies, or at least in the company of each other. To the non-buff, to those unfortunate souls who remain anesthetic to him, nothing can seem more pointless or painful than observing two such persons quote their favorite passages to one another!

Unfortunately, humor differs from serious literature in at least two important respects. In the first place, it is more often than not topical—that is to say, it is aimed at the current scene and at contemporary figures and problems. When those figures and problems are no longer around, its appeal is greatly diminished. This is true even of the very greatest comic writers, men like Aristophanes and Rabelais. No one argues their originality, their importance, or the entertainment which their work is still capable of providing, but it takes a classical scholar familiar with Athenian politics and culture in the fourth century B.C. to explain the endless allusions in Aristophanes, and it takes someone extraordinarily well versed in the history of the medieval Church to appreciate Rabelais's barbs and jests to the fullest. The rest of us can enjoy them, of course, but there is simply no getting around the fact that humor which has to be explained in footnotes has lost much of its point.

So with Mencken, and the essay on Veblen, delightful as it is, may be taken as another proof of this thesis. When, in the same year (1919), he reworked the *Smart Set* version for inclusion in the first volume of *Prejudices,* the few changes that it pleased him to make were in the nature of stylistic improvements; but when he came back to it again, almost thirty years later, to prepare it for the *Chrestomathy,* he had to update many of its allusions simply so that it would be more intelligible to a new generation of readers. Alas! since then another whole generation has come and gone, and the result is that the piece almost demands annotation to explain many of its lines. How many modern readers know who Otto Kahn was, or Professor Scott Nearing? How many have ever heard of, much less read, Baxter's *Saint's Rest?* Who recalls the crazes for paper-bag cookery and twilight sleep? To how many, indeed, does the name of Thorstein Veblen himself mean anything? True, the lack of such knowledge does not really constitute an insuperable obstacle to our enjoyment of the essay, but as with the great classical humorists we are inevitably missing a great deal even if we do not know it.

The second point to be made about humor is that, precisely because it is humor, it is not taken seriously—and therefore the person who creates it is not taken very seriously either. All too often we tend to think of him as a mere "entertainer," and to at least some extent this is his own fault. The idea that he wishes to put over may be solemn, or even profound, but he cloaks it in a leaven of wit, jests, puns, farce, buffoonery, irony, satire, and exaggeration, and our reaction to all of this is so instantaneous that we let the idea go right by us without even noticing that it is there. It is the icing on the cake that attracts us, and the icing is so delicious that we fail to appreciate the cake.

There can be little doubt that this sort of fate befell Mencken, both in his own time and in retrospect. Setting aside his special reputation as a language scholar, he is usually referred to as a "wit," a "satirist," an "iconoclast," a "curmudgeon," as "irreverent," as the "bad boy from Baltimore." He was, of course, all of these things. There is nothing wrong with appreciating him for his humor, heaven knows, but to appreciate only his humor is to miss much of what he has to say to us. Even so astute a critic as Alistair Cooke, it seems to me, comes dangerously near falling into this trap. In the otherwise very perceptive introduction which he wrote to his excellent little anthology, *The Vintage Mencken*, Cooke says that he was "overrated in his day as a thinker" (which he never really was) and that he "was vastly underrated as a humorist." He was, Cooke adds, a "humorist by instinct." This is certainly true, but it is one of those truths that do not go quite far enough.

Neither can there be any doubt that Mencken was himself responsible for this view. Humor was his weapon, even if he did use it for ends that were to him very serious. Most—one is strongly tempted to say all—that he wrote was written with the deliberate intent to shock. The incredible exaggeration, the outlandish similes, the mockery, the gratuitous insults hurled at so many things that the majority of people hold in reverence or at least in respect—all these techniques were designed to call attention not so much to himself as to the ideas that he wished to drive home. They succeeded a bit too well: almost any other American critic of his day could have written an essay on Thorstein Veblen that would lead the reader to think only of Veblen, but the effect of Mencken's is to leave him thinking only of Mencken.

The point is, as he himself insisted so many times, that he never wrote a line he did not sincerely believe. (He usually added "at the moment," but what he believed at the moment was never inconsistent with what he believed his whole life long.) Beneath the brilliant fireworks of the style there lie the deepest conviction and the most firmly held opinions. When Mencken calls William Jennings Bryan "a somewhat greasy bald-headed man with his mouth open," when he defines Puritanism as "the haunting fear that somebody, somewhere, may be having a good time," when he describes Protestant Fundamentalism as "shocking nonsense" propounded by "sorry bounders of God" who are at war with "every decency that civilized men cherish," he means exactly what he says—he could not have expressed himself more precisely if he had used mathematical formulae. One recalls the long years of diatribes against Roosevelt and the New Deal, and it might seem that all of this was a mere journalistic ploy designed to shock readers of the *Sun* and *Mercury*, but an incident that took place long afterward confirms how genuine his feelings were. Richard Dunlap, a youth who had lived and grown up in the next block of Hollins Street, once asked him if that was all it was. Dunlap, who was attending the University of Maryland's School of Journalism, had asked to interview Mencken for the college paper, and his request was graciously granted. The interview took place in the boardroom of the *Sun* building, and in the course of it the young man put his question in pretty much those terms. Mencken's face reddened, Dunlap recalled later; his neck thickened, and he exploded, "I think Roosevelt was a son of a bitch!"

It was precisely this sort of thing, of course, that made him so hard for so many people to take. If you were an admirer of Roosevelt, Mencken's writings about him constituted an outrageous attack not only upon a very great man, but upon the office of President of the United States and quite possibly upon the sanctity of government itself; even if you were against him (and it should be remembered that thousands of people in the thirties and forties were), you may still have felt that it was not quite the thing to do to call him a son of a bitch. A generation earlier it had seemed equally disrespectful to wave Bryan away as a "yap" and a "bald-headed man with his mouth open." If you were a lover of literature and the criticism that elucidated it, you would doubtless consider that it was in bad taste to dismiss scholars like Brander Matthews and Paul Elmer More and Irving Babbitt as mere hollow frauds. Above all, if you had any religious belief—and the vast majority of the American people had at least some—Mencken's books and articles on the subject constituted the most unforgivable irreverence and blasphemy, and he himself could only be the Antichrist come to earth. To all such groups, and to numerous others, Mencken is anything but funny.

Does this mean that it is necessary to agree with all of his ideas in order to appreciate his humor as well? I do not think that it does, and in support of this I offer the undeniable—even if somewhat puzzling—fact that he has always had a disproportionately large number of admirers among the clergy, a class of men whom one would expect would be required to detest him by the very nature of their calling. It is among those who take not only their own ideas but Mencken's as well just a bit too seriously that the bitterest opposition to him is to be found—but of course it was precisely such people at whom he aimed his attacks and deliberately sought to infuriate.

His thought, it should be unnecessary to say, was seldom original and never profound. There is no point in making him out to have been a great thinker, and any suggestion that he was one would have evoked a violent reaction from him—either he would have burst into guffaws or disappeared quietly into a nearby ocean. "Great Thinkers" were precisely the kind of people whom he distrusted most. His ideas are chiefly notable for their solid common sense—but common sense was a rather rare commodity in the America of his time, and perhaps that is the reason why he seemed so unusual and irritatingly different. If there is a larger supply of it today, if life is saner and more intelligent and a bit pleasanter to live, he deserves much of the credit for that fact. We also have to be grateful to him for giving us a body of literature that, a generation after his passing, is still capable of reminding us that laughter is the best antidote for our troubles, and that it remains the only really effective way for disposing of the "charlatans," "mountebanks," and "frauds" which, despite his best efforts, continue in our midst.

CHRONOLOGY

YEAR	LIFE	NEWSPAPER WORK
1880	Born W. Lexington St., Baltimore, Md., Sept. 12	
1883	Family moves to 1524 Hollins St.	
1884		
1886	Enters Professor Friedrich Knapp's Institute	
1889	Discovery of *Huckleberry Finn*	
1892	Enters Baltimore Polytechnic Institute	
1899	Death of August Mencken, Sr., Jan. 13	Goes to work as reporter for Baltimore *Morning Herald*; 1st story Feb. 24, 1899
1900	Trip (because of illness) to Jamaica, British West Indies	
1901		Drama critic of *Herald*, Sept. 1901 to 1903; editor, *Sunday Herald*, Oct. 1901 to Oct. 1903
1903		City editor, *Morning Herald*, Oct. 1903 to Aug. 31, 1904
1904	First formation of the Saturday Night Club	*Herald* printed in Washington and Philadelphia because of the Great Fire
		Republican National Convention, Chicago, June 19–24
		Democratic National Convention, St. Louis, July 5–11
		City editor, *Evening Herald*, Aug. 25, 1904, to 1905
1905		Managing editor, *Herald*
1906		*Herald* ceases publication, June 17
		News editor, Baltimore *Evening News*, June–July

MAGAZINE WORK	BOOKS	CONTEMPORANEOUS EVENTS
		Publication of *Huckleberry Finn*
1st poem, addressed to Kipling, published in Dec. 1899 issue of *The Bookman*		
		Dreiser's *Sister Carrie*
	Ventures into Verse	
		Great Baltimore Fire, Feb. 7
	George Bernard Shaw: His Plays	
		Upton Sinclair's *The Jungle*

YEAR	LIFE	NEWSPAPER WORK
1906 (Cont.)		Editor, Baltimore *Sunday Sun,* July 30, 1906, to April 18, 1910
1908	First meeting with George Jean Nathan (or 1909?)	
1909		
1910		Editor, Baltimore *Evening Sun,* April 18, 1910, to Dec. 1916
1911		Beginning of the "Free Lance" column, May 8, 1911, to Oct. 23, 1915
1912		
1913		
1914		
1915		Suspension of the "Free Lance" column
1916		Program notes for Baltimore Symphony Orchestra, reprinted in *Evening Sun;* continued for 2 years

MAGAZINE WORK	BOOKS	CONTEMPORANEOUS EVENTS
Book editor, *The Smart Set*	*The Philosophy of Friedrich Nietzsche*	
	Ibsen's *A Doll's House* and *Little Eyolf*, translated & edited with Holger A. Koppel	
	What You Ought to Know About Your Baby by Leonard K. Hirshberg (ghost-written by HLM)	
	The Gist of Nietzsche	
	Men versus the Man (with Robert Rives La Monte)	
		Dreiser's *Jennie Gerhardt*
	The Artist (reprinted from *The Bohemian* magazine, Dec. 1909)	Dreiser's *The Financier*
(W. H. Wright becomes editor of *The Smart Set*)		
Mencken and Nathan co-editors of *The Smart Set*	*Europe After 8:15* (with Nathan and W. H. Wright)	Outbreak of First World War in Europe
		Dreiser's *The Titan*
		Dreiser's *The "Genius"*
		Masters' *Spoon River Anthology*
		Cather's *The Song of the Lark*
	A Book of Burlesques	
	A Little Book in C Major	

YEAR	LIFE	NEWSPAPER WORK
1917		War dispatches from Germany, Jan.– March
		Also from Cuba on revolution, March
		Articles in New York *Evening Mail,* June 18, 1917, to July 8, 1918
1918		
1919		
1920		Pan-American Conference, Havana, Jan. 18–25
		Beginning of "Monday Articles" in *Evening Sun,* continuing into 1938
		Republican National Convention, Chicago, June 7–13
		Democratic National Convention, San Francisco, June 26–July 7
1921		
1922		
1923	First meeting with Sara Powell Haardt	
1924		Articles for Chicago *Tribune,* Nov. 9, 1924, to Jan. 29, 1928

MAGAZINE WORK	BOOKS	CONTEMPORANEOUS EVENTS
	A Book of Prefaces	America enters First World War
	Pistols for Two (by "Owen Hatteras") with Nathan	Cabell's *The Cream of the Jest*
		Hergesheimer's *The Three Black Pennys*
	Damn! A Book of Calumny	End of First World War, Nov. 11
	In Defense of Women	
	The American Language, 1st ed.	18th Amendment and Volstead Act begin Prohibition
	Prejudices: First Series	
		Cabell's *Jurgen* and *Beyond Life*
	Prejudices: Second Series	Lewis' *Main Street*
	The American Credo (with Nathan)	
	Heliogabalus (with Nathan)	
	Nietzsche's *The Antichrist* (translated)	
	The American Language, 2d ed.	Dos Passos' *Three Soldiers*
		Cabell's *Figures of Earth*
	Prejudices: Third Series	Eliot's *The Waste Land*
		Lewis' *Babbitt*
Mencken and Nathan relinquish editorship of *The Smart Set* with Dec. 1923 issue	*The American Language,* 3d ed.	
Founding of *The American Mercury,* Jan. 1924	*Prejudices: Fourth Series*	

YEAR	LIFE	NEWSPAPER WORK
1924 (Cont.)		Republican National Convention, Cleveland, June 9–13
		Democratic National Convention, New York, June 23–July 29
1925	Death of Anna Abhau Mencken, Dec. 13	Scopes "Monkey Trial," Dayton, Tenn.
1926		
1927		
1928		Republican National Convention, Kansas City, June 11–16
		Democratic National Convention, Houston, June 23–30
		Al Smith Campaign Tour, Oct. 12–30
1929		
1930	Marriage to Sara Powell Haardt, Aug. 27; moves to 704 Cathedral St.	London Naval Conference, Jan. 27–Feb. 10
1932		Republican National Convention, Chicago, June 13–18
		Democratic National Convention, Chicago, June 26–July 2

MAGAZINE WORK	BOOKS	CONTEMPORANEOUS EVENTS
Nathan withdraws as *Mercury* co-editor, Feb. issue	*Americana*, 1925	Dreiser's *An American Tragedy*
		Founding of *The New Yorker* magazine
Banning of *Mercury* in Boston because of "Hatrack" article	*Notes on Democracy*	
	Prejudices: Fifth Series	
	Americana, 1926	
	Prejudices: Sixth Series	
	Selected Prejudices	
	Menckeniana: A Schimpf-lexikon	
		Beginning of Depression
		Hemingway's *A Farewell to Arms*
		Wolfe's *Look Homeward, Angel*
Nathan separates completely from *Mercury*	*Treatise on the Gods*	
	Making a President	

YEAR	LIFE	NEWSPAPER WORK
1933		
1934		
1935	Death of Sara Haardt Mencken, May 31; moves back to Hollins St.	
1936		Republican National Convention, Cleveland, June 8–13
		Democratic National Convention, Philadelphia, June 22–28
		Townsend Convention, Cleveland, July 14–20
		Coughlin Convention, Cleveland, Aug. 13–18
		Landon Campaign Tour, July 23–Aug. 30
1937		
1938		Temporary editor, *Evening Sun*, Jan. 24–May 9
1939		
1940		Republican National Convention, Philadelphia, June 22–29
		Democratic National Convention, Chicago, July 13–19
		Willkie Campaign Tour, Aug. 16–Nov. 3
1941		Withdrawal from *Sunpapers* because of their war policy; final article, Feb. 2

MAGAZINE WORK	BOOKS	CONTEMPORANEOUS EVENTS
Retirement from editorship of *Mercury*		Repeal of 18th Amendment ends Prohibition
	Treatise on Right and Wrong	
		Wolfe's *Of Time and the River*
	The American Language, 4th ed., revised & enlarged	
	Ed., *The Charlatanry of the Learned* by Johann Burkhard Mencken	
	Co-author, *The Sunpapers of Baltimore*	
		German invasion of Poland begins Second World War
	Happy Days	
	Newspaper Days	Japanese attack on Pearl Harbor brings U.S. into war

YEAR	LIFE	NEWSPAPER WORK
1942		
1943		
1945		
1946		
1947	Stroke, Aug. 6; recovery after few days	
1948	Suffers massive stroke, Nov. 23, which prevents any further reading or writing	Rejoins *Sun* staff Republican National Convention, Philadelphia, June 19–22 Democratic National Convention, Philadelphia, July 10–15 Progressive Party Convention, Philadelphia, July 23–26 Articles, Aug. 1–Nov. 9
1949		
1956	Dies in sleep at 1524 Hollins St., Jan. 29	

MAGAZINE WORK	BOOKS	CONTEMPORANEOUS EVENTS
	A New Dictionary of Quotations	
	Heathen Days	
	Supplement I, *The American Language*	End of Second World War
	Christmas Story	
	The Days of H. L. Mencken (1-vol. ed. of *Days* books)	
	Supplement II, *The American Language*	
	A Mencken Chrestomathy	
	Minority Report	

BIBLIOGRAPHICAL NOTE

◇◇

THE FOLLOWING LIST is in no sense a bibliography of the works of H. L. Mencken, and indeed I have not attempted any, since a very full and detailed one may be found in Betty Adler's *H.L.M.: The Mencken Bibliography*. Its purpose is simply to indicate the abbreviations by which, in order to save space, works frequently referred to in the text are indicated in the notes. References to all other works are in full. Except where otherwise indicated, the publisher is Alfred A. Knopf, Inc., New York.

AC   *The American Credo: A Contribution Toward the Interpretation of the National Mind* (in collaboration with George Jean Nathan). 1920; revised and enlarged edition 1921.

AL1, 2 . . .   *The American Language: An Inquiry into the Development of English in the United States.* 1st edition, 1919; 2d, 1921; 3d, 1923; 4th edition corrected, enlarged, and rewritten, 1936; Supplement I, 1945; Supplement II, 1948.

BP   *A Book of Prefaces.* 1917.

Chrestomathy   *A Mencken Chrestomathy* (edited and annotated by the author). 1949.

DW   *In Defense of Women.* New York: Philip Goodman, 1918; 1st Knopf edition, 1919; paperback reprint, Time Reading Program, 1963.

GBSP   *George Bernard Shaw: His Plays.* Boston: John W. Luce & Co., 1905.

HaD   *Happy Days.* 1940.

HeD   *Heathen Days.* 1943.

MR   *Minority Report: H. L. Mencken's Notebooks.* 1956.

NeD   *Newspaper Days.* 1941.

NoD   *Notes on Democracy.* 1926.

PFN   *The Philosophy of Friedrich Nietzsche.* Boston: John W. Luce & Co., 1908; 3d edition, 1913.

P1, 2 . . .   *Prejudices: First Series,* 1919; *Second Series,* 1920; *Third Series,* 1922; *Fourth Series,* 1924; *Fifth Series,* 1926; *Sixth Series,* 1927.

TG   *Treatise on the Gods.* 1930; 2d edition corrected and rewritten, 1946; paperback reprint, Vintage Books, 1963.

TRW   *Treatise on Right and Wrong.* 1934.

In addition, certain other works on which I have drawn heavily are referred to (after their initial occurrence in the notes) by the following short titles:

Adler   Betty Adler (with the assistance of Jane Wilhelm), *H.L.M.: The Mencken Bibliography.* Baltimore: Johns Hopkins Press, 1961.

Angoff   Charles Angoff, *H. L. Mencken: A Portrait from Memory.* New York: Thomas Yoseloff, Inc., 1956; paperback reprint, A. S. Barnes & Co., Inc., 1961.

Bode   Carl Bode, *Mencken.* Carbondale, Ill.: Southern Illinois University Press, 1969; paperback reprint, 1973.

Forgue   Guy J. Forgue, ed., *Letters of H. L. Mencken.* New York: Alfred A. Knopf, Inc., 1961.

Goldberg   Isaac Goldberg, *The Man Mencken: A Biographical and Critical Survey.* New York: Simon & Schuster, 1925.

Kemler   Edgar Kemler, *The Irreverent Mr. Mencken.* Boston: Little, Brown & Co., 1950; paperback reprint, 1963.

Manchester   William Manchester, *Disturber of the Peace: The Life of H. L. Mencken.* New York: Harper & Brothers, 1950; paperback reprint (as *H. L. Mencken: Disturber of the Peace*), Collier Books, 1962.

Mayfield   Sara Mayfield, *The Constant Circle: H. L. Mencken and His Friends.* New York: Delacorte Press, 1968; paperback reprint, Dell Publishing Co., 1969.

McHugh   Robert McHugh, ed., *The Bathtub Hoax and Other Blasts and Bravos from the Chicago Tribune* by H. L. Mencken. New York: Alfred A. Knopf, Inc., 1958.

Moos   Malcolm Moos, ed., *A Carnival of Buncombe.* Baltimore: Johns Hopkins Press, 1956; paperback reprint (as *H. L. Mencken on Politics*), Vintage Books, 1960.

There are, of course, many other studies of Mencken, some of them relatively small and restricted in scope, and my indebtedness in one way or another to most of them is evident throughout the book. Among those that have appeared since his death in 1956, mention may be made of the following: Marvin K. Singleton, *H. L. Mencken and the* American Mercury *Adventure* (Durham, N.C.: Duke University Press, 1962), an exhaustively documented and, on the whole, judicious study of the founding, content, influence, and decline of the *Mercury.* —William H. Nolte, *H. L. Mencken: Literary Critic* (Middletown, Conn.: Wesleyan University Press, 1966; paperback reprint, University of Washington Press, 1967): a thorough and authoritative analysis of Mencken's ideas on literature and literary criticism, and of his influence on the subsequent literary history of the nation. —Philip M. Wagner, *H. L. Mencken* (Minneapolis, Minn.: University of Minnesota Press, 1966): written by a friend and colleague on the staff of the *Sunpapers,* this is a delightful tribute whose modest dimensions belie its real importance. —Guy J. Forgue, *H. L. Mencken: l'Homme, l'Oeuvre, l'Influence* (Paris: Minard, 1967): an encyclopedic work, far and away the biggest and most important treatment of Mencken in any language other than English; it is to be hoped that it will eventually be available in translation. —Bud Johns, *The Ombibulous Mr. Mencken* (San Francisco, Calif.: Synergistic Press, 1968): a minor piece of curiosa, dealing with Mencken's drinking habits; it is especially interesting for its illustrations, many of which are not reproduced elsewhere. —Douglas C. Stenerson, *H. L. Mencken: Iconoclast from Baltimore* (Chicago: University of Chicago Press, 1971): a serious and, on the whole, adequate study of the ethnic, familial, cultural, and intellectual forces which shaped Mencken's life and thought; unhappily, it comes to an abrupt halt just a little more than midway through his career. —Fred C. Hobson, Jr., *Serpent in Eden: H. L. Mencken and the South* (Chapel Hill, N.C.: University of North Carolina Press, 1974): a study both of Mencken's treatment of the South and of the way the South treated him in turn, with special emphasis (naturally) on the famous "Sahara of the Bozart" essay.

Also, since Mencken's death, there has been a steady stream of volumes anthologizing from his work, and particularly from the enormous mass of his hitherto uncollected magazine and newspaper pieces. The McHugh and Moos volumes listed above were among the earliest of these; the former reprints some fifty of the articles which Mencken wrote weekly for the Chicago *Sunday Tribune* between November 1924 and January 1928, while the latter selects from the incredible richness of the "Monday Articles" in the *Evening Sun*, about seventy that treat specifically of politics, political conventions and campaigns, and candidates for public office. The two best and most representative collections are undoubtedly *The Vintage Mencken*, compiled by Alistair Cooke (New York: Vintage Books, 1955), and *The American Scene: A Reader*, selected and edited, with an introduction and commentary, by Huntington Cairns (New York: Alfred A. Knopf, Inc., 1965). Louis Cheslock's *H. L. Mencken on Music* (New York: Alfred A. Knopf, Inc., 1961) is referred to in the footnote on page 287. *H. L. Mencken's Smart Set Criticism*, edited by William H. Nolte (Ithaca, N.Y.: Cornell University Press, 1968), recovers from the magazine's files, as its editor says, about one-sixth of the some 900,000 words that Mencken wrote for it between 1908 and 1924; most of what is in it had not previously been used elsewhere, even by Mencken himself. Carl Bode's anthology *The Young Mencken* (New York: Dial Press, 1973) gathers together a rich selection of the early work done for the *Herald*, the *Sun*, and *The Smart Set*; it stops in the early twenties. *A Gang of Pecksniffs*, edited by Theo Lippman, Jr. (New Rochelle, N.Y.: Arlington House Publishers, 1975), is a collection of some little-known pieces on journalism, newspaper work, and salient figures of that world. Finally (at least for the moment), *Mencken's Last Campaign*, edited by Joseph C. Goulden (Washington, D.C.: New Republic Book Co., Inc., 1976), reprints some of the last things that Mencken ever wrote as he covered for the *Sun* the national political conventions of 1948 and the Truman, Dewey, and Wallace campaigns.

Most of these collections have critical introductions and commentary which situate their contents within the general frame of Mencken's life and thought, as well as the social, political, and cultural background of the time.

I have already listed the late Betty Adler's exhaustive bibliography of Mencken's work, which includes as well virtually everything ever written about him. She brought it up to date in *A Ten-Year Supplement, 1962–1971* (Baltimore: Enoch Pratt Free Library, 1971). It is only fitting to list two other indispensable research tools for which scholars are indebted to this most knowledgeable, resourceful, and courteous of all Menckenians: *A Descriptive List of H. L. Mencken Collections in the U.S.* (Baltimore: Enoch Pratt Free Library, 1967), giving a detailed listing of Mencken holdings in thirty-four American universities, libraries, and private collections, and the incredible *Man of Letters: A Census of the Correspondence of H. L. Mencken* (Baltimore: Enoch Pratt Free Library, 1969), a 335-page inventory of his enormous, and even unbelievable, correspondence.

The Pratt Library's quarterly journal, *Menckeniana*, founded by Miss Adler, carried on after her death by the late Maclean Patterson, and edited since his death by Frederick N. Rasmussen, keeps the bibliography current and prints numerous brief biographical and critical pieces about him.

Lastly, this seems as appropriate a place as any to say something about the principles which have guided me in quoting from Mencken's works. As I have indicated when treating of his style, he ceaselessly revised and edited them, with the result that the same piece may exist in two or even three different versions. An article or review that originally appeared in *The Smart Set, The American Mercury,* the Baltimore *Sunpapers,* or the Chicago *Tribune* might be greatly revised and expanded for inclusion in one of the volumes of *Prejudices,* and many of these were revised yet again when he gathered them into the 1949 *Chrestomathy.*

In general, I have used the text of the *Chrestomathy* for all the things that are included in it, since it must be assumed to represent the final form in which Mencken wished his work to be preserved. In the case of those pieces which he did not see fit to include in this omnibus volume, I have used the latest version so far as it was possible to determine it. There are, however, a very few cases where it served my purpose better to quote from an earlier rather than a later version.

The foregoing does not apply, of course, to *The American Language* in any of its editions, to the *Days* books, or to *Treatise on the Gods.* For the last-named, I have worked from the text of the revised edition published in 1946, save that here, too, there were one or two instances where it seemed more useful or interesting to quote from the original (1930) edition.

Since the above was written and set in type, Octagon Press, a division of Farrar, Straus & Giroux, has issued thirteen books by H. L. Mencken in a set of uniformly bound hardcover reprints, thus making available again works which have been out of print and unobtainable for many years. The books are: the six volumes of *Prejudices, A Book of Prefaces, In Defense of Women, Notes on Democracy, The Bathtub Hoax, Treatise on Right and Wrong, The American Credo,* and *Menckeniana: A Schimpflexikon.*

NOTES

INTRODUCTION

1. *Letters of H. L. Mencken*, ed. Guy J. Forgue (New York: Alfred A. Knopf, Inc., 1961), p. 444.
2. MR, p. 118.
3. Forgue, "A Personal Note" (Hamilton Owens), pp. vii–viii.
4. Letter to Theodore Dreiser, April 19, 1939 (Forgue, p. 433).
5. "On Metaphysicians," P6, p. 79.
6. *Ibid.*, p. 81.
7. GBSP, "By Way of Introduction," pp. xiv–xv.
8. "Footnote on Criticism," P3, p. 93.
9. MR, p. 140.
10. Aristotle, *Works*, ed. Sir David Ross (Oxford University Press), Vol. XII, pp. 27–28.
11. *Summa Theologiae*, I, Q. 2, a. 1, obj. 3.
12. Letter to Gamaliel Bradford, after Oct. 17, 1918 (Forgue, p. 129).
13. "The Divine Afflatus," P2, p. 164; *Chrestomathy*, p. 447.
14. *Chrestomathy*, preface, p. vii.
15. Letter to Jim Tully, Jan. 22, 1940

16. "The American Tradition," P4, p. 10.
17. *Chrestomathy*, p. 624.
18. Mencken, *James Branch Cabell* (New York: Robert M. McBride & Co., 1927), p. 3.
19. BP, p. 197.
20. AL1, pp. 126–28.
21. P2, pp. 15–16.
22. Mencken's typed introduction to the bound volumes of the "Free Lance" in the Enoch Pratt Free Library, Baltimore. Quoted in Betty Adler, *H.L.M.: The Mencken Bibliography* (Baltimore: Johns Hopkins Press, 1961), p. 49.
23. Letter to Roscoe Peacock, April 24, 1934 (Forgue, pp. 374–75).
24. In a review of *Notes on Democracy* in the *Saturday Review of Literature*, Dec. 11, 1926.
25. *On Native Grounds* (New York: Reynal & Hitchcock, 1942), p. 198.
26. Carl Bode, *Mencken* (Carbondale, Ill.: Southern Illinois University Press, 1969), p. 242.

27. *H. L. Mencken's Smart Set Criticism,*
    ed. William H. Nolte (Ithaca, N.Y.:
    Cornell University Press, 1968), p. 117.

                CHAPTER I

1. Forgue, p. 280.
2. *Ibid., p.* 286.
3. *Ibid.,* p. 298.
4. *Menckeniana* 26 (Summer 1968), p. 4.
5. *The Constant Circle* (New York:
   Delacorte Press, 1968), p. 264.
6. HaD, preface, p. v.
7. *Ibid.,* p. viii.
8. "The National Letters," P2, p. 82.
9. NeD, preface, p. viii.
10. HaD, p. 99.
11. *Ibid.,* p. 93.
12. *Ibid.,* p. 249.
13. *Ibid.,* pp. 6–7.
14. *Ibid.,* p. 69.
15. *Ibid.,* p. 136.
16. "On Living in Baltimore," P5, pp.
    240–43.
17. Bode, p. 18.
18. HaD, preface, p. vii.
19. From a sheaf of miscellaneous
    autobiographical notes housed in a
    solander case in the Pratt Library's
    Mencken Room. Few of them are dated,
    but they appear to have been written for
    the most part around 1941 and the years
    immediately following. Hereafter
    referred to as AN1941.
20. HaD, preface, p. vii.
21. *Ibid.,* p. 93.
22. From the 200-page bound manuscript,
    housed in the Mencken Room, which
    Mencken wrote and supplied to Isaac
    Goldberg for the latter's book about him.
    Hereafter referred to as AN1925.
23. HaD, p. 97.
24. AN1941.
25. Manchester, *Disturber of the Peace: The
    Life of H. L. Mencken* (New York:
    Harper & Brothers, 1950), p. 138.
26. Forgue, pp. 288–89.
27. HaD, p. 255.
28. AN1925, p. 39.
29. AN1941.

30. HaD, preface, p. vii.
31. *Ibid.,* p. 252.
32. *Ibid.,* p. 251.
33. *Ibid.*
34. AN1925, p. 42.
35. HaD, pp. 78–79.
36. *Ibid.,* preface, p. vii.
37. AN1941.
38. HaD, p. 164.
39. *Ibid.,* preface, p. viii.
40. *Ibid.,* p. 170.
41. AN1925, pp. 66–67.
42. HeD, p. 53.
43. *Ibid.,* p. 40.
44. HaD, p. 158.
45. *Ibid.,* p. 167.
46. Nolte, ed., *H. L. Mencken's Smart Set
    Criticism,* p. 179.
47. The article is included in *The Bathtub
    Hoax and Other Blasts and Bravos from
    the Chicago Tribune,* ed. Robert
    McHugh (New York: Alfred A. Knopf,
    Inc., 1958), pp. 86–90.
48. AN1925, p. 73.
49. William H. Nolte, *H. L. Mencken:
    Literary Critic* (Middletown, Conn.:
    Wesleyan University Press, 1966), p. 37.
50. NeD, p. 61.
51. GBSP, "By Way of Introduction," p. xi.
52. *Ibid.,* preface, p. vii.
53. AN1925, p. 74.
54. BP, p. 74.
55. Baltimore *Evening Sun,* May 4, 1925.
56. Forgue, p. 414.
57. PFN, p. 19. (All page references are to
    the "third" edition, published in 1913.
    Actually, there never was a second
    edition; what goes by that designation is
    simply a reprint of the original 1908
    volume.)
58. *Ibid.,* p. 9.
59. *Ibid.,* p. 29.
60. *Ibid.,* p. 8.
61. *Ibid.,* p. 28.
62. *Ibid.,* p. 49.
63. NeD, preface, p. ix.
64. *Ibid.,* p. 24.
65. *Ibid.*
66. *Ibid.,* p. 23.
67. HaD, p. 216.

68. NeD, p. 37.
69. *Ibid.*, preface, p. vii.
70. *Ibid.*, pp. 37–38.
71. *Ibid.*, p. 94.
72. AN1925, pp. 124–25.
73. *Ibid.*, p. 109.
74. NeD, p. 70.

CHAPTER II

1. *Mercury*, I, 5 (May 1924), p. 60. The passage is reprinted in *Chrestomathy*, pp. 84–85, under the title "Sabbath Meditation."
2. TG, p. 246.
3. *Ibid.*, pp. 246–47.
4. MR, p. 140.
5. *Chrestomathy*, p. 331.
6. *Ibid.*, p. 335.
7. *H. L. Mencken: The American Scene, A Reader,* ed. Huntington Cairns (New York: Alfred A. Knopf, Inc., 1965), intro., p. xiii.
8. *Life*, 21 (Aug. 5, 1946), p. 46.
9. P1, pp. 150–51.
10. *Chrestomathy*, p. 317.
11. *Smart Set*, LVI, 1 (Sept. 1918), pp. 138–39. The article, entitled "Rattling the Subconscious," is included in William H. Nolte's anthology *H. L. Mencken's Smart Set Criticism*, pp. 147–51.
12. TG, p. 262.
13. AL4, Supp. I, p. 419 n.
14. HeD, p. 4.
15. Charles Angoff, *H. L. Mencken: A Portrait from Memory* (New York: Thomas Yoseloff, Inc., 1956), p. 172.
16. *Chrestomathy*, p. 86.
17. P3, pp. 267–68.
18. AN1941.
19. TG, preface, p. vi.
20. *Ibid.*, p. 4.
21. *Ibid.*, p. 95.
22. *Ibid.*, p. 96.
23. *Ibid.*, p. 110.
24. P6, p. 143.
25. MR, p. 207.
26. *Mercury*, I, 5 (May 1924), p. 60.
27. TG, p. 285.
28. MR, p. 37.
29. Letter to Herbert F. West, Aug. 9, 1940 (Forgue, p. 446).
30. TG, p. 232.
31. *Ibid.*, preface, p. vi.
32. *Ibid.*, p. vii.
33. *Ibid.*, pp. 286–88.
34. MR, pp. 130–31.
35. TG, pp. 150, 191.
36. MR, p. 256.
37. TG, p. 234.
38. NoD, p. 66.
39. *The World of George Jean Nathan*, ed. Charles Angoff (New York: Alfred A. Knopf, Inc., 1952), p. 50.
40. Angoff, p. 144.
41. AC, p. 45.
42. TRW, pp. 247–50.
43. AN1925, p. 158.
44. TG, p. 280.
45. *Ibid.*, p. 281.
46. *Ibid.*, pp. 242–45.
47. MR, p. 214.
48. "Protestantism in the Republic," P5, p. 106.
49. TG, p. 282.
50. TRW, p. 265.
51. P5, p. 111.
52. NeD, p. 161.
53. DW, p. 171.
54. TG, p. 281.
55. "The Husbandman," P4, p. 54.
56. "From the Memoirs of a Subject of the United States," P6, pp. 75–76.
57. *Mercury*, III, 11 (Nov. 1924), p. 292; P6, pp. 278–79.
58. MR, pp. 262–63.
59. TG, preface 1st ed., p. viii.
60. Forgue, p. 371.
61. *Damn! A Book of Calumny* (New York: Philip Goodman, 1918), pp. 91–94. The passage is reproduced in *Chrestomathy*, pp. 82–84.
62. TRW, p. 88.
63. TG, preface 1st ed., pp. viii–ix.
64. Forgue, p. 219.
65. "Officers and Gentlemen," P5, p. 265.
66. *Chrestomathy*, p. 111.
67. "The Butte Bashkirtseff," P1, p. 127.
68. Forgue, p. 27.

69. Owen Hatteras (pseud.), *Pistols for Two* (New York: Alfred A. Knopf, Inc., 1917), p. 32.
70. AN 1925, p. 167.
71. AN 1941.
72. TRW, p. 45.
73. "Meditations in the Methodist Desert," P4, pp. 173–74.
74. AN 1925, p. 196.
75. See his 1920 letter to Burton Rascoe, included in Forgue, pp. 184–90, and in Cairns, *The American Scene*, pp. 470–77.
76. Isaac Goldberg, *The Man Mencken: A Biographical and Critical Survey* (New York: Simon & Schuster, 1925), p. 84.
77. "The Campaign Opens," Baltimore *Evening Sun*, Aug. 27, 1928; included in *A Carnival of Buncombe*, ed. Malcolm Moos (Baltimore: Johns Hopkins Press, 1956), p. 186.
78. "The Pedagogy of Sex," P6, p. 205.
79. MR, preface, p. v.
80. "Rondo on an Ancient Theme," P5, pp. 100–1. Cf. also MR, pp. 67–69.
81. TRW, p. 263.
82. "The Blushful Mystery," P1, p. 199.
83. *Ibid.*
84. *Ibid.*, pp. 199–200.
85. DW, intro., p. vii.
86. *Ibid.*, pp. 21–22.
87. *Ibid.*, p. 3.
88. *Ibid.*, p. 129.
89. *Ibid.*, p. 185.
90. *Ibid.*, pp. 207–9.
91. All of these are taken from the "Sententiae" section of *Chrestomathy*, pp. 619–21.
92. Letter of Dec. 2, 1927, to Charles Green Shaw; Forgue, p. 306.
93. "Human Monogamy," Chicago *Tribune*, Jan. 16, 1927; reprinted in McHugh, pp. 155–60.
94. Mayfield, p. 3.
95. Mayfield, p. 213.
96. HaD, p. 251.
97. NeD, preface, p. ix.
98. Nietzsche, *The Antichrist*, translated with an introduction by H. L. Mencken (New York: Alfred A. Knopf, Inc., 1920),

pp. 80, 123, 180. The italics are in all cases in the original German text.
99. Forgue, p. 417.
100. PFN, p. 153.
101. "Bugaboo," P4, p. 212.
102. NoD, p. 11.
103. MR, p. 91.
104. "A Blind Spot," *Smart Set*, LXI, 4 (April 1920), p. 43; *Chrestomathy*, p. 162.
105. *Men versus the Man*, p. 32.
106. *Ibid.*, p. 115.
107. MR, p. 121.
108. "The National Letters," P2, pp. 76–77.
109. MR, p. 168.
110. *Ibid.*, p. 224.
111. *Ibid.*, p. 17.
112. Quoted in William H. Nolte, *H. L. Mencken: Literary Critic* (Middletown, Conn.: Wesleyan University Press), p. 56.
113. "The Politician," P4, p. 126.
114. See "On Living in Baltimore," Baltimore *Evening Sun*, Feb. 16, 1925; reprinted in expanded form, but with the same title, in P5, pp. 237–43.
115. *Mercury*, I, 3 (March 1924), pp. 292–96; "The Husbandman," P4, pp. 43–60; *Chrestomathy*, pp. 360–64. All of the remaining quotations in this section are taken from "The Husbandman."
116. PFN, p. 217.
117. "Education," P3, pp. 247–48; *Chrestomathy*, pp. 306–7.
118. *Ibid.*, pp. 238–39; *Chrestomathy*, p. 301.
119. Baltimore *Evening Sun*, March 12, 1923; *Chrestomathy*, p. 316.
120. P5, pp. 140–41.

CHAPTER III

1. AN 1941.
2. DW, rev. ed., intro., pp. xvi–xvii.
3. *Mercury*, I, 1 (Jan. 1924), p. 30.
4. "The Impending Combat," Baltimore *Evening Sun*, May 28, 1928; reprinted in Moos, p. 156.
5. HeD, pp. 279–80.
6. Moos, p. 2.

7. "Post-Mortem," Baltimore *Evening Sun*, July 14, 1924; reprinted in Moos, p. 79.
8. "The Politician," P4, pp. 129–30.
9. MR, p. 174.
10. Forgue, p. 171.
11. "On Controversy," Chicago *Tribune*, Oct. 24, 1926; reprinted in McHugh, pp. 275–76; P6, p. 94.
12. "Matters of State," P3, p. 292.
13. *Ibid.*, p. 289.
14. *Ibid.*
15. PFN, p. 202. Here, as on so many pages in this early work, it is Mencken rather than Nietzsche who is speaking.
16. "From the Memoirs of a Subject of the United States," P6, p. 38.
17. MR, pp. 203–4.
18. "On Government," P4, pp. 224–25.
19. From a review of Albert Jay Nock's *Jefferson*, written for the September 1926 issue of *The American Mercury* and included in P6, pp. 145–50.
20. Forgue, pp. 184–85.
21. "Matters of State," P3, p. 292.
22. NoD, p. 3.
23. *Ibid.*, p. 7.
24. *Ibid.*, p. 120.
25. "A Blind Spot," *Smart Set*, LXI, 4 (April 1920), p. 43; *Chrestomathy*, p. 162.
26. "Das Kapital," P3, p. 106.
27. "The Forward-Looker," P3, p. 222.
28. "Birth Control," P5, p. 29.
29. "Making Ready for 1924," Baltimore *Evening Sun*, April 2, 1923; Moos, p. 52.
30. "Who's Loony Now?" Baltimore *Evening Sun*, Dec. 27, 1921; Moos, p. 47.
31. NoD, p. 117.
32. AN1925, p. 171.
33. P3, p. 10.
34. *Ibid.*, p. 22.
35. "The American Tradition," P4, p. 24.
36. BP, p. 22.
37. "On Government," P4, pp. 235–36.
38. *Chrestomathy*, preface, p. viii.
39. "Al," Baltimore *Evening Sun*, April 23, 1928; reprinted in Moos, p. 150.
40. "Who's Loony Now?" Baltimore *Evening Sun*, Dec. 27, 1921; reprinted in Moos, p. 47.
41. "The Dismal Science," P3, p. 280.
42. "The Last Round," Baltimore *Evening Sun*, Oct. 4, 1920; reprinted in Moos, p. 23.
43. "The Believing Mind," Chicago *Tribune*, Aug. 8, 1926; reprinted in McHugh, p. 22.
44. "Das Kapital," P5, p. 109.
45. "The National Letters," P2, p. 70.
46. *Ibid.*
47. Mencken, intro. to translation of Nietzsche's *Antichrist*, p. 30.
48. "Golden Age," P5, pp. 271–72.
49. AC, p. 29.
50. AN1925, pp. 168–69.
51. "In the Rolling Mills," P6, p. 248.
52. "On Being an American," P3, p. 46.
53. AN1925, p. 106.
54. "Government by Blackleg," Baltimore *Evening Sun*, Sept. 27, 1920.
55. "Matters of State," P3, p. 296.
56. "A Carnival of Buncombe," Baltimore *Evening Sun*, Feb. 9, 1920; reprinted in Moos, p. 8.
57. "Campaign Notes," Baltimore *Evening Sun*, Sept. 13, 1920; reprinted in Moos, p. 22.
58. "Essay in Pedagogy," P5, pp. 230–31.
59. *The Days of H. L. Mencken* (New York: Alfred A. Knopf, Inc., 1947), "Author's Note," p. vi.
60. *Mercury*, XXVIII, 112 (April 1933), p. 390; reprinted as "Coolidge" in *Chrestomathy*, p. 254.
61. "The Tune Changes," Baltimore *Evening Sun*, March 27, 1933; reprinted in Moos, p. 275.
62. "The Piper Passes His Hat," Baltimore *Evening Sun*, April 16, 1934.
63. "Götzendämmerung," Baltimore *Evening Sun*, April 4, 1935.
64. "Meditations for March 15," Baltimore *Evening Sun*, March 11, 1935.
65. "Three Years of Dr. Roosevelt," *Mercury*, XXXVII, 147 (March 1936), p. 264.
66. "Burying the Dead Horse," Baltimore

Evening Sun, Aug. 17, 1936; reprinted in Moos, p. 314.

67. "Coroner's Inquest," Baltimore *Evening Sun,* Nov. 9, 1936; reprinted in Moos, pp. 331–32.

68. "The Call of Service," Baltimore *Evening Sun,* April 21, 1940.

69. "From the Journal of a Plague Year," Baltimore *Evening Sun,* June 2, 1940.

70. HeD, p. 200.

71. "Thirteen Years," Baltimore *Evening Sun,* March 20, 1933.

72. "Optimist vs. Optimist," Baltimore *Evening Sun,* Aug. 6, 1923; included in "Meditations in the Methodist Desert," P4, pp. 161–62.

73. HeD, p. 209.

74. MR, p. 103.

75. TRW, p. 298.

76. "Meditations in the Methodist Desert," P4, p. 159.

77. The article is reprinted as "The Perihelion of Prohibition" in *Chrestomathy,* pp. 411–15.

78. "The Dry Millennium," P2, p. 219.

79. "Si Mutare Potest Aethiops Pellum Suam," *Smart Set,* LIII, 1 (Sept. 1917), p. 138. The title is taken from Jeremiah 13:23: "Can the Ethiopian change his skin, or the leopard his spots?"

80. "Gropings in Literary Darkness," *Smart Set,* LXIII, 2, (Oct. 1920), p. 141.

81. P. 619n.

82. P2, p. 149; *Chrestomathy,* p. 192.

83. MR, p. 152.

84. "On Being an American," P3, p. 13.

85. *Chrestomathy,* preface, pp. vii–viii.

CHAPTER IV

1. Sherman's judgment occurs in his essay "Beautifying American Literature," *The Nation,* CV (Nov. 29, 1917), p. 594. More's is in *The Demon of the Absolute, New Shelburne Essays,* Vol. I (Princeton, N.J.: Princeton University Press, 1928), pp. 2, 76. The remaining references for the foregoing paragraphs are as follows: Calverton, *The Newer Spirit* (New York: Boni & Liveright, 1925), p. 165; Bromfield, "The New Yorker," *Bookman,* LXI (July 1925), p. 582; Kemler, *The Irreverent Mr. Mencken* (Boston: Little Brown & Co., 1950), p. 123; Farrar, "Mustard Plaster Mencken," *Bookman,* LXIV (Dec. 1926), p. 389; De Casseres, *Mencken and Shaw* (New York: Silas Newton, 1930), p. 187; Wilson, "The All-Star Literary Vaudeville," *A Literary Chronicle: 1920–1950* (New York: Doubleday Anchor Books, 1956), p. 81.

2. *The Smart Set: A History and Anthology,* ed. Carl R. Dolmetsch (New York: Dial Press, 1966), p. 24.

3. Behrman, in *ibid.,* intro., p. xx. It has to be borne in mind, of course, that Mencken and Nathan did not actually become co-editors of *The Smart Set* until the issue for November 1914.

4. Angoff, p. 19.

5. Carl Van Doren, *Many Minds* (New York: Alfred A. Knopf, Inc., 1924), pp. 122–23.

6. Boyd, p. 67.

7. Cairns, *The American Scene,* p. 53.

8. Frank Harris, *Contemporary Portraits: Fourth Series* (New York: Brentano's, 1923), p. 154; Vincent O'Sullivan, "The American Critic," *The New Witness* (London), Nov. 28, 1919.

9. Goldberg, p. 251.

10. "The National Letters," P2, p. 15.

11. *Ibid.,* p. 16.

12. Van Wyck Brooks, *The Confident Years* (New York: E. P. Dutton & Co., Inc., 1952), p. 394.

13. BP, pp. 135–36.

14. "Pedagogues A-Flutter," *Mercury,* XX, 77 (May 1930), p. 127.

15. "Puritanism as a Literary Force," BP, pp. 275–76.

16. Nolte, *H. L. Mencken: Literary Critic,* p. 37.

17. BP, p. 164.

18. *Ibid.,* p. 163.

19. "Huneker, a Memory," P3, pp. 65–66, 68.

20. AN1925, p. 74.

21. Mencken's letter to Dreiser is reprinted in its entirety in Forgue, pp. 12–14.

22. Angoff, ed., *The World of George Jean Nathan*, pp. 19–20.

23. Mencken, *James Branch Cabell*, pp. 18–19.

24. AN1925, p. 182.

25. BP, pp. 153–54.

26. "Critics Wild and Tame," *Smart Set*, LIII, 4 (Dec. 1917), p. 138.

27. "Fifteen Years," *Smart Set*, LXXII, 4 (Dec. 1923), pp. 138–44.

28. "The Monthly Feuilleton," *Smart Set*, LXIX, 4 (Dec. 1922), p. 141.

29. AN1925, p. 112.

30. *Ibid.*, p. 145.

31. Angoff, p. 107.

32. Forgue, p. 427.

33. *Ibid.*

34. "Footnote on Criticism," P3, pp. 88–89; *Chrestomathy*, p. 431.

35. "The Fringes of Lovely Letters," P5, p. 207.

36. "Criticism of Criticism of Criticism," *Smart Set*, LII, 4 (Aug. 1917), p. 138. (In the revised form of the article appearing in P1, the wording is different.)

37. "Footnote on Criticism," P3, pp. 84–85; *Chrestomathy*, p. 429.

38. "A Road Map of the New Books," *Smart Set*, XXVII, 1 (Jan. 1909), p. 153.

39. "The National Letters," P2, pp. 40–41.

40. "Prose Fiction Ad Infinitum," *Smart Set*, XXXVIII, 1 (Sept. 1912), p. 153.

41. "Suffering Among Books," *Smart Set*, LI, 1 (Jan. 1917), p. 267; "The Dean," P1, p. 55.

42. MR, p. 238.

43. BP, p. 45.

44. *Ibid.*, p. 12.

45. *Ibid.*, pp. 92–93.

46. "Arnold Bennett," P1, pp. 43–44.

47. "The Late Mr. Wells," *ibid.*, p. 22.

48. *Ibid.*, pp. 28–29.

49. "Arnold Bennett," *ibid.*, pp. 36–37.

50. "Essay in Pedagogy," P5, p. 219.

51. "The Poet and His Art," P3, p. 147.

52. "Exeunt Omnes," P2, p. 182; "The Poet and His Art," P3, pp. 154–55; "Toward a Realistic Aesthetic," P4, p. 237; AL4, Supp. I, p. 323n.

53. HaD, p. 162.

54. "Five Little Excursions," P6, p. 177.

55. "Hints for Novelists," Chicago *Tribune*, Dec. 27, 1925; reprinted in McHugh, p. 67.

56. "The Poet and His Art," P3, p. 169; *Chrestomathy*, p. 458.

57. "George Jean Nathan," P1, p. 216.

58. "Reflections on the Drama," P3, pp. 300–1; *Chrestomathy*, p. 565.

59. *Ibid.*, p. 301; p. 565.

60. "Toward a Realistic Aesthetic," P4, p. 240; *Chrestomathy*, p. 551.

61. *Ibid.*, p. 239.

62. MR, p. 63.

63. HaD, p. 201.

CHAPTER V

1. Forgue, p. 395.

2. AN1941.

3. It is reproduced in Carl Bode's anthology *The Young Mencken* (New York: Dial Press, 1973), pp. 318–32.

4. Forgue, p. 189.

5. AL1, preface, p. vi.

6. AL4, preface, p. v.

7. AL2, p. 4.

8. McDavid, *The American Language . . . abridged*, intro., p. v.

9. *Chrestomathy*, p. 583.

10. Philip Wagner, *H. L. Mencken* (Minneapolis: University of Minnesota Press, 1966), p. 45.

11. AL4, p. 194 n.

12. Supp. I, p. 260.

INDEX

A NOTE ABOUT THE AUTHOR

CHARLES A. FECHER was born in Baltimore in 1917, was educated there, and lives there still. Since 1963 he has been employed by the Roman Catholic Archdiocese of Baltimore. He is the author of *The Philosophy of Jacques Maritain* (1953, 1969) and has written articles for *The Critic, The Catholic World,* and *The Sign.* He contributes a weekly book review column to *The Catholic Review,* for which he received in 1977 the Catholic Press Association's award for the best regular column. He is married and has two daughters.

A NOTE ON THE TYPE

This book was set in Caledonia, a VIP version of a Linotype face designed by W. A. Dwiggins. It belongs to the family of printing types called "modern face" by printers—a term used to mark the change in style of type letters that occurred about 1800. It borders on the general design of Scotch Modern, but is more freely drawn than that letter.

Composed by Typesetting Services of California, Pleasant Hill, California. Printed and bound by Haddon Craftsmen, Scranton, Pennsylvania.

Designed by Margaret M. Wagner